Electoral Management

Design

Revised Edition

Electoral Management Design

Revised Edition

Helena Catt
Andrew Ellis
Michael Maley
Alan Wall
Peter Wolf

International IDEA's resources on electoral processes

Handbook Series
The International IDEA Handbook Series seeks to present comparative analysis, information and insights on a range of democratic institutions and processes. Handbooks are aimed primarily at policymakers, politicians, civil society actors and practitioners in the field. They are also of interest to academia, the democracy assistance community and other bodies.

© International Institute for Democracy and Electoral Assistance 2014

International IDEA publications are independent of specific national or political interests. Views expressed in this publication do not necessarily represent the views of International IDEA, its Board or its Council members.

The map(s) presented in this publication does not imply on the part of the Institute any judgement on the legal status of any territory or the endorsement of such boundaries, nor does the placement or size of any country or territory reflect the political view of the Institute. The map is created for this publication in order to add clarity to the text.

Applications for permission to reproduce or translate all or any part of this publication should be made to:

International IDEA
Strömsborg
SE-103 34 Stockholm
Sweden

International IDEA encourages dissemination of its work and will promptly respond to requests for permission to reproduce or translate its publications.

The electronic version of this publication is available under a Creative Commons Licence (CCl)—Creative Commons Attribute-NonCommercial-ShareAlike 3.0 Licence. You are free to copy, distribute and transmit the publication as well as to remix and adapt it provided it is only for non-commercial purposes, that you appropriately attribute the publication, and that you distribute it under an identical license. For more information on this CCl, see: <http://creativecommons.org/licenses/by-nc-sa/3.0/>.

Graphic design by: Pernilla Ottenfelt Eliasson
Cover Design by: Pernilla Ottenfelt Eliasson
Cover illustration: © Jing Jing Tsong c/o theispot.com
Printed by: Bulls Graphics, Sweden

ISBN: 978-91-87729-66-9

Foreword

The world entered the third millennium with 140 countries holding multiparty elections, which represents a historic shift in the nature and profile of political participation.

Since then, the democratic world has expanded further; new states have resulted from socio-political movements for individual freedom. Many of these new states are still struggling to establish viable democratic governance systems and structures to fulfil their citizens' aspirations.

Sustaining the process of democratization is more challenging in the least developed and developing countries, which face pervasive poverty, multiethnic conflicts and social tensions between the powerful and powerless. Countries that are economically rich yet poor in other human development indicators are another difficult category to deal with.

Many present-day democracies are called representative democracies, in which people elect representatives to make decisions on their behalf. In some, the electoral management system itself is under pressure, if not direct attack, and in need of immunity and insulation. Competitive elections, in addition to being expensive and wasteful, are increasingly being manipulated by political parties, propaganda machines and clever demagoguery; they need healthy, constructive debates on public policy.

Election managers thus continuously face formidable challenges to keep the electoral system functional and provide a level playing field for everyone, and struggle to retain their autonomy and integrity.

The larger issue is making democratic systems and processes work for all four principles: popular control, political equality, constitutional governance and individual freedom. This revised and updated publication is relevant in this context. If meticulously followed and intelligently implemented, its guiding principles can keep the electoral oversight and regulatory agencies in strategic fitness and failsafe condition against undue pressure and motivated interference.

This publication focuses on how electoral management bodies (EMBs) can protect their autonomy, exercise management control, safeguard integrity, maintain transparency, ensure efficacy, and professionally implement rules and procedures while keeping the system voter friendly. From registering eligible voters to counting votes and declaring results, the pathways of election managers are full of risks that require competencies and high-order skills. I am sure that

EMBs and their staffs will find this document useful, and that it will help improve the professional and effective management of the complex electoral process.

Dr. S.Y. Quraishi
Former chief election commissioner, India

Preface

International IDEA's vision is to be the primary global actor in sharing comparative knowledge and experience in support of democracy, and aims to make this knowledge and experience available to inspire national dialogue and catalyse political will.

Electoral frameworks, including the choice of electoral system and the design of electoral administration, determine both the outcomes and the credibility of electoral processes and thereby trust in democracy. The development of professional electoral administration is not merely a technical and managerial issue, but a process that crucially engages political stakeholders who have their own interests and objectives. Its role in the overall development and strengthening of democracy cannot be overstated.

This Handbook brings together a core global comparative knowledge base on the design, establishment, financing, training and assessment of electoral management bodies. The first edition was published in 2006 and has since formed the basis of training materials and online tools; it is one of International IDEA's most popular knowledge resources and it has been translated into several languages.

Much has happened since the publication of the first edition of this handbook. New electoral management bodies (EMBs) have been formed, old ones have been revised in response to allegations of fraud and corruption, the role of technology in elections is much more prevalent, the field of professional development for EMB members and staff has grown, and progress in the field of gender and elections has been made. It is therefore time to publish a revised edition, with the most relevant sections updated and expanded, current country-level data and several new case studies which will help highlight the diversity, creativity and innovations in the field of electoral management globally.

The Handbook will be a valuable resource for everyone involved or interested in the strength and legitimacy of their electoral process.

Yves Leterme
Secretary-General
International IDEA

Contents

Foreword	III
Preface	V
Contents	VI
Acronyms and Abbreviations	XIV
Introduction	1

Chapter 1. Who Organizes Elections? 5

What Is an EMB?	5
Three Models of Electoral Management	6
The Independent Model of Electoral Management	7
The Governmental Model of Electoral Management	7
The Mixed Model of Electoral Management	8
What Can Be Expected of EMBs under the Different Electoral Management Models?	10
EMBs Attributes under the Three Broad Models of Electoral Management	12
Permanent and Temporary EMBs	12
Centralized or Decentralized EMBs	17
EMBs in Federal Countries	18
Transitional International EMBs and National EMBs	18
Representation of the EMB before Cabinet and the Legislature	19
Some Guiding Principles for All EMBs	21
Independence	21
Impartiality	22
Integrity	23
Transparency	23
Efficiency	24
Professionalism	24
Service-mindedness	24
Chapter Summary	25

Chapter 2. The Legal Framework: The Context for an EMB's Role and Powers 43

How Legal Instruments Define Electoral Processes	43
International and Regional Treaties and Agreements	45
The Constitution	46
Electoral Laws: Acts and Ordinances	49
EMB Rules, Regulations and Proclamations	50
Chapter Summary	52

Chapter 3. The Powers, Functions and Responsibilities of an EMB 73

Powers and Functions	73
Extent of Powers, Functions and Responsibilities	75
Direct Democracy Instruments	77
Functional Divisions between Electoral Institutions	77
Boundary Delimitation	78
Voter Registration	79

Registration and Funding of Political Parties	80
Election Campaigns	81
Voter Education and Information	82
Validation of Election Results	84
Electoral Observation	84
International Activities	84
Electoral Dispute Resolution	85
EMB Responsibilities as a Public Organization	85
Avoidance of Conflicts of Interest	86
EMB Responsibilites to Promote Democracy and Equity	87
Gender Balance	87
Ethnicity	90
Broad-based Access	91
Chapter Summary	92

Chapter 4. The Composition, Roles and Functioning of an EMB — 107

EMB Membership	107
Status of EMB Members	108
The EMB Chair: A Special Role?	109
EMB Members: Respected Experts or Watchdogs for Each Other?	110
Multiparty-based EMBs	110
Expert-based EMBs	111
EMBs with Both Expert and Multiparty Membership	112
Full-time or Part-time EMB Members?	112
How Many EMB Members?	114
Term of Office of Members of Permanent EMBs	114
Recruitment and Appointment of EMB Members	116
Recruitment Through Open Advertisement	116
Appointment of EMB Members	117
Qualifications for Appointment	118
Conditions of Service and Security of Tenure for EMB Members	121
Oath/Pledge-taking or Affirmation	122
Internal Regulations	122
EMB Decision-making Processes	123
Meetings of EMB Members	124
Closed or Open EMB Meetings	124
EMB Member Committees	125
EMB Members' Relationships with the EMB Secretariat	125
Chapter Summary	126

Chapter 5. Planning and Implementing EMB Activities — 145

The EMB Secretariat	145
The EMB Secretariat and the Public Service	146
Structuring the Secretariat	148
Organizational Structure Charts	149

How to Develop an Organizational Chart	150
Model Secretariat Structures	150
Strategic Planning	152
Operational Planning	158
The Electoral Calendar	159
Chapter Summary	164

Chapter 6. The Development of Professional Electoral Management — 177

Use of Public Service Staff for EMB Secretariats	178
Permanent and Temporary Staff	179
Employment Conditions: EMB-Specific or Public Service Staff	179
Staff Pensions	180
Career Patterns of Professional Electoral Officers	180
Procedures for Recruiting EMB Staff	180
Procedures for the Appointment of EMB Secretariat Staff	182
Staff Training and Development	183
EMB Organizational and Staff Development for Permanent Staff	183
Using International Experience	185
Mentoring	185
Education and Development Courses for EMB Staff	186
Operational Training	187
Training Methods	187
Cascade Training	188
Training by Mobile Teams	188
Simultaneous Training	188
Training Materials	189
Instructions	189
Training Manuals	189
Simulations and Videos	189
Factors that May Inhibit EMB Professionalism	190
Chapter Summary	191

Chapter 7. The Financing of EMBs — 207

Common EMB Financing Issues	207
What Electoral Costs Need to be Financed?	208
Who Finances EMBs and How?	210
State or Public Funding	210
Method of Disbursing State Funding	210
Integrated or Distributed Electoral Budgets	210
Donor Funding	210
Other Sources of EMB Funding	212
Budget Formulation Methods for EMBs	212
Budget Formulation and Approval Process	214
Availability of Budget Funds	215

Control of EMB Funding	215
EMB Procurement Policies and Procedures	216
EMB Financial Control Measures	217
Asset Management	218
Records Management	218
Principles of EMB Financial Management	219
Transparency	219
Efficiency and Effectiveness	219
Integrity	220
Chapter Summary	220

Chapter 8. Stakeholder Relationships — 229

Who are the Stakeholders and What Is Their Role in the Electoral Process?	229
Primary Stakeholders	229
Political Parties and Candidates	230
EMB Staff	231
The Executive Branch	231
The Legislature	232
Electoral Dispute Resolution Bodies	233
Judicial Bodies	234
Election Monitors/Certification Teams and Citizen and International Election Observers	234
Traditional Media	235
Social Media	236
The Electorate	236
Civil Society Organizations	237
The Donor Community and Electoral Assistance Agencies	238
Secondary Stakeholders	238
EMB Suppliers	238
The Public at Large	239
Regional and International Networks	239
Maintaining Relationships With Stakeholders	239
How To Deal With Difficult Stakeholders	242
Chapter Summary	243

Chapter 9. Electoral Technology — 257

Elections Technology in Recent Decades	257
Types and Main Features of Elections Technology	257
Selected ICT Concepts with Impact on Elections Technology	259
ICT Innovation Cycles and their Relation to the Electoral Cycle	259
The 'Bathtub Curve' and Electoral Cycles	259
Total Cost of Ownership of ICT Systems	261
ICT Security and Costs	262
Election Technology Vendors	262

IX

      Needs-driven Approach 263
      Procurement 263
      Vendor Lock 263
      Open Source vs. Proprietary Systems 264
      Commercial Off-the-shelf Systems vs. Customized System Development 264
   Voter Education and Public Information 265
   Training and Expertise 265
   Administrative and Operational Objectives 266
      Maintaining EMB Oversight 266
      Accountability and Integrity 266
      Focus on the Whole Electoral Process 267
      Inclusiveness 267
      Sustainability of Donor-funded Technology 267
      Selecting Appropriate Technology 268
   Issues of Electronic Voter Registration 268
   A Brief Background of Electronic Voting and Vote-counting Systems 269
      System Requirements, Certification and Audits 270
      Voter Verified Paper Audit Trails 271
      Costs 271
   Chapter Summary 272

Chapter 10. Assessing EMB Performance 285
   Why is EMB Accountability Important? 285
   Principles and Best Practices for EMB Accountability 285
   Stakeholder Accountability 286
   Consultation and Communication 286
   Performance Accountability 286
      Internal Performance Accountability 286
      External Performance Accountability 287
   Financial Accountability 288
      Internal Financial Accountability 288
      External Financial Accountability 289
   Accountability for the Use of Technology-based Systems 290
   EMB Assessment Mechanisms 290
      Internal Quality Controls 290
      Auditing EMBs 291
      Performance Audits 292
      Financial Audits 294
      Programme Evaluation by EMBs 295
      Peer Reviews 298
      External Oversight Issues 299
   Chapter Summary 299

Chapter 11. EMB Sustainability 313
   What Is Sustainability? 313
   Why Is EMB Sustainability Important? 314
   Needs Assessment 314
   Electoral Sustainability and Donor Support 316
   Practices Favouring Sustainability 318
   Staffing for Sustainability 318
   Office Systems 319
   Electoral Materials 320
   Structural and Technological Sustainability Implications 321
      Electoral Systems 322
      Electoral Boundary Delimitation 322
      Voter Registration 322
      The Polling Process 323
   Automated Voting and Counting Processes 325
   Chapter Summary 326

Chapter 12. EMB Networks 343
   What Are Electoral Networks and Why Do They Matter? 343
   National Electoral Networks 343
   Regional EMB Networks 344
   Global Electoral Networks 346
   Electoral Support Networks 347
   Chapter Summary 347

Chapter 13. Reforming Electoral Processes 365
   What Is Electoral Reform? 365
   Failing EMBs 367
   The EMB's Role in Electoral Reforms 368
   The Scope of Electoral Reform 369
   Managing Electoral Change 372
   Risks Associated with Electoral Reform 372
   Chapter Summary 373

Annexes
World Survey: Electoral Management Bodies in 217 Countries and Territories 374
Electoral Management Glossary 396
References and Further Reading 409
EMB Websites and Social Media Platforms 414
About the Authors 426
Acknowledgements 434
About International IDEA 435

Index 436

Tables

Table 1	Characteristics of the Three Broad Models of Electoral Management and their Component EMBs	9
Table 2	What an EMB under the Independent Model Is, May Be and Is Not	11
Table 3	What an EMB under the Governmental Model Is, May Be, and Is Not	13
Table 4	Examples of Attributes of EMBs under Mixed Model Electoral Management	14
Table 5	Advantages and Disadvantages of the Three Different Electoral Management Models	20
Table 6	Advantages and Disadvantages of Assigning Some Electoral Functions to Institutions Other than the EMB	78
Table 7	Advantages and Disadvantages of Multiparty, Expert and Combined EMBs	113
Table 8	Number of Members in a Selection of Party-based and Expert-based EMBs as of 2012	115
Table 9	Some Advantages and Disadvantages of Open Advertising for Members of EMBs	116
Table 10	Qualifications Stated in the Electoral Law for Appointment to Two Reformed Expert-based EMBs: South Sudan and Bhutan	120
Table 11	The Policymaking and Implementation Components of the Three Models of Electoral Management	145
Table 12	Possible Advantages and Disadvantages of Using Public Servants as EMB Secretariat Staff	147
Table 13	Attributes and Examples of Electoral Core, Diffuse and Integrity Costs	209
Table 14	Some Key Advantages and Disadvantages of International Donor Funding for Electoral Processes	212
Table 15	Election Performance Audit: Criteria and Issues	293
Table 16	Possible Performance Audit Findings and Recommendations	294
Table 17	The Botswana Post-election Review 2004: Terms of Reference	297
Table 18	EMB Post-election Review Cycle Checklist	298

Figures

Figure 1	Characteristics of the Three Broad Models of Electoral Management and their Component EMBs	10
Figure 2	The Electoral Cycle	16
Figure 3	Organizational Structure of the South African Independent Electoral Commission	153
Figure 4	Organizational Structure of the Afghan EMB	154
Figure 5	Organizational Structure of the New Zealand Electoral Commission	155
Figure 6	Organizational Structure of Electoral Management in Costa Rica	156
Figure 7	Organizational Structure of Electoral Management in Tonga	157
Figure 8	Extract from the Australian Electoral Commission (AEC) Strategic Plan, 2009–14	160

Figure 9	The Elections Calendar for the 2011 Presidential, Parliamentary and Local Elections in Zambia	162
Figure 10	National Assembly Elections Calendar, Bhutan, 2013	163
Figure 11	Stakeholder Engagement – Statement of Principles	240
Figure 12	How ICT Equipment Has Evolved Between Elections	260
Figure 13	The Bathtub Curve	261

Boxes

Box 1	Checklist for Electoral Management Legal Framework	51
Box 2	The Indian Code of Conduct for Use of Official Resources for Electoral Purposes	82
Box 3	Some Important Steps toward Developing Electoral Administration as a Profession	187

Case Studies

Republic of Seychelles	27
Mexico	32
Cambodia	54
Afghanistan	61
Costa Rica	93
Armenia	98
Nigeria	128
Norway	137
Senegal	165
Republic of Korea	171
Liberia	192
Timor-Leste	200
Tonga	222
United States	245
Tunisia	250
Kenya	273
United Kingdom	302
Bosnia and Herzegovina	328
Ukraine	335
Haiti	349
India	358

Acronyms and Abbreviations

A-WEB	Association of World Election Bodies
ACEEEO	Association of European Election Officials
AEA	Association of Electoral Administrators (UK)
AEC	Australian Electoral Commission
AEOBiH	Association of Election Officials in Bosnia and Herzegovina
ANFREL	Asian Network for Free Elections
AU	African Union
BCEN	National Office of Electoral Disputes (Haiti)
BEC	Bureau Electoral Communal (Haiti)
BED	Bureau Electoral Déparemental (Haiti)
BiH	Bosnia and Herzegovina
BON	Broadcasting Organisation of Nigeria
BRIDGE	Building Resources in Democracy, Governance and Elections
CAA	Constitutional Appointments Authority (Seychelles)
CEC	Central Election Commission (Bosnia and Herzegovina, Georgia, Russia, Armenia, Ukraine)
CEMC	Central Election Management Council
CENA	Commission Electorale Nationale Autonome (National Autonomous Electoral Commission) (Senegal)
CEO	chief electoral officer
CEP	Conseil Electoral Provisoire (Haiti)
CNE	National Elections Commission (Timor-Leste)
CNRA	Conseil National de Regulation de l'Audiovisuel (National Council for the Regulation of TV and Radio) (Senegal)
CNRV	Commission Nationale de Recensement des Votes (National Commission for the Tallying of the Votes) (Senegal)
ConEC	Constituency Electoral Commissions (Armenia)
CORE	Cost of Registration and Elections (Project)
CPP	Cambodian People's Party
CSO	civil society organization
CTA	chief technical advisor
CTCEP	Transitional College of the Permanent Electoral Council (Haiti)
CTV	Centre de Tabulation de Vote (Vote Tabulation Centre) (Haiti)
DEC	District Election Commission (Ukraine)
DRE	direct recording electronic (system)
EAC	Election Assistance Commission (USA)
EBDC	Election Broadcasting Debate Commission (South Korea)
EC	Election Commission (Bosnia and Herzegovina, South Korea, Seychelles)
ECC	Electoral Complaints Commission (Afghanistan)
ECF	Electoral Commissions' Forum (of SADC countries), also Electoral Commission of the Federation (Nigeria)
ECI	Election Commission of India

ECK	Electoral Commission of Kenya
ECOWAS	Economic Community of West African States
EISA	Electoral Institute of Southern Africa
ELECT	Enhancing Electoral and Legal Capacity for Tomorrow (Afghanistan)
EMB	electoral management body
ERC	Electoral Reform Committee (Nigeria)
EVM	electronic voting machine
FCT	Federal Capital Territory (Nigeria)
FEC	Federal Election Commission (United States)
FPTP	First Past The Post
FUNCINPEC	Front Uni National pour un Camobdge Indépandant, Neutre, Pacifique, et Coopératif (United Front for an Independent, Neutral, Peaceful and Cooperative Cambodia)
FYROM	Former Yugoslav Republic of Macedonia
GEO	Global Electoral Organization
HAVA	Help America Vote Act (United States)
ICCPR	International Covenant of Civil and Political Rights
ICT	information and communications technology
IDEA	International Institute for Democracy and Electoral Assistance
IEBC	Independent Electoral Boundaries Commission (Kenya)
IEC	Independent Election (or Electoral) Commission (Afghanistan, Timor-Leste, Botswana)
IEIS	integrated election information system
IENDC	Internet Election News Deliberation Commission (South Korea)
IFE	Federal Electoral Institute (Mexico)
IFES	International Foundation for Electoral Systems
IIEC	Interim Independent Electoral Commission (Kenya)
INE	National Electoral Institute (Mexico)
INEC	Independent National Electoral Commission (Nigeria)
IOM	International Organization for Migration
IREC	Independent Review Committee (Kenya)
ISAF	International Security Assistance Force (Afghanistan)
ISIE	Independent High Authority for Elections (Tunisia)
IT	information technology
JEMB	Joint Electoral Management Body (Afghanistan)
LEMNA	Law on the Election of the Members of the National Assembly (Cambodia)
MINUSTAH	United Nations Stabilization Mission in Haiti
NCTR	National Commission of Television and Radio (Armenia)
NEB	National Electoral Board (Riksvalgstyret) (Norway)
NEC	National Election Committee (Cambodia)
	National Election Commission (Liberia, Nigeria, South Korea)
NGO	non-governmental organization
OAS	Organization of American States

OCV	out-of-country voting
ODIHR	Office for Democratic Institutions and Human Rights (OSCE)
OMR	optical mark recognition
ONI	National Identification Office (Haiti)
OSCE	Organization for Security and Co-operation in Europe
OSD	organizational and staff development
PEC	Precinct Electoral Commission (Armenia)/ Provincial Election Committee (Bosnia and Herzegovina, Cambodia)
PEO	principal electoral officer (Afghanistan)
PIANZEA	Pacific Islands, Australia, New Zealand Electoral Administrators Network
PPLC	Political Parties Liaison Committee (Kenya)
PR	proportional representation
REC	Resident Electoral Commissioner (Nigeria)
RS	Republika Srpska
SADC	Southern African Development Community
SIEC	State Independent Electoral Commission (Nigeria)
SRP	Sam Rainsy Party (Cambodia)
SRSG	Special Representative of the (UN) Secretary-General (Afghanistan)
STAE	Technical Secretariat for Electoral Administration (Timor-Leste)
SVR	State Voter Register (Ukraine)
TCO	total cost of ownership
TSE	Tribunal Supremo de Elecciones (Supreme Electoral Tribunal) (Costa Rica)
UK	United Kingdom
UN	United Nations
UNAMA	UN Assistance Mission in Afghanistan
UNDP	United Nations Development Programme
UNEAD	United Nations Electoral Assistance Division
UNIORE	Inter-American Union of Electoral Organizations
UNOPS	United Nations Office of Project Services
USAID	United States Agency for International Development
VVPAT	voter-verified paper audit trail

Introduction

The credibility and legitimacy of electoral processes is inextricably linked to electoral integrity. The Global Commission on Democracy, Elections and Security identified five major challenges to the conduct of elections with integrity in its 2012 report: building the rule of law to substantiate claims to human rights and electoral justice, developing professional and competent electoral management bodies (EMBs) with full independence of action, creating institutions and norms of multiparty competition and division of power, removing barriers to universal and equal political participation, and regulating political finance. Each of these challenges requires a multidimensional response that combines political will, effective institutional design and effective mobilization, implementation and management in practice.

The organization and administration of multiparty democratic elections was not previously considered newsworthy. An election or direct democracy poll—such as a referendum—is, however, often the single largest activity that is ever organized in a country. It is a very complex administrative task, which is implemented in a politically charged atmosphere. When it is done well, it may attract little comment. When it is not done well, or when it is undermined, the effects can be catastrophic.

The administration of many electoral events, however, passed largely unnoticed, except by those directly affected, even though the losing political parties often challenged the conduct of the election and its results. From around the mid-1980s, this began to change. The conduct of democratic elections began to be seen, and reported, as a central element of transitions from authoritarianism or conflict resolution. Elections came to be more closely scrutinized by political parties, the media, and international and citizen election observers.

Since the mid-1980s, there has also been an unprecedented commitment to electoral reforms around the world, driven by the realization in political and electoral administration circles that changing social environments required a rethink of electoral arrangements, by the critical attention of the media and election observers and by the emergence of global and regional organizations promoting democracy. As scrutiny of elections increased, from the early 1990s the lack of experience and the 'knowledge gap' in the technical know-how for election management was overtaken by a 'credibility gap' in many electoral institutions—a diminished public confidence in the integrity and diligence of their activities.

Public interest has more often been focused on reforming electoral systems to enhance representation. Yet reforms to the machinery for organizing and administering electoral events are of equal importance. These include a trend toward establishing autonomous electoral management bodies with wide-ranging powers and responsibilities, and the improvement of electoral organization in order to deliver higher-quality electoral services more effectively, while enhancing the freeness and fairness of electoral events.

As the administration of elections has received more scrutiny, it has also become more professional. Electoral managers have learned from experience—their own and that of non-electoral organizations—and have formed links and networks through which ideas and practices are shared and electoral standards may be raised. There are different organizational approaches to the design and conduct of elections, but there are many common themes and issues faced by all electoral administrators.

As electoral administration has developed through greater professionalism, it has had to respond to greater challenges. In addition to their tasks related to implementing election laws and managing electoral technicalities, some EMBs have assumed responsibilities in highly political areas, for example the oversight of political finance, the registration and oversight of political parties, the role and activities of the media during elections, and the promotion of political participation. In addition, the ingenuity of those who wish to undermine the integrity of elections means that electoral administrators can never rest on their laurels: protecting electoral integrity can require a continual leapfrog process for the EMB to keep ahead.

This Handbook is intended to be a resource to directly support those who are responding to the challenge identified by the Global Commission to build professional, competent and fully independent EMBs. In doing so, it may also support those who are responding to the commission's other four challenges. It seeks to bring together the knowledge and expertise that has been gathered worldwide about EMB roles and functions, and the organization, financing and management of election administration. It identifies examples of practices that have been successful and those that have been less successful. It recognizes that different models may be appropriate in different contexts, and does not in general seek to be normative or prescriptive beyond the basic characteristics sought in good electoral processes: freedom, fairness, equity, integrity, voting secrecy, transparency, effectiveness, sustainability, service-mindedness, efficiency, impartiality and accountability.

The prime objective in compiling this publication has been to provide practical information in a form that is easily accessible and (to the greatest extent possible) free of theorizing and electoral or management jargon. It contains information that is useful not only to those establishing institutions involved in managing elections, those in newly established electoral institutions and those in emerging democracies. The Handbook also offers a wide range of experiences and information on good practices for those interested in assessing performance and improving administration in well-established EMBs. Equally, it provides useful data to all who have an interest or stake in electoral administration—whether in governments, political parties, the media or civil society organizations, or as interested observers of political and electoral matters.

CHAPTER 1

Who Organizes Elections?

What Is an EMB?

The complexity and specialist skills necessary for electoral management require that an institution or institutions be responsible for electoral activities. Such bodies have a variety of shapes and sizes, with a wide range of titles to match, such as Election Commission, Department of Elections, Electoral Council, Election Unit or Electoral Board. The term electoral management body (EMB) has been coined to refer to the body or bodies responsible for electoral management, regardless of the wider institutional framework in place.

An EMB is an organization or body that has the sole purpose of, and is legally responsible for, managing some or all of the elements that are essential for the conduct of elections and direct democracy instruments—such as referendums, citizens' initiatives and recall votes—if those are part of the legal framework. These essential (or core) elements include:

a. determining who is eligible to vote;
b. receiving and validating the nominations of electoral participants (for elections, political parties and/or candidates);
c. conducting polling;
d. counting the votes; and
e. tabulating the votes.

If these essential elements are allocated to various bodies, then all bodies that share these responsibilities can be considered EMBs. An EMB may be a stand-alone institution, or a distinct management unit within a larger institution that may also have non-electoral tasks.

In addition to these essential elements, an EMB may undertake other tasks that assist in the conduct of elections and direct democracy instruments, such as voter registration, boundary delimitation, voter education and information, media monitoring and electoral dispute resolution. However, a body that has no electoral responsibilities other than, for example, boundary delimitation (such as a boundary delimitation commission), electoral dispute resolution (such as an electoral court), election media monitoring (such as a media monitoring commission), or the conduct of voter education and information (such as a civic education commission) is not considered an EMB because it is not managing any of the essential elements identified above. Similarly, a national population or statistics bureau that produces electoral registers as part of the general process of population registration is not considered to be an EMB.

Different EMBs may be established for different electoral processes. In Mexico and Poland, the EMBs are responsible for both presidential and parliamentary elections; in Australia, the national EMB deals with national-level elections, while state-level elections are the responsibility of separate state-level EMBs. In the United Kingdom (UK), the arrangements for the conduct of elections and referendums are separate.

Some bodies that are not engaged in any of the essential elements of elections may nonetheless be popularly regarded as EMBs. The US Federal Election Commission (FEC) defines its mission as 'administering and enforcing federal campaign finance laws'. However, such institutions do not qualify as EMBs under the definition above.

In addition to the division of functional responsibility for different elements of the electoral process, electoral responsibilities may be divided between bodies at different levels. For example, some elements of the conduct of elections may be managed by a national-level electoral commission, a ministry (such as the Ministry of the Interior) or a national government agency, while others are implemented by local-level commissions, regional branches of government departments or local authorities (as in Spain). The term EMB may also apply to a national electoral commission that co-manages elections together with local authorities, such as the Swedish Election Authority, which coordinates ballot paper printing, the distribution of seats and the announcement of results at the national level.

Three Models of Electoral Management

A country's electoral management model may either result from a holistic design process or be grafted onto an existing system of state administration. In post-colonial countries, the model may be strongly influenced by colonial administrative patterns. While there are many variations, there are three broad types or models of electoral management: Independent, Governmental and Mixed Models. The form of electoral management and the individual EMBs of 217 countries and territories are detailed in Annex A, which is based on International IDEA's Electoral Management Design Database (<http://www.idea.int/elections/emd/electoral-management-design-database.cfm>).

The three broad electoral management models are:

- Independent Model
- Governmental Model
- Mixed Model

The Independent Model of Electoral Management

The Independent Model of electoral management is used in countries where elections are organized and managed by an EMB that is institutionally independent and autonomous from the executive branch of government; its members are outside the executive. Under the Independent Model, the EMB has and manages its own budget, and is not accountable to a government ministry or department. It may be accountable to the legislature, the judiciary or the head of state. EMBs under this model may enjoy varying degrees of financial autonomy and accountability, as well as varying levels of performance accountability. Many new and emerging democracies have chosen this model, including Armenia, Bosnia and Herzegovina, Burkina Faso, Canada, Costa Rica, Estonia, Georgia, India, Indonesia, Liberia, Mauritius, Nigeria, Poland, South Africa, Thailand and Uruguay.

In some countries, two bodies are established to manage elections, both of which are independent of the executive and can be considered independent EMBs. One of these bodies is likely to have responsibility for policy decisions relating to the electoral process, and the other to be responsible for conducting and implementing the electoral process. There may be provisions to insulate the implementation EMB from interference by the policy EMB in staffing and operational matters. Examples of this 'double-independent' framework under the Independent Model include Jamaica and Romania.

The Governmental Model of Electoral Management

In countries with the Governmental Model of electoral management, elections are organized and managed by the executive branch through a ministry (such as the Ministry of the Interior) and/or through local authorities. Where EMBs under this model exist at the national level, they are led by a minister or civil servant and are answerable to a cabinet minister. With very few exceptions, they have no 'members'. Their budget falls within a government ministry and/or under local authorities.

Countries that use this model include Denmark, Singapore, Switzerland, the UK (for elections but not referendums) and the United States. In Sweden, Switzerland, the UK and the United States, elections are implemented by local authorities. In Sweden and Switzerland, the central EMB assumes a policy coordinating role.

Electoral Management Design

The Mixed Model of Electoral Management

The Mixed Model of electoral management usually involves two component EMBs and a dual structure: (1) a policy, monitoring or supervisory EMB that is independent of the executive branch (like an EMB under the Independent Model) and (2) an implementation EMB located within a department of state and/or local government (like an EMB under the Governmental Model). Under the Mixed Model, elections are organized by the component governmental EMB, with some level of oversight provided by the component independent EMB. The Mixed Model is used in France, Japan, Spain and many former French colonies, especially in West Africa, for example Mali and Senegal.

The powers, functions and strength of the component independent EMB in relation to the component governmental EMB vary in different examples of the Mixed Model, and the classification of a particular country as using this model is sometimes not very clear. In the past, the component independent EMB was sometimes little more than a formalized observation operation, although this version is dying out, having been abandoned, for example, in Senegal. In other cases, the component independent EMB supervises and verifies the implementation of electoral events by the component governmental EMB, and tabulates and transmits results, as in Congo (Brazzaville). In some Francophone countries, the Constitutional Council is engaged in the tabulation and declaration of results and can be considered a component independent EMB within the Mixed Model. In Chad, this applies to referendums only, and not to elections. In Mali, where elections are organized by the Ministry of Territorial Administration, both the Independent National Electoral Commission and the Constitutional Court undertake their own tabulation of results; the country thus has three component EMBs (one governmental and two independent).

The relationship between the component EMBs in a Mixed Model is not always clearly defined in legislation or practice, and friction can result. In the 1999 elections in Guinea (which used the Mixed Model at that time), the majority and opposition representatives in the component independent EMB had conflicting approaches to its role in supervising and verifying the elections; thus its effectiveness was heavily disputed.

International IDEA's 2014 survey of electoral management in 217 countries and territories worldwide showed that 63 per cent followed the Independent Model, 23 per cent the Governmental Model and 12 per cent the Mixed Model (the remaining 2 per cent corresponds to countries that do not hold national-level elections).

Table 1: Characteristics of the Three Broad Models of Electoral Management and their Component EMBs

Aspect of the Model and the Component EMB(s)	Independent Model — Independent EMB(s)	Governmental Model — Governmental EMB(s)	Mixed Model — Independent Component — Component Independent EMB	Mixed Model — Governmental Component — Component Governmental EMB
Institutional arrangement	Is institutionally independent from the executive branch of government.	Is located within or under the direction of a department of state and/or local government.	Is institutionally independent from the executive branch of government.	Is located within or under the direction of a department of state and/or local government.
Implementation	Exercises full responsibility for implementation.	Implementation is subject to executive branch of government direction.	Has autonomy to monitor or supervise, and in some cases set policy for, implementation.	Implementation is subject to executive branch of government direction, and monitoring or supervision and in some cases policy setting by independent component.
Formal accountability	Does not report to executive branch of government but with very few exceptions is formally accountable to the legislature, judiciary or head of state.	Fully accountable to executive branch of government.	Does not report to executive branch of government and is formally accountable to the legislature, the judiciary or the head of state.	Fully accountable to executive branch of government.
Powers	Has powers to develop the electoral regulatory framework independently under the law.*	Powers are limited to implementation.	Often has powers to develop electoral regulatory framework independently under the law. Monitors or supervises those who implement elections.	Powers are limited to implementation.
Composition	Is composed of members who are outside the executive branch while in EMB office.	Is led by a minister or public servant. With very few exceptions has no 'members', only a secretariat.	Is composed of members who are outside the executive branch while in EMB office.	Is led by a minister or public servant. Has no 'members', only a secretariat.
Term of office	Offers security of tenure, but not necessarily fixed term of office.	Usually no members, therefore N/A. Secretariat staff are civil servants whose tenure is not secured.	Offers security of tenure, but not necessarily fixed term of office.	Term of office is not secured.
Budget	Has and manages its own budget independently of day-to-day governmental control.	Budget is a component of a government ministry's budget or local authority budget.	Has a separately allocated budget.	Budget is a component of a government ministry's budget or local authority budget.

*A few countries which use the Independent or Mixed Model of electoral management do not have independent EMBs with regulatory powers.

Figure 1: Characteristics of the Three Broad Models of Electoral Management and their Component EMBs

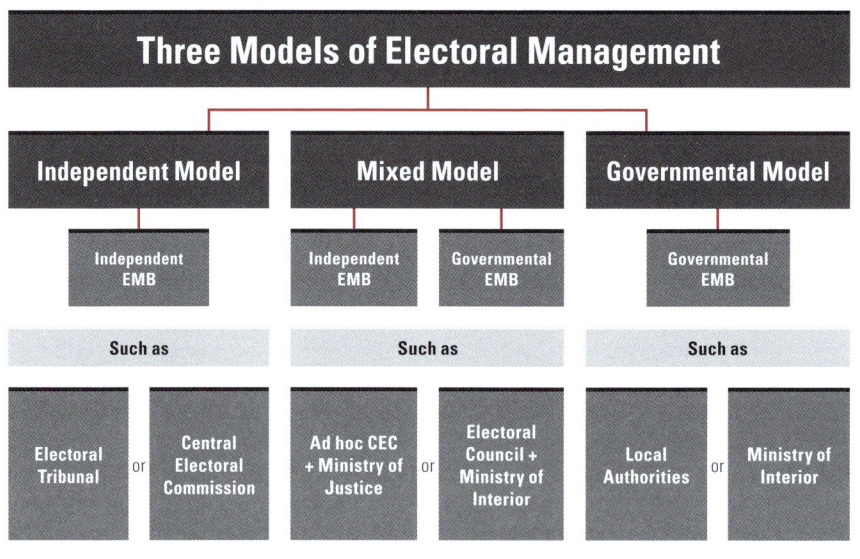

CEC = Central Electoral Comission

What Can Be Expected of EMBs under the Different Electoral Management Models?

A country's electoral management model is an important factor in EMB behaviour, but far from the only one; it is simplistic to think of three different behaviour patterns. EMB behaviour also depends on the electoral framework, political and social expectations, and the cultural environment within which each EMB operates. Influences include the political commitment to allow an EMB to act freely and impartially, the range of powers and functions given to an EMB, the qualifications of members or staff for appointment and their terms of office, the way in which members and/or staff are selected and appointed, the oversight and accountability framework, and whether the EMB has a legal personality and is thus able to sue and be sued. For example, an independent EMB comprising representatives of competing political parties and an independent EMB comprising non-aligned academics or others free of political association may both follow the Independent Model, but are likely to operate differently. Similarly, an EMB under the Governmental Model with a sponsoring department that controls local electoral management offices is likely to behave differently from one that depends on numerous local authorities to implement electoral activities.

However, there are some general characteristics, advantages and disadvantages of the three Models and their EMBs. Tables 1, 2, 3, 4 and 5 list some key issues.

Table 2: What an EMB under the Independent Model Is, May Be and Is Not

Aspect	Essential Attributes	Possible Attributes	What It Is Not
Institutional arrangement	Institutionally independent from the executive branch of government.		Is NOT part of the structure of a department of state and/or local government.
Implementation	Exercises full responsibility for implementation.	May be a legal entity which can sue and be sued in its own right (e.g. Azerbaijan, Botswana, Democratic Republic of Congo, Kenya and Lithuania) or not a legal entity (e.g. Mozambique).	Is NOT above the constitution or law.
Accountability	Is subject to good governance constraints.	Typically is formally accountable to the legislature, the judiciary or the head of state. May have varying levels of financial autonomy and accountability. May have financial autonomy through drawing up its own budget and receipt and use of public funds with minimal involvement of the executive branch of government. May have varying levels of performance accountability.	Is NOT formally accountable to the executive branch of government. Is NOT free of policy, financial, and performance accountability and good governance constraints.
Powers	Has powers to make policy decisions independently under the legal framework.	Typically has powers to develop the electoral regulatory framework independently under the law. Usually has broad overall powers and functions for electoral implementation. May have powers to hire, fire and discipline its own staff. May have power to establish its own procurement and accounting procedures.	
Composition	Is composed of members who are outside the executive while in EMB office.	Members may be non-aligned 'experts' or politically affiliated.	
Term of office	Members have security of tenure.	Members have a fixed term of office.	Members can NOT be removed/dismissed arbitrarily by the executive branch.
Budget	Has and manages its own budget independently of day-to-day governmental control.	May have a separately allocated budget from the legislature. May receive funding from the executive branch or the donor community.	Does NOT fall within the budget of any government ministry.
Staff	Has autonomy to determine its staff needs, rules and policies.	May be able to access personnel from within the public service.	Staff members are NOT necessarily public servants.

Electoral Management Design

EMBs Attributes under the Three Broad Models of Electoral Management

Mixed Model electoral management encompasses a variety of structures, internal relationships and attributes. Apart from the characteristics noted in Table 1, it is difficult to codify their essential and possible attributes. The relationship between the component EMBs in a Mixed Model is significant in determining its attributes and methods of operation. Effective legal frameworks for Mixed Model electoral management clearly specify the division of powers and functions between the component policy, monitoring or supervisory EMB(s) and the component implementing EMB(s) and their interactions. Table 4 shows some examples of attributes of component EMBs under Mixed Model electoral management.

Permanent and Temporary EMBs

There are many phases to the electoral process: in an election, for example, these include the design and drafting of legislation, the recruitment and training of electoral staff, electoral planning, voter registration, the registration of political parties, the nomination of parties and candidates, the electoral campaign, polling, counting, the tabulation of results, the declaration of results, the resolution of electoral disputes, reporting, auditing and archiving. After the end of one electoral process, it is desirable for work to begin on the next. The entire process is described as the electoral cycle, illustrated in Figure 2.

In determining whether a permanent or temporary EMB is appropriate, workloads throughout the electoral cycle need to be considered, and the expense of maintaining a permanent institution has to be compared with the expense and time required to establish a new body for each election. Where a temporary EMB appears appropriate, it is important to consider how institutional memory relating to elections will be maintained. Where electoral events occur regularly—such as regular partial or by-elections and continuous voter registration—or where continuing electoral development work, such as ongoing voter education and information or advocacy of electoral law reform is needed, a permanent electoral institution is justifiable. Countries such as Armenia, Australia, Brazil, Canada, Indonesia, Mexico, the Philippines, South Africa and Thailand maintain permanent EMBs.

Some countries have temporary EMBs that function only during the electoral period. Such countries may follow any of the Independent, Governmental or Mixed Models. In some cases, the governmental EMB has to be temporary because the civil servants who run elections have other full-time duties and are assigned to the EMB only during electoral periods. However, some countries with a Governmental Model of electoral management, such as Sweden, maintain a small skeleton staff to take care of electoral issues between elections, including updating the electoral register. In some countries that use the Mixed Model, the component governmental EMB is permanent in order to preserve institutional memory, while the component independent EMB is temporary and is set up only during electoral periods.

Table 3: What an EMB under the Governmental Model Is, May Be, and Is Not

Aspect	Essential Attributes	Possible Attributes	What It Is Not
Institutional arrangement	Is located within a department of state and/or local government.	May be a department, an agency or a local authority.	Is NOT an institution that is independent of the executive branch of government.
Implementation	Implementation is subject to direction by the executive branch of government.	Implementation responsibilities may be shared with ministries, departments or local authorities.	
Accountability	Is fully accountable for policy, finance, performance and governance to the executive branch of government.		
Powers	Powers are limited to implementation.	May often share electoral implementation responsibilities with other departments and local governments.	Does NOT have independent regulatory powers.
Composition	Is led by a minister or civil servant.	With very few exceptions has no members, only a secretariat. Selection of members (if any) and secretariat may be done exclusively by the executive.	
Term of office		Usually has no members and therefore no term of office.	
Budget	Budget is a component of a government ministry's budget.	May receive funding from donor community.	Does NOT decide on its own budget.
Staff	Is primarily staffed by public servants.	May be able to access personnel from outside the public service.	Can NOT hire and fire its own staff.

Electoral Management Design

Table 4: Examples of Attributes of EMBs under Mixed Model Electoral Management

Country	France		Japan	
Component EMBs	**Component Independent EMB**	**Component Governmental EMB**	**Component Independent EMB**	**Component Governmental EMB**
Title	Constitutional Council	Ministry of Interior, Bureau of Elections	Central Election Management Council (CEMC)	Ministry of Internal Affairs and Communications, Election Division
Composition	Body defined in the constitution with 9 appointed members, 3 each appointed by the president, the national assembly and the senate.	N/A	5 members appointed by the parliament	N/A
Structure	Permanent	Permanent	Temporary. Term of office 3 years.	Permanent
Relationship between Component EMBs	Oversight and some dispute resolution only.	Organization and piloting of the electoral process, the major functions.	A secretariat within the ministry gives the CEMC administrative support; the minutes of the CEMC meetings are available on the ministry's website.	Implementation of CEMC instructions and decisions and ensuring their implementation by highly decentralized EMBs at regional and local level.
Distinct powers and functions of the Component EMBs	Acceptance of nominations in presidential elections. Watching over the regularity of presidential elections and referendums, and declaration of their results. Ruling on disputes over the results of parliamentary elections.	Organization and administration of all elections.	Exercise of general direction and supervision of the administrative conduct of national elections.	Administrative conduct of all aspects of elections.

N/A = Not applicable

Country	Senegal		Spain	
Component EMBs	Component Independent EMB	Component Governmental EMB	Component Independent EMB	Component Governmental EMB
Title	Autonomous National Election Commission	Ministry of the Interior, General Directorate of Elections	Central Electoral Board	Ministry of the Interior, General Directorate of Elections
Composition	12 members sworn in by the Constitutional Council	N/A	8 judges of the Supreme Court + 5 experts (professors of political science, law, sociology, etc.) jointly proposed by parties represented in parliament. Chairman and vice-chairman are elected by Central Electoral Board from among the 8 judges.	N/A
Structure	Permanent	Permanent	Permanent. Renewed every 4 years after each parliamentary election.	Permanent
Relationship between Component EMBs	Independent supervision, review and verification of the electoral process.	Organization and administration of the entire electoral process.	Supervision of the entire electoral process.	Exercise of all electoral implementations functions. Must consult with the other component for important decisions.
Distinct powers and functions of the Component EMBs	Independent supervision, review and verification of registration and of the electoral process.	Organization and administration of the entire electoral process.	Supervision of electoral events, nomination of candidates, handling of complaints, declaration of results and allocation of seats.	Registration of voters, polling, counting, electoral logistics.

N/A = Not applicable

Figure 2: The Electoral Cycle

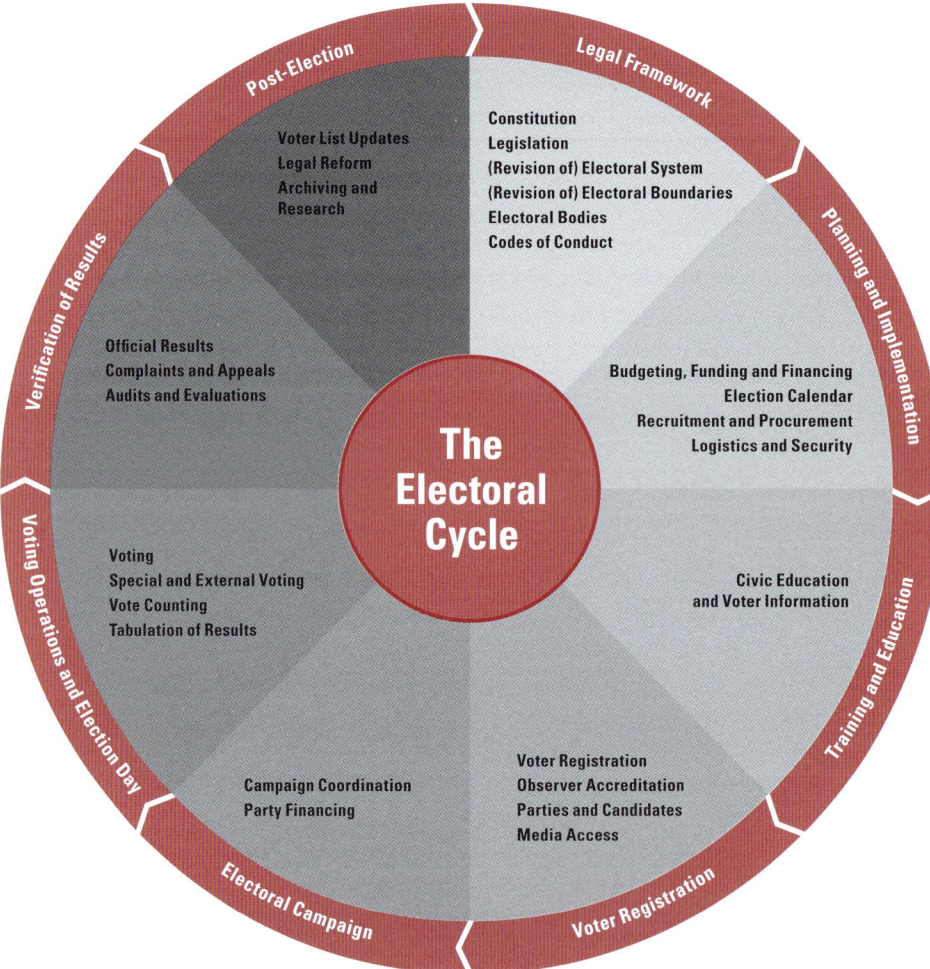

Countries such as Bulgaria, Niger and Romania, whose electoral management follows the Independent Model, have permanent central EMBs that coexist with temporary subordinate EMBs at lower levels. The Russian Federation has permanent EMBs at both the federal and constituent unit levels, and Georgia has permanent EMBs at both the central and district levels. Both have temporary EMBs at the local level during the election period. Depending on the responsibilities of the subordinate EMBs and the logistics required, these structures are usually appointed from one to six months before polling day. Permanent EMBs were created in much of Central and Eastern Europe following encouragement from the Association of Central and Eastern European Election Officials (ACEEEO) (now the Association of European Election Officials) and the recommendation of Organization for Security and Co-operation in Europe Office for Democratic Institutions and Human Rights (OSCE/ODIHR) election observer missions that such structures would enhance institutional memory and operational continuity.

Centralized or Decentralized EMBs

The level of an EMB's power concentration or devolution depends very much on the system of government in the country. In unitary countries, the responsibility for elections will be determined at the national level. Federal countries may have separate EMBs at the national level and in each state/province, which often operate under different legal frameworks and may implement different electoral systems.

The nature of the EMB will usually be defined in the electoral law, whether this takes the form of a single omnibus law—as in the Philippines—or a separate law specifically relating to electoral administration—as in Indonesia. The legal framework may distinguish between powers and functions that are given to a central or national EMB and those given to regional or lower-level EMBs. In unitary countries, such vertical divisions of power and functions may be between different branch levels of the one national EMB, or between national and local EMBs, as in the UK. It is common in a unitary system, as in Costa Rica, Ghana and the Philippines, to have one central EMB that is responsible for all elections, which has subordinate offices at both the provincial and local levels. Countries with laws that define separate, hierarchically accountable EMBs at national, regional, administrative district and even village level often assign devolved or different powers and responsibilities to each level. Many countries, such as Indonesia, Lithuania and Slovakia, have a central EMB that devolves responsibilities for implementing some electoral functions.

Countries that use the Governmental or Mixed Model may rely on local authorities to conduct all or part of the electoral activities. For example, Sweden operates a highly decentralized electoral management structure that consists of a national EMB for policy coordination and local authorities that manage elections, and Hungary and Switzerland devolve some powers to local EMBs. Devolving electoral powers and responsibilities to local authorities without appropriate oversight may make it more difficult to maintain electoral consistency, service, quality and—ultimately—the freedom and fairness of elections. The United States is a good example of this difficulty.

Decentralized EMB structures can ensure continuity in the EMB's work, especially where it has responsibility for recurring tasks such as continuous voter registration.

Decentralized EMBs, even if only temporary at the lower levels, can enhance inclusiveness and transparency in electoral management. However, decentralized EMBs may face a management challenge in maintaining consistent quality in service delivery.

The sustainability and relative costs of permanent vs. temporary EMBs at the regional and/or lower levels need to be considered, as well as the advantages.

Electoral Management Design

EMBs in Federal Countries

In federal countries, the national- and provincial-level EMBs may each have separate, devolved structures. The nature of the relationship between such EMBs, and the powers and responsibilities of each, depend on the provisions of the law. There are a variety of approaches to this relationship.

- In Australia and Canada, the national EMB is responsible for national (federal) elections, while provincial EMBs are responsible for provincial and local elections.

- In Brazil, the state EMBs are generally responsible for running all elections, and the national EMB is involved in the tabulation and declaration of the results for national offices.

- In India, the national EMB exercises overall superintendence, control and direction over state elections. The conduct of these elections is the direct responsibility of the state chief electoral officer, who is a senior civil servant appointed by the national EMB.

- In Nigeria, the national EMB assumes responsibility for federal and state elections and referendums, while the provincial EMBs are only responsible for local elections.

- In the Russian Federation, a central EMB at the national level is responsible for all federal elections; regional EMBs are responsible for elections in the 89 regions that make up the federation; and lower-level EMBs are responsible to the central EMB for federal elections and to the regional EMB for republic, regional and local elections.

- In Switzerland, a national EMB is responsible for policy coordination, while local authorities manage elections.

While there are often rivalries between EMBs at the national and provincial levels in federal systems, there are examples of cooperation. For example, in Australia, state electoral laws specifically provide that the electoral registers for provincial and local elections are to be jointly maintained with the national EMB, rather than the provinces maintaining their own registers. Such coordination in electoral laws has significant cost-saving benefits.

Transitional International EMBs and National EMBs

Transitional EMBs are set up temporarily to facilitate transitional elections. They are normally set up under the auspices of the international community, for example through the United Nations (UN), and consist of or include international experts as members. Countries where transitional international EMBs have been set up include Cambodia (1993), Bosnia and Herzegovina (1996), and Timor-Leste (2000).

An advantage of transitional international EMBs is that they benefit from the presence of international election experts who have vast technical knowledge and comparative electoral experience. This type of EMB structure is useful in deep-rooted conflict situations that require consensus building through mediation and dialogue. The presence of international experts on the EMB may bolster domestic and international stakeholder confidence in supporting the electoral process. However, local ownership of the electoral process may be significantly diminished, and the more usual approach is to provide international expertise for rather than international control of the transitional election.

While not strictly 'international', the EMBs in Afghanistan (2004) and South Africa (1994) were national institutions with provision for the appointment of international members. The 1994 South African EMB consisted of five international experts, but since 1996 it has had a national EMB following the Independent Model.

Transitional EMBs may also consist of nationals only, often political party representatives; an example was the 53-member EMB of Indonesia in 1999. This EMB was larger than usual in an effort to provide representation and inclusiveness. In 2001, Indonesia amended its Electoral Law to provide for an 11-member expert-based EMB, and membership was subsequently reduced to seven in 2007.

Representation of the EMB before Cabinet and the Legislature

Regardless of the model or type of EMB, it needs to deal with the executive branch of government and the legislature on issues such as electoral law and budgets. It is a good practice for a multiparty committee of the legislature, such as the Joint Standing Committee on Electoral Matters in Australia, to deal with EMB matters, and for a cabinet member to handle all EMB issues in cabinet and speak on its behalf in cabinet and the legislature. For a governmental EMB, the relevant minister would usually be from the department in which the EMB is located.

Unless an independent EMB within an Independent or Mixed Model also has someone to speak on its behalf—a task that may be allocated to a specified minister—it is difficult for EMB matters to attract sufficient attention from either the legislature or the cabinet. For example, the arrangement in Namibia—under which the speaker of parliament handles all EMB matters, including electoral law and the EMB budget—has in the past presented some problems for the EMB because the speaker is not represented in cabinet, and cabinet rules in Namibia state that proposals for legislation must first be presented to the cabinet by one of its members. A crisis over delays in electoral law reform in 2003 led to the appointment of a temporary 'guardian' minister to the EMB and the Ministry of Regional and Local Government being given the legislative task. However, the general interests of the ministry led to a perception that it might not be fully neutral in undertaking this task, and debate on an effective channel between the EMB and the legislature continued.

Table 5: Advantages and Disadvantages of the Three Different Electoral Management Models

	Advantages	Disadvantages
Independent	• Provides a conducive environment for the development of electoral corporate identity and staff professionalism. • Is less likely to be subject to restrictions on who can be involved in electoral management, as it may be able to draw on outside talent. • Concentration on electoral business may result in better planning and more cohesive institutionalization of election tasks. • Is in control of its own funding and implementation of electoral activities. • Electoral administration tends to be under unified control even if different service providers are used. • Electoral legitimacy is enhanced as the EMB is perceived to be impartial and not subject to political control.	• May be isolated from political and electoral framework decision-makers. • May not have sufficient political influence to acquire sufficient or timely funding. • Member turnover may reduce corporate experience and institutional memory. • May not have the skills or experience to deal with bureaucratic and corporate environments. • May be higher cost, as institutional independence makes it difficult to co-opt low-cost or no-cost governmental structures to assist in electoral implementation.
Governmental	• Has self-renewing corporate memory and sustainability. • Has available a pool of bureaucratically experienced staff. • Is well placed to cooperate with other government departments in providing electoral services. • Has cost advantages through resource synergies within and between government departments. • Has a power base and influence within government.	• Credibility may be compromised by perception of being aligned with the current government or subject to political influence. • Is subject to internal decisions of government departments or local authorities on funding allocations and electoral policies. • May not have staff with the appropriate electoral skills. • Bureaucratic style may not be appropriate to electoral management needs. • Electoral administration may be fragmented among a number of arms of the executive branch of government with differing agendas.
Mixed	• Credibility of prominent members of independent EMB may enhance electoral legitimacy. Implementation EMB has self-renewing corporate memory and sustainability. • Has available a pool of bureaucratically experienced staff augmented by outside independent talent. • Implementation EMB is well placed to cooperate with other government departments in providing electoral services. • Independent EMB is in control of its policies and funding. Implementation EMB has cost advantages through resource synergies within and between government departments. • Dual structure provides checks independent of external observation.	• Credibility may be compromised as electoral activities are implemented by governmental bodies and monitoring powers may not be sufficient to rectify electoral irregularities. • Member turnover in independent EMB may reduce corporate experience and institutional memory. • Independent EMB may not have sufficient political influence to acquire sufficient or timely funding. Implementation EMB is subject to internal departmental or local governments' decisions on funding allocations and electoral policies. • Independent EMB may be lacking in real-world political skills. Implementation EMB bureaucratic style may not be appropriate to electoral management needs. • Electoral administration may be fragmented among a number of arms of the executive branch of government with differing agendas.

Some Guiding Principles for All EMBs

Regardless of which model is used, every EMB should be certain that it can ensure the legitimacy and credibility of the processes for which it is responsible. This can be done if electoral management is founded on fundamental guiding principles.

Guiding principles for EMBs:

- independence
- impartiality
- integrity
- transparency
- efficiency
- professionalism and
- service-mindedness

These guiding principles form the basis of electoral administration and are essential to ensure both the actual and perceived integrity of the electoral process.

Independence

There is some confusion over the meaning of EMB independence because the term 'independent' embraces two different concepts: (1) structural independence from the government (the Independent Model) and (2) the 'fearless independence' expected of all EMBs, no matter which model is used, in that they do not bend to governmental, political or other partisan influences on their decisions. While one issue is formal and the other is normative, they are seen as linked; in many parts of the world, the Independent Model is regarded as the one most likely to ensure an EMB's independence of decision and action.

Institutional or 'structural' independence can only be found in the constitution or the law. The simplest way to promote independence of decision and action in an EMB is to create a legal framework that embeds EMB independence, as provided in the constitutions and principal EMB laws of many countries, such as Mexico, South Africa, Uruguay and Zambia. While this is always feasible with the Independent Model and may be feasible when the Mixed Model is used, it may be more difficult to embed under the Governmental Model, apart from strict requirements for impartiality of action, given the integration of the EMB(s) into ministries or local governments.

For both Independent and Mixed Model electoral management, a culture of independence and the commitment of EMB members to independent decision-making are more important than formal 'structural' independence. Strong leadership is important for maintaining an EMB's independence of action. For example, a senior member of the judiciary may fill the position of chair of an independent EMB within either model. Such a link to the judiciary may make undue interference by the government or opposition parties in EMB operations less likely. However, it would not be appropriate where the judiciary is not regarded as impartial or free of corruption, or does not have enough members for it to be able to avoid conflicts of interest in election-related court cases. Countries that use judges or former judges as EMB chairs include Australia, Brazil, Costa Rica and Zambia.

Alternatively, the appointment of a respected public figure who is known for political non-alignment may advance the independence of the EMB. For example, Burkina Faso tackled this issue by appointing a civil society leader as the EMB chair. In governmental EMBs, the appointment as executive head of a public servant known for his or her integrity and unwillingness to be politically directed, as in Northern Ireland, can have a similar effect.

Impartiality

To establish the integrity and credibility of electoral processes, and promote the widespread acceptance of election results, an EMB must not only conduct electoral events in a fearlessly independent manner; it must also be impartial in its actions. Without impartial electoral management and independent action, the integrity of the election is likely to fail, making it difficult to instil widespread belief in the credibility of electoral processes, especially among the losers.

Every EMB is expected to manage elections impartially. Irrespective of the model, its source of accountability, management control or funding, the EMB should treat all election participants equally, fairly and even-handedly, without giving advantage to any political tendency or interest group.

In theory, an independent EMB made up of non-aligned 'expert' appointees might be best able to achieve impartiality. Other independent EMBs, for example where nominees of the contesting political parties are appointed to the EMB, may have a more difficult time establishing their credentials with the public as completely impartial bodies. Except in countries that have a tradition of a non-aligned civil service, the decisions and activities of EMBs under the Governmental or Mixed Models may be publicly regarded as likely to favour the incumbent government.

Yet governmental EMBs in some countries that use the Mixed Model (such as Spain) and some countries that use the Governmental Model (such as Finland and Sweden) are generally regarded as impartial. Conversely, some EMBs that follow the Independent Model may be independent in name only. Impartiality may be imposed by the legal framework or EMB structure, but it has to be put into practice through the EMB's behaviour and attitudes toward its stakeholders. Impartiality is a state of mind more than a statement in law, although it can be encouraged by a constitutional and legal framework that enables the effective external review of EMB decisions and by an EMB code of conduct with strong sanctions that are independently administered.

It is important that the general public perceives EMBs as impartial. This can best be achieved by ensuring that all EMB actions are transparent and just, and are effectively publicized and communicated.

Integrity

The EMB is the primary guarantor of the integrity and purity of the electoral process, and EMB members are directly responsibility for ensuring this. Integrity may be easier to maintain if the EMB has both full independence of action and full control of all essential electoral processes, including full control over budgets and staffing. Where other bodies have electoral functions, EMBs need to be empowered to monitor their activities closely to ensure that they meet the highest integrity standards.

Electoral law and EMB regulations benefit from incorporating clear powers for the EMB to deal with electoral officials who threaten electoral integrity by acting to benefit political interests or who are corrupt. Ignoring such problems can create larger public issues of integrity and credibility than the public use of disciplinary powers. To the extent that it is possible, it is in the EMB's interest to ensure that breaches of the electoral laws, rules and codes of conduct are followed by appropriate sanctions.

Transparency

Transparency in operational and financial management lays out for public scrutiny the decisions and reasoning of the EMB. Transparency is a basic good practice for all EMB activities. It can help an EMB combat perceptions of and identify actual financial or electoral fraud, or a lack of competence or favouritism toward particular political tendencies, which can enhance its credibility. Electoral transparency may be backed by electoral law, for example by a requirement that the EMB inform the public of its activities, as in Indonesia. Or it may be required by the EMB's code of conduct, for example the frequent media briefings and releases and stakeholder consultations undertaken by the Liberian EMB for the 2011 elections. Even without such formal backing, an EMB may adopt a transparency policy.

The absence of transparency in electoral processes invariably leads to the suspicion that fraudulent activities are taking place. For example, where observers and the public are unable to access progressive vote count and aggregation data, and where there are significant delays in announcing and validating election results (as in Belarus and Ukraine in 2004 and Ethiopia in 2005) the credibility of the election suffers.

Efficiency

Governments and the public expect that funds for elections will be used wisely and services delivered efficiently. In the face of expanding and ever more expensive technological solutions, and demands for increased effort in high-cost areas such as voter education and information, EMBs have to be careful that their programmes sustainably serve electoral efficiency, as well as integrity and modernity.

A successful EMB is one that has displayed integrity, competence and efficiency. These qualities help generate public and political party confidence in electoral processes. The legal framework can assist by defining efficient standards for electoral and financial management. However, sometimes members of an EMB may be unfamiliar with electoral practices and procedures; at other times they may not be used to dealing with contracting for equipment and materials in a cut-throat corporate environment. The resulting inefficiency in election organization may easily be perceived as corrupt and fraudulent behaviour, which may lead to more serious challenges to the EMB's credibility. Where trust is lacking in the political process generally, an EMB is unlikely to be given the benefit of the doubt.

Professionalism

Professionalism in electoral managements requires accurate, service-oriented implementation of electoral procedures by suitably skilled staff. EMBs need to ensure that all election officials, whether core staff or temporary workers, are well trained and have the necessary skills to apply high professional standards in their technical work. Professional training prompts public trust that the entire process is 'in good hands'. However, while a continuous training and skill development programme is an essential part of creating and maintaining a professional EMB, professionalism depends just as much on the attitude of every member and secretariat staff person. A personal commitment from each individual in an EMB to equity, accuracy, diligence and service in all they do, and to self-improvement, is necessary to maintain professionalism in electoral management.

Visible professionalism in an EMB also gives political parties, civil society, voters, donors, the media and other stakeholders the confidence that electoral managers are capable of undertaking their tasks effectively. A lack of visible professionalism in electoral management, on the other hand, will create public suspicions of inaccurate and perhaps fraudulent activity, and a lack of trust. It will make it easier for complaints from election losers to find public support, whether the complaint is valid or not.

Service-mindedness

EMBs not only have a responsibility to provide a service to their stakeholders— it is the major reason for their existence. Developing and publicizing service delivery standards for all their activities provides both internal motivators for

EMB members and staff to provide high-quality service, and external yardsticks with which stakeholders can assess the EMB's performance. Some basic service standards are often included in the electoral legal framework, as in Canada: these include time-based standards such as deadlines for announcing election results, compiling the electoral registers, distributing voters' identification (ID) cards or distributing information on voting location.

Further useful service delivery standards can be adopted by the EMB itself as part of its procedures for each electoral process. These may be time-based service standards such as the average, maximum and minimum times voters spend queuing to receive ballot papers, the time within which an enquiry from a member of the public will be answered, or the average time taken to process voter registration data for an elector. They may also be quality-based standards such as the percentage of electors being refused a vote due to errors on the electoral register, the proportion of materials missing or not delivered on time to polling stations, the proportion of polling stations that did not open on time on election day, or the accuracy and timely availability of preliminary voting results.

As well as such hard facts, stakeholder perceptions of EMB service performance are critical in influencing public judgements of the EMB's integrity and effectiveness. Regular public or stakeholder surveys (for example, after elections) can provide useful information to help an EMB assess and improve its service delivery. These may be conducted by the EMB itself or be external, for example as part of the EMB's accountability responsibilities—such as a performance review by the legislature.

Chapter Summary

- Elections are complex and specialized processes that are most effectively managed by a body with specific electoral management responsibilities.
- An EMB is an institution or body founded for the sole purpose of managing some or all of the essential elements of electoral management, which include:
    - determining who is eligible to vote;
    - receiving and validating the nominations of electoral participants (for elections, political parties and/or candidates);
    - conducting polling;
    - counting the votes; and
    - tabulating the votes.
- Essential and other electoral tasks may be conducted by a single body, or be allocated to multiple bodies.

- There are three broad models of electoral management:
  - Independent Model
  - Governmental Model
  - Mixed Model
- Each model of electoral management may encompass one or more EMBs with varying functions.
- An Independent Model of electoral management consists of an EMB (or sometimes two) that is institutionally independent from the executive branch of government. In the Governmental Model, EMBs are part of and accountable to the executive branch.
- A Mixed Model typically consists of two component EMBs: an independent EMB with policy and/or monitoring powers, and a governmental EMB responsible for the implementation of the electoral process.
- A critical issue for all EMBs, whether institutionally independent or not, is independence of decision-making and action. An EMB's behaviour and attitudes are more important for building public trust in the credibility of electoral management than the institutional framework within which it operates.
- Each model of electoral management has some basic attributes, but also many variations. The way in which EMBs work depends not merely on the model used, but also on other electoral framework, social, cultural and political factors.
- There are many types of EMBs within the three broad models. They may be permanent or temporary, and may be centralized or decentralized to varying degrees. Each structure has its advantages and disadvantages that need to be carefully assessed according to the particular country's conditions.
- Special coordination considerations may be necessary for EMBs in federal countries and in transitional environments, where an international presence on the EMB may assist in conflict management.
- EMBs preferably have an allocated minister to represent their views to the cabinet and a multiparty committee of the legislature that deals with electoral matters.
- Regardless of which model is used, all EMBs need to follow some guiding principles, including independence of decision-making and action, impartiality, integrity, transparency, efficiency, professionalism and service-mindedness. These principles are sometimes more fully achieved under the Independent Model than by the other models.

CASE STUDY

Republic of Seychelles: A New Electoral Commission

Marie-Thérèse Purvis

Background

Seychelles became an independent republic in 1976 under the leadership of a newly elected coalition government of the two main political parties at the time. One year later this government was deposed in a coup d'état led by the Seychelles People's United Party, which established a one-party constitution in 1979. The National Assembly was dissolved and replaced by a one-party People's Assembly, whose members were selected through a general election in 1979. Other one-party presidential and assembly general elections took place in 1987 and 1991.

The country returned to multiparty democracy in the early 1990s, with a new constitution approved through a referendum in 1993. This change required the appointment of an independent electoral commissioner responsible for establishing and maintaining the voters' register, delimiting the electoral boundaries, oversight of political campaigning, organizing elections and registering political parties. Under the new constitution, presidential and National Assembly elections, which are based on universal franchise, take place every five years.

Calls for electoral reforms after the general elections of 2007 and 2011 resulted in a sixth amendment to the 1993 constitution, which changed the office of the electoral commissioner to that of an Electoral Commission (EC) in 2011. One of the EC's mandates was to recommend electoral reforms that would further enhance democracy.

The Legislative Framework

In addition to the constitutional provisions that established the EC and stipulated procedures for presidential and National Assembly elections, two other main statutes provide the detailed legal framework for elections in Seychelles. The Elections Act of 1995 regulates the registration of voters, the organization of presidential and National Assembly elections, and referendums. The Political Parties (registration and regulation) Act of 1991 establishes the EC as the registrar of political parties, with responsibility for maintaining a register of political parties, allocating public funds to parties and reporting to the National Assembly accordingly. Section 3 of the Public Order Act of 1959 deals with control of public gatherings, which also include political party public meetings and rallies. Other regulations pursuant to the Elections Act include the Election Advisory Board Regulations of 2010 and the Elections Regulation of 2006, which address issues of signage and the use of government vehicles in polling activities.

Institutional Structure

The EC comprises five members (one woman and four men) who are independent professional persons, not aligned with the interests of any political party or government. They are appointed for seven years, with the possibility of renewing their applications after that period.

The positions were advertised by the Constitutional Appointments Authority (CAA) in accordance with article 115a of the constitution, and the CAA made recommendations to the president, who appointed the five members, including a chairperson. The latter is the only full-time member of the commission; he heads the EC secretariat of four other permanent staff. Other electoral officers are recruited on a temporary basis during election periods or for specific purposes such as voter registration.

Since the Seychelles electoral system is small, the commission has responsibility for both policy decisions relating to the electoral process and overseeing the implementation of the electoral process. It is independent of any government ministry or department. It operates autonomously and manages its own budget, for which it is accountable only to the Ministry of Finance and the auditor general. The commission reports annually to the National Assembly on the conduct of all elections it is responsible for, and on the public funding of political parties.

Powers and Functions

As mandated by the constitution, the Elections Act and the Political Parties Act, the EC is responsible for ensuring that all eligible persons can exercise their right to present themselves as candidates for election and that all voters have access to the electoral system by:

- maintaining the national register of voters;
- informing voters about the electoral system and elections;
- maintaining a register of political parties;
- ensuring the registration of candidates for elections;
- overseeing the conduct of election campaigns;
- administering access to the public media for campaign purposes;
- reviewing and adjusting electoral boundaries;
- training electoral staff;

- conducting presidential and National Assembly elections and referendums, in accordance with the legal framework;
- reporting to the National Assembly on the administration of elections and referendums; and
- periodically making recommendations to the government for further reforms.

Financing

The commission is financed through public funds. Each year the chairperson submits a budget to the Ministry of Finance, following the same procedure as other government ministries or departments. All expected costs are normally covered. The budgets for elections are prepared separately, and all election expenses are covered under the consolidated revenue fund.

Accountability

The EC is fully accountable to the Ministry of Finance for all expenditure of public funds. Its accounts are also subject to audits by the auditor general. As the registrar of political parties, the commission also reports annually to the National Assembly on the public financing of political parties and on all elections that are organized, and it may be taken to court by any aggrieved person or political party.

Professionalization

Members of the commission and secretariat staff participate in regional and international training programmes and other professional development activities. This is often through contacts with regional and international organizations active in the areas of electoral management and democracy promotion. EC members also take part in election observation missions in the region and elsewhere.

Some training of temporary staff responsible for electoral administration is conducted during election periods. However, the EC still lacks a coordinated professional development programme for all its members and staff.

Relations with the Media, Other Institutions and Agencies

Access to public media for campaign purposes is regulated by the Elections Act, and the commission ensures that all candidates and parties have equal access to airtime on national radio and television. However, it has no control over campaign opportunities through privately owned media, although political parties and candidates generally agree to abide by a voluntary code of conduct for elections. The EC collaborates with the Media Commission, which is a relatively new organization and is still in the process of finalizing a code of ethics for the local media. Under the one-party system the media was completely controlled by the government, and this legacy is only gradually being challenged.

The EC works closely with a number of government ministries and departments, including the statistics department, civil status office, immigration, and information and communications technology departments. It is relatively easy for the EC to communicate with the executive, legislature and judiciary on matters related to elections and electoral reforms, as it deems necessary.

The EC is a member of the SADC Electoral Commissions Forum, and its members participate actively in their professional development programmes. Close ties are maintained with the Commonwealth Secretariat, and the EC has welcomed observers from these organizations as well as from local observer groups.

New Technologies

An electronic voter register is updated and maintained annually. The EC is considering the introduction of biometric identification cards and the use of barcode scanners and existing GIS databases to carry out a voter census that should considerably improve the accuracy of the voter register.

Electoral Reform Management

The EC was mandated to undertake electoral reforms, in particular to review existing legislation governing electoral matters and make recommendations to government. The process began in October 2011 with setting up a forum for electoral reform comprising representatives of all registered political parties and civil society, and the establishment of an agreed roadmap to guide its work. It was agreed that, as a general rule, forum decisions would be by consensus. The views of voters were sought through a series of regional public meetings and other avenues of direct communication with the EC. The forum's deliberations on electoral reform were open to the public, and many of the issues debated were also taken up in the local media.

All legislation relating to elections was reviewed, and the EC submitted its first set of recommendations on section 3 of the Public Order Act to the president in 2012. Recommendations on the other statutes were forwarded to the government in 2013. The major aim of the recommendations was to strengthen the democratic process governing elections in Seychelles.

The main areas proposed for reform include:

- enacting new laws that enable citizens to exercise their right to assemble peacefully in public places, as opposed to having to seek police permission for such assemblies;
- holding elections within 90 days of a president resigning or dying;
- the institutionalization of a regular voters' census to ensure an accurate voter register at all times;
- the streamlining of the nomination procedures for candidates for elections;
- setting limits on and control of campaign financing;
- obligatory disclosure of sources of campaign funding;

- streamlining procedures for the registration of political parties; and
- reviewing the basis for financial support to political parties and the public disclosure of political party financing.

By mandating the newly appointed EC to undertake reforms, the government has, at one level, made a commitment to pursuing such reforms. However, recommendations for legislative changes can only happen if they are enacted by the National Assembly. Still, government support would remain a very important element in this process. The commission is also in a position to play a relatively strong advocacy role in the reform process.

Gender

The EC advocates for gender equality in all its principles, procedures and activities. And although the majority of electoral officials are women, and women make up the majority of voters in most age categories, women's participation on the national political scene—such as women parliamentarians, senior government executives and leaders of political parties—remains relatively low compared to men. Fewer women are to be found on the executive committees of political parties, and generally parties field more male than female candidates. The argument often put forward for this is that 'the best candidates' are selected anyway. However, the untenable underlying assumption here is that since the majority of committee members and candidates are men, they are therefore the best candidates.

There is clearly a need for the EC to further mainstream gender in its voter education and outreach programmes, as well as in its overall practices.

Opportunities and Constraints

The small size of the country—a voter population of about 60,000 out of a total population of 88,000—has the advantage of facilitating access, shortening the power distances between people and their elected representatives, and providing greater opportunities for change. However, the highly dispersed nature of the Seychelles archipelago, the emergent democratic governance and limited citizens' engagement in it so far, make for a unique situation and present particular challenges for the new EC. The recent consultative process for electoral reform has strengthened the commission's position as an independent body and helped it to gain the trust of all stakeholders. The commission has to build on these strengths over the next five years of its mandate if it is to succeed in effecting the changes that should help consolidate democracy through the electoral process.

CASE STUDY

Mexico: A Sophisticated Scheme for Addressing a Serious Distrust Issue

Carlos Navarro

In 1988, a systematic crisis of confidence in the Mexican electoral system ensued after the official results of a rather controversial presidential election were announced. Until then, elections had been controlled by successive governments belonging to a hegemonic political party that had remained in power for nearly 60 years.

In order to face this crisis and address all the demands and expectations of democratic change, a series of constitutional and legal reforms was agreed upon between 1989 and 2007. These reforms significantly modified the rules, institutions and electoral procedures in order to adhere to standards of rigor, impartiality and transparency. These reforms contributed to creating a solid multiparty system and promoting important guarantees and equity conditions in the competition for the vote.

The creation of the Federal Electoral Institute (IFE) in 1990 was a key piece of this transformation process. The IFE was conceived as a public, permanent, independent and specialized body, responsible for conducting federal elections in Mexico.

Mexico is a federal state, made up of 32 autonomous entities (31 states and the capital, which is the venue of the federal powers) that comprise its internal governmental regime. From 1946–2014, this federal arrangement expressed itself, in electoral terms, as a clear division of competences between the federation and its 32 entities; even when they shared a series of common precepts, each governmental order had its own rules, institutions and electoral procedures.

This legal-institutional arrangement functioned for almost seven decades, until a constitutional reform agreed on at the end of 2013 and in place since the beginning of 2014 brought substantial change. An essential component of this change is the replacement of the IFE with the National Electoral Institute (INE). The INE has most of the same characteristics and structure as the IFE, but its range of powers is broadened.

Although the creation of the INE does not imply the elimination of the bodies responsible for conducting elections in the 32 entities, its name does accurately suggest the implications of changes in the legal-institutional design. The INE is not only responsible for organizing federal elections, but it also has the power to collaborate and intervene in local elections (executive and legislative authorities at the municipal and state levels). All this, governed by the laws of the national political parties and electoral procedures.

This case study analyses the origin, nature and scope of the IFE, and sketches some of the implications and challenges of its replacement by the INE. IFE has played a key role in the reform and modernization process of the Mexican electoral regime during the last three decades and the fact is, as of May 2014, neither the new electoral laws nor the electoral procedures common to all the states have yet been approved. The characteristics and scope of the new electoral organization model will be examined, particularly those related to the INE's powers and organization.

It is also worth pointing out that the Mexican model of electoral institutions assigns administrative competences (preparing, organizing and conducting the elections) and jurisdictional roles (solving controversies and applying electoral justice) to different, specialized organizations at each level of government. This text is solely focused on the IFE/INE as an EMB.

Background

Mexico, like most Latin American countries, obtained its independence from Spain at the beginning of the 19th century. Even though a large share of its first 100 independent years was characterized by intense political instability due to the fact that access to power was frequently settled in the battlefield, elections—even if they were a mere formality—took place regularly.

Originally inspired by political slogans such as 'Sufragio Efectivo, No re-elección' (Effective suffrage, no re-election) the country experienced one of the first social revolutions of the 20th century. Once the turmoil it caused was over, a new political regime was established at the end of the 1920s. The regime was characterized by the centralization of political power in the president of the republic, and was structured around a hegemonic party system with accentuated authoritarian characteristics.

While the four decades that followed the Mexican Revolution saw profound social and economic transformations, the political regime was practically unaltered. There was a formal multiparty system and elections were duly observed, but the nominal opposition was very weak.

It was not until the mid-1970s that intense social pressure and mobilizations contributed to the first important changes in the political regime. Legal means were opened for the political participation and representation of different social forces (particularly leftist) that had been systematically excluded from the political arena until then.

By the end of that decade, new forces had burst into politics and the growing electoral competition was quite visible. However, even though political plurality had been encouraged, the rules and practices related to electoral management had not been modified. The operation of the electoral machinery was set in motion only during electoral periods under the control of the executive, which caused great distrust. The organizing of elections and their results were, for many Mexicans, synonymous with manipulation and fraud.

Such circumstances turned the federal elections of 1988 into a landmark. The crisis came to a head when, amid questions and doubts regarding the fairness of the process and the certainty of its results, the victory of the ruling party and its candidate was announced. It became inconceivable to all political forces and actors to hold another election without comprehensive and thorough reform of the legal and institutional framework governing the electoral competition.

In this context, a very important cycle of constitutional and legal reforms took place between 1989 and 1996 to progressively answer the demands for greater transparency and impartiality in the organizing of elections. The reforms also helped strengthen the multiparty regime and guarantee an equitable context for electoral competition.

That set of reforms, and the ones approved in 2007 and 2008, had two distinctive features. The first was its inclusiveness, not only by involving all the political forces represented in congress in the entire process of negotiation and agreement, but also by taking into account the reflections and proposals made by specialized and interested groups and stakeholders. The second feature was the comprehensive scope and completeness of the reforms, which responded to a number of demands about the regime's composition.

It is important to remember that the negotiations and agreements for this first cycle of reforms took place from 1989 until 1996, when the hegemonic political party was still in power—it held control of the executive and had an absolute majority in both chambers of congress.

Creation and Powers of the Federal Electoral Institute

The 1989–90 constitutional and legal reforms substantially modified the institutions and procedures that govern federal elections in Mexico. One of the most important changes in the new Mexican electoral architecture was the creation of the IFE. Following the mandate of the constitution and the issuing of a new electoral law in 1990, the IFE was founded that year as a permanent public organization, autonomous in terms of its decisions and professional in its performance—which represented a fundamental change in the nature of the institution responsible for organizing federal elections.

The constitution states that the IFE must abide by five fundamental principles when executing its powers: certainty, legality, independence, impartiality and objectivity. While the various constitutional and legal reforms that have been approved over the 20 years since the IFE's foundation have altered some of the formulae and mechanisms conceived for its composition, organization and functioning, the intention of each change has been to safeguard or heighten those principles.

The significant expansion of the IFE's powers through reforms was also meant to respond to the demands that have emerged from new circumstances and dynamics in the competition for votes. There are now higher expectations around the world that electoral rules and institutions will guarantee free, fair and credible elections and ensure an equitable competitive environment.

Thus the two main elements of the electoral reforms in Mexico focused on impartiality in the organization of elections and equity during the competition, in efforts to build trust and strengthen the electoral regime. The shaping of the IFE's structure, along with its powers and the ways it has wielded them for over two decades, are clear examples of these reforms.

True independence of EMBs includes a financial dimension related to their ability to plan their own budget and, just as importantly, receive and spend funds promptly. In this sense, attention must be drawn to the budgetary independence of the IFE from its creation (since only congress can modify it) and its very generous and timely public funding, which has enabled it to efficiently carry out its responsibilities.

The budget that the IFE administered, and now administered by the INE, comes solely from public funds. During the 2012 elections, USD 473.3 million was allocated for ordinary operational expenses, USD 316.3 million for organizing the electoral process and USD 392.0 million as public funding for political parties to meet their own ordinary and campaign expenses, for a total of USD 1.2 billion.

To demonstrate its proper management of resources, the INE is compelled to abide by rules on transparency and public accountability, and is overseen by a General Comptroller's Office with broad powers to perform its duties; the head of that office is independently appointed by congress.

In order to ensure that the IFE's responsibilities were carried out in a professional manner, the 1990 legislation stipulated the creation of an electoral civil service, which was effectively established in 1992. All IFE officers in the executive areas that handle key functions related to planning, organizing, conducting and surveilling elections had to be part of this electoral civil service. In this regard, no major changes should be expected for the INE.

An Increasing Repertoire of Functions and Responsibilities

Since its creation, the IFE was empowered to directly perform all activities related to preparing, organizing, conducting and surveilling every federal electoral process, as well as other activities attendant to the law (such as contributing to the enhancement of democratic life, preserving the political parties' regime and contributing to the dissemination of civic education).

In this regard, perhaps the most important feature of the reforms approved during the IFE's existence was the systematic enlargement and diversification of its powers. In addition to its essential electoral organizational and logistical powers (e.g. candidate registration; accreditation of citizen and international observers; selection and training of polling site officers; design, printing and distribution of all electoral materials; provision of preliminary results and official vote tallying), the IFE was also responsible for many other tasks that have been inherited by the INE, which are discussed below.

Periodic Revision and Adjustment of Electoral Boundaries

The composition of the Lower Chamber of the Federal Congress is a variation of the German mixed-member proportional representation (PR) system, in which 300 of the 500 representatives are elected using a first past the post (FPTP) system in an equal number of single-member districts distributed among the 32 entities of the federation according to the population distribution. The IFE was responsible for conducting a periodic revision of those 300 single-member districts in order to preserve the principle of equal representation. The INE also exerts this power for state-level constituencies.

Integration and Permanent Updating of the Federal Registry of Voters and the Issuing of the Voting Card

The IFE was—and now the INE is—responsible for the integration and permanent updating and refining of the electoral roll that is used for all the country's elections. Registration in the electoral roll is voluntary, so each citizen must do so personally. Upon registration, the INE issues a voting card with a photograph, free of charge, which is valid for a period of ten years. Since Mexico has no national identification document, this photo-voting card has in practice become Mexicans' most common ID. There were 79.5 million citizens enabled to vote in the 2012 federal elections.

Control and Oversight of Parties and Campaign Financing

During the last two decades, Mexico has developed one of the world's most generous permanent public financing systems for political parties. The constitution stipulates that public financing must prevail over private financing. The IFE was (and the INE is) responsible for administrating the public subsidy assigned to the national political parties (nearly USD 400 million in 2012).

At the same time, private financing is subject to very precise regulations and restrictions regarding its origin and amounts. Consequently, political parties have very strict obligations to account for the origin, management and use of all the resources they get for both their organization and functioning and for campaigning.

The exercise of its very ample powers regarding national political parties' finance control and oversight, as well as that of federal campaigns, was the IFE's sole responsibility during its existence. In order to achieve this, it constructed one of the most complex and sophisticated systems imaginable. This important and delicate function has now been taken over by the INE, but it has significantly expanded: it also has to control and oversee the financing of parties and campaigns at the level of the 32 federal entities. These functions also include independent candidates, who may now run for office for all kinds of elections, after a reform was approved in 2012.

Administering State Times in the Media

Until 2008, Mexico had a regime that combined a generous allowance of free media (radio and television) access for parties' electoral propaganda, subsidized by the state, and a basic group of regulations to purchase additional time under equal conditions. In 2008, a set of important constitutional and legal reforms brought about a dramatic transformation: neither political parties nor individual or legal entities were allowed to buy time to broadcast any political propaganda or electoral publicity in the media.

Since then, any access to or use of the public or private media for political-electoral propaganda is reserved for political parties and candidates. This access is only granted through the (very generous) time the state provides in all radio stations (around 1,600) and TV channels (around 750) that operate in Mexico.

All the arrangements and facilities comprised in this free service for parties and candidates, which also reserves time for messages from the electoral authorities, is now the INE's responsibility. Its realization has required the installation and operation of an enormous and very sophisticated technical-administrative mechanism in charge of distributing the 42 minutes of programming available to the political parties and candidates every day during campaigns; the technical validation and national distribution of the material produced by the parties; the verification of its broadcasting in the space and time previously agreed on; and the generation of the consequent informative reports.

Organizing Electoral Debates

A 2008 reform gave the IFE the power to organize two debates between the registered candidates for presidential elections. The most recent constitutional reform requires the new legislation to set the rules for the electoral authorities to organize mandatory debates among candidates to all electoral posts. Therefore the INE's powers in this matter may expand to at least the legislative elections.

A Complex Organizational Structure

To fully accomplish its purposes and powers, the IFE established—and the INE is expected to maintain and even expand, according to its new and extended powers—a vast and complex organizational structure, in which four different kinds of bodies can be highlighted:

- councils: directive and decision-making bodies in all areas of jurisdiction of the institution, are composed in a collegiate fashion;
- executive boards: composed of members of the electoral civil service; they are in charge of implementing the policies, programmes and approved resolutions agreed by the directive bodies;
- technical bodies: specialized organs that provide technical advice upon request from other areas in the IFE; and
- surveillance bodies: commissions formed mainly and equally by representatives of the political parties; their function is to oversee the tasks related to integrating, updating and verifying the electoral roll.

Aside from its headquarters in the capital city, the IFE operated and the INE now operates in a decentralized fashion, with 332 permanent offices all over the country (where the directive, executive and surveillance bodies have representation).

A Steering Body that Guarantees Independence and Impartiality

The most important mechanisms for guaranteeing the independence and impartiality of an institution are the integration of its directive bodies and decision-making methods. Although each of the INE bodies has equal representation of the political parties, and parliamentary groups are represented at the highest council, the only members with the right to vote are those with no partisan affiliation.

The main directive body of INE is its General Council, formed in April 2014, which consists of 11 members who have a right to voice and vote, and a variable number of members who are entitled to participate in debates, but not vote. The 11 voting members are the president councillor and ten electoral councillors. All of them shall be elected, as a general rule, by a vote of two-thirds of the members of the Lower Chamber, following a complex procedure that involves different stages that are clearly established by the constitution. Their eligibility depends on meeting certain requirements that guarantee, first and foremost, their independence and impartiality, but also their ability to perform their duties. All voting members shall serve a nine-year term and be replaced on a staggered basis.

Non-voting members include one representative of each nationally registered political party (currently seven); one for each parliamentary group with party affiliation in either chamber of Congress (currently also seven); and the executive secretary of the INE. The General Council is currently made up of 26 members. All General Council sessions are public and take place in a facility that is equipped for media coverage and live transmission on the Institute's website. Debates are regulated, decisions are taken by majority vote and the voting members do so openly.

Intensive Usage of New Technologies

Even though the essential electoral procedures such as casting a vote, scrutinizing and tallying the votes at the polling stations (roughly 143,000 were installed at the July 2012 federal elections) are done manually, the IFE used (and now the INE uses) technology intensively to carry out many of its organizational and electoral process activities. For instance, technology is used to establish a permanent connection between its offices throughout the country and provide the mass media, and all other interested audiences, with timely information.

In addition to the impressive technological platform used for the integral management of state broadcasting times, biometric systems are used to create the electoral registry and produce photo-voting cards (which also have visible and invisible security measures that make them almost impossible to forge or alter). Another key use of new technologies is the design and operation of an intranet devoted solely to the real-time dissemination of preliminary elections results on more than 25 public websites.

Final Comments

The Mexican electoral architecture, and particularly the IFE's (and now INE's) nature, organization and powers, are clear examples of how far efforts (and regulations) can go to guarantee the transparency, trust and credibility of elections and their results in an environment that can be characterized by systematic distrust, which is particularly apparent among the main contenders.

A little over 20 years after its creation, and after conducting eight federal elections (four general and four mid-term elections), the IFE was able to fully accredit the impartiality, rigour and professionalism with which all of its powers and responsibilities were carried out. In this regard, the IFE's existence very much contributed to the strengthening and dissemination of democratic rules, institutions, values and practices.

From this perspective, it was very surprising that the constitutional reform approved by Congress at the end of 2013, as part of a wide consensus between the federal government and the main political parties, involved not only the substitution of the IFE with the INE, but also altered in a very significant and unconventional sense the bases on which the model of distribution of competences between the federation and the 32 federal entities had been structured and conducted in the political-electoral field.

Most analysts think this was a reform that went astray. The original idea behind it, which, even if arguable, made sense: to confer on a single body the responsibility for conducting all the elections and popular consultations in the country. This would have served to avoid administrative and budgetary duplicity and to guarantee homogeneity and impartiality in the management of all electoral processes. Moreover, and in contrast with the previous reforms of 1989–90, this reform does not solve a real problem or address clearly identified insufficiencies, but rather is the result of strict negotiations and trade-offs among the main political actors.

A hybrid model for electoral management without precedent among federal states has been adopted with the new constitutional reform. This model will require the law to clarify and specify the INE's scope of competencies and collaboration powers with the 32 local electoral authorities. There is also the aggravating factor that the national authority will not only have the power to choose the voting members in the highest decision-making bodies in the local entities, but will also be able to directly assume functions related to the organization of elections in the states, as well as handle legal matters regarding these elections that may require its intervention or set a court precedent.

In any case, during the IFE's existence, it systematically enlarged the scope of its powers. With the creation of the INE, and more generally, with the adoption of the new electoral management model for the federal agreement, this logic has remained, and is likely to be intensified and reinforced.

Thus the Mexican model may well be an excellent example with which to evaluate, deeply and rigorously, the challenges and risks of enlarging and making electoral regulations more sophisticated (especially those regarding the competition for the vote, which involves a more 'referee' than managerial role)—and, consequently, of broadening the scope of powers of the authority in charge of putting them into practice or ensuring their compliance.

It is still a paradox that neither the IFE during its time nor the INE currently, as a national authority, has any formal power to participate in the process of creating or reforming legal rulings in electoral matters, as other EMBs in the region do. This, despite the densely regulated and sophisticated model of electoral management and competition of the Mexican system, which has a huge constellation of permanent electoral bodies that are independent and highly specialized.

CHAPTER 2

The Legal Framework: The Context for an EMB's Role and Powers

How Legal Instruments Define Electoral Processes

The structure, powers, functions and responsibilities of EMBs are defined in those parts of a country's legal framework that deal with electoral processes. Especially in newer democracies, the current trend is to develop a comprehensive legal framework that guarantees the independence and integrity of the electoral process, promotes consistency and equality in electoral management, and supports full and informed participation in electoral events by political parties, civil society organizations (CSOs) and electors. The full legal framework for elections can be based on a variety of sources, including the following:

1. International documents, for example article 25 of the International Covenant on Civil and Political Rights (ICCPR): 'Every citizen shall have the right and the opportunity, without any of the distinctions mentioned in article 2 and without unreasonable restrictions:

   a) To take part in the conduct of public affairs, directly or through freely chosen representatives;

   b) To vote and to be elected at genuine periodic elections which shall be by universal and equal suffrage and shall be held by secret ballot, guaranteeing the free expression of the will of the electors;

   c) To have access, on general terms of equality, to public service in his country'.

2. Regional documents, for example the African Charter on Democracy, Elections and Governance: 'State Parties re-affirm their commitment to regularly holding transparent, free and fair elections in accordance with the Union's Declaration on the Principles Governing Democratic Elections in Africa' (article 17)

3. The constitution

4. National laws, which may take the form of one comprehensive electoral code, as in Albania, Argentina, Armenia and the Philippines. Alternatively, there may be a set of laws covering different aspects of the electoral process. Indonesia, for example, has a Law on General Elections, a Law on Election Organisation, a Law on Presidential Elections, a Law on Political Parties, a Law Establishing the Constitutional Court (one of whose functions is the resolution of certain electoral disputes) and a Law on Local Governance, which includes provisions for elections for the heads of the regional executive branches of government. Some countries (e.g. Latvia, South Africa, Uzbekistan and Zambia) define the structure, composition and powers of their EMB in a separate law, as does Thailand, where this law has the higher status of an organic law. Other laws, such a voter registration law, ID law or a law on the organization of the national territory, can also be part of the legal framework.

5. Provincial or state laws, which in federal countries may govern the processes for provincial or state and local electoral events (as in Australia) or for national electoral events (as in the United States)

6. Ordinances and regulations made by national or lower-level authorities

7. Regulations, proclamations and directives issued by an EMB, if it has the power to do so

8. Customary laws and conventions that may be integrated into electoral law, or EMB regulations or policies dealing with issues such as separate voter registration and voting arrangements for women and men

9. Administrative policies made by an EMB or other bodies, and

10. Codes of conduct (voluntary or otherwise) that may have a direct or indirect impact on the electoral process, for example, for EMBs, election participants, observers and election reporting by the media.

The organization and administration of electoral processes is complex, and always involves a substantial mass of detail. It is therefore usually specified in written laws and regulations, rather than determined by unwritten tradition or administrative policymaking. Written laws and regulations provide the benefits of certainty, visibility and transparency; are easier to subject to judicial review; and are accessible to interested parties, including electors. The legal certainty provided by a detailed exposition of electoral processes embedded in law, backed by constitutional authority, will tend to promote confidence in the consistency, fairness and even-handedness of electoral administration, and provide clear opportunities for legal redress. The level of detail specified at different levels of the legal framework will vary from country to country, depending on factors such as systems of law and the level of trust in EMBs' willingness and ability to make fair and consistent decisions and policies.

International and Regional Treaties and Agreements

Many UN member countries incorporate into their domestic law (using a variety of constitutional means) key UN decisions and treaties, such as the 1966 ICCPR and the 1979 Convention on the Elimination of All Forms of Discrimination against Women (CEDAW). In such cases, domestic electoral laws, and EMB policies and actions, need to consider the treaties' provisions as treaty obligations that their country has voluntarily adhered to, especially in relation to issues such as universal and non-discriminatory suffrage, secret and free voting, the rights of women to be elected and hold public office, and the rights of minority language groups. Bilateral agreements between countries and regional treaties on supranational bodies (e.g. the European Union) may also contain electoral requirements. While complementary laws are usually required to give effect to such treaties, EMB actions that contradict rights contained in ratified treaties may still be legally challengeable.

Member states of regional bodies, such as the OSCE, the Organization of American States (OAS) and the African Union (AU), are increasingly committing themselves through either legislative or executive ratification to implement treaties and decisions adopted by the regional bodies. In 1990, the OSCE adopted the Copenhagen Commitments, through which its participating states 'solemnly declare that among those elements of justice which are essential to the full expression of the inherent dignity and of the equal and inalienable rights of all human beings are…free elections that will be held at reasonable intervals by secret ballot or by equivalent free voting procedure, under conditions which ensure in practice the free expression of the opinion of the electors in the choice of their representatives'. The AU Charter on Democracy, Elections and Governance provides that 'State Parties shall:

1. Establish and strengthen independent and impartial national electoral bodies responsible for the management of elections.

2. Establish and strengthen national mechanisms that redress election-related disputes in a timely manner.

3. Ensure fair and equitable access by contesting parties and candidates to state controlled media during elections.

4. Ensure that there is a binding code of conduct governing legally recognized political stakeholders, government and other political actors prior to, during and after elections. The code shall include a commitment by political stakeholders to accept the results of the election or challenge them through exclusively legal channels'.

The AU has backed up the charter in practice by establishing an electoral support unit within its secretariat.

Similar frameworks have been developed by subregional bodies, such as the Southern African Development Community (SADC) and the Economic Community of West African States (ECOWAS). One example of such a regional and enforceable treaty that affects the legal frameworks for EMBs is the ECOWAS Protocol on Democracy and Good Governance of 2001, under which member countries commit themselves to independent or impartial electoral administration and timely electoral dispute resolution.

In addition to ratified, binding treaties and decisions, there are non-binding decisions by international and regional bodies. In October 2005, the Global Declaration of Principles and Code of Conduct for International Electoral Observation was adopted by the United Nations and by a wide range of global and regional organizations; many more organizations have adopted it subsequently. In the SADC region, the Electoral Institute of Southern Africa (EISA) and the Electoral Commissions' Forum of SADC countries (ECF) have jointly developed and adopted the Principles for Election Management, Monitoring and Observation (PEMMO), while the SADC Parliamentary Forum has established its own electoral norms and practices. These sets of principles and guidelines serve as benchmarks against which observer missions in the region assess whether an election is free, fair and credible.

The Constitution

A growing number of countries are incorporating fundamental electoral provisions in their constitutions, often including the type, composition and responsibilities of the EMB. Countries such as Bangladesh, Costa Rica, Ghana, India, Indonesia, South Africa and Uruguay have set up their respective EMBs as constitutional bodies, which makes it more difficult to alter their status and other constitutionally defined elements. Constitutional provisions are almost always more entrenched than mere laws; constitutional amendments require, for example, a qualified majority in the legislature or a referendum. The barrier that constitutional entrenchment presents to ruling parties that wish to change electoral provisions to their advantage gives opposition parties a sense of greater protection than they would have if those provisions were contained in government regulations or statute law, which can be altered by a majority in the legislature.

Some electoral provisions whose principles are often included in constitutions include:

- EMB independence;
- EMB composition and appointment system;
- EMB term of office;
- EMB powers and functions;
- suffrage rights or voter registration qualifications;
- political party rights;
- boundary delimitation authority or parameters;
- presidential election systems;
- national legislative election systems;
- the right or qualifications to stand for election;
- the intervals or maximum intervals at which elections must be held; and
- mechanisms for settling electoral disputes.

The range and nature of electoral provisions that are considered appropriate to be set out in a country's constitution vary widely according to local considerations.

- Austria's constitution defines EMB membership, franchise, the Constitutional Court's role in electoral disputes and the electoral system.
- The constitution of Bangladesh defines the powers, independence and functions of the EMB, the franchise, candidate qualifications, and the maximum period between elections.
- Cameroon's constitution specifies political party rights, candidate qualifications, the intervals at which elections must be held, and the powers of the Supreme Court and Constitutional Council related to electoral disputes.
- In Costa Rica, the constitution establishes the independence, membership and functions of the EMB, and deals with the franchise, political party rights (including government funding), electoral systems and qualifications for candidacy.
- For elections in the Czech Republic, the constitution defines the franchise, the electoral system and the maximum period between elections.
- Ghana's constitution deals with the franchise, the establishment of the EMB, the right to form or join a political party, and the delimitation of electoral districts.
- In India, the constitution has provisions establishing an EMB and addresses the franchise and electoral register, barring court interference in electoral matters and reserving seats for legally defined 'castes' and 'tribes' in the House of the People.

- Madagascar's constitution sets out candidacy rights, the electoral systems for the senate and presidency, and the Constitutional Court's role in elections and election disputes.
- The Namibian constitution enunciates the qualifications and procedures for presidential elections.
- Peru's constitution deals with the autonomy, membership and functions of the National Elections Tribunal, which supervises electoral processes and is responsible for party registration, announcement of results and electoral dispute resolution. The constitution also empowers the National Office for Electoral Processes to organize materials and logistics, funding and vote count information for all electoral events; sets out the qualifications for its chief executive; and empowers the National Registry of Identification and Civil Status to create the electoral register from its civil registry database.
- The constitution of Romania sets out the citizens' right to elect and be elected, and requires an organic law to regulate the establishment and functioning of the Permanent Electoral Authority.

Similarly targeted electoral provisions in constitutions may also be drafted in very different ways. Consider the following two examples of constitutionally defined EMB 'independence':

'Except as provided for in this Constitution or any other law not inconsistent with this Constitution, in the performance of its functions, the Electoral Commission shall not be subject to the direction or control of any authority or person' (article 46 of the constitution of Ghana).

'General elections shall be organized by a general election commission of a national, permanent, and independent character' (article 22E(5) of the Indonesian constitution).

While enshrining major electoral provisions in the constitution generates confidence in the electoral system, there may be disadvantages if these provisions are too detailed. The legal framework may then be difficult to change in practice because it is difficult to satisfy the conditions for amending the constitution, or due to the length of time it takes to amend the constitution.

The extent to which electoral provisions are incorporated into the constitution is significantly affected by the level of public trust in the country's election administration. In many established democracies with a high level of public trust in lawmaking and public administration in general, and the organization of elections in particular, constitutions do not make provision for the design of the EMB. Yet it is common—and not only among fledgling democracies—to have independent and robust EMBs that are supported by sophisticated and detailed legal frameworks that incorporate key electoral provisions in the constitution. The authority and clarity of the constitution foster stakeholder confidence in the electoral process.

Electoral Laws: Acts and Ordinances

An EMB may be established by statute, through an act of the legislature. For example, Australia, Burkina Faso and Canada established their respective EMBs entirely by statute law. It is unusual for governmental EMBs to be defined specifically in law; tasks are more frequently allocated to government agencies in an electoral law. However, in the UK (see the case study), which has no written constitution, the Electoral Commission—the EMB for referendums—is defined in statute law.

It is generally good practice when drafting such electoral statutes:

- to transparently lay down the legislative framework for electoral processes and clearly allocate the responsibility for filling in the gaps and/or details through secondary legislation, regulations or EMB administrative procedures;
- to define the status of the national EMB(s) and any subsidiary EMBs, including their accountability, powers, responsibilities and functions; and
- for legislation to provide a clear and sufficiently detailed framework to ensure effectiveness and integrity in all matters relating to electoral administration, such as EMB member and staff appointments and tenure; operational management issues related to voter registration, political party and candidate registration, political campaigns, and voter education and information; EMB transparency; voting, vote counting and the announcement of results; financial and asset management issues; and electoral offences and resolving electoral disputes.

Other issues that may be covered in electoral legislation include boundary delimitation principles and processes, and codes of conduct for EMB members and staff, political parties, publicly-owned media and election observers.

Parts of the legal framework may also be enacted as secondary legislation, for example, by an EMB with the power to make regulations by some form of executive decree; by a state or provincial legislature in the form of secondary legislation in a federal country; or by municipal authorities in the form of ordinances.

Provisions for the conduct of provincial and local elections are often contained in separate legislation. In federal countries, national and provincial electoral legal frameworks may need to be separately defined, depending on the constitutional split of powers between the national and provincial levels. Inconsistencies or overlapping provisions between national and provincial electoral legislation, for example for voter registration or voting procedures, may confuse electors. Regular consultations between federal and provincial lawmakers and electoral administrators can help minimize confusion and duplication.

In addition, where elections to a supranational body are contemplated, national legislation is likely to be necessary to define the electoral management structure within the overall supranational agreement. Looking at the example of the European Parliament, the provisions contained in the European-level legal instruments are for the most part very general in nature, and the definition of the electoral management structure for European Parliament elections is left to each member state.

As with the balance between electoral provisions in the constitution and in legislation, the balance between electoral provisions in legislation and subsidiary regulations or procedures needs to be carefully judged. Electoral legislation needs to be detailed enough to ensure integrity and effectiveness, but not so detailed that legislative amendment would be required to permit EMBs to deal with minor changes in their operations. Too much detail in the legislation can result in, for example, an EMB being unable to change its staffing structure or the design of an administrative form, or to introduce office automation systems without a change to the law. Particularly in environments where election processes take place after legislatures' terms of office have ended, electoral legislation needs to allow EMBs the flexibility to respond to changing electoral circumstances.

A modern electoral legislative scheme may entail one or several different laws. Traditional legal drafting for electoral legislation has often been precise, but in a structure and language that are not very accessible. The legislation may become particularly difficult to understand if it is subject to successive amendments over time, without a fully revised and consolidated law being produced.

A single omnibus law covering all electoral activity can be cumbersome, but may facilitate reference and review. Separate laws on individual issues—as in Indonesia, for example, such as the EMB, political parties, electoral registers, elections to the legislature, presidential elections and local government elections—provide clear and easy reference to specific electoral activities, but it may be too time consuming or difficult to ensure that there are no conflicts of content between them. Another possible solution (as in Hungary) is that the substantive norms (such as suffrage rights, eligibility, number of election rounds and the electoral system) are embodied in separate laws (on elections to the legislature, local elections and referendums), while the electoral process is regulated in a common law that consists of a general part (binding on all types of elections) and special norms for each type of election.

International IDEA's publication *International Obligations for Elections: Guidelines for Legal Frameworks* discusses a number of issues to consider when designing or reviewing a legal framework for electoral management. Key considerations are summarized in Box 1 (on page 51).

EMB Rules, Regulations and Proclamations

In some countries, an EMB has legal powers to regulate the electoral framework either by enacting new laws or by making rules and regulations that complement existing primary legislation. Such an arrangement is efficient and allows for the speedy amendment of the legal framework. For example, Uruguay's EMB can make decisions and dictate actions that cannot be reviewed by any other branch of government. Thus it has *legislative powers* (making laws that govern elections), *judicial powers* (reviewing and interpreting laws with binding effect) and *implementation powers* for the laws and norms it has enacted.

A more usual practice is for an EMB, particularly an independent EMB, to be empowered to make reviewable regulations by filling in the detail of concepts contained in the law, or filling existing gaps in the law. For governmental EMBs, this power may be held by the ministry within which the EMB is located. Such regulations in most countries are subject to review, generally by a court or constitutional court, to test whether they are within the powers of the EMB (or ministry) to make, and whether they are otherwise consistent with the law.

Box 1: Checklist for Electoral Management Legal Framework

1. Does the legal framework provide for the EMB to be constituted as an independent and impartial institution?
2. Does the legal framework require and enable the EMB to operate in an impartial and transparent manner?
3. Does the legal framework protect EMB members and staff from arbitrary dismissal?
4. Does the legal framework define the accountability, powers, functions and responsibilities of the EMB at each level, as well as relationships between the levels?
5. Does the legal framework adequately define the EMB's relationships with external stakeholders?
6. Does the legal framework provide clear guidance for all EMB activities, yet allow it practical flexibility in its implementation?
7. Does the legal framework allow the timely and enforceable review of EMB decisions?
8. Does the legal framework allow the EMB sufficient time to organize electoral events effectively?
9. Does the legal framework ensure that the EMB has sufficient and timely funding to manage its functions and responsibilities effectively?

In countries such as the Gambia, Thailand and Yemen, the EMBs have the power to make regulations to facilitate their mandate, including the conduct of elections. In Namibia, the EMB has the power to issue proclamations that by law must be gazetted, and that cover issues such as political parties' code of conduct, some procedural issues on voter registration and parties' disclosure of foreign donations. The Indonesian EMB has specific regulatory powers in some critical areas, including voter registration, candidate registration, the conduct of election campaigns and voting processes.

EMB powers to make regulations should always be exercised in such a way as to ensure consistency with both the constitution and the electoral law.

Many EMBs have the power to formulate administrative policies and directions on operational issues such as their relationships with their own staff (on matters such as gender equality, affirmative action, performance management and staff development) and with external stakeholders. External stakeholders include government ministries, in particular finance ministries, the legislature, political parties, CSOs and the media.

Unlike regulations, which by law must be issued publicly, an EMB may have no legal obligation to publish its administrative directives and policies, although it is always good practice for it to do so. Where EMB policies have to be formally approved by the EMB, they can be made publicly available through the minutes of EMB meetings. It is important that an EMB consult its stakeholders when formulating new policies or reviewing old ones in order to foster stakeholder awareness and buy-in.

Chapter Summary

- Electoral processes are complex, standardized activities that require clear, simple and relatively comprehensive legal definition in order to promote consistency, equity and a common understanding of electoral frameworks by all electoral stakeholders.

- The electoral legal framework within which an EMB operates may be defined in many different types of instruments—including international and regional treaties, the constitution, national and subnational statute law, and EMB and other regulations.

- International and regional treaties and agreements provide a framework of norms against which a country's electoral legal arrangements can be defined and assessed.

- There is a trend toward defining key electoral issues in the constitution, as this may provide a workable means of protecting electoral norms from manipulation by the ruling party. Electoral arrangements may be further defined in statute law, secondary legislation and regulations.

- Electoral statute law may either be a single law or multiple laws that need to be kept in harmony. EMBs or the executive branch of government may be able to issue regulations to fill in gaps in the law; usually these would be subject to some form of judicial or other review. EMBs may also be able to set their own administrative policies. For confidence in election processes, it is important that all parts of the electoral framework—treaties, constitution, statute laws, and EMB and other regulations, as well as administrative policies—are freely and publicly available, and that changes are discussed and shared with key stakeholders.

- A balance needs to be struck between providing for certainty and consistency in the legal framework, on the one hand, and allowing an EMB the flexibility to respond effectively to changing electoral circumstances on the other. The amount of electoral detail in higher-level instruments—constitutions and statute laws—will often depend on the level of trust in political participants and the EMB's performance.

- International IDEA's publication *International Obligations for Elections: Guidelines for Legal Frameworks* provides guidelines for assessing electoral legal frameworks.

- EMBs' powers to make regulations should always be exercised in line with both the constitution and the electoral law.

CASE STUDY

Cambodia: Lack of Confidence in the National Election Committee*

Eric des Pallières

Background

Since emerging from devastating civil and international conflict, Cambodia has held regular elections, first at the national level and then at local levels. Under the 1991 Paris Peace Agreements, the first national elections were organized by the United Nations Transitional Administration in Cambodia (UNTAC) in May 1993. Although deemed technically credible, they were marred by widespread intimidation and political violence. In September 1993, a new constitution was adopted, which established the Kingdom of Cambodia as a multiparty state and stipulated that elections to the National Assembly would be held every five years. In January 1988, the National Election Committee (NEC) was established, and further national elections were administered nationally in 1998, 2003, 2008 and 2013. The first multiparty local elections ever conducted were in 2002 for 1,621 Commune Councils,[1] whose mandates were renewed in 2007 and 2012. Indirect elections were held in 2006 and 2012 for the senate, and in 2009 for newly established councils at the district and province levels.

Until 2013, successive elections had been marked by the ever-increasing domination of Hun Sen's Cambodian People's Party (CPP), which has ruled the country since Vietnam overthrew the Khmer Rouge regime in 1979. After it lost the 1993 elections to the royalist FUNCINPEC[2] 38 to 45 per cent, the CPP rejected the results and a power-sharing agreement was brokered under which Hun Sen became the second prime minister. In 1997, the coalition fell apart amid armed confrontation, and Hun Sen assumed sole leadership of the country. In 1998, the CPP received 40 per cent of the votes and formed a new coalition with FUNCINPEC. In 2003, the CPP received 47 per cent of the votes but the elections were followed by protracted political deadlock as it had not achieved the two-thirds majority of seats then required by the constitution to form a government of its own, and the opposition again refused to recognize the

---

* A case study on Cambodia also appeared in the original edition of the Handbook: Peter Bartu, 'Cambodia: Tensions around the National Election Committee', *Electoral Management Design: The International IDEA Handbook* (Stockholm: International IDEA, 2006), pp. 284–88.

results. Eventually, another CPP/FUNCINPEC coalition was formed. In 2008, the CPP received 58 per cent of the votes and secured a two-thirds majority in the National Assembly. Meanwhile, support for FUNCINPEC had evaporated and the Sam Rainsy Party (SRP) became the main opposition party with 22 per cent of the votes.

In 2012, the two largest opposition parties, SRP and the Human Rights Party (HRP), merged to form the Cambodian National Rescue Party (CNRP). The 2013 parliamentary elections were marked by significant losses by the ruling party, as official results gave the CPP 48.8% (68 seats) to the newly unified opposition's 44.5% (55 seats). The integrity of the electoral process was called into question by national and international observers, who documented record levels of irregularities[3], notably pertaining to voter registration and identification. Claiming victory, the opposition rejected the official results, calling for an independent investigation into electoral irregularities and a reform of the NEC, accused of pro-government bias. This led to massive street protests and the longest post-election crisis in Cambodia's recent history.

Until 2013, the overall administration of elections had generally improved over time. However, two decades after the UN-run elections, the electoral process in Cambodia still fell short of key international obligations for democratic elections. In fact, issues that have undermined successive elections since 1998 have remained essentially the same: the independence of the NEC, the registration of voters and the settlement of disputes, not to mention a general environment that is not conducive to a level playing field, particularly regarding media access and the use of state resources. Whereas recent elections had underlined the need for substantial enhancements in these areas, lack of political reform and the record level of irregularities observed in the 2013 elections have further eroded confidence in the electoral administration, which is now in need of complete overhaul.

Legislative Framework

Whereas constitutional provisions outline key principles for the conduct of national elections,[4] they do not address the establishment, composition and responsibilities of an EMB, nor is this the subject of a distinct organic law. The NEC was legally established under the relevant provisions of the Law on the Election of the Members of the National Assembly (LEMNA) in December 1997. Further electoral laws were subsequently adopted as new elected assemblies were created. In the absence of a consolidated electoral code, the legal framework for elections thus consists of distinct pieces of legislation for elections to the National Assembly, the Senate, Commune Councils, and the recently established councils at the province and district levels. Other applicable instruments include the Law on Political Parties, the Law on the Press and the Law on the Constitutional Council.

Since 1998, the LEMNA has been progressively enhanced through regular amendments drawn from lessons learned, notably in 2002 and on two occasions in 2006, bringing some improvements to the general framework of electoral procedures related to voter registration, dispute resolution and the composition of the NEC. Lack of political will has since hampered reform. Minimal amendments pertaining to voter registration in 2011 failed to address core shortcomings. As for election management, the law defines the NEC as 'an independent and neutral' body,[5] but provisions pertaining to its composition and appointment have consistently raised concerns about its actual independence. Further, important electoral administration functions are delegated to other branches of the government.

Composition and Appointment Methods

There has been a persistent lack of confidence in the neutrality and impartiality of the NEC among electoral stakeholders. Despite successive reforms of its composition, an adequate formula has yet to be found that would lead to more consensual acceptance. Further concerns relate to legal shortcomings that affect the NEC's ability to ensure a fully independent administration of elections. Its members are nominated by the Ministry of Interior and appointed by royal decree at the request of the Council of Ministers, upon approval by a simple majority of the National Assembly. These institutions are all dominated by the CPP, and there is no requirement for public consultations among political parties or with other sectors of society. In addition, commissioners do not serve a definite term and are not explicitly protected from removal without cause by the National Assembly.

The composition of the NEC initially featured elements of multiparty membership, with eleven commissioners drawn from a variety of parties, including government officials and representatives of each political party represented in the National Assembly. It was widely criticized for lacking independence and impartiality in both the 1998 legislative and 2002 commune elections, particularly in its handling of complaints. While opposition members were largely outnumbered, internal strife also affected decision-making during the contested 1998 parliamentary elections. Many critics demanded reform that would remove party influence, while others argued in favour of an openly multiparty NEC with sufficient checks and balances. Before the 2003 elections, it was reformed to a smaller, 'neutral' board, whose five members were to be selected 'from among dignitaries experienced in politics, with work experience and good reputation'.[6] New procedures were also introduced for appointing members of subordinate provincial and communal election commissions. In an environment characterized by partisanship and obedience to authority, the switch to an expert EMB failed to ease accusations of pro-government bias by opposition parties and civil society watchdogs.

In 2006, a new amendment to the law enlarged the NEC's membership from five to nine, tacitly reinstating some multiparty representation as it allowed FUNCINPEC and the opposition SRP to second two members each, while the five others were deemed aligned with the ruling party. In practice, however, FUNCINPEC had become a coalition partner of the ruling CPP, and the balance tilted to seven to two on most decisions. With NEC decisions being made by simple majority vote and its internal regulations requiring a minimum of three members to put forward any proposition, the influence of opposition representatives remained extremely limited beyond accessing information. Subordinate provincial and communal commissions often remained largely dominated by CPP affiliates, as documented by national and international observers.[7] In 2011, the main political parties other than the CPP issued a joint call for multiparty representation at all levels of electoral administration, but their demand was not taken into consideration.[8] Following the 2013 elections, the opposition has made a complete overhaul of the NEC a key condition of any political settlement.

Institutional Structure and Capacity

Cambodia's elections are administered by a four-tier structure. At the central level, the NEC is headed by a permanent nine-member committee: one chair, one vice chair and seven commissioners. It is supported by a General Secretariat, which oversees the work of five departments: operations, administration, finance, training and public information, and legal services. The General Secretariat has developed significant technical expertise over the years, and has demonstrated the capacity to efficiently plan and execute electoral activities, although the use of new technologies has been underexplored to date, particularly as regards voter registration processes and results management. Activated for the election period, lower-level structures consist of 24 provincial election commissions and 1,633 commune election commissions. Between elections, the NEC maintains smaller secretariats at the province level so as to ensure continuity and oversee annual voter registration updates.

Powers and Functions

The LEMNA grants the NEC wide-ranging powers to prepare and conduct the electoral process. Its core electoral functions include: publishing the election timetable; appointing and supervising lower electoral commissions; preparing, reviewing and validating the voter lists; registering political parties and candidates for elections; conducting polling and counting operations; and establishing and announcing the results. The NEC also has jurisdiction to 'adopt regulations, procedures and directives for the electoral process within the framework of applicable laws'. The committee has plainly exercised this power in an effort to strengthen and clarify existing legal provisions with a comprehensive, though lengthy and fragmented, set of regulations, directives, instructions and guidelines.

The NEC's functions also encompass substantial regulatory powers over political contestants, the media and other players. The NEC is required by law to take all measures to ensure fair elections—including monitoring electoral campaigns, ensuring equal access to the media, auditing campaign finances and settling electoral disputes. The LEMNA thus requires stakeholders to comply with the rules and specific codes of conduct developed by the committee. Yet the NEC's power to regulate the media during elections is undermined by legal uncertainty regarding law enforcement and the imposition of sanctions. The same applies for campaign finance, especially in the absence of any limitations on contributions or expenses.

Furthermore, important electoral functions have been delegated to local authorities that are largely controlled by the ruling party, which calls into question the true independence of electoral administration. With the introduction of a permanent voter registry ahead of the 2003 elections, related amendments to the LEMNA stated that the NEC 'shall delegate any of its powers to commune councils' to perform annual voter registration activities on its behalf. The NEC retains ultimate responsibility for 'reviewing and validating voter lists' without the effective capacity to do so. Finally, the power to determine the number of seats in the National Assembly and their distribution per constituency rests with a special committee formed by the Council of Ministers, with one representative of each party represented in the Assembly, two officials of the Ministry of Interior and the director of the National Institute for Statistics.

Responsibility for Electoral Justice Processes

Among its key functions, the NEC is responsible for 'deciding on all complaints and appeals relating to the election, except for those that fall under the jurisdiction of the Court'. For national elections, this jurisdiction is subject to recourse before the Constitutional Council, which rules in final instance. One unique aspect of the Cambodian system is that it grants the NEC quasi-judicial competences as regards penal offences related to elections, notwithstanding possible criminal proceedings. A lack of confidence in the judiciary, among other reasons, accounts for such a choice. As a complement to the law, NEC regulations have established clear jurisdiction for lower electoral commissions in the settlement of electoral complaints.[9] They shall attempt conciliation between the concerned parties before formal proceedings are conducted, and act as critical filters to prevent the congestion of legal services at the national level. Their decisions may be appealed to the next level up to the NEC, and ultimately to the Constitutional Council for National Assembly and Senate Elections.

Despite these valuable features, the adjudication of complaints and appeals remains one of the most contentious aspects of the electoral process. As documented by national and international observers in recent elections, Cambodia's electoral justice system has failed to remedy the most significant alleged irregularities. Given the environment in which they operate, lower electoral commissions are often reluctant to embark on politically charged proceedings; many complaints are thus summarily dismissed at the entry point, on formal grounds or for 'lack of evidence', and complainants may be pressed to accept conciliation even when serious offences are alleged. Despite successive amendments, there remain critical flaws in the applicable provisions, including overly complex procedures, the absence of a general jurisdiction for the NEC to address violations other than specifically listed electoral offences, and unreasonably short timelines for the submission and settlement of post-election challenges. Finally, notwithstanding the competence of its legal services, the NEC is not perceived as an impartial arbiter, particularly as it has failed to enforce sanctions on ruling party affiliates in a number of recent high-profile cases.

Media Relations

In response to a deficit in public confidence, the NEC has made substantial efforts in recent years to improve its external communication strategy, making greater use of a variety of techniques and instruments, notably by its Public Information Bureau. The NEC has improved the dissemination of timely information on the electoral process to all stakeholders through a designated spokesperson, regular press conferences, press releases and posts on its website. During election periods, the LEMNA requires all media to make their services available to the NEC free of charge for voter education and information purposes. Finally, particular attention has been paid to issuing methodical answers to and clarifications of the various reports issued by election observers, development partners and national watchdogs, though often in a dismissive manner that may prove counterproductive.

The NEC's responsibility concerning the conduct of electoral campaigns includes 'taking measures to ensure equal access to the public media'. NEC rules include special programming on state television offering equal, though limited, slots to political contestants for their promotion. In addition, the NEC issued guidelines requiring all media to provide pluralistic coverage of the elections and refrain from using inflammatory or offensive language. State media are also given the responsibility to apply principles of equity and distinguish between government and party activity in their news coverage. In practice, however, most broadcast media are controlled by the CPP, which continues to receive overwhelming coverage. The respective responsibilities of the NEC and the Ministry of Information remain unclear as regards law enforcement and the imposition of sanctions. In 2008, the NEC issued warnings to broadcast media for breaking campaign rules but took no further action, despite manifest evidence of continued violations.

Financing and Sustainability

The NEC is funded by the Cambodian Government and donor contributions. With the sole exception of foreign grants, all subsidies must be credited to a dedicated trust fund account of the National Treasury. Since the first NEC-administered elections in 1998, Cambodia has made significant progress toward financial sustainability of the electoral process. While donor funding has been substantial over the years, it has decreased with each election between 1998 and 2013 from nearly 80 per cent of the overall budget to limited donations in kind, as a result of cost reductions and increased government input. Between 1998 and 2003, the budget for elections was cut in half. Costs reductions were driven in part by the reform of voter registration, from a full registration drive conducted anew before each electoral event to a permanent registry updated annually by commune authorities. While enhancing financial sustainability, this move nevertheless resulted in the transfer of critical electoral functions to local authorities dominated by the ruling party. Electoral expenses have increased since: the NEC requested a budget of USD 17 million in 2008 and USD 21 million in 2013. Voter registration was again a factor, as extension of registration periods induced higher costs. International contributions have continued to dwindle, partly due to donor fatigue, stalled electoral reform and the absence of substantial democratic development.

Electoral Reform Management

After two decades of sizeable international assistance, the electoral process in Cambodia still falls short of key international obligations for democratic elections. While the overall conduct of the electoral process has generally improved over time, critical issues that have undermined successive elections since 1998 have remained essentially the same: the independence of the NEC, voter registration and the settlement of disputes, not to mention a political environment that is not conducive to a level playing field. As documented by national and international observers, the parliamentary elections in 2008 had already highlighted the need for further, substantial reform in these critical areas: the electoral campaign saw overwhelming media bias toward the ruling party and widespread abuse of state resources, voter registration flaws left hundreds of thousands disenfranchised on election day, and the dispute resolution system failed to remedy the most significant irregularities. Although minimal adjustments were made to the legislative and regulatory provisions governing voter registration in 2011, these were too late and limited in scope and failed to address well-documented, core shortcomings. As a result, the 2013 elections were marred by the same serious flaws in the registration and identification of voters as previous elections, but their magnitude reached unprecedented levels. Their potential impact on the credibility of the election results has been well documented by the complementary findings of many civil society watchdogs coalesced in the Electoral Reform Alliance (ERA).[10]

Lack of progress was largely due to absence of political will on the part of Cambodian authorities and the NEC to genuinely address any of the key recommendations formulated over the years by national watchdogs, international observer missions and development partners alike. Critical reports were being almost systematically met with dismissive rebuttals, as exemplified in the white paper[11] published by the government in the aftermath of the 2013 elections. Despite its past role in electoral reform, the NEC has put forward a restrictive reading of its mandate that excludes any involvement in debating changes to the electoral legislation, hence depriving the executive and legislature of irreplaceable technical expertise. The last elections have thus contributed to worsening public discredit of an institution now deemed a constitutive part of the problem and in need of complete overhaul.

Notes

[1] Since 2012, Cambodia has had 1,633 Commune Councils.
[2] Acronym (in French) for United Front for an Independent, Neutral, Peaceful and Cooperative Cambodia.
[3] See notably: Electoral Reform Alliance (ERA), *Joint Report on the Conduct of the 2013 Cambodian Elections,* November 2013.
[4] The constitution guarantees the right to vote or stand as a candidate in a free, universal, equal, direct and secret ballot (articles 34, 76), sets a five-year term for the National Assembly (article 78) and establishes the Constitutional Council as the highest jurisdiction for disputes related to its elections (article 136).
[5] LEMNA, article 12, as amended in 2002.
[6] LEMNA, articles 12, 13.
[7] See COMFREL and NICFEC's reports on the elections 2003, 2007, 2008, and EU EOM, *Final Report on the National Assembly Elections,* 2008.
[8] NRP, SRP, HRP and FUNCINPEC, *Recommendations for Reforming the Composition of the National Election Committee to Build Trust Among Political Parties Contesting Elections,* May 2011.
[9] With the exception of those pertaining to voter registration, which are lodged to Commune Councils.
[10] ERA, *Joint Report on the Conduct of the 2013 Cambodian Elections,* November 2013. Contributing organisations: Cambodian Human Rights and Development Association (ADHOC), Coalition for Integrity and Social Accountability (CISA), Committee for Free and Fair Elections in Cambodia (COMFREL), Cambodian League for the Promotion and Defense of Human Rights (LICADHO), National Democratic Institute (NDI), Neutral and Impartial Committee for Free and Fair Elections in Cambodia (NICFEC), People Center for Development and Peace (PDP-Center Phnom Penh) and Transparency International Cambodia (TIC).
[11] Office of the Council of Ministers' Press and Quick Reaction Unit, *White paper on the 2013 General Election for the 5th Mandate of the National Assembly of the Kingdom of Cambodia,* September 2013.

CASE STUDY

Afghanistan: An Electoral Management Body Struggles to Deal with Executive Interference*

Andy Campbell

In late 2001 the Taliban regime was removed from controlling much of Afghanistan by a US-led international coalition. Since that time, much has changed. The Transitional Islamic State of Afghanistan created via the Bonn agreement of 2001 is now the Islamic Republic of Afghanistan, and the US-led Operation Enduring Freedom gave way to a NATO-led International Security Assistance Force (ISAF), which was initially restricted to Kabul. Armed factions, a serious destabilizing factor, were for the most part disarmed and demobilized, and many warlords renounced violence. It was hoped that electoral and political gains made would be built upon, that lessons learned would be acted upon and that weaknesses identified would be addressed. It was also hoped that the Taliban would be defeated, and that the remaining warlords would be forced to accept the status quo and relinquish the past. The reality in Afghanistan, however, is far from ideal.

In 2012 Afghanistan still had the Taliban (in various factions) and other insurgent groups seeking to reassert their control through wanton acts of violence, for the most part directed against Afghans. ISAF combat troops were drawing down during 2014. Localized warlords, although disarmed, now exist in the guise of provincial governors, presidentially appointed ministers and elected officials to the National Assembly. The Joint Election Management Body (JEMB) was closed down and the Independent Electoral Commission (IEC) took over but suffered from extreme executive office interference and the embarrassment of running possibly the worst electoral event in living memory in 2009. It involved industrial-scale fraud, the active collusion of senior EMB staff, and an incredibly strained relationship with the international community that funded it and the United Nations Development Programme (UNDP) that provided advisors to support it. It remains to be seen what the next ten years will hold in terms of the EMB's ability to run credible electoral events.

---

* A case study on Afghanistan also appeared in the original edition of the Handbook: Reginald Austin, 'Afghanistan: An Electoral Management Body Evolves', *Electoral Management Design: The International IDEA Handbook* (Stockholm: International IDEA, 2006), pp. 113–17.

Historical Background and Recent History

Since mid-2004 Afghans have participated in a series of elections: presidential (2004); Wolesi Jirga (lower house of the National Assembly) and Provincial Council (for 34 provinces) in 2005; Presidential and Provincial Council (2009) and Wolesi Jirga in 2010. In addition, as a result of the Provincial Council events, two-thirds of the upper house of the National Assembly (the Meshrano Jirga) is selected by each of 34 Provincial Councils, and one-third is appointed by the president. In 2004 out-of-country voting (OCV) for Afghan refugees was held in Pakistan and Afghanistan for the presidential election, run by the International Organization for Migration (IOM); this was not repeated for any subsequent events.

The timeframe for elections is based on various sections of the Afghan constitution, which has given the EMB an extremely unrealistic and unworkable election calendar with elections scheduled almost every year. When combined with other factors, including climate and the ongoing insurgency, the election calendar has hindered the full maturity of an Afghan EMB.

The development of the Afghan EMB has also been hampered by external influences for most of its existence, in particular the executive, elements from within the UN system and strong personalities in regional centres around the country. To make matters worse, the evolution of the Afghan EMB was not a smooth, well-planned process; achieving the outcome of an elected president and an elected National Assembly with reduced influence from illegally armed groups and warlords were the primary drivers for the international community and the Afghan elite, rather than the long-term viability of an EMB. As a result, the foundation of the EMB has been messy.

The evolution of the Afghan EMB has been an unnecessarily complex process. From 2003 to 2006 there were five different phases. The first entity (2002) was purely a UN construct housed in the United Nations Assistance Mission in Afghanistan (UNAMA) offices. In mid-2003 an interim hybrid Afghan and international entity (the JEMB) was formed to supervise the existing UNAMA function via a decree from the interim president. In early 2004 the UNAMA function was crafted into an Afghan-led secretariat that answered to the JEMB. This entity ran the 2004 presidential event. There was no provision in the 2004 election law to appeal decisions, hence in 2004 the office of the Special Representative of the Secretary-General (SRSG) and the United Nations Electoral Assistance Division (UNEAD) hastily convened the Impartial Panel of Election Experts with investigators drawn from the IOM-run OCV programme in Iran and Pakistan. This panel was created in response to allegations of interference as well as issues surrounding the use of indelible ink.

In early 2005 most of the original JEMB commissioners were replaced, and the lead implementing agency was shifted to the UN Office of Project Services (UNOPS). A heavy international-led presence managed the 2005 events. At its height, over 500 internationals were assigned to support the process, although many were engaged for only a few months. In May 2005, the 2004 Electoral Law was replaced with a new presidential decree that called for the creation of an Electoral Complaints Commission (ECC) with five commissioners (three international, appointed by the SRSG, and two

Afghan: one appointed by the Supreme Court and one from the Afghan Independent Human Rights Commission). The Media Commission reported to the JEMB as per article 51 of the amended law (now article 60 of the 2010 law).

In late 2005, after the National Assembly met for the first time, the JEMB was dissolved and the Afghan IEC was formally established. In 2006 the UNDP established the Enhancing Electoral and Legal Capacity for Tomorrow (ELECT) programme to provide advisors to the IEC. There was a delay in commencing the ELECT programme, and delays in funding the new IEC resulted in a number of quality staff leaving. This delay was in part because of a USD 11 million shortfall due to the increased cost of the 2005 elections, as effectively UNDP owed UNOPS the money for running the 2005 event.

The IEC developed a strategic plan for 2006–09 that was not overly ambitious, but it was never fully adopted. The key task of voter registration reform was again deemed too expensive, both economically and politically. Discussions on electoral reform and related issues, such as a nationwide census that would have enabled boundary delimitation, a critical task for the yet-to-be-held district council elections, did not occur. The IEC continued planning for the 2009 presidential election, but did not have the money or the capacity to run the event according to the timetable. Another voter registration exercise was conducted from 2008. Support continued from UNDP-ELECT when staff were eventually recruited. Recruitment of international advisors has continued to be a weakness, primarily through the cumbersome UNDP recruitment system, even though most were on the UNEAD roster of experts. The event was delayed and then came the fiasco of an election in which almost one in four ballots was invalidated and five principal electoral officers (PEOs) were eventually dismissed. In 2010 changes came with a new election law, as well as a new chairman and new chief electoral officer (CEO).

Legislative Framework

The legal basis for the establishment of the IEC is the constitution and the Electoral Law. Article 33 states that 'citizens shall have the right to elect and be elected', and article 156 states that the 'Independent Election Commission shall be established to administer as well as supervise every kind of election'. There have been three electoral laws, all of which have been presidential decrees: 2004, 2005 (which introduced the ECC provisions) and 2010. There are also a number of other decrees and adjunct laws, such as the Political Parties Law of 2009, that affect the IEC.

Presidential Decree No. 23 of January 2005 established the structure and workings of the IEC, and limited the role of the JEMB until the establishment of the National Assembly (article 10). A previous presidential decree from 2003 established the Interim IEC. The original Electoral Law of 2004 contained article 61 (Elections during the Transitional Period), which referred to this as 'the end of the transitional period'. Article 66 of the 2010 Election Law gives the IEC the power to issue binding regulations; to date, it has issued regulations on a wide range of topics. Article 50 specifies that the IEC will determine the rights and obligations of the agents, observers and media.

As mentioned above, the Media Commission, which reports to the IEC, was created in the Election Law (article 51 of the amended law, now article 60 of the 2010 law). The ECC received its mandate from article 61 of the Election Law. The structural and legal arrangements of the ECC are awkward and subject to extreme interference, as witnessed in 2009 and 2010. The ECC is a temporary body, which presents significant institutional memory issues.

The IEC is not responsible for political party registration; this is handled by the Ministry of Justice. Nor is it responsible for boundary delimitation.

Electoral Reform

Electoral reform is a staple discussion in Afghanistan; it is much talked about and seldom implemented. Fundamentally, Afghanistan has not progressed from an electoral base that is founded not in debated law, but rather in successive presidential decrees. The 2010 Election Law was issued under article 79 from the president; it allows for legislative decrees in times of 'immediate need'. This process bypassed section 109, which prohibits changes to the law 'during the last year of the legislative term'. Because the Wolesi Jirga delayed the vote even though the chamber voted the law down in a 'sea of red cards', the Meshrano Jirga refused to debate it on administrative grounds.

The new law in 2010 enforced the president's right to appoint all members of the ECC and made what some described as 'mere administrative changes'. For example, the 2010 law removed article 9 (Commitment to Impartiality and Confidentiality) for electoral officials, a section that was lost on many commentators in Kabul, both Afghan and international. Another change was the replacement of the 'majority of valid votes' with the broad notion of a 'majority of votes over 50 percent'. These 'mere administrative changes' are subtle yet profound, and have a significant impact on the fundamental principles of an EMB as well as the rule of law.

The secretariat staff of the JEMB was involved in drafting the amended 2005 Election Law, and the IEC staff have provided support to this mechanism, including the 2010 decree. In addition, in 2012 the IEC produced its own complete revision of the Election Law, which it sent to the Ministry of Justice for review. Although the stakeholder engagement was minimal, this is the first time the IEC has successfully embarked on such a task. Various entities, however, mostly domestic, are seeking to steer the electoral reform debate in their own direction. Within the National Assembly, one of the registered 'parliamentary' groups is working on electoral reform, and US-funded entities are seeking to create a space for Afghans to participate in the process. A large multiparty coalition is also pursuing electoral reform, as is at least one diplomatic mission. All these groups have a vested interest in electoral reform in Afghanistan, yet voters are seldom engaged in the process.

Institutional and Operational Issues

Like the JEMB in 2004 and 2005, the IEC has a secretariat to perform electoral operations. For the 2004 election, the secretariat was managed by an Afghan; in 2005 the SRSG appointed an international CEO with an Afghan counterpart who in 2006 became the first Afghan CEO and later ran the 2009 elections. Nearly all the Afghan PEOs of 2004–05 were appointed as PEOs in 2006 within the IEC, ensuring a continuity of knowledge and experience. Ironically, for the most part UNDP-ELECT did not rehire as advisors the international staff from 2004–05 that had a wealth of experience to offer. In early 2010 the CEO was replaced with a former JEMB/IEC staff member who inherited a dysfunctional IEC. The chairman was also replaced, but most commissioners remained. The CEO supervised the 2010 election and resigned in mid-2012 to return to development work.

There are three primary institutional and operational issues that affect the EMB: intimidation (in relation to independence), fraud and a declining turnout. The institutional issues of intimidation and fraud have plagued the EMB since its creation. The notion of independence is not uniformly entrenched or respected, and this issue continues to impede the functioning of the IEC. Although the international staff from 2004–05 and UNDP-ELECT have generally been very experienced electoral managers in their own right, more than a few were unable to adequately impart capacity or provide guidance on independence and withstanding interference.

There are, unfortunately, many examples of interference across all events. In 2005, extreme pressure was placed on the JEMB's staff to find a way to remove some Wolesi Jirga and Provincial Council candidates in a certain province; pressure came from both the president's office and that of the SRSG. In 2009, there was frequent direct 'contact' from the president's office to the IEC over the anticipated result of the presidential election, and a number of PEOs interfered with the results in their provinces after direct and unprecedented pressure from strong local entities. In the 2010 election, the Ministry of Defence announced its own list of polling stations that it would protect, in direct contrast to the (shorter) official IEC list; the implication was that these additional stations were likely to experience fraud. As has been stated by seasoned electoral experts, the possible responses to this type of interference are to 'bend, break or flee'.

UNDP-ELECT assigned a chief technical advisor (CTA) to support the CEO and to manage the ELECT programme; thus far there have been five CTAs. On more than one occasion, the CTA has clearly operated as a member of the UN first and foremost and reported to the SRSG. This partly explains why the relationship between the CEO and CTA deteriorated significantly in the lead up to the 2009 election.

The third issue that affects the EMB, declining voter turnout (but increasing voter registration), is a growing concern. Voter turnout, expressed by the number of valid ballot papers that are presented on election day, has decreased from 8.0 million in 2004 to 6.4 million in 2005, 4.2 million in 2009 and 4.0 million in 2010. In the same period, due to reliance on a fundamentally flawed voter registration system, the number of registered voters increased from 12.4 million in 2004 to over 17.5 million in 2010. The primary reason for this was the decision to have a voter registration 'top up' between 2008 and 2010, rather a complete reregistration, which would have been far better if the systems were in place to capture the data.

The most often-cited reason for the decline is the deteriorating security situation, which explains only part of it. Another important reason is that voters do not perceive the electoral process as a means to improve their lives. The process, the EMB and democracy are viewed with growing distrust and scepticism.

Acquiring and Managing New Technologies

Afghanistan, although a fragile state, is able to use new media and technologies; mobile telephones are widespread and Internet usage is growing. Like much of Africa, it has no need to use landline technology before jumping to the next level. Unfortunately, this has not been embraced by the IEC due to cost restrictions, both initial and recurring. Climate constraints also hamper the IEC's ability to use new technologies.

The most glaring gap in terms of using new technology is the voter registration database, or lack thereof. The voter registration method as mentioned above is flawed. It is effectively a handwritten piece of paper with the person's province or district (but not their address); it may or may not have a photo (women have the right to decline having their photograph taken).

As early as 2006, it was planned that the IEC, jointly with the Ministry of Interior, was to establish a joint civil voter registry (CVR) to provide a national identification system within a comprehensive national database. The project's pilot phase involved the use and testing of two biometric technologies: facial recognition and iris recognition as search tools for verification and identification of multiple registrations in the database. The UN High Commissioner for Refugees has used iris technology for refugee repatriation, but the IEC is not in a position to use such technology. Facial recognition proved too costly in the pilot and was dropped. Since 2007 the Ministry of the Interior has indicated that it wanted to undertake civil registration autonomously from voter registration, although to date this has not proved effective either. A modified voter registration plan was considered again, and under pressure from UNDP-ELECT, new voter registration cards were issued without effective safeguarding against multiple or proxy registration.

Powers and Functions

The IEC has some, but not all, of the basic attributes of an impartial and independent EMB. It is responsible for voter registration and the conduct of elections as well as the handling of nominations, polling, counting and announcing the results. The IEC is not responsible for registering political parties; this task is handled by the Ministry of Justice. The EMB has no capacity to undertake boundary delimitation, which is an ongoing issue for organizing the district council elections.

The IEC is also a key actor in vetting candidates for links to armed groups. Yet the ECC is empowered in the Electoral Law to be the final arbiter regarding candidates. This part of the system has been the subject of much discussion and executive interference. The ECC performed its functions moderately well in 2005, as dictated by the Election Law, although it was established very late. The ECC structure in 2009 was the same as 2005, with three internationals and two Afghans. But it is a temporary body with no institutional memory. During the 2009 election it was seen as a last bastion of independence due to the very questionable actions of the IEC executive, although it lost a great deal of credibility when it sought to use a sampling methodology to remove tampered ballot papers. It used this method on the advice of a few and as the result of the IEC refusal to recount 10 per cent of ballot papers. In almost a reversal of fortunes, the IEC of 2010 was more independent, whereas the ECC was seen as operating at the behest of the executive, especially in its very questionable decision not to be the final arbiter of complaints, as required by the Electoral Law. The role of the ECC will continue to be an Achilles heel in electoral management in Afghanistan until the IEC is capable of handling complaints.

Financing

The IEC is a permanent institution, and its daily activities and electoral events are technically funded from the national budget. Senior staff are employed under the auspices of the Afghan Civil Service Commission. The IEC prepares its own annual budget as well as the electoral budget, which are submitted through the Ministry of Finance for approval by the National Assembly. Donors then agree to contribute what they can to the process, in particular voter registration. Herein lies the problem.

Consistency in funding the EMB has hindered its development, and directly affects its long-term sustainability. As it stands, the UNDP-ELECT II (the new UNDP programme that commenced in 2012), is the preferred basket for donors to contribute to, both for UN support to the IEC and for its ongoing daily costs. The Afghan state lacks the fiscal capacity to sustain the IEC and undertake significant programmes such as voter registration and elections, and has relied heavily on international donor support, which has been inconsistent in application and delivery.

The costs associated with the four cycles of elections held thus far are not unexpected, but their frequency has resulted in calls to adjust the electoral calendar, which would require constitutional amendment. The minimum estimated costs for the four election years is over USD 758 million: USD 105 million for 2004 (the original budget was USD 130 million), USD 168 million for 2005 (the original budget was USD 159 million), and over USD 485 million for 2009 and 2010. These amounts do not include the considerable contribution from ISAF for the distribution and retrieval of sensitive material and force protection. After its departure, these costs will have to be borne by the Afghan government.

Accountability

As with many things in Afghanistan, the fundamentals are still a work in progress. The president appoints and can dismiss the chairman, deputy and the other members of the commission, as well as the CEO. In the past these appointments have been subject to executive whim. Although the National Assembly has requested a role in issuing a vote of confidence and a stamp of approval for these roles, to date this has not occurred. The EMB sits in legal limbo within the government machinery. The 2005 Presidential Decree No. 23 on the Structure and Working Procedure of the IEC is still current. Presidential Decree No. 21, also from 2005, appointed the members of the first IEC by name, but created no enduring appointment mechanism. The president has since followed this precedent and named commissioners or the CEO unilaterally. One former

CEO was appointed three days after being asked to submit his resume to the presidential palace for consideration.

Decree 21 refers to article 156 in the constitution, which speaks of the establishment of the IEC but not who it answers to. Article 2 of the decree states that the IEC shall be independent in its duties, but again does not stipulate who it answers to. As a matter of governance, all government departments, whether they are independent bodies or not, should give an account of their work. The IEC's only reporting requirement is through the annual accountability week reporting in March, in which all state agencies report on their achievements through the media.

Accountability issues also extend to the continued practice of the executive rewarding electoral staff for what could be perceived as 'favourable outcomes'. Article 6 of decree 21 clearly prohibits members of the IEC 'for a period of one year (to) be appointed to top official positions'. This ban has been violated on a number of occasions: a previous CEO (2006–10) was put forward as a minister in 2010 by the president well within the 12-month moratorium; an IEC chairman (2007–10) was appointed to the post of chairman of the High Office for Oversight and Anti-Corruption in 2010 shortly after resigning; and the original director of the JEMB secretariat (2004) was appointed as a cabinet secretary in early 2005.

Professionalism

Throughout the various forms of the EMB in Afghanistan, capacity building has been inconsistently applied. In 2003–04 the notion of counterparts through pairing was used widely. In 2005, while every international role had an Afghan counterpart and capacity building was seen as a primary aim, it was not uniformly implemented. This unfortunately is not unique to Afghanistan. Both the JEMB and the IEC extensively used the Building Resources in Democracy, Governance and Elections (BRIDGE) methodology and this has had a positive outcome, although the BRIDGE training was frequently an internal affair; little cross-pollination from outside sources has been achieved. Over time, there have been some modest steps to professionalize electoral officials. There is now an Afghan Association of Electoral Officials, which was founded by the deputy CEO of the IEC. It is also open to non-IEC staff, and is an associate institutional member of the Association of European Election Officials. Frequent study tours for election officials are conducted to examine how other countries run their EMB and events.

Training and membership in networks, however, can only go so far if interference permeates at all levels. The unfortunate reality in Afghanistan is that very experienced electoral staff succumbed to executive and regional power broker interference. As well as the eventual removal of the chairman and CEO of the IEC, the aftermath of the 2009 elections saw five PEOs, all with many years of experience, dismissed; in addition, several hundred district field coordinators and over 6,000 polling day staff were black-listed from working for the IEC again. While the fraud was extreme in 2009, it was also fairly significant in 2005, but due to political pressure to have a successful election it was not adequately investigated. The 2010 election was better, but primarily because the IEC was quick to invalidate over 1.3 million ballot papers and the ECC chose not to deal with many matters in a robust manner as expected.

Relations with other Entities

The EMB has had a mixed relationship with other domestic and international entities. The diplomatic community has maintained a relationship with the senior executive of the IEC, which was demonstrated by the challenges of the 2009 election and the replacement of the chairman and CEO in 2010. This is symptomatic of the political space in which the EMB operates; elections are, after all, essentially a political activity—and none more so than Afghanistan.

The IEC's primary relationship is with the UNDP via its ELECT programme; significant support sometimes comes from other entities such as the International Foundation for Electoral Systems (IFES) via its Support to the Electoral Process in Afghanistan (STEP) role (which has now ended). The relationship between UNDP-ELECT and the IEC has been incredibly acrimonious at times, in part due to the personalities involved, but also because of deeply conflicting perceptions of programme implementation. The low point in the relationship coincided with the 2009 elections and the murder of UNDP-ELECT staff in Kabul, but improved considerably with a new CEO for the IEC and a new CTA of UNDP-ELECT from 2010. In 2011 the CEO advised IFES that they no longer required any more advisors.

Other internationally funded organizations have continued to support the IEC, such as the Asia Foundation (with its role in implementing the BRIDGE course); party institutes, primarily the National Democratic Institute in training clients for the IEC; and political parties, candidates and their agents. However, this ancillary support is likewise donor driven, and the follow-up impact when these programmes have been discontinued is significant. Domestically, the IEC and the main electoral monitoring organization Free and Fair Election Forum of Afghanistan (FEFA) have had a challenging relationship; the latter has sometimes reported on issues without prior consultation with the IEC. Likewise, the IEC has reacted to such reporting in a manner not entirely conducive to the principles of free speech and transparency.

Sustainability

There has been ongoing debate about the viability of the IEC, as various international actors have dithered at times over funding arrangements. This has had a negative impact, as was seen in early 2006. Regardless, the IEC is a permanent institution, and it has developed functioning strategic plans, budgets and contingency planning—all of which demonstrate an internal administrative maturity. In 2012 the IEC published its latest strategic plan.

There have been various attempts at reforming the EMB's operational model. The IEC is required to have a presence in all 34 provinces in addition to Kabul, and eight regional offices. In the JEMB phase, the IEC operated out of UN offices; in 2006 a purpose-built headquarters was established in Kabul. Not all of the 34 province offices are in stand-alone facilities yet, and some still rely on leveraging off government facilities. The total number of Afghan staff of the IEC when not in an election year is around 405, although this number increases significantly in an election year. The number of temporary staff has decreased from over 120,000 in previous events to 86,000 as polling station staff for the 2010 event. The current budget (2012–14), which excludes voter registration, is approximately USD 60 million—which includes both UNDP-ELECT and IEC staff.

Opportunities and Constraints

The challenge of supporting a viable and independent EMB needs to be assessed in the context of what has not worked well in the past. The notion of electoral reform is part of the answer—in particular, having a law passed by legislators, which ideally was drafted by them in consultation with the EMB and key stakeholders. The voting system is a moot point. A commitment from the donor community to providing core funding between electoral years for the EMB would ensure continuity. Significant and hard decisions on options to create a viable voter registration database through a voter registration exercise or a civil registration exercise led by the Interior Ministry with EMB support is critical. Unfortunately, these options have been explored more than once, yet a declining voter turnout is a significant concern that should be addressed. Senior members must be appointed through an impartial and transparent process that is vetted by the National Assembly; it is an opportunity to renew the people's trust in democratic institutions. All members of the EMB must be strictly apolitical; a partisan EMB will not work in Afghanistan. It is likely that issues such as gender balance and minority engagement, including the disabled, will take a back seat until these core matters are resolved.

CHAPTER 3

The Powers, Functions and Responsibilities of an EMB

There is often no clear distinction in electoral law or practice between the powers and functions of an EMB. In some electoral laws, all EMB activities sanctioned by law are referred to as powers. In many countries, powers and functions are listed in both the constitution and legislation so that EMBs have both constitutional and statutory powers and functions. In many electoral laws, such as those of Australia, Indonesia and South Africa, 'powers and functions' are referred to jointly; in others, such as Bosnia and Herzegovina, the law merely lists activities that the EMB 'shall' perform. It could be argued that a legally described power gives the EMB the *authority* to do something, and a legally described function is an activity that the EMB is *expected* to perform. Responsibilities, such as gender equity, often come from separate national and international laws that cover the work of all government-funded bodies, or are adopted as an extension of democratic principles.

Many factors influence EMBs' powers and functions. The results of the negotiation processes among political forces, within the country or beyond, that paved the way for the EMB's establishment are generally a strong influence, particularly in countries recently emerging into democracy. Other specific political, administrative and geographical influences can include the structure of the state (e.g. unitary or federal, presidential or parliamentary), demographics, the electoral system (e.g. single- or multi-member electoral districts) and the existence of other electoral service providers. The historical interaction of these factors within each country has created a wide variety of models for EMB powers, functions and responsibilities.

Powers and Functions

The majority of EMBs have the powers to make rules, regulations and determinations that are binding on all players in the electoral process—voters, political parties and candidates, the media and observers—provided they are consistent with both the constitution and the electoral laws. These powers may be limited by law to specific aspects of the electoral process, or the law may give the EMB a general regulation-making power.

Some EMBs have executive, legislative and judicial powers. For example, the establishment of powerful EMBs was necessary to curtail the dominance of the executive over the other branches of government under the oligarchic governments of Latin America. In countries such as Costa Rica and Uruguay, EMBs became known as the fourth branch of government. These EMBs can make regulations, directions and reviews of regulations that are binding on the electoral processes, and their decisions cannot be reviewed by any other branch of government. They also have executive powers to call and conduct elections, to certify or nullify election results, and to resolve electoral disputes.

In other parts of the world, EMBs have some power to investigate and enforce laws related to the conduct of elections. The Bhutan EMB has the powers of a court, and the Thai EMB has the legal powers of a law enforcement agency. In Bosnia and Herzegovina and Liberia, the EMBs can compel anyone to appear before it during an investigation. In the Philippines and Russia, the EMB is obliged to carry out inquires in connection with complaints that the law has been breached. In Canada the EMB has the power to investigate possible breaches, but it usually delegates these to the police.

The Liberian, Mexican and Portuguese EMBs can impose fines. In Thailand, the EMB can indict those who break election laws. In Bosnia and Herzegovina the EMB can impose civil penalties for non-compliance, but must first seek to achieve compliance. The Canadian EMB can enter into a compliance agreement with any person who has committed or is about to commit an offence against the Elections Act. In Cambodia and South Africa, the EMBs have the power to investigate and resolve disputes of an administrative nature or disputes that do not necessarily fall within the courts' jurisdiction. In many other countries (such as Australia, Bhutan, Tonga and Ukraine), the EMB refers any suspicions of a breach of electoral law to the police.

The majority of EMBs have powers that are primarily of an executive nature, related to implementing electoral activities. Many EMBs, such as Bhutan, Cambodia, Ghana, Liberia, Russia, South Africa, Thailand, Tonga and Zambia, can make binding regulations and prescribe penalties for their breach. Regulations issued by EMBs are subject to review by the courts, and they must be consistent with the electoral laws. In South Africa, such reviews are conducted by an electoral court.

In some countries the EMB's powers extend to determining election dates, within parameters set by law that are often fixed to a time period defined by the end of an elected body's term of office. In some countries with fixed terms of office for the legislature and executive, the EMB is responsible for formally determining the election date. In India, the EMB has the power to draw up an election schedule and issue the election writ. The Russian EMB can call an election if the legislature has failed to do so. Many EMBs have the power to order re-polling or re-counting if an election at a particular location has violated the law. For example, local government election commissions in Indonesia can order re-polling or re-counting in individual polling stations if processes have not been correctly followed, and the Namibian EMB can order a re-poll in the event of violence or an emergency. In some cases, such as in Bhutan, Thailand, Uruguay and Zambia, the EMBs have a broader power to order re-polling if an election did not proceed in a fair and honest manner as defined by law.

However, many EMBs have no influence over when an election is called. For example, in countries such as Mexico and the United States, which have presidential constitutions that stipulate the separation of legislative and executive powers, elections are held on a fixed date. However, in countries with parliamentary systems that follow the Westminster model, the government's tenure depends on its ability to retain the support of a majority of members of the legislature. The power to call elections may belong either formally or in practice to the leader of the government, who can use it for political advantage. Even where the government has the power to nominate the election date, there have been cases, such as Nepal in 2007 and 2012, where the EMB has successfully postponed the election date that was initially announced by the government.

Extent of Powers, Functions and Responsibilities

Particularly in emerging democracies, electoral legal frameworks are being designed to cover all electoral process matters that are relevant to the delivery of free, fair and credible elections. This can have the advantage of promoting electoral integrity by ensuring that EMBs exercise control over the entire process. In many countries, EMBs have powers and functions across a wide range of activities throughout the electoral cycle.

The core functions in the conduct of an election are:

1. *Determining who is eligible to vote:* the right of adult citizens to participate in elections is one of the cornerstones of democracy, and ensuring that only eligible people vote helps confer legitimacy on the election process.

2. *Receiving and validating the nominations of electoral participants* (for elections, political parties and/or candidates): the right to stand for election is a fundamental political right, and ensuring that all contestants have followed the law helps confer legitimacy on the election.

3. *Conducting polling:* the ability to safely cast a vote is at the core of an election.

4. *Counting the votes* cast so that the election result reflects the will of the voters.

5. *Tabulating the votes* in accordance with the electoral system so that the winners can be identified.

6. *Running a credible organization* so that the legitimacy of the election is not compromised by the actions of those conducting the election.

Most of these functions may be expanded in some situations, giving EMBs a range of other functions:

- Determining who is eligible to vote
    - identifying and registering voters
    - identifying and registering voters living in another country who are still eligible to vote
    - developing and maintaining a national electoral register
- Receiving and validating the nominations of electoral participants (for elections, political parties and/or candidates)
    - registering political parties
    - regulating political party financing
    - overseeing political party pre-selections or primaries
- Conducting polling
    - planning and implementing electoral logistics
    - hiring and training temporary electoral staff
    - training political parties' and candidates' poll watchers
    - directing the police or other security services to ensure a peaceful election
    - accrediting and regulating the conduct of election observers
    - adjudicating electoral disputes
    - organizing external voting for those not in the country
- Counting the votes
- Tabulating the votes
    - announcing and certifying election results
- Running a credible organization
    - making national or regional electoral policies
    - planning electoral services
    - training electoral staff
    - reviewing and evaluating the adequacy of the electoral framework and the EMB's own performance after elections

Other common functional areas of work are:

- Delimiting electoral district boundaries
- Regulating the election campaign period

- Regulating the conduct of political parties and candidates, in particular during the election campaign
- Registering third parties and regulating their behaviour
- Regulating the conduct of the media during elections
- Regulating opinion polls
- Controlling and where possible preventing electoral fraud
- Instilling community responsibility to encourage democracy at home and elsewhere:
    - conducting voter information/education and civic education
    - supporting access for all
    - promoting equality and equity policies and practices
    - providing electoral research facilities
    - advising the government and legislature on electoral reform issues
    - participating in international electoral assistance services
- Providing services for conducting private organizations' (such as trade unions, civil society organizations) elections

Direct Democracy Instruments

The conduct of electoral direct democracy instruments—referendums, citizens' initiatives and recall votes—raises issues that are for the most part similar to those raised by the conduct of elections. Additional issues may include verifying that the processes for calling direct democracy votes have been correctly followed—a contentious issue, for example, in Venezuela's presidential recall vote in 2004—and regulating campaigning and voter education and information. In the US state of Oregon, the EMB is required to distribute to every household a collection of the position statements submitted by citizens on each issue submitted to referendum.

It is usual for EMBs to be responsible for organizing both elections and direct democracy instruments. However, the UK Electoral Commission, which does not perform the role of EMB for elections (for which a Governmental Model electoral management structure is used), is tasked with the role of EMB for referendums.

Functional Divisions between Electoral Institutions

It is common for some of the potential non-core functions of an EMB to be assigned in the electoral legal framework to another institution. It is becoming more common for some non-core functions to be contracted out by an EMB or supported by other institutions or civil society organizations (CSOs), but this is a management rather than a legal framework issue. Functions that are often assigned in the legal framework to an institution separate from the EMB(s) include boundary delimitation, voter registration, the registration and funding of political parties, electoral dispute resolution, the certification and announcement of election results, and voter education and information. If electoral functions are assigned to more than one institution, the legal and policy framework needs to be very clear on each institution's functional responsibilities, and on the hierarchy of authority and coordination mechanisms between the institutions.

Table 6: Advantages and Disadvantages of Assigning Some Electoral Functions to Institutions Other than the EMB

Advantages	Disadvantages
• May insulate EMBs from some politically sensitive decisions (e.g. political party registration, electoral boundary delimitation). • Allows EMBs to concentrate on core functions. • May locate electoral activities in institutions with more relevant technical skills than the EMB possesses. • May result in successful bids for funding for functions that EMBs may find difficult to fund. • May provide a check and balance on functions implemented by EMBs.	• Other institutions may not have as much credibility as an EMB to undertake electoral functions in an impartial manner. • There may be lack of coordination and shared goals between institutions with different agendas. • May locate electoral functions in institutions for which these are not a high priority, and with little or infrequent electoral experience. • May not be cost-effective. It may also be difficult to identify funding expended on electoral functions, to prevent funds allocated for electoral functions from being diverted to other activities. • May be used as a tool to thwart the independent actions of an EMB that refuses to take instructions from a government.

Boundary Delimitation

It is common in many countries—especially those that follow the Commonwealth tradition such as Australia, Botswana, Canada and India—for the electoral legal framework to create a separate body or commission to assume responsibility for boundary delimitation. Countries where the EMB takes responsibility for boundary delimitation include Indonesia, Nigeria and Uganda. In Barbados and Belize, the EMB is called the Electoral and Boundaries Commission. In some examples, such as in Australia, the boundary delimitation authority, while separate from the EMB, includes the senior EMB secretariat and may be supported by staff deputed from the EMB. There are countries such as the United States in which the electoral law assigns responsibility for boundary delimitation to the legislature. However, this practice can easily lead to the imposition of electoral district boundaries that are favourable to the current majority party in the legislature, thus institutionalizing their hold on power.

There are operational and cost-effectiveness advantages of an EMB taking responsibility for electoral district boundary delimitation. Boundary delimitation is, however, a politically divisive issue, and leaves an EMB open to attack by those who perceive the results as not serving their interests. Some electoral analysts therefore argue that boundary delimitation is best handled by a body other than an EMB, in order to shield it from potential politically motivated attacks that may damage the EMB's credibility.

Voter Registration

In some countries the electoral legal framework requires voter registration to be linked to a national identification or civil registration system that is controlled by an authority other than the EMB. Countries that have used this method include Colombia, Hungary, the Netherlands, Romania and Sweden. In these cases, voter registration is a purely administrative action. If there is any dispute (for example, if someone is alleged to be registered who is not qualified to vote, or has allegedly been wrongly omitted from the electoral register), the EMB has to determine voter eligibility, not the civil registration authority. In other countries, a body other than the EMB is responsible in electoral law for developing and compiling the electoral register. In Spain, the Electoral Census Office of the National Institute of Statistics is the responsible body, and in countries such as Moldova and South Korea, local authorities prepare the electoral register for the independent EMB.

However the electoral register is compiled, the basic concern is that the data contained in it must be accurate and credible. Voter registration conducted by an EMB under the Independent Model may give electoral registers greater credibility with the public than those derived from or compiled by a government department, even though using existing civil registration or ID system data may be more cost effective. Whatever institution prepares the electoral register data, an EMB must verify that the electoral registers used at polling stations are accurate.

The EMBs in Costa Rica and the Dominican Republic are responsible for creating the civic list. In Bangladesh and Guyana, the EMBs have the responsibility of issuing national identification documents and voter registration cards. This has worked well in these countries and has made the task of compiling and maintaining the electoral register significantly easier for the EMB. Quality control measures on voter registration, such as opportunities for public inspection by voters, are commonly embedded in electoral laws. In South Africa, as in many developed countries that have (electronic) population registers, the EMB regularly compares its voter registration records with the population register to identify unqualified or 'phantom' voters for removal.

One of the most important aspects of an effective voter registration process is ensuring that all eligible voters, women and men, are enfranchised and have access to information and infrastructures for voter registration purposes. Planning and administering a voter registration process that gives women equal access to information and infrastructure is critical for ensuring their right to universal and equal suffrage. This objective can be pursued by strategies such as an active voter registration process in which an EMB is tasked to reach out to potential voters and help them register door to door or using other procedures canvassing large groups of the population. It may also include conducting a broad-based voter information campaign in connection with the planned voter registration process, to explain basic legal and democratic principles underpinning the voter registration process to members in rural and traditionally marginalized communities or groups, or in settings where women may face gender-based barriers that limit their participation in social and political processes.

Registration and Funding of Political Parties

The registration of political parties, when required, may also fall outside the functions assigned to EMBs by the electoral legal framework. In other countries such as India, Mexico, South Africa and Thailand, the EMB administers political party registration, serves as the guardian of political party symbols and independent candidates' logos, and holds copies of party constitutions and selection rules. Party registration may take place either throughout the electoral cycle or occur in the months prior to each election.

It is uncommon for an EMB to assume responsibility for parties' procedures for selecting candidates, but the increasing pressure for internal party democratization has caused some election analysts to support this role for EMBs. Many EMBs in the USA are involved in running primary elections for party candidates for elected office. The EMB in the Australian state of Queensland has the power to conduct inquiries and audits of pre-selection or primaries of candidates for state and local elections. The Indian EMB insists that registered parties hold periodic internal elections.

The supervision of political parties' contributions and/or expenditures, and the disbursement of any public funding for parties and candidates, also sometimes falls outside the functions given to EMBs by the electoral legal framework. Party funding and expenditure are controlled by a body other than an EMB in countries such as Spain and the USA. In Canada, Kenya, Lithuania and Russia, candidates and political parties have to report all financial contributions they receive to the EMB and provide an audited report of their expenditures during election campaigns (and in some cases each year). In New Zealand these reports are received and made public, while in Cambodia, Liberia, Nigeria and Russia the EMB checks these reports and makes the results public. In France and India, the EMB checks that campaign spending limits are adhered to. In Mexico and Zambia, the EMB distributes state funding to political parties annually and for each election campaign. Some EMBs have a role in regulating media allocations for party campaigns. The EMBs in Canada, India, Mexico and Russia regulate the allocation of public media air time to parties and candidates. In Canada, the EMB appoints a broadcasting arbitrator to allocate paid and free time to registered political parties on the electronic broadcasting networks. In Bosnia and Herzegovina, the EMB ensures equitable treatment in the provision of public places and facilities for use during the campaign.

Election Campaigns

Political party and candidate campaign codes of conduct may be included in the legal framework, as in Angola, Lesotho, South Africa and Nepal, or be an EMB-brokered voluntary arrangement between parties, as in Cambodia, India, Indonesia, Kenya, Liberia, Malawi and Nigeria. These codes are more effective if they are voluntarily agreed upon by the parties, but benefit from the EMB or electoral dispute resolution bodies being legally empowered to impose sanctions for breaches.

Equal access to the media and balance in their reporting on the election are intrinsic to a free, fair and credible election. Several EMBs, such as those in Indonesia and Tonga, have a mandate in the electoral legal framework to regulate political parties' campaign methods and conduct in general. In a few cases, the EMB prescribes campaign behaviour. For instance in Bosnia and Herzegovina, the distribution of campaign material that depicts women or men in stereotypical, offensive or humiliating ways is forbidden. In Nepal, the media code of conduct prohibits reporting that could potentially harm principles of gender equality and social inclusion, and messages that are likely to provoke violence. In other countries, such prohibitions are part of laws on media regulation or behaviour in public places or equity and anti-violence legislation. Jurisdiction issues relevant to the media's treatment of election 'news' are more commonly left either to self-regulation or to a media council. This is the case in Zambia. An agreed upon code of conduct for the media is used in Liberia and Nepal.

Some EMBs also seek to regulate the conduct of the party in power to ensure that it does not use public resources in the election campaign. The quality of non-partisanship and the ability to create a level playing field for all political participants are pillars on which an EMB can build good-practice electoral management. A lack of electoral equity—for example, an electoral environment that favours the governing party—can undermine transparency and the credibility of elections and EMBs. While some of the factors and practices that contribute to electoral equity may lie outside the strict ambit of an EMB's powers and functions, EMBs can work to ensure that the legal framework is fully utilized to promote equality and equity.

Some emerging democracies are unfamiliar with the concept of a level playing field. In countries that are influenced by Westminster models of government, or where the public service and state media have been required to be strictly loyal to the ruling party, the government has electoral advantages. Such advantages could include the power to determine an election date without consultation, the use of public resources for campaign activities and favourable media access.

In some countries, the electoral law for transitional elections has attempted to level the playing field by strictly controlling and limiting media advertising by the political contestants, requiring the EMB to allocate all campaign activities equally among the contestants and forbidding the use of any public resources for election campaigns.

The use of public resources for election campaigns is a challenge to EMBs in all countries. This area is rarely covered in electoral legislation. The Indian EMB has issued a code of conduct to govern the electoral use of public resources by government ministers to ensure that no cause is given for any complaint that the ruling party has used its official position during the election campaign (see Box 2).

Box 2: The Indian Code of Conduct for Use of Official Resources for Electoral Purposes

The Indian Code of Conduct applies to parties in power at the national and state levels and requires equal access to public facilities for opposition party campaigns.

The code prohibits:

- ministerial use of government machinery or personnel for campaigns;
- combining official ministerial visits with campaigning;
- the use of government transport for campaigning;
- the use of public funds for campaign-related media advertising;
- the misuse of government media for partisan coverage of political news;
- the awarding of grants and payments from discretionary funds after the election date has been announced; and
- announcing or commencing public works or making appointments or undertakings that may influence voters after the election date is announced.

Source: Extracted from the 'Model Code of Conduct for the Guidance of the Political Parties and Candidates' of the Election Commission of India (<http://www.thehinducentre.com/multimedia/archive/01828/Model_Code_of_Cond_1828248a.pdf>, accessed 30 June 2014).

Elements of election campaigns that are not directly related to political party activities are also under the jurisdiction of some EMBs. For example, electoral law in Bosnia and Herzegovina and in Russia regulates the publication of political opinion polling. In countries such as Albania, Peru and Singapore, the EMBs are empowered to enforce bans on the publication of opinion polls during specified periods before voting day. However, courts in Canada and India have overturned or restricted EMB powers in this regard.

Voter Education and Information

Voter information and broader democracy or civic education is a role that is increasingly being added to EMB functions. Some EMB legal frameworks have clearly provided for EMB conduct of voter information and education campaigns as in Bhutan, Cambodia, Kenya, Latvia, Lithuania, Singapore, South Africa, Thailand and Tonga, while others, including Sweden, have not. Some EMBs have a wider remit to promote democratic values (Costa Rica), the democratic process (Lesotho), the purpose of elections (Ghana) and active citizenship (Costa Rica). Education efforts are often targeted at groups that are less likely to vote or face hurdles in participation. The Nepalese EMB has created an education centre based on the Australian EMB's education centres. The Costa Rican EMB's Institute for Training and Education in Democracy has a mandate to conduct relevant academic research, support the wider education system and incorporate new technologies in its work.

It is preferable for an EMB's legal framework to include a voter education and information function, as this is indispensable for democratic consolidation, especially in emerging democracies. It is important for the legal framework to empower an EMB to conduct voter education and information campaigns in its official mandate in order to help consolidate democracy, since otherwise the government will be reluctant to fund such efforts.

However, it would be harmful for the EMB or any other body to be given exclusive voter education and information rights or powers to restrict who may educate and inform voters. Voter education and information is too important, and its implementation too complex, to be left to an EMB alone. Political parties, civil society, corporations and government agencies such as education systems may all have an important complementary role to play to help ensure that voters have all the information they need to make informed choices. An EMB's voter education and information responsibilities could be partially or wholly delegated to other institutions, including CSOs. In Ghana, for example, the EMB is responsible for voter information, while its sister commission is responsible for civic education. The Thai EMB is empowered to outsource voter education and information to private organizations, while the Liberian EMB has guidelines for non-governmental organizations (NGOs) involved in civic education.

EMBs have an intrinsic responsibility to ensure that their activities and operations benefit all citizens. This responsibility naturally entails targeting voter information campaigns to groups that may have traditionally experienced specific and disproportionate difficulties in accessing information and knowledge about their basic democratic rights and freedoms, such as the right to vote and the right to be elected. Women in many societies have traditionally been subjected to such forms of exclusion. Voter information campaigns are a particularly important tool to help eliminate barriers to women's political participation and representation. In Senegal, in 2011 and 2012 in the wake of the adoption of important gender parity provisions in the electoral legislation, the National Election Commission organized a series of activities with the support of various national and international partners to raise awareness of the new provisions among prospective women candidates, as well as political party representatives responsible for monitoring the candidate nomination and registration processes.

Validation of Election Results

It is common for electoral legal frameworks to make EMBs responsible for certifying and announcing election results, and to prescribe a time period within which the results must be announced. This is the case, for example, in Armenia, Cambodia, Honduras, Poland and South Africa. In Niger these functions are given to the Constitutional Court, and in Cameroon and France to the Constitutional Council. In Denmark, the legislature is responsible for validating the results of national elections.

The chief justice of Zambia is the returning officer for the presidential election and is thus responsible for announcing its results. Following a recommendation of the National Technical Committee on Elections, the draft revised constitution released for discussion in April 2012 makes the chair of the Election Commission the returning officer for the presidential election.

Electoral Observation

While independent election observation, by its nature, is conducted outside EMB control, electoral legal frameworks often assign EMBs observation-related functions. It is good practice for an EMB to accredit observers, guarantee their rights of observation, provide them with comprehensive background briefing materials and define observers' responsibilities, often in a legally enforceable code of conduct. Independent observation, especially in emerging democracies, can be a critical component of building public confidence in electoral processes.

Independent observation, by both citizen and international observers, by its nature must be free of control and interference by EMBs or any other authority, except those controls necessary to ensure observers' authenticity, impartiality and safety, and to prevent the disruption of electoral processes. Just as electoral laws take into account a country's international treaty obligations, an EMB's observer-related powers and functions must recognize international obligations and good practices—such as the UN-endorsed Global Declaration of Principles and Code of Conduct for International Electoral Observation. Attempts to place impediments in the way of observation—such as charging a high fee for the registration of each observer—or to over-regulate observation may be contrary to international principles. EMBs often insist that observers are accredited before being admitted to polling places, and have created agreed upon codes of conduct in some places, such as Cambodia and Liberia.

International Activities

It is important that the legal framework for elections provides a mandate for the EMB to participate in international electoral activities. No EMB or country is an island unto itself, and many EMBs are called on from time to time to assist other EMBs, either as observers or technical advisers, or to host study missions from other EMBs.

Although many EMB legal frameworks do not provide for participation in international electoral assistance missions, many EMBs do undertake these tasks on both small and large scales. EMBs that regularly participate in international technical cooperation include those of Australia, Canada, France, Ghana, India, Mexico and South Africa; such cooperation is both bilateral and multilateral. Many other EMBs regularly participate in international observation missions, or in professional contact and exchange activities facilitated by regional networks of election officials. The mandate of the Bangladeshi EMB provides for EMB 'support to the United Nations and its member states in organizing elections by fielding of election monitors and observers and organising training for electoral personnel'. The law in Bhutan tasks the EMB with providing assistance to foreign countries and organizations in matters relating to elections in situations approved by the Ministry of Foreign Affairs.

Electoral Dispute Resolution

An EMB's powers to investigate and prosecute a suspected breach of electoral rules were covered at the start of this chapter. When the electoral dispute relates to the election result, other bodies are often involved. Complaints about the results come first to the EMB in many countries, including Afghanistan, Australia, Bosnia and Herzegovina, Costa Rica, Timor-Leste, Lesotho, South Africa and Thailand. Such complaints go to the regular courts in Bangladesh, Botswana, Guyana, Ireland and Sierra Leone, and to the Constitutional Court in Burkina Faso, Germany and Indonesia. The EMB has the final say in disputes over the election result for legislative and other elections in some places including Bolivia, Costa Rica, Sweden and Uruguay, while the final say goes to the regular court in Bosnia and Herzegovina, Botswana, Timor-Leste, Ireland, Lesotho and Russia; to the Constitutional Court in Cambodia and Mozambique; and to a specialized electoral court in Mexico and South Africa.

EMB Responsibilities as a Public Organization

As a state-funded organization, the EMB will be expected to behave with integrity and to follow the country's public sector standards, which may include measures of transparency and accountability. Such measures often include standard public sector accountability measures, such as annual reporting on activities to an external body such as the relevant minister (as in Botswana) or directly to the legislature (e.g. in Australia, Canada, Liberia and South Africa). Important responsibilities, such as accountability for performance and finances, relationships with stakeholders and developing sustainable electoral processes, are examined in detail later in this Handbook. Requirements to follow good financial and audit standards are covered in Chapter 7.

EMBs have overarching obligations to adopt good practices so that their levels of integrity promote free, fair and credible elections, their efficiency ensures that public funds are not wasted, and their service standards meet with public approval. If the best practice in electoral organization could be identified, it would be the goal that EMBs would strive to achieve. It is perhaps more realistic to aim to achieve targeted elements of good practice, which can be applied regardless of the differences between electoral systems, while still delivering free, fair and credible elections.

An EMB's responsibilities may also include more normative elements of how it is expected to behave, which may be further elaborated in its code of conduct. Detailed codes of conduct for EMB members and more senior staff may also include transparent and accountable actions based on law, professional behaviour in all actions and accuracy in all work. It may be more appropriate to have a simpler code for lower-level or temporary staff with limited responsibilities. For example, for polling station officials, a simple statement committing them to obey all relevant laws, regulations and directions, and maintain impartiality and ballot secrecy, may be sufficient.

South Africa has a code of conduct for EMB members and another for election staff. Cambodia and Liberia also have a staff code of conduct. When the EMB staff and secretariat comes from the country's civil service, then they will be responsible for the codes and standards of the civil service. Electoral legislation in Indonesia includes obligations for the EMB to provide good service to all election participants and treat them fairly, determine and implement quality standards for election materials, maintain comprehensive electoral archives, fully inform the public of its activities, be accountable for its funding and report regularly to the president on the conduct of each election.

A code of conduct embodying the above principles is essential for all EMBs, regardless of their model or composition. Members and staff of all EMBs are expected to uphold the integrity of electoral processes and to refrain from acting in a manner that conflicts with their role as impartial electoral referees.

Avoidance of Conflicts of Interest

EMBs make decisions involving the fast and effective spending of large budgets. High-value individual supply agreements—for items such as ballot boxes, ballot papers and computer equipment—can be of huge benefit to the winning supplier. Connections between EMB members or staff and suppliers, other election participants or stakeholders who can benefit from EMB decisions can lead to perceived conflicts of interest which jeopardize an EMB's public credibility, or real conflicts of interest which damage its integrity. General public service legislation may cover these issues in relation to public servants serving in EMBs.

Conflict of interest provisions could be included in legislation or EMB regulations, and can be part of an enforceable code of conduct for EMB members and staff. They usually specify that EMB members and staff who have an interest or potential interest in a matter that comes before the EMB for consideration and decision should notify the EMB in a timely manner and refrain from participating in the consideration of that matter. To be effective, realistic enforceable sanctions for breaches of conflict of interest provisions are necessary, such as dismissal from the EMB or other disciplinary action. Examples of such provisions (in relation to an EMB member) are contained in the Australian electoral legal framework.

The same is true of EMB staff and members' contacts with or links to political parties and candidates. Such contacts or links should be disclosed in a timely manner, and affected EMB members and staff should refrain from participating in any decision that might benefit the relevant parties or candidates.

EMB Responsibilities to Promote Democracy and Equity

Electoral legislation in some countries defines not only EMB powers and functions, but also their responsibilities and obligations. Other international and national laws apply to the EMB as a public body, such as human rights and laws seeking to ensure equal treatment for women, ethnic minorities, people with disabilities and internally displaced persons.

As upholders of democratic values, EMBs have behavioural and access responsibilities to the community they serve, even where these are not defined in the electoral legal framework. Some of these responsibilities relate to issues such as transparency, gender balance, sensitivity to customs and traditions, treatment of ethnicity, providing electoral access to marginalized groups and creating conditions that are conducive to fair electoral competition. The South African EMB has created a Governance and Ethics Committee that will develop a policy of social responsibility.

Gender Balance

EMBs have a responsibility to ensure that they reflect the society's gender composition in their internal and external activities. Elements of this responsibility may be defined in electoral and gender equity laws, and some may be adopted voluntarily by an EMB. In much of the world gender equity relates to women, as they generally constitute less than half of participants in elections despite making up half of the population. Across much of Asia, gender balance also considers the third gender.

Gender balance within the legislature or among candidates is included within electoral law in many countries. EMBs may have a role, such as ensuring that political parties nominate at least the number of women candidates required by law and rejecting any candidate list that does not comply (as in Argentina, Belgium, Costa Rica, Guyana, Iraq, Mexico, Mongolia, Palestine, Paraguay and Poland). Albania fined political parties, including the main government and opposition parties, for failing to meet quota requirements in 2013. Some may be taken on by an EMB as a social campaign; in 2004 the Indonesian EMB returned party candidate lists for reconsideration where they did not meet the recommended (but not enforceable) 30 per cent women candidate quota. It is good practice for EMBs to promote equity by advocating the inclusion of gender balance measures in electoral legislation and by including such measures in their own regulations or codes of conduct.

The provision and enforcement of sanctions is the most important way to ensure that gender quotas are effective. In the context of legislated quotas, the presence and enforcement of timely and proportionate sanctions greatly increases the likelihood of party compliance. Sanctions are usually provided in electoral laws, and EMBs are generally responsible for monitoring compliance. A majority of countries that use legislated candidate quotas have sanctions for non-compliance; the EMB rejects candidate lists (or sections thereof) that violate the quota rules. Some countries instead use a financial sanction; EMBs usually perform the function of detecting non-compliance and enforcing financial sanctions as well. EMBs' determination to carefully oversee these processes is critical for upholding international obligations and the rule of law in this field.

Where gender quota rules provided in the electoral laws are ambiguous and open to various interpretations and exploitations from political actors, some electoral courts and tribunals have proven effective in strengthening the implementation of these rules through their rulings. In Costa Rica, a quota rule of 40 per cent was implemented in the 1998 elections, but the electoral authorities failed to reject lists that did not meet the quota requirement. In response, the Supreme Electoral Tribunal ruling the following year clarified the method in which the quota law should be implemented, specifying that lists should comprise a minimum of 40 per cent of either sex, and that women should have 40 per cent of electable seats, interpreted as the number of seats the party received in the district in the previous election. In Mexico, in 2011 the Federal Electoral Court upheld the appeal of several women who had challenged the practice of waiving the gender quota requirement of 40 per cent in candidate lists for parties that selected their candidates through primary elections. The court ruled that all parties had to abide by the quota requirement, and clarified that women members could only be substituted by women alternates.

Gender balance among EMB members and election staff at all levels is gaining greater attention. As of the end of 2013, women headed the EMBs in Albania, Georgia, Guatemala, Lesotho, Namibia, Saint Lucia, Sierra Leone, South Africa, Taiwan and Zambia. At least one-third of EMB members are women in several countries, including Armenia, Ghana, Guam, Liberia and Costa Rica, as well as most of those who have a woman chair.

It is equally important to ensure that women are fully represented at all levels of the EMB secretariat and in its temporary election staff—as polling station staff and managers. Some electoral laws have a gender quota on the composition of the board and staff (Timor-Leste) and employees (Kenya). In Nepal, parliamentary guidelines require that at least half of election staff who work with voters are women, and that each polling place must have a woman staff member to mark women's fingers and a woman staff member to manage the women's queue. In Guinea, the selection process for EMB members states that gender must be taken into account. In Bosnia and Herzegovina, the rules on the composition of municipal election commission and polling station committees stipulate that effort should be made to ensure that each gender is represented by at least 40 per cent of members.

Commitments to increase women's participation in EMB leadership positions and attain a gender balance across all levels of the electoral administration system need to be implemented in good faith, so that such efforts meet the intended standards and avoid the relegation of women to lower-level positions across the electoral administration system. For example, in Ukraine's 2012 elections, women formed 72 per cent of staff in precinct election commissions, while there were only four women out of 15 members (26 per cent) of the Central Election Commission (CEC). In the 2012 Georgian parliamentary elections, women constituted two-thirds of the precinct election commissions and about half of the district election commissions, while only one woman served at the CEC level.

Ensuring that there is a gender balance in its own personnel and activities, whether or not this is required by electoral legislation or government policy, will promote an EMB's credibility and allow it to fully tap the available resources for its membership, professional and support staff, consultants, advisers, and permanent and temporary staff.

Adopting an internal gender policy, carrying out a gender audit or mapping of all activities, following a gender mainstreaming policy and having a designated senior staff member who oversees gender inclusion who checks for gender inclusion are all ways that an EMB can ensure that women can participate fully in all aspects of an election. The EMB needs to provide a good example on gender balance issues in all its activities.

Creating a professional working environment within an EMB at all levels, in which there is zero tolerance of gender-based discrimination or harassment of any member of the institution, whether permanent or temporary staff, is vital for advancing the goal of true gender equality within the EMB. Cases of gender-based harassment and exploitation of staff by senior managers frequently go unreported or undocumented, which prevents the investigation and elimination of such practices. In this context, EMBs should strive to review and reform their internal oversight procedures, institute effective non-discrimination and anti-harassment policies, and encourage the reporting and thorough investigation of such instances with adequate sanctions against perpetrators.

The staffing and set-up of registration process and polling places can have a major impact on women's ability to cast a vote. In some places, women are effectively disenfranchised when their vote is cast by their father or husband. Where this is common, EMBs have been working to ensure that women cast their own vote, in secret. In the Former Yugoslav Republic of Macedonia (FYROM), the EMB adopted a strategy to prevent this practice and issued a strong directive to all staff. In addition, pregnant women and those with young children are routinely allowed to the front of the queue in polling places in Afghanistan, Cameroon, Nepal, Tanzania and Uganda, and Uzbekistan has a special room for mothers at all polling places.

Where women wear a veil, then women workers are needed at the polling station and during voter registration if a photo is required as part of the process. In such

Electoral Management Design

countries, separate polling places for women and men are used (for instance in Afghanistan, Lebanon, Pakistan and Palestine). Different polling places for women and men are also common in South America.

The inclusion of gender-based issues in the content of training and voter education and information programmes is an important measure. When all images of an election contain men as polling place workers, security staff, candidates and voters, then women may gain the impression that their participation is not welcome. Thinking about the portrayal of elections in all materials promotes women's participation in political life and enables the EMB to communicate more effectively with and respond to the needs of the whole society. Voter awareness posters that include women as polling place staff and voters have been used in Ghana, Kenya and Kosovo.

If women are known to constitute less than half of the electoral roll or to be less likely to vote, then targeted voter education can be effective. Many EMBs will assist relevant CSOs in such work. Such organizations are also more likely to conduct work encouraging women to stand as candidates for election. In the 2010 Tanzanian election, a booklet was distributed that encouraged women to stand as candidates and to vote, and reminded them that they have the right to cast their own vote for the candidate of their choice.

Ethnicity

Ethnicity and diversity have become important factors in the organization of multiparty democratic elections, especially in many emerging democratic societies, such as Bosnia and Herzegovina. As with gender balance, ethnic balance relates to enforcing any candidate quotas, the composition of the EMB members and staff, as well as internal policies and the delivery of voter information and education.

In Tanzania, the chair and vice-chair must be representatives of the two sides of the union—the mainland and Zanzibar. The composition of the EMB in Bosnia and Herzegovina must contain two Croats, two Bosniacs and one 'other'; a member from each group holds the presidency of the commission on a 21-month rotation.

The ethnic mix of local commissions and staff is also specified by law in Bosnia and Herzegovina. This approach is more likely to gain the confidence and support of all ethnic groups for the EMB's credibility and even-handedness, which will have positive effects on the eventual acceptance of election results. The preparation of election materials and voter information, including the EMB website, in the full range of languages spoken in the country is an important component of recognizing ethnic diversity and the right of all to participate.

Broad-based Access

Electoral law and public pressure are increasingly requiring EMBs to provide services to ensure that all eligible electors have genuine access to the electoral process. For example, the 2002 international Bill of Electoral Rights for People with Disabilities promotes equal rights of access to all electoral processes for people with disabilities. All access-extending services are costly and need to be considered by the EMB (and legislators) in relation to its budgetary constraints.

Voters' special access needs may include mobile registration and voting facilities for those in hospitals, confined to the home or in prison; external voting; the provision of voter registration and voting facilities for internally displaced persons, and in locations outside the country for significant refugee populations (as in Afghanistan, Iraq and Sierra Leone); providing facilities for voting by post or before election day; ensuring that registration, polling stations and equipment are accessible to voters with disabilities; providing electoral information materials suitable for those with visual or aural disabilities, and providing registration or voting assistance to them where needed; and providing voting equipment such as ballot paper templates for the visually impaired. EMB processes may also adopt preferential treatment for pregnant women, nursing mothers, the elderly and people living with disability, especially during voter registration and polling.

In Albania, the EMB pays for the installation of ramps in any building that it uses as a polling place that needs a ramp to allow wheelchair access, thus providing long-term access to such buildings outside the election period. Bosnia and Herzegovina permit people without identity papers to register, and Liberia allows internally displaced persons to register for their county of origin while residing in a different county.

Partnerships with CSOs or relevant government entities will assist the EMB in identifying the precise needs of marginalized groups, and may even help defray the costs of providing access to them.

The legal framework or EMB policies on electoral access may be informed or constrained by customary rules or traditions. These may relate to issues such as who may nominate candidates for particular offices, or the need to establish separate voting queues or locations for men and women. Other issues on which custom or tradition may impinge on access (and electoral integrity) include photographing women for electoral ID cards, voting methods and the use of visible indelible ink to mark voters. Where customary laws are deeply entrenched, an EMB can enhance its acceptance throughout society if its structures, policies and procedures can demonstrate respect for such customary practices, as long as this will not contradict the electoral laws and EMB policies, hinder its activities or prevent people from participating in elections.

Chapter Summary

- An EMB's powers and functions may not be separately identified in its legal framework. Apart from the essential elements of an EMB, these powers and functions can cover a greater or lesser variety of tasks, depending on factors such as the structure of the state, the electoral system, and the number and type of organizations that provide electoral services.

- Essential or core powers and functions of an EMB are:
  - determining who is eligible to vote;
  - receiving and validating the nominations of electoral participants (for elections, political parties and/or candidates);
  - conducting polling;
  - counting the votes; and
  - totalling the votes.

- Non-core functions that may be undertaken by an EMB include voter registration, boundary delimitation, political party regulation and the adjudication of electoral disputes.

- Most EMBs have 'executive' powers and functions that relate to the conduct of elections; some have adjudicative and a very few have legislative powers. Most EMBs' activities are reviewable by judicial or other bodies.

- There may be advantages and disadvantages, which need to be carefully assessed, of assigning some electoral activities—such as boundary delimitation, compiling data for electoral registers, registering and funding political parties, monitoring political campaigns, voter education and information, and validation of election results—to specialist bodies other than an EMB.

- EMBs have behavioural and access responsibilities to the communities they serve, which may extend beyond the minimum requirements of the electoral legal framework. These include promoting gender balance within the EMB itself and political life more broadly, dealing fairly with issues of ethnicity, promoting equality and equity in electoral contests, providing equality of access to electoral services for all and especially for marginalized members of society, and recognizing customary practices where these are in harmony with electoral management principles.

- The electoral legal framework and EMB policies can help guard against inappropriate behaviour by EMBs by requiring members and staff to avoid conflicts of interest.

- An enforceable code of conduct, which all EMB members and staff are required to sign, helps the EMB maintain electoral integrity, ethics, impartiality, service and professional standards.

CASE STUDY

Costa Rica: The Supreme Tribunal of Elections*

Luis Antonio Sobrado González and Ileana Aguilar Olivares

Background

The Supreme Electoral Tribunal (TSE) was one of the main institutional innovations of the country's Political Constitution of 1949. During a historical situation in which disrespect for elections led to a war, the constituents chose to create a top electoral body that safeguarded its independence and professionalism. The Costa Rican model of electoral organization represented a milestone in Latin American public law that technically gave the TSE the status of a fourth state branch, equivalent to the legislative, executive and judicial powers.

Institutional Judicial Framework

The work of the TSE is comprised within the country's current legal regulations under the hierarchy of the electoral legislation (see Electoral Code, article 3): the political constitution, current international agreements, electoral laws, regulations, guidelines and press releases issued by the Tribunal, statutes of registered political parties, and other provisions under the regulations and party statutes.

Non-written norms such as electoral jurisprudence, the main general principles of law, the principles of electoral law and custom are also part of the applicable judicial regulation with the rank of the norm they interpret—and are part of, or delimit—and they are binding toward everyone except the Tribunal. Thus changes in its jurisprudential criteria should be enacted through well-founded reasoning, and all interested parties must be duly informed.

---

* A case study on Costa Rica also appeared in the original edition of the Handbook: Rubén Hernández Valle, 'Costa Rica: A Powerful Constitutional Body', *Electoral Management Design: The International IDEA Handbook* (Stockholm: International IDEA, 2006), pp. 76–9.

Mission and Functions

In accordance with its philosophical context, the mission of the TSE is to organize and arbitrate transparent and reliable electoral processes that can foster democratic coexistence and provide civil registry and identification services to Costa Rican citizens.

To accomplish its mission, the TSE performs four main functions:

1. *Electoral administration:* organizes, directs and controls all suffrage-related acts.
2. *Civil registry:* issues ID documents, and registers and certifies all events related to civil matters including birth, adoption, marriage, divorce, death or adoption of Costa Rican nationality.
3. *Jurisdictional:* breaking away from the classic scheme of the monopoly of the jurisdictional function under the Judicial Branch, the Political Constitution of 1949 granted the TSE the power to dictate resolutions that are unappealable in electoral matters.
4. *Formation in democracy:* promotes democratic values and civic participation through the formulation and execution of training programmes; and research on and publication about topics related to democracy and elections geared toward electoral employees, political parties, students and citizens in general.

Institutional Structure

The TSE is the highest authority in electoral and administrative matters. It has 32 regional offices throughout the country and directly supervises a number of other offices. It is comprised of three tenure magistrate judges and three substitute magistrates, who must satisfy the same requirements as the magistrates of the Supreme Court of Justice. The court appoints the magistrates of the Tribunal for a six-year term through a public contest in which the professional and academic merits of the candidates are assessed without intervention from the political parties or congress. During an electoral period, the Tribunal is comprised of five magistrate judges.

Financing

The TSE is wholly financed with public funds. Its institutional budget includes the needs of all its functional and operational areas. The budget is presented to the authorities of the Ministry of the Treasury, and is approved by the legislative branch.

Accountability

The philosophical framework that governs the TSE incorporates transparency as a constant attitude toward justice, impartiality, truth, objectivity, openness and accountability. The Budget Law assigns public funds to the TSE on a yearly basis, and all contracts and payments are subject to control and revision by the General Comptrollership of the Republic, which is an auxiliary constitutional body of congress that deals with matters concerning the supervision of the National Treasury.

The TSE also belongs to an Inter-institutional Network of Transparency, which has the aim of fostering citizens' access to information related to the administration of public funds through its Internet publications.

The TSE publishes on its webpage all the minutes of its sessions, the institutional budget, financial information, details of purchases and acquisitions, payroll information as well as its Annual Work Report. The latter is presented publicly each year before local authorities and citizens.

The Professionalism of Electoral Officers

Since its creation, the TSE has recruited and trained its staff to guarantee transparent and efficient elections with the highest standards of electoral organization. Due to the continuous modernization of electoral processes, there is ongoing training for electoral workers.

Many years ago the TSE established a process of staff assessment that is linked to a programme of professional upgrading and career development, with a view to developing a cadre of election administration professionals. The stability and professionalism of electoral staff has been a strength of Costa Rican electoral administration.

Along with the regular staff, the TSE engages temporary election personnel to carry out some of the tasks of electoral administration (electoral aides and the National Board of Delegates). To successfully accomplish its tasks, the TSE provides them with training on all matters concerning the electoral process, current regulations and election logistics.

Media Relations

The Electoral Code regulates polling organizations and the dissemination of electoral propaganda in the mass media, which grants the TSE some control over these areas.

- Only those enterprises and mass media previously registered with the TSE will be able to provide electoral propaganda services. They must guarantee equal treatment to all political parties participating in the electoral process. Polling and surveying organizations must also register with the TSE.
- There is an advertising ban effective during Christmas (16 December–1 January) and three days prior to election day.
- The publication or dissemination of polls and surveys concerning the electoral process is prohibited for three days before the elections. The director of any mass media organization that violates this norm is subject to monetary sanctions.

In regard to referendum processes, the regulation states that the mass media must inform the TSE of propaganda spots negotiated by the participants in the election, and about the people responsible for the publication, on a weekly basis. The mass media also have to report the current fees and any modification that may affect them.

It is important to point out that the TSE does not have control over the content of electoral propaganda. Thus, in the event that someone is offended by its content, he/she should consult with the appropriate judicial body.

It is also important to note that due to a provision established in Law no. 1758, 'The Radio Law', after a call for elections has been made, the TSE is granted free 30-minute spots on commercial radio and TV stations every week to give directions regarding cultural and civic topics.

Relations with Other Institutions

The Political Constitution of 1949 granted the TSE the rank of a constitutional body with financial and functional independence from the three government branches. Therefore its relationship with the other state institutions is similar to that of a fourth branch of government.

The TSE can establish alliances with national and international institutions with related institutional objectives. Some of its key local collaborators are the Ministry of Education, the National Institute for Women, public universities, the judicial branch and the General Comptrollership of the Republic. At the international level, it has relationships with International IDEA, UNDP, OAS, the Konrad Adenauer Foundation and the Inter-American Institute of Human Rights (IIDH), among others.

The TSE is also part of the Association of Electoral Bodies of Central America and the Caribbean (Tikal Protocol) and the Inter-American Union of Electoral Organizations (UNIORE). Both institutions foster the exchange of information and cooperation among participating electoral bodies.

New Technologies Management

The TSE has a General Direction of Technological Strategy that aims to promote and develop projects that have a high institutional impact in terms of information technology as a tool to improve the electoral processes and services that the institution provides. Some of the main projects currently underway are automation of processes in the General Direction of Electoral Registry, an electoral geographic information system, and strengthening the system for issuing ID documents.

Electoral Reform Management

In accordance with the constitution, the TSE must be consulted before legislation related to electoral matters is passed by congress. If a decision by congress goes against the wish of the TSE or if the TSE is not consulted, congress can pass election related legislation only with the support of at least two-thirds of its members. Likewise, the constitution states that six months prior to a popular election and four months after it, congress cannot pass laws related to electoral matters without the agreement of the TSE.

The current Electoral Code is the result of a proposal presented by the TSE to congress. The bill went through many delays and changes over two legislative periods; however, there was finally political consensus to approve the new code in 2009. It represents significant progress in the Costa Rican electoral system, such as the inclusion of a broad chapter on electoral justice, regulation of internal democratization of political parties, establishment of parity and power shift to achieve gender equity, improvement of party finance control mechanisms, the creation of the Electoral Registry and the Institute of Formation and Studies on Democracy (IFED) within the structure of the TSE, and the authorization of absentee voting as of the 2014 election.

Bibliography

Código Electoral 2009, *Decreto Legislativo No. 8765,* República de Costa Rica

International IDEA, *Experiencias de reforma política y electoral en Colombia, Costa Rica y México desde la perspectiva comparada latinoamericana* [A Comparative Latin American Perspective of Political and Electoral Reform Experiences in Colombia, Costa Rica and Mexico] (Stockholm: International IDEA, 2009)

Tribunal Supremo de Elecciones, *Informe de Labores* 2011 [Activity Report 2011] (San José: TSE, 2012)

CASE STUDY

Armenia: Electoral Administration in South Caucasus

Arpine Galfayan

Background

Armenia is a small country with a population of about 3 million; it is situated in the South Caucasus region and neighbours Azerbaijan, Georgia, Iran and Turkey. Russia is not an immediate neighbour, but has a major influence on the country's political processes, including elections. Armenia became an independent republic in 1991 after the collapse of the Soviet Union. Its history of a multiparty political system dates back to 1918–20, the First Republic of Armenia. From 1920–90, the Communist Party was the only legal political entity in the country, and elections were rather a formal event, similar to all other places in the USSR.

Armenia's first EMB was formed in 1995, following the adoption of the Law on the Elections of the National Assembly Members, which also set out procedures for the formation of its EMB, the Central Electoral Commission (CEC). While the EMB falls under the Independent Model, genuine independence of the electoral administration is seriously under question. The EMB is believed to be one of the instruments for reproducing the corrupt governing elites. Although the composition of the EMB has changed several times and the party model was replaced by a professional model, this has done little to improve public trust in the electoral process. The Organization for Security and Co-operation in Europe (OSCE) Office for Democratic Institutions and Human Rights (ODIHR) report on the 2012 parliamentary elections recommends that 'special measures should be undertaken to increase public trust in the integrity of the election process. They could include, but not be limited to, increased transparency in the work of the electoral and state authorities, additional voter education on the secrecy of the vote, and enhanced campaigns against vote buying and vote selling.'[1]

Legislative Framework

Armenia's constitution has no provisions about electoral administration, but rather states general electoral principles and defines the basic provisions for conducting presidential, parliamentary and local elections and referendums, such as who can run for elections, when elections shall be conducted and what the basic responsibilities of the elected public offices are. The Electoral Code of 2011 is the main legal document that regulates the administration of elections, as well as virtually all other aspects of elections. Section 2 of the code is dedicated to the structure, roles, responsibilities and competences of the EMB. It empowers the EMB to adopt normative acts/decisions on technical and procedural issues that are not regulated in the code (e.g. candidate registration procedures, ballot paper design).[2]

Institutional Structure of the EMB

Elections in Armenia are administered by a three-level commission: the CEC, Constituency Electoral Commissions (ConECs) and Precinct Electoral Commissions (PECs). The CEC is the main body responsible for organizing national elections and supervising their legality. ConECs are formed according to the number of electoral constituencies, which is presently 41. At national elections, they collect and transfer results from polling stations and handle electoral disputes at the precinct level; at local elections, they carry out functions similar to the CEC—they are responsible for the overall organization and supervision of local elections. PECs are formed to organize polling and counting in electoral precincts (1,800–2,000 voters on average). The CEC and the ConECs are permanent bodies with a six-year term of office, while PECs are formed for the election period only.

EMB Powers and Functions

Under the electoral law, the EMB has the powers of:

- supervising the uniform application of the Electoral Code and ensuring that all subordinate legal acts correspond to the code;
- adopting rules and procedures for the CEC and subordinate commissions;
- nominating and registering candidates and parties, and supervising parties' financial activities;
- delimiting electoral constituencies (delimitation of precincts is carried out by the police, which is also responsible for voters' lists);
- professional development and accreditation of electoral officers;
- accrediting observers and the media;
- supervising the electoral budget;
- defining forms and samples of electoral documents (ballot papers, tabulation protocols, etc.) and the procedures for filling and keeping them; and
- voter information, etc.

Voter lists are compiled by the police, and the National Commission of Television and Radio (which licenses and monitors private broadcasters) and the Council of Public TV and Radio regulate media campaigns.

Composition of the EMB

The 2011 Electoral Code changed the composition of the EMB from party based to professional. The CEC is composed of seven members who are appointed by the president of Armenia upon the proposal of the human rights defender (three members), the Chamber of Advocates (two members) and the Court of Cassation (Armenia's supreme court, two members).

The CEC has a secretariat of 25 permanent civil service staff members. ConECs are also composed of seven members, appointed by the CEC from among applicants to an open public announcement. Gender quotas require that at least two commissioners in the CEC, and in each ConEC, are of the under-represented gender. PECs are composed of seven or more members, who are assigned by political parties in parliament and CECs (two members). The chairpersons, deputy chairpersons and secretaries of the CEC and ConECs are elected by commission members from among themselves. The positions of PEC chairpersons and secretaries are distributed by the CEC among political party appointees, proportional to the number of seats the parties won in the proportional component of the last parliamentary elections, which in recent elections resulted in a diverse countrywide distribution of these positions. Regarding the composition of electoral commissions, OSCE/ODIHR observers reported in 2012 that representatives of parliamentary parties at the regional level generally expressed trust in the election administration since they could nominate PEC members and appoint proxies (party observers) at all levels of the election administration, while the largest extra-parliamentary force, which was not represented in PECs, expressed its lack of trust.[3] The OSCE/ODIHR observation report of 2012 parliamentary elections also expressed concern about the lack of provisions to prevent possible conflicts of interest in the election administration which, resulted in a number of ConEC appointments that may have affected the impartiality of these commissions.[4]

Financing of the EMB

The funding for organizing and conducting elections, and for operating the electoral commissions, is provided from the state budget. If early elections are held, or if the state budget does not have a sufficient reserve fund, the reserve fund of the Central Bank of Armenia shall be used for elections. When this is impossible, the CEC can obtain credit from private banks. The EMB drafts its own budget for both electoral and non-electoral periods and presents it to the government, which embeds it in the draft annual state budget for parliamentary approval.

The law prohibits the EMB from accepting money from any other source, including foreign donors. On the one hand, this regulation makes the EMB self-reliant and ensures that the state budget pays all necessary election costs. On the other hand, this limits its opportunities to fundraise for additional innovative development projects that the state budget would not be able (or would consider inappropriate) to fund.[5]

In the non-electoral period, the EMB's funding is limited to staff and maintenance expenditures, yet this period would be ideal for starting new projects, such as electoral education campaigns, professional development projects for various election stakeholders and institutional development activities. This gap is partly filled by Article 38.7 of the

Electoral Code, which allows the EMB to use 15 per cent of the candidates' electoral deposits for institutional development and acquisition of new technologies, for example.[6]

Accountability of the EMB

The CEC submits one annual financial report on expenditures to the Control Chamber of the Republic of Armenia (parliamentary body), and another to the Oversight and Audit Service, which is composed of independent experts and CEC secretariat members. In addition to financial reporting, within three months after each election the CEC chair reports to the National Assembly about the implementation of the electoral process. The ConECs contribute to this CEC report.

EMB and Electoral Justice

Under the Electoral Code, decisions, actions and inactions of the electoral commissions can be appealed to the superior commission, while all complaints against the CEC are under the jurisdiction of the Administrative Court. Local and international election observers have criticized the EMB's handling of electoral disputes. The OSCE/ODIHR observation report on the 2012 elections mentions that 'The manner in which election commissions and courts dealt with election complaints often left stakeholders without effective consideration of their claims.'[7] Both the electoral commissions and the courts often take a formalistic approach to dealing with complaints. The vast majority of reported complaints were either denied consideration or rejected for technicalities.[8]

The OSCE/ODIHR election observation report for the 2012 parliamentary elections also recommends that:

> Election commissions, law enforcement bodies, and courts should interpret, implement and enforce the electoral legal framework taking into consideration the spirit and intent of the law, which aims to ensure an equal playing field for contestants, free will of the voters, and the integrity of the electoral process. This would include a wider interpretation of vote buying and enforcement of the ban on campaigning in schools and on involvement of educational staff and students in campaigning. In addition, the Criminal Code could be amended to include offenses for abuse of official position and administrative resources for campaigning. The criminal offense for distribution of libellous campaign material should be repealed.

The Professionalism of Electoral Officers

The Electoral Code stipulates the professional requirements for all levels of electoral commissions, which include educational background and professional experience. CEC members are required to have:

- higher legal education and at least three years of professional experience in the last five years;
- a scientific degree in law and at least three years of professional experience in the last five years;
- higher education and at least five years of professional experience of public service in state bodies in the last ten years; and

- higher education and at least three years of professional experience in the last five years in a standing electoral commission or in the staff thereof. [9]

There are similar criteria for ConEC members. PEC members must complete an accreditation process. At least once each year, the CEC organizes professional development courses in all provinces of the country. Citizens with the right to vote can individually apply to and participate in the courses, and political parties can submit lists of their members or supporters. Upon completion of the course, those who successfully pass a qualification test receive certificates that allow them to be selected as precinct election commissioners. The qualification tests can be taken by any citizen, irrespective of their prior participation in the professional development course. Both the courses and tests are open for monitoring by mass media representatives and NGOs. In addition to these courses, training is carried out (in 2012 in collaboration with IFES) upon appointment to the PEC. Despite these efforts, a large number of PEC members withdraw from the commission shortly before election day; their replacements have not attended the second round of training, which results in poorer professionalism of the polling officials and more violations on election day.[10] Training for ConECs is carried out upon formation of the commission.

There is no training requirement for CEC members. All secretariat members are civil servants, and therefore must pass a standard legal test every three years in order to maintain their position.[11] The civil servant position for CEC secretariat members was introduced in 2004 in order to preserve institutional memory and protect the secretariat staff from the frequent changes that previously occurred after the formation of every new commission.

According to the final report of OSCE/ODIHR on the 6 May 2012 parliamentary elections, 'before election day, the election process was administered in an overall professional and efficient manner. The CEC and TECs [ConECs] worked in an open and transparent manner, granting to proxies, observers and media representatives information and access to their sessions. However, CEC and TEC decisions were taken with limited open discussion, somewhat reducing transparency. All necessary election preparations were made within legal deadlines.' The same report points out that the CEC 'also organized nationwide training for the majority of TEC and PEC members; PEC training was overall assessed positively by OSCE/ODIHR long term observers, although many PECs faced problems with counting procedures on election night'. The OSCE/ODIHR further recommends that 'training of election commission members on election procedures should be continued and enhanced, with a particular focus on counting and tabulation procedures.'[12]

Relationship with the Media

No public relations problems were reported by international and local observers, the media or the EMB. The EMB usually provides public information in a professional manner, informs the media about upcoming events, organizes frequent briefings and press conferences during the election period, and updates its official website. CEC events are usually well attended by the media, especially during the election period.

Criticism usually concerns issues of the media campaign. The Electoral Code regulates free and paid campaign airtime on public television and radio. Public and private broadcasters are required to ensure non-discriminatory conditions and to provide unbiased information in their news programmes. The responsibility of regulating campaign airtime on public and private broadcasters was moved from the CEC to the National Commission of Television and Radio (NCTR, for monitoring private broadcasters) and the Council of Public TV and Radio. The EMB's role is to develop a timetable for allocating airtime to all parties and candidates. The CEC and NCTR work closely together, and the CEC relies on NCTR data when reporting on elections or dealing with election complaints regarding the media campaign.

Half of the NCTR's eight members are elected for a six-year term by parliament, and half are appointed by the president. The president also appoints the five members of the Council of Public TV and Radio. Election observation reports since 2003 consistently identify problems with regard to balanced media coverage.[13] The coverage is usually more balanced for parliamentary elections, while for presidential campaigns the incumbents or governmental candidates have continuously had overwhelmingly positive coverage and more time than opposition candidates. While public broadcasters, which are strongly controlled by the government, have never been sanctioned for violations, two private TV broadcasters faced administrative cases for biased coverage in the 2012 parliamentary elections; one of them was fined about EUR 2,000 for breach of the election silence period. Violations regarding biased coverage were not punished.

Relations with Other Institutions and Agencies

The EMB works well and coordinates with other state agencies involved in elections. This includes the police (which are responsible for voters' lists), the NCTR and Council of Public TV and Radio (which are responsible for media monitoring), and local governments (which allocate space for polling stations, design the polling stations, etc. in accordance with CEC decisions).[14]

The EMB's relations with the executive, legislative and judiciary branches are also rather cooperative. In Armenia, the executive, legislative and judiciary branches are strongly linked, with little independence or opposition to each other. The EMB is perceived and acts as part of the 'team' in the ruling political elite.

Independent NGOs, especially the prominent human rights and election watchdog organizations, are critical of the EMB's status and work. Other, more technically focused organizations have some formal cooperation with the EMB and coordinate, for example, on voter education campaigns and disability-friendly polling stations.

The CEC collaborates with international organizations that carry out electoral observation or provide technical assistance. Although foreign organizations do not fund elections and are not officially considered donors to the CEC, election-related projects are usually coordinated with the CEC.

Sustainability of the EMB

The Electoral Code guarantees that elections and the EMB are funded from the state budget in election and non-election periods. The fact that the EMB's secretariat is composed of civil servants with long-term contracts also supports sustainability and the institutional memory of the organization.

During the election period, about ten temporary staff are hired to organize elections. The restricted funding provides little possibility for the implementation of innovative or development projects in non-election periods.

New Technologies

The Armenian EMB considers one of its achievements to be the creation of a network between CEC and ConECs that facilitates the transparency of election results tabulation. As soon as the data is filled in by computer at the constituency level, the results appear in the network at the CEC and are immediately publicized in the CEC media centre. Future plans include broadcasting of all CEC meetings, so that ConECs in their constituencies can follow them online.

During the past year the CEC revamped its website, which is now available in Armenian and English. The website provides information about the CEC and past and future elections, and provides access to a range of electoral and legal documents.

Limited electronic voting was also introduced in 2011. It only involved personnel and family members of embassies and consulates, and staff members of legal persons registered in Armenia who have branch offices in foreign countries (altogether around 200 people). For all other citizens, voting abroad is unavailable.

Electoral Reform Management

The EMB does not have the power to initiate legal reform in the legislature. This is normally done through the government, which has the constitutional right to submit legal initiatives. In practice, the EMB drafts a good portion of electoral law reforms, but it must negotiate with the government before going to parliament, which limits the independence of the EMB.

Opportunities and Constraints

Armenian legislation provides a sound foundation for the conduct of democratic elections. The technical (if not ethical) professionalism of electoral administration has also substantially improved over the last 20 years. However, electoral integrity is the biggest issue faced by the EMB today. It is largely controlled by the ruling political elites, and is not an impartial and ethical institution. Political will and positive systemic change are needed to change this, as well as a major increase in democratic awareness among the citizenry, particularly an increased appreciation of democratic processes by the people, and active and responsible engagement from voters and civil society.

A diversification of funding opportunities would allow the creation of projects such as a professional development centre and a youth electoral and citizenship education centre within the EMB, together with academic and civil society institutions, which in the long run can contribute to democratization and the improvement of electoral practices.

Staffing the EMB with fully independent and ethical election professionals is another way in which it can win voters' trust and conduct independent, impartial electoral processes. Stricter individual responsibility for electoral violations can also be an instrument for enforcing more democratic electoral processes.

Notes

[1] OSCE/ODIHR, *Armenia, Parliamentary Elections, 6 May 2012: Final Report*, 2012.
[2] Article 36.1 of the 2011 Electoral Code of Armenia states that 'The Central Electoral Commission shall adopt regulatory and individual legal acts, whereas constituency and precinct electoral commissions – individual legal acts.'
[3] OSCE/ODIHR 2012.
[4] OSCE/ODIHR long-term observers were informed about several cases of conflict of interest. For example, the chair of the CEC was the wife of one of the candidates. See ibid, p. 8.
[5] In an interview with Liana Simonyan, head of the CEC Foreign Relations Department, she mentioned the idea of creating a Training Center and Youth Electoral and Citizenship Education centre within the EMB, which cannot be done with the existing resources.
[6] All parties and candidates have to pay an electoral deposit to participate in elections; the deposits of those who do not pass the prescribed threshold go to the state budget.
[7] OSCE/ODIHR 2012.
[8] Transparency International Anti-Corruption Center's iditord.org website, which offered citizen reporting during the May 2012 parliamentary elections in Armenia, received frequent reports of violations of campaign rules (e.g. a period of silence on the election eve and election day, bribing voters, voter list inaccuracies, violations of voting day procedures, etc.).
[9] Electoral Code of Armenia, Article 40.3.
[10] Interview with Ruben Sargsyan, APR Group (Free Public Law Protective Youth), local NGO, 30 October 2012.
[11] Exceptions: the CEC media speaker, chairperson's assistant and referent may be selected based on merit and do not have to be civil servants.
[12] OSCE/ODIHR 2012.
[13] Vardanyan, Edgar, 'OSCE/ODIHR and Armenian Elections', *The Changing World: A Glance from Yerevan*, 1, ACNIS, 2012.
[14] The CEC's decisions (normative acts) are binding for all institutions involved in organizing elections.

CHAPTER 4

The Composition, Roles and Functioning of an EMB

An EMB's activities generally require both the determination of policy and the implementation of major administrative and logistics operations. Where the Governmental Model of electoral management is used, both of these functions are undertaken by civil servants, who are employed by one or more bodies of the executive. While members of the executive branch of government, such as ministers, may also take an active role in EMB policymaking under the Governmental Model, it is more common for the head of its secretariat, who may be termed director of elections or have a similar title, to be responsible for policy. It is not usual for governmental EMBs to have members; rather, they are composed entirely of secretariat (public service) staff. An exception is the Czech Republic, where EMB members are appointed from the executive branch.

In EMBs under the Independent Model, the policy function is undertaken by individual(s) (i.e. the EMB's 'members') from outside the executive branch who are specially appointed for this task. Their role is similar to that of the board of a corporation—to guide the direction of the EMB—although in many cases EMB members have a full-time and more 'hands on' role than would be usual for a corporate board. Similarly, under the Mixed Model, the component independent EMB is guided by a 'board' of members.

The use of the terms 'independent model' or 'independent members' should not be confused with the independence of the EMB, which depends on its actions (see Chapter 1). People appointed by political parties can act independently, and people appointed for their expertise can act partially.

EMB Membership

EMB members need a very high level of management skills and commitment to maintaining integrity under pressure. Ideally, an EMB should include members with a wide range of the skills needed to ensure that it can function effectively, such as legal, communications, education, logistics, technology and corporate management skills. Public confidence in EMBs is enhanced where the electoral legislation contains (1) qualifications for appointment to EMBs that are clearly defined and appropriate for the complex task of managing electoral processes impartially and (2) selection and appointment mechanisms that are transparent and based on the candidates' merits. The mode of selection and appointment, and the tenure, of EMB members vary by country. Details of the composition, appointment and tenure of EMB members are available in Annex A.

There are various titles for EMB members; each has its own nuances that are related to the basis, role and powers of the policymaking members of the EMB. In Canada, the chief electoral officer is both the chief and sole policymaker and the head of the administration (secretariat), and is the sole EMB member. The frequently used term 'commissioner' is not applied consistently. In many countries that use the Independent or Mixed Model, EMB members are referred to as commissioners. In Australia, the electoral commissioner is both the head of the secretariat and a full voting member of the EMB (although not the head of the EMB), while the deputy and assistant commissioners are the staff of the secretariat. In India, the EMB has three members, the chief election commissioner and two election commissioners, and the most senior members of the secretariat are known as deputy election commissioners. In Francophone countries and Latin America, an EMB head may be termed 'president', and in Latin America the term 'councillor' is sometimes used to describe EMB members.

The chairs of EMBs in Bangladesh, Nigeria and Pakistan, who by law are known as chief electoral commissioners, serve as the EMBs' chief executive. The role of such a chair is similar to that of an executive chair or executive director in the corporate world. Unlike chairs in some other EMBs, this type of chief electoral commissioner has executive powers and is more 'hands on' in directing the electoral process. Although he or she may be assisted by other commissioners and the secretariat, the chief electoral commissioner in these countries will have the final say in matters of finance and administration, and also on key aspects of the electoral process.

Status of EMB Members

For an EMB to operate effectively, its members need to have a status that entitles them to respect from and a relationship of equality with the government, the legislature and society. In India, the three EMB members—the chief election commissioner and the two election commissioners—have the status of judges of the Supreme Court. The head of an EMB especially needs a status that affords her or him access to the highest levels of government and ensures adherence to the EMB's decisions. The chair of the EMB in Pakistan (the chief electoral commissioner) has the same conditions of service as the chief justice, as do his counterparts in numerous other countries.

While it is important that EMB members have a high status, it is also important that members do not behave as though they are bigger than the EMB institution they serve, or come to be regarded by society as 'the EMB'. Personality-based institutions can be highly polarizing. A good-practice model for EMB members to follow is to personalize the institution they serve, rather than institutionalize the person or persons leading the EMB. For example, decisions may be described as the 'decision of the commission' rather than 'the decision of the commissioners'.

The EMB Chair: A Special Role?

In some countries, the legal framework provides for a two-stream procedure for the appointment of EMB members: one for the chair and another for all other members. In Ghana, Guyana, Lithuania, Pakistan, Thailand and Uruguay, the EMB chair (sometimes called the EMB president) serves as a 'first among equals' and is appointed by the head of state/government at a level higher than the other members. The chair of the Ghanaian EMB is appointed at the level of a senior judge, while other members are at the level of judges of a lower court. In the Solomon Islands, the speaker of parliament becomes the chair of the EMB.

Where the EMB chair is appointed on different terms than the other members and at a higher level, he or she tends to play a more prominent role, over and above that of presiding over the EMB's meetings. He or she may have additional powers related to matters such as chairing various EMB internal subcommittees, actively supporting the secretariat in policy implementation and monitoring, and liaising with stakeholders. In Lithuania, for example, the EMB chair has specified powers to hire and fire staff; to keep and direct the use of the EMB seal; and to represent the EMB in state institutions, in court and in international organizations. In Liberia, the chair of the National Elections Commission is also by law the official spokesperson for the commission, although secretariat staff carry out the day-to-day work of maintaining contact with the media.

In countries such as Bosnia and Herzegovina, Costa Rica, Guam, Moldova, Russia, South Korea, Ukraine and Uzbekistan, all EMB members are appointed on the same terms, and the chair (and in some cases the vice chair and secretary) is elected by his/her peers after the first meeting. In Mozambique, the chair is elected from among the civil society representatives. In Bosnia and Herzegovina and in Guam, the elected chair serves for only part of the commission's term. When the chair is elected from within the EMB, the chair's main responsibility is to preside over the meetings of the commission and/or its subcommittees if necessary.

There are no specific advantages or disadvantages associated with appointing the EMB chair as a first among equals or having members of the EMB select their chair from among themselves. The appropriate practice depends on the context in which the EMB structure was originally designed and continues to function.

The case for a 'first among equals' EMB chair is stronger where an EMB is nascent and requires some nurturing, and the position is full time. This may also apply where the chair is a full-time position and other members are part time. Where the EMB is a part-time body, it may be more appropriate for the chair to be elected by his or her peers and for him or her to have the same conditions of service as all other EMB members.

EMB Members: Respected Experts or Watchdogs for Each Other?

In countries where the Independent or Mixed Model is used, electoral legislation specifies the framework for EMB membership. There are myriad different legal provisions that govern this critical issue. A basic difference is between a multiparty-based EMB and an expert-based EMB. Broadly, a multiparty-based model assumes that decisions are often political and allows each political party to choose some of the members, on the assumption that each will ensure that decisions do not unduly favour other parties. By contrast, an expert-based model assumes that decisions are primarily legal or technical and seeks people with the expertise to deal with these issues competently.

Multiparty-based EMBs

Many countries, especially those that have experienced difficult transitions from authoritarian rule to multiparty democracy, have chosen multiparty-based EMBs. In such societies, public servants are likely to have been largely discredited as electoral policymakers because of a history of being agents of the authoritarian former ruling party or military regime. The fight against authoritarianism may also have polarized society to the extent that it is difficult to find public figures who are widely accepted as impartial to serve on an EMB for a transitional election. Many Central and Eastern European countries adopted multiparty-based EMBs during their transitions.

Multiparty EMBs comprise a mixture of political party nominees. The legal framework may entitle all recognized or registered political parties contesting an election to be represented equally on the EMB (as in Guam), or a threshold may restrict representation—for example, to parties represented in the legislature or with more than a specified proportion of members in the legislature. Of the 20 members nominated by political parties in Guinea, half are nominated by the political party of the president and the others by the opposition parties. In Albania, the party-affiliated members represent the distribution of seats in the legislature. In Venezuela in the mid-1990s, the larger parties each had their own representative, while smaller parties of the left and right were represented collectively.

Political party-based appointment often implies that EMB members are serving on the EMB as political party representatives or agents and, as well as impartially managing electoral processes, serve to protect their nominating parties' interests. However, while each individual member is seen from the outside as partisan, each also ensures that the others do not take partisan advantage—so the EMB can nonetheless be credibly perceived as an impartial body. Political party-based members often hold office for a fixed term and cannot be dismissed except for cause, such as a breach of their duties, or upon their withdrawal by their nominating authority. Frequent replacement by parties of their representatives, however, has the potential to disrupt the work of the EMB.

In Guinea and Mozambique, political party nominees to an EMB are eminent persons who are required to maintain high standards of impartiality and professionalism, and thus they do not serve as political party representatives.

Many electoral analysts believe that having political party representatives on an EMB engenders consensus among actors in the electoral contest and enhances transparency, both of which improve confidence in the electoral process. Voters may feel more encouraged to participate in elections if the leaders of political parties play an active role in the electoral process, specifically through representation on the EMB.

Yet a political party-based EMB can imperil or cripple decision-making, especially where political parties' critical interests are at stake. The presence of politicians on the EMB may undermine confidentiality in matters such as the security of ballot materials. Multiparty-based EMBs also tend to generate dissatisfaction, especially among minority parties that might be excluded from the EMB either because they are not represented in the legislature or because they did not participate in the negotiation that led to the initial appointments of EMB members.

> Multiparty EMBs may help promote trust and confidence in electoral processes in the initial stages of democratic transitions. Depoliticization of EMBs may be more appropriate as confidence in the electoral process grows.

Expert-based EMBs

Expert-based or non-party-based EMBs are those that the legal framework requires to be made up of individuals appointed on the basis of their professional standing. In some cases, members of an expert-based EMB may be nominated by political parties or civil society, but this does not imply that they will be directed by their nominating parties or act in a partisan manner. In Mexico, although the EMB is a permanent body with 11 expert voting members, each political group in the legislature and each national political party also provides one non-voting representative.

Qualifications to be a member of an expert-based EMB may include impartiality, a minimum age, professional qualifications and electoral knowledge. Expert-based EMB members are often eminent public figures renowned for political neutrality who have expertise in fields such as law, public administration, political science or the media. Expert-based EMBs are found in countries such as

Australia, Bangladesh, Canada, Costa Rica, India, Indonesia, Poland, Thailand and Ukraine. The law in many of these countries stipulates that EMB members must not have been active in party politics in the recent past, and must not be a political party member while serving as a member of the EMB. Nevertheless, in highly politicized situations, nominees may be seen as friendly to a particular party or faction, and there may be the perception that the parties have divided the positions between them rather than choose impartial members who are acceptable to all.

One common form of the expert-based model is judicial EMBs. In Brazil, for example, elections are the responsibility of national and state electoral tribunals, which are considered a specialized segment of the judicial branch, comprising judges of various categories along with a small number of expert lawyers; below the tribunals, regular judges are detailed for a short time to oversee electoral preparations and operations in each electoral district. The EMBs of Costa Rica and Guatemala are also judicial; all of their members are judges.

EMBs with Both Expert and Multiparty Membership

Some electoral legal frameworks specify that EMBs have a mixed membership of party representatives and politically non-aligned members, such as judges, academics, civil society representatives and career public servants. For example, in Côte d'Ivoire, EMB members are appointed by political parties, law and judicial societies, and government ministries. This may combine advantages from both models, producing even-handed bodies that have both political party buy-in and transparency in their operations.

This combined model can be implemented in various ways. In Mexico, the members nominated by political parties can take part in debates but cannot vote on decisions. In Mozambique, the five members designated by the parties in the legislature then select the eight expert members from nominees provided by CSOs. In Croatia, a standing national EMB comprising Supreme Court judges and other distinguished lawyers is expanded for the electoral period by representatives of the majority and opposition blocs of political parties in the national legislature. Each electoral district has similarly constituted EMBs.

Like multiparty EMBs, combined EMBs can find decision-making difficult. For example in the 1999 Indonesian elections, the combined EMB was unable to validate the election results because members representing some very minor political parties refused to sign the validation unless their parties were allocated seats to which they were not entitled by their votes. Table 7 on page 113 shows some key advantages and disadvantages of multiparty, expert and combined EMBs.

Full-time or Part-time EMB Members?

Whether it is more appropriate for EMB membership to be a full-time or part-time position depends on the electoral and administrative circumstances. In a permanent EMB, workloads may be high throughout the electoral cycle and

Table 7: Advantages and Disadvantages of Multiparty, Expert and Combined EMBs

	Advantages	Disadvantages
Multiparty EMBs	• May promote electoral participation by opposing political forces. • May encourage voter participation. • Enhances electoral transparency. • Ensures political party input to the EMB's policy development. • Ensures links with critical electoral stakeholders. • Brings political experience to the management of electoral processes.	• Members' actions may be motivated by political interest. • May not have appropriate professional experience or qualifications. • May be unwieldy if all parties are represented. • May lack credibility if some parties are excluded or if political parties are not respected. • May find consensus decision-making difficult. • EMB unity may suffer due to public disputes between parties.
Expert EMBs	• Impartial and neutral membership promotes the credibility of the EMB. • Likely to reject political pressure. • Professionalism of members. • Makes a range of expert knowledge available on the EMB. • Eminent public figure members raise the profile of the EMB. • May have a broad range of professional networks on which the EMB can draw.	• May not always be aware of relevant political factors. • Political actors may have limited access to EMB activities. • May not have good links with critical electoral stakeholders. • Members may need to address conflict of loyalties between the work of the EMB and the views of the organizations they come from. • The best 'experts' may not be willing to serve. • It may be difficult to find 'non-partisan' members in transitional environments.
Combined EMBs	• May achieve balance between political and technical considerations. • May encourage participation, and expert members may counterbalance any attempt at partisan actions. • The EMB is transparent to political participants and has some professional credibility. • Both expert knowledge and political input are available to the EMB. • Links with both critical electoral stakeholders and public figures. • Has both political experience and professional networking capacities.	• Political and expert elements may have different agendas. • EMB may experience competitive leaking of information between its components. • May be unwieldy if all political and expert elements are represented. • May lack credibility if some parties are excluded. • May find consensus decision-making difficult. • High-calibre experts may not be willing to work with political elements.

require that EMB members are full time and thus readily available for speedy consultation and decisions. Full-time EMB members may be a good option where there are recurring activities, such as regular partial or by-elections, ongoing voter education and information, continuous voter registration or continuing electoral law reforms. In a temporary EMB, the electoral period workload may be such that full-time members are preferable. Full-time EMB membership may also be appropriate where there are doubts about the impartiality and skill levels of the EMB's secretariat.

The benefit of having full-time EMB members must always be weighed against the cost of their services, when it may be years before the next election. There is also the risk of a potential conflict between senior members of the secretariat and full-time EMB members, especially when the former begin to interpret the full-time presence of the EMB members as interfering in the implementation of policy.

Some electoral legal frameworks, such as Indonesia's, require that EMB appointments are full time. Countries such as Gambia appoint full-time EMB members even though it is not a legal requirement.

In countries where election dates are fixed and EMBs have limited responsibility between elections, it may be advisable to have part-time EMB members. In Ghana and South Sudan, EMB members are part time, while the chair and deputy are full time. It is also possible for members to serve part time in non-electoral periods and full time during electoral periods.

How Many EMB Members?

The electoral legal framework will generally specify the number of EMB members. However, when the membership of a multiparty EMB is determined by criteria such as party representation in the legislature, it is not possible to specify an exact number of members, as this number may vary over time.

The number of members of EMBs varies considerably worldwide, and need not be related to the size of the country. For example, in the small country of Lesotho, the EMB has three members, while Nigeria, a much bigger country, has a 13-member EMB. However, Canada, despite its sizeable land mass, and India, which has about 700 million voters, have one- and three-member EMBs, respectively. Having a larger number of EMB members may provide broader representation, whereas a smaller number can facilitate discussion and decision-making. Having an uneven number of members ensures that simple majority vote decisions can be made without having to resort to measures such as giving the EMB chair a casting vote. EMBs that include political party nominees tend to have more members than expert-based EMBs, in order to accommodate a credible range of political interests.

Electoral law in countries such as Guatemala and Turkey allows for the appointment of alternate or deputy members to EMBs. Under certain circumstances, a deputy member can automatically take the place and exercise the powers of a member.

Term of Office of Members of Permanent EMBs

In many permanent EMBs, members have a specified term of office. As of the end of 2013, terms of office were three years in Malta and Rwanda; four years in the Dominican Republic, Honduras, Jamaica, Latvia and Palau; five years in Kiribati, Lesotho, and Trinidad and Tobago; six years in Nepal; seven years in

Table 8: Number of Members in a Selection of Party-based and Expert-based EMBs as of 2012

Number of Members in Party-based EMBs	
31	Israel
11	Liechtenstein
5	Eritrea
Number of Members in Expert-based EMBs	
15	Ukraine
7	Philippines, Turkey, Uganda
5	Ecuador, Gambia
1	Papua New Guinea

the Philippines, South Africa, Uganda and Ukraine; eight years in Romania and ten years in Botswana (see Annex A). Some EMBs' terms of office are defined in relation to the legislature's term of office. In Botswana, the EMB has a permanent secretariat, but EMB members are operative only during elections and hold office for two successive terms of the legislature (equivalent to ten years). In Bhutan, India and Nepal, if a member turns 65 before the end of their appointed term, they must retire.

The EMBs in Cambodia, Canada, Ghana and Malaysia have an unspecified term of office; once appointed, members remain in office until they reach retirement age, unless they resign or are removed. In Canada and Malaysia the chair remains in office until he or she reaches the age of 65.

The advantage of limiting the term of office is that it promotes the constant generation of new ideas through new appointments. However, it may undermine institutional experience, especially if EMB members' terms coincide with a single electoral cycle. Many electoral laws that specify limited terms of office for EMB members allow for reappointment by mutual consent between the appointee and the appointing authority. South Africa and Zambia limit EMB members to two terms of office, while Pakistan and Russia do not limit EMB members' terms of office. Reappointment is prohibited by law in Mexico and the Philippines.

In South Africa, the terms of EMB members are staggered. Every new appointment is made for a period of seven years and not for the remainder of other members' terms. In Senegal, one-third of EMB members are appointed every three years; Mexico similarly staggers appointments. In Guam, Guinea and Senegal, if a vacancy occurs then the replacement serves only until the end of the term of the person they are replacing.

Staggering EMB members' terms of office greatly helps retain institutional experience and provides for smooth leadership succession. If appointments are not staggered, the new EMB members should be appointed long enough after the last election to allow the former EMB members to complete and report on their election evaluation, and long enough before the next election for the new EMB members to master their responsibilities before the election period commences. This may often be around mid-way between elections.

Recruitment and Appointment of EMB Members

The process of appointing EMB members involves nomination or advertisement, selection and appointment. In some countries the law has specific rules for all three stages in the process, but in others only the body that makes the appointment is specified.

Recruitment Through Open Advertisement

In Iraq, members of the expert-based EMB are recruited through open advertisement. Interested candidates may apply directly to be considered for appointment or be nominated by members of the public. Applications are received and screened (through public interviews) by an independent body. The names of shortlisted candidates are submitted to the head of state for final appointment.

While open advertising and screening mechanisms can provide a broad range of applicants for EMB member positions and promote competence in the selection of members, they do not necessarily guarantee that the most appropriate candidates are chosen. Where the mechanism for screening and appointing EMB members is dominated by one political grouping, competent candidates who are not in favour with this grouping may have lesser chances of selection.

Table 9: Some Advantages and Disadvantages of Open Advertising for Members of EMBs

Advantages	Disadvantages
• Fosters transparency in appointment. • Provides a wide pool of prospective members. • Allows for open selection on merit. • Promotes inclusiveness by allowing all stakeholders to nominate candidates. • Contains checks and balances in the appointment process as the responsibilities for nomination, screening and appointment can lie with different bodies. • Opens opportunities for candidates outside the favoured elites.	• Eminent professionals may be unwilling to submit themselves to public screening. • People may be discouraged from applying, as failure to be appointed will be publicly known. • Cost of advertising and screening processes. • Time taken to complete appointment process. • Oversight of membership and operations of screening committees may be required. • Open advertising and selection processes may disguise the fact that a dominant political group still determines EMB membership.

Appointment of EMB Members

The head of state appoints EMB members in many countries. In Canada, Latvia and Mexico, the legislature is responsible for appointment, while the court is responsible for appointment in Costa Rica. The division of EMB appointment powers between the executive and legislature (and judiciary) provides checks and balances in appointment procedures and enhances the appointment process. If one branch of government (especially the executive) has the sole right to appoint EMB members, there is a danger that such appointees, even if they are men and women of integrity, may be perceived by the public, and especially the opposition parties, as pawns of the appointing authority.

Even if the power to appoint EMB members is divided between the executive and the legislature, this arrangement will be fettered if the same party dominates both branches, or if the executive effectively controls the legislature. In this case, the requirement of a two-thirds majority in the legislature to approve EMB appointments could be a useful remedy, because it may give minority parties a veto power; this voting rule is used in Mexico, Nigeria, Uruguay and Yemen.

The extent to which the head of state makes his or her own choice, chooses after consultation or follows the decision of others varies. In Pakistan, the head of state chooses all members, while in Guyana and Saint Lucia the head of state appoints all members but chooses only some of them. The unilateral appointment of EMB members, especially by the executive branch, has been criticized by many analysts, who argue that it could encourage the appointment of government and ruling party sympathizers rather than impartial arbiters.

Some form of consultation in appointing members of the EMB is more common. Involving the legislature, including opposition parties, in the confirmation process can help provide some degree of multiparty support for the appointments. Parliamentary factions and groups are consulted in Ukraine, and in Trinidad and Tobago appointments are made based on the advice of the prime minister following consultation with the opposition leader.

Whether the final choice is made by the head of state or the legislature, a nominating committee or less formal grouping of individuals is used for part of the process in some cases. In Guatemala, the nominating committee is composed of university rectors and deans of law and a representative of the bar association. In Bhutan, a short list is jointly proposed by the prime minister, the chief justice, the speaker, the chairperson of the National Council and the leader of the opposition party. In Papua New Guinea, the Electoral Commission Appointments Committee is made up of the prime minister, the leader of the opposition, the chair of the Parliamentary Committee on Appointments and the chair of the Public Service Commission. In Vanuatu, the president appoints based on the advice of the Judicial Service Commission. In Malaysia, the president appoints after consulting the conference of rules (comprised of the heads of each Malay state). In the Philippines, the president appoints with the consent of the Commission on Appointments. In Zambia, the president uses a selection committee comprising members of the Supreme and Constitutional Courts, the Civil Service Commission, the Judicial Service Commission, a representative of church bodies and the ombudsman. In South Africa, candidates are nominated by a panel made up of the president of the Constitutional Court, a representative of the Human Rights Commission, a representative of the Commission on Gender Equality and the public prosecutor. In South Sudan, the selection process must include consultation with women and civil society groups. In Zambia, the shortlist is advertised to all for public scrutiny.

In many cases the nominating committee decides who to appoint, but in some cases a committee presents a list of names that includes more names than there are places to be filled, and another body makes the final choice from within that group. In Indonesia and South Africa, the legislature chooses from the names proposed by the panel. In Brazil, the president selects two from a list of six provided by the Supreme Federal Court. In Lithuania, the minister of justice and the bar association each provide a shortlist and the members are selected by drawing lots.

Another way to share the role of appointing EMB members is to let specified bodies select a certain percentage of members instead of appointing all members in the same way. For instance in South Korea, three of nine are appointed by the president, another three are elected by the National Assembly and the final third is nominated by the chief justice of the Supreme Court. In Lithuania, some members are nominated by the minister of justice and the bar association. In Latvia, the Supreme Court elects one member of the EMB and in Botswana the Judicial Service Commission chooses five of the seven members from a list of recommendations from the all-party conference. Key government departments each designate a member of the EMB in Portugal.

In some cases, individuals are EMB members because they hold another position, such as auditor general (Tonga), head of the Department of Statistics (Germany) or chief judge of the Maori Land Court (New Zealand prior to 2010).

Qualifications for Appointment

Whether the personal qualifications required for appointment to an EMB are detailed in the electoral law generally depends on whether the EMB is expert based or multiparty based. For multiparty EMBs, political parties usually use their own criteria for appointing their representatives to the EMB, such as seniority in the party hierarchy, party membership or professional qualifications.

There are some multiparty EMBs for which the law defines criteria for members' qualifications, such as not being a party activist or not having recently held political office. In Mozambique for example, members of the multiparty EMB are required by law to be professionally qualified and to carry out their work with integrity, independence and impartiality. This means that political parties are obliged to nominate candidates who meet the qualifications of non-partisanship and independence. Such nominees are in many cases eminent members of the community rather than members of the political parties that nominated them.

In the case of expert-based EMBs, the electoral law may define an extensive set of personal qualifications for EMB members, as it does in Indonesia. Alternatively, the law may rely on its definition of the EMB's expected behaviour and functions to define the qualities of EMB members to be appointed, such as being known for their their moral integrity, intellectual honesty, neutrality and impartiality (Senegal).

It is typical to expect EMB members to meet the criteria of professional competence and political neutrality. In Mexico, the Philippines and Vanuatu, previous election candidates are not eligible, and in Bosnia and Herzegovina, Mexico, Moldova, Nepal and South Africa, those with a high political profile are not considered.

In some countries, appointment is open only to those with legal training. All members of the EMB in Pakistan, Poland and Turkey must be a current or former senior judge, and the chair must hold such a position in Australia, Botswana, Portugal and Tanzania. In Lithuania, Mexico, Nepal, the Philippines, Russia and Ukraine, EMB members must have at least a university degree. In Bosnia and Herzegovina, Mauritius and the Philippines, a law degree and time practicing as a lawyer are required.

Other formal requirements for EMB membership generally include citizenship and often age. Requirements for gender and ethnic balance in EMB membership was discussed in Chapter 3. Citizenship requirements are common (for instance Liberia, Lithuania, the Philippines, Senegal and South Africa). However in Iraq, two of the nine members do not need to be citizens; in Tonga and Fiji, citizenship is not a requirement for the chair; and citizenship is not a requirement in New Zealand. A minimum age is mentioned but varies from 25 in Guinea to 30 in Mexico, 35 in Liberia and the Philippines, 40 in Pakistan and 45 in Nepal.

The manner in which EMB members are nominated for appointment may influence the type of person chosen, which may work in favour of or against certain sectors of society. For example, in Indonesia in 2001, it appears that the initial nominations for potential members of the new EMB were sought solely from distinguished academics; thus most nominees were also academics. Open processes can hide a more controlled environment of appointment to EMBs. For example, the 1999 EMB law in Azerbaijan required that half the EMB members be appointed by the legislature and half by the president. Since the president's party controlled the legislature, this resulted in a nominally non-partisan but in reality government-influenced EMB.

While some electoral laws specify that EMB members must have a certain occupation, few specify any appropriate mix of experience or skills. Where qualifications are required, these are generally legal. In the corporate world, a company with activities as large and broad as an EMB's would be unlikely to have a narrowly focused board.

Table 10: Qualifications Stated in the Electoral Law for Appointment to Two Reformed Expert-based EMBs: South Sudan and Bhutan

	South Sudan	Bhutan
Impartiality	Yes	None
Personal integrity and fairness	Yes	None
Citizenship essential	Yes	Yes, by birth (and not married to a person who is not a citizen of Bhutan)
Minimum age	35	None
Professional qualifications	At least a secondary school leaving certificate or equivalent	None
Knowledge of electoral issues	None	None
Physically and mentally healthy	None	None
Not politically active	A person who has not been a candidate in general elections or an agent of a candidate for three years prior to becoming a commissioner	None
Registered as a voter	None	None
Requirement to hold another office	None	None
Bans on holding other office	None	None
Character requirement	Not convicted over the past seven years of a crime involving dishonesty or moral turpitude or contravention of the election conduct, even if he or she enjoys a pardon	Not convicted of any criminal offence or in arrears of taxes or other dues to the government
Residence in country	None	None

Conditions of Service and Security of Tenure for EMB Members

In countries with full-time EMB members, their conditions of service, especially salaries and benefits, are generally publically known. As constitutional public bodies, the conditions of service for many EMBs are determined by the independent body that sets terms for parliamentarians, judges and other public bodies—such as the Commission on Remuneration of Representatives (South Africa) or the Law on Remuneration of Public Officials (Latvia). EMB members may be appointed under the same conditions of service, including pay levels, as senior judicial officers or other senior public officials. For instance in Ghana, the chair has the same terms as a justice of the Court of Appeal, and the other commissioners are equivalent to a justice of the High Court. In some places such as Bangladesh and Liberia, EMB members receive police protection in recognition of their senior public position.

Part-time EMB members usually receive a sitting allowance when they attend EMB meetings. Some countries augment this with a monthly retainer allowance. Such allowances are determined by the government in line with its own policies and regulations.

EMB members' remuneration is often charged directly to the consolidated fund. This arrangement assures members' benefits and salaries during their term of office, and helps them maintain full independence in their work.

EMB members' security of tenure and immunity from unwarranted harassment—such as salary cuts, reductions in conditions of service or malicious prosecution—and from the danger of removal from office by either the executive or any other authority, provides a framework within which members of the EMB can carry out their work impartially, professionally, without fear and favour, and resisting political pressures. EMB members may be less confident about taking decisions that are unpopular with the executive or legislature if they know that they may be removed from office, or their salaries and conditions may be reduced, without due process of law.

In many countries, the tenure protection for EMB members in the electoral law is the same as that for senior judicial officers: they can only be removed from office for a cause, such as misconduct or mental and physical incapacity. This is the case in Malaysia, Pakistan and Zambia. In India, a two-thirds majority of the legislature is required to remove an EMB member, even when misconduct is proven. In other places, EMB members are less secure in their positions and can be recalled by parliament (Latvia) or on proof of misconduct (Liberia). In South Sudan, a commissioner can be removed by the president for repeated absence from EMB work; if convicted of a crime involving fraud, dishonesty or moral turpitude; or if two-thirds of commissioners recommend removal on the grounds of partiality, incapacity or gross misconduct in the work of the EMB. Protection from arbitrary reductions in salary and conditions of service may also be guaranteed by law.

Electoral Management Design

Another safeguard for commissioners who may be taking decisions that are unpopular with some political groups is immunity from prosecution for activities undertaken while serving on the EMB. In Senegal EMB members cannot be investigated, arrested or prosecuted for their work on the EMB, and in Mozambique they have legal immunity except for actions that would have an improper effect on the election result. In Guinea and South Sudan, commissioners can only be prosecuted if they are caught in the process of committing a crime.

Protecting the tenure of party representatives on multiparty-based EMBs can be a complex issue. If parties are responsible for appointing and removing their EMB representatives, they may also be free to replace them when they wish, as they are in Mexico.

Oath/Pledge-taking or Affirmation

In many countries, such as Botswana, Lithuania, Nigeria, Pakistan, Senegal, South Sudan and Ukraine, EMB members take a formal oath or a pledge of allegiance, loyalty and integrity before taking office. The oath or pledge may be administered by a senior official or judicial officer, for example, the chair or deputy of the Seimas (the legislature) in Lithuania. The oath/pledge-taking binds the EMB members to uphold the country's constitution and electoral laws. The text of the oath or pledge may be simple, or more detailed. It may also include or refer to the code of conduct or any law governing conflicts of interest for EMB members.

For example, the oath used in Guinea is: 'I .... swear on my honor to faithfully and honestly fulfill my duties as a member of the CENI, to obey only the sole authority of the Act, not to engage in any activity that may affect the Independence, neutrality, transparency and impartiality of the Independent National Electoral Commission (INEC), to keep strictly secret deliberations and vote, even after the termination of my functions. For perjury, I face the rigors of the law.'

Internal Regulations

An EMB will generally need to issue and maintain a series of regulations governing the internal functioning of its operations. These may cover administrative, financial and technical issues, such as staff safety and security, authorizations to speak to the media, meeting procedures and standing orders, the membership of internal committees, logistics controls, purchasing, asset controls, financial disbursements and records management. These regulations may have more impact if the EMB members (or the head of the secretariat in a governmental EMB) are required to agree on and formally issue them.

EMBs can delegate powers to make less critical internal rules to specified members of the secretariat. Distribution of these rules to all EMB members and staff (in regional/local as well as central offices) will promote adherence. Clear and enforceable sanctions for breaches of these regulations are necessary.

Enforcement procedures also need to be fully and openly defined, and to follow accepted principles of justice. For governmental EMBs, and other EMBs using public service staff, the appropriate public service regulations may apply automatically; modification for EMB use may also be possible and desirable.

EMB Decision-making Processes

Methods of making EMB decisions vary according to the model of electoral management, a country's decision-making culture and the requirements of the electoral law. Where the Governmental Model is used, EMBs rarely have 'members', and administration may be directed by the executive branch of government; thus the role of a governmental EMB may be as much one of proposing as determining action. Powers to determine policy and administrative issues may be delegated to the chief of the EMB secretariat by the government institution within which it is located.

For EMBs under the Independent Model and component independent EMBs under the Mixed Model, electoral law may specify some decision-making issues, such as the election of the chair, the decision-making powers of the EMB chair and/or members meeting in plenary, the requirements for majority or super-majority votes, the role of the chair in voting and the use of casting votes.

While some key aspects of decision-making may be covered by the electoral law, it is usual for the details of the EMB's decision-making processes to be defined in standing orders or administrative procedures determined by the EMB members. Many use the normal standing orders employed in their country rather than create a unique set. Such documents may define a range of issues, including EMB members' authorities, such as:

- the role of the chair;
- responsibilities for decision-making and the ability to delegate these;
- methods of calling EMB meetings;
- frequency of meetings;
- responsibility for meeting agendas;
- the processes of decision-making: proposals, rules of discussion, and types of voting and/or requirements for consensus;
- attendance at meetings and quorums;
- rights and roles of secretariat staff at meetings;
- invitations to outsiders to attend EMB meetings;
- taking, authenticating and issuing meeting minutes;
- method of issuing EMB policies and directions;
- methods of suspending or altering standing orders; and
- responsibilities for media conferences.

Electoral Management Design

Meetings of EMB Members

Regular EMB member meetings help develop agreed policy directions, review EMB performance and provide guidance on policies to EMB secretariat staff. The level of detail considered will depend on the extent to which the role of implementing policy is delegated to the secretariat or chief election officer.

In many instances, a quorum consists of 50 per cent of the members; sometimes, as in Botswana, one of those must be the chair or their designated deputy. A number of decision rules apply. In many places, including Bhutan, Botswana and Latvia, a majority of those present can take a decision, which given a quota of half of the members means a decision can be made by a quarter of members. In Georgia, a decision is made by a majority vote of those at the meeting, as long as that also comprises a third of the total membership. In Guam and Saint Lucia, decisions need the agreement of half of all members, while in Bosnia and Herzegovina two-thirds of members need to agree, although if that does not occur on an issue at two successive meetings, then a majority of all members must approve the decision. In Georgia and Latvia, a member with a dissenting opinion on a matter has the right to put his or her views in writing and to attach them to the minutes; however, he or she cannot prevent the majority decision being executed. It is common for the minutes of EMB member meetings to be signed by both the chair and the secretary, and in some cases (especially in multiparty EMBs) by all members of the EMB, in order to authenticate them.

While full-time EMB members may be available daily to provide direction to EMB secretariat staff, part-time members are more likely to meet only occasionally to deliberate policies and activities that shape the EMB's operations. Outside electoral periods, full-time EMBs may meet every week, while part-time EMBs usually meet less frequently, often monthly. During peak electoral event periods, more frequent meetings are usual; full-time EMBs may meet as often as daily.

Closed or Open EMB Meetings

EMB meetings that are open to the public may promote greater trust in the EMB. Where meetings are open to the public by law, it is important that the EMB publicizes the dates of its meetings. It is also important that it cooperates with the police to ensure the maintenance of security and protocol during EMB sessions. In Bosnia and Herzegovina, Lithuania and Moldova, the law provides for EMB meetings to be open to members of the public, and members of the public may record or film EMB sessions provided that such activities do not disrupt the proceedings. In Lithuania, EMB meetings are broadcast live on their website. In Guam, the EMB holds a public meeting at 4 p.m. on the third Thursday of every month.

In South Africa, EMB meetings are closed to any person who is not a member, unless he or she attends by special invitation, and often only for a specific item. Closed EMB meetings may allow more open discussion, especially on sensitive matters, and members do not have to fear public reprisals for personal views on any matter brought before the EMB. Decisions can be presented as agreed upon by the entire EMB, with no report on how close the vote was, and so give a unified voice to the EMB, similar to the idea of cabinet decisions in the Westminster model. However, closed meetings reduce the transparency of EMB decision-making and can lead to public suspicions about the influences on the EMB. Any closed EMB meetings need to be followed quickly by a public announcement or media conference on their deliberations and results.

Decisions taken during each meeting still need to be publicized, and the law often specifies that certain decisions must be included in the formal gazette or government newsletter. Many EMBs list all decisions on their website.

EMB Member Committees

For EMBs with a relatively large number of members it can be advantageous for the EMB to form committees to oversee or manage some of its activities. In Indonesia, the formation of such committees, which are responsible to the full membership of the EMB, has allowed greater specialization and concentration by EMB members on key policy tasks. They may be an advantageous means of rationalizing oversight workloads during periods of peak electoral activity. In some cases, such committees have the power to co-opt non-EMB members, such as professionals from outside the EMB, or EMB secretariat staff. Some EMBs establish a smaller group that is entirely or mainly made up of their members, which interacts with the EMB secretariat on behalf of the members as a whole. In Mexico, the law provides for the permanent use of six committees: electoral training and civic education; electoral organization; political parties; professional electoral service; voter register and reports and complaints. The Nigerian EMB has 15 committees covering core election roles such as logistics as well as organizational matters such as tendering and staff welfare.

EMB Members' Relationships with the EMB Secretariat

Where Independent or Mixed Models of electoral management are used, the relationship between EMB members and EMB secretariats is critical. Appropriate roles for EMB members can vary widely. EMBs made up of part-time members are more likely to adopt a more hands-off approach of providing broad policy review and oversight, while full-time members may be more directly involved. Members of component independent EMBs under the Mixed Model may be less likely to be involved in detailed administration issues, and more involved in overall integrity and quality control. In elections marking a transition to multiparty democracy, members of EMBs under the Independent Model that use a public service secretariat, and members of component independent EMBs under the Mixed Model, may find it particularly prudent to assume a publicly visible operational management role in order to enhance the public credibility of the electoral process. In some countries, EMB members may assume the responsibility of head of a department of the secretariat. Where EMB members are involved in the day-to-day leadership and management of the EMB's activities, as was the case in Indonesia in 2004, allocating specific direction and oversight tasks in this manner clarifies responsibilities and provides greater clarity to the secretariat staff. Individual members of the EMB in Thailand take on a similar management-oriented role.

Elements that can promote an effective working relationship between EMB members and the secretariat include a clear delineation of powers and tasks between the members and the secretariat, clear hierarchical authority between the two, and competent appointments that generate mutual respect. Where public servants make up the secretariat of an EMB under the Independent Model, it is important that they report directly and only to the EMB—not also to an outside government department. Where the Mixed or Governmental Model is used, a single departmental reporting responsibility for electoral issues handled by the secretariat staff of a governmental EMB is highly preferable for the same reasons.

Attendance by the head of the secretariat or his/her nominee at all EMB plenary meetings as an invited speaker or guest, a non-voting EMB member or as an EMB member with full rights (as in Australia) reinforces the links between EMB members and the secretariat staff, and ensures that all meetings have the benefit of advice on the practical operations of the EMB.

Chapter Summary

- Independent EMBs are found under both the Independent and Mixed Models and are guided by a board of EMB members. With very few exceptions, EMBs under the Governmental Model, and governmental EMBs under the Mixed Model, do not have EMB members, only secretariat staff.

- There is no optimal number of EMB members, and no general principle to indicate that either full- or part-time EMB membership is preferable. The size of the country and its population, economic and geopolitical issues; the EMB's powers and functions; the strength of its secretariat; and whether electoral management follows the Independent or the Mixed Model may determine the size and work schedule of the EMB membership.

- EMB members need to have sufficient status to entitle them to respect from their counterparts in other sectors of society, and constitutional or legal guarantees of their conditions of service and security of tenure sufficient to enable them to act without fear or favour.

- Independent EMBs under the Independent and Mixed Models may have a membership that is multiparty (nominated by political parties qualified to do so) or expert (politically non-aligned members appointed on the basis of their professional skills) or a combination of political and professional appointees. The type of membership that is suitable for a particular country will depend on its political environment and stage of democratic development.

- Fixed and secure terms of office for EMB members allow for institutional confidence and renewal. Staggering EMB members' terms of office minimizes disruption and helps retain an EMB's institutional memory.

- A quality EMB membership selection process can be achieved by open advertising for candidates and ranking all applicants according to a transparently applied 'fit and proper' test. The most widely accepted procedure for EMB appointments is for one branch of government to nominate and another to confirm. This process could start with the executive or judiciary and end with the legislature, or vice versa.

- Electoral law usually specifies the qualifications for EMB membership, which generally include citizenship, good repute, ability to act impartially, and professional qualifications or knowledge. They may include other factors such as age, health, holding or not holding specified positions, and residence.

- EMB members need to develop decision-making and management mechanisms that are suitable for the type of EMB and the country's management culture. They also need to adopt standing orders that ensure transparent EMB meeting and decision-making processes, and internal regulations for the effective administration of the EMB. It may be useful for the EMB membership to form subcommittees that deal with different aspects of electoral administration.

- EMB meetings can be either closed or open to the public. Open meetings may promote greater trust in the EMB and its activities, while closed meetings may allow more open discussion on sensitive matters.

- A good working relationship between EMB members and its secretariat is critical for effective functioning of the EMB.

CASE STUDY

Nigeria: Independent National Electoral Commission*

Olufunto Akinduro

Background

Nigeria gained independence from Britain in 1960. Like most former British colonies, its elections have been managed by a permanent EMB. Nigeria's political history is characterized by years of military rule and four republics of civil rule. With every transition programme, an election management authority was established. Overall, Nigeria has had five EMBs: the Electoral Commission of the Federation (ECF) that conducted the 1964 federal elections and 1965 regional elections; the Federal Electoral Commission (FEDECO) that conducted the transitional elections in 1979 and the controversial 1983 elections that ended in a return to military rule; the National Electoral Commission (NEC) that managed the three-year transition programme and ended with the annulled 1993 elections; the National Electoral Commission of Nigeria (NECON) that was established by General Sani Abacha to manage his transition programme, which was aborted after his death in 1998; and the Independent National Electoral Commission (INEC). INEC, which is the focus of this case study, is the longest-serving EMB in Nigerian history. It has conducted four elections: the 1999 transition election; the historic 2003 election, which was the first election successfully conducted under civil rule in Nigeria; the critical 2007 elections, which facilitated the first civilian regime change in Nigeria; and the 2011 elections.[1]

Legislative Framework for Elections in Nigeria

Nigeria has a long history of constitutional and electoral reforms dating from the period of colonial administration up to 2010, and the debate on electoral reforms has continued since the 2011 elections. It is also important to note that the major constitution-making processes that have taken place have been closely linked to Nigeria's history of transition programmes. All EMBs since independence have been appointed by the president,

---

* A case study on Nigeria also appeared in the original edition of the Handbook: Carl Dundas, 'Nigeria: A Need for Modernization', *Electoral Management Design: The International IDEA Handbook* (Stockholm: International IDEA, 2006), pp. 253–55.

subject to legislative ratification. EMBs established during the military regime were appointed by the Federal Executive Council. It is also important to mention that since the introduction of the Federal Character Principle (principle of regional or state representation) in the 1979 constitution, it has remained one of the criteria for the appointment of members of the electoral commissions.[2]

Elections in Nigeria are currently regulated by the 1999 constitution (as amended) and the Electoral Act of 2010 (as amended). As in previous constitutions, INEC was established as a federal executive body. The constitution broadly defines the scope of the commission's powers and responsibilities, and provides for its independence and funding. The 1999 constitution introduced the establishment of 36 Independent Electoral Commissions (SIECs) in each state of the federation, which are mandated to conduct local government elections.[3] The constitution also provided for the appointment of the chairman and members of the commissions by the president, subject to confirmation by the senate. At the state level, the governors appoint the chair and members of the SIECs with confirmation from the State House of Assembly. The constitution also stipulates the criteria for registering political parties.[4]

The Electoral Act provides further detail on the structure of the commission, its powers and guidelines for registering voters, procedures for the conduct of elections, the registration and regulation of political parties, electoral offences and the determination of election offences.

The legal framework for elections in Nigeria has undergone a number of reforms since 1999. The Electoral Act was passed in 2001, and three other pieces of legislation have since been passed, in 2002, 2006 and 2010. Among many other changes introduced by the 2006 act, it empowered the commission to appoint its secretary, to undertake voter education and to prosecute offenders. The law also addressed the ambiguities surrounding the appointment and dismissal of resident electoral commissioners (RECs). The 2010 Electoral act was passed to address the shortcomings of the 2006 act and harmonise the act with the amended constitution. It is important to note that the debates on the passage of the act coincided with the debates on constitutional reforms ahead of the 2011 elections. The 2010 Electoral Act therefore concentrated on certain issues that previous electoral reform efforts could not address because they required the amendment of the 1999 constitution. The act was also amended once before the 2011 elections to increase the time for voter registration and to postpone the elections from January to April 2011, and further streamline its powers to regulate political parties' activities—especially the process of nominating candidates through party primaries.[5] The 2010 act also prohibits parties from changing the names of persons nominated as candidates, provides new ceilings on campaign expenditures, empowers INEC to deregister political parties on the basis of conditions provided in the law, and limits the powers of an election petition tribunal to nullify the results of an election, but restrains tribunals from declaring candidates as winners of an election. The act mandates the announcement and posting of election results at polling stations, introduces penal provisions for electoral offences, and empowers INEC to prosecute offenders.

The 1999 constitution was amended twice in 2010, after over ten years of national discourse on constitutional reforms. Following the conduct of the 2007 elections, which were reported as the worst in the country's history,[6] the late President Yar'Adua set up the Electoral Reform Committee (ERC) to review the electoral history of Nigeria and the legal and institutional framework for the conduct of elections, and make proposals for reforms. The ERC undertook wide consultations and received 1,466 memoranda. Its report, submitted in 2008, was widely accepted as reflecting Nigerians' thoughts on electoral reform. The report also greatly contributed to the constitutional and electoral reforms that preceded the 2011 elections. In its extensive analysis of the challenges of electoral governance in Nigeria, the ERC noted that INEC is an overburdened institution and proposed the creation of three other institutions to undertake its responsibilities. The ERC also proposed to transfer the powers of appointment of the INEC from the president to the National Judicial Council, and recommended that the commission be recruited through an open process. As part of its report, the ERC proposed five bills for reforming different aspects of the electoral process in Nigeria, three of which were focused on unbundling and restructuring INEC.

Though the executive did not fully adopt the content of the ERC report, it did set the tone for the national deliberations on constitutional and electoral reforms prior to the 2011 elections. In 2010, the executive drafted and submitted to the National Assembly a bill for amending the 1999 constitution. While there was a list of pressing national issues to address in a constitutional review process, priority was given to electoral matters. The first amendment of the 1999 constitution provided for the financial autonomy of INEC by charging its budget and the salaries of its chair and members to the Consolidated Revenue Fund. The neutrality and non-partisanship of commission members was also addressed in the amendments, in addition to the timing of elections, the jurisdiction of the courts in determining election petitions, the composition of election petition tribunals and the time limits for determining election petitions.[7] The second bill for amendment of the 1999 constitution involved re-examining the new timelines for the conduct of national elections.[8]

Institutional Structure

Nigeria has a three-tiered federal system of government, with a bicameral legislature. The first tier is the federal level, the second is state level—there are 36 states and a Federal Capital Territory (FCT)—and the third tier of government consists of 774 local government areas. Each tier of government has an executive and legislative branch; at the state level there are State Houses of Assembly, and at the local level there are Local Government Councils. Federal and state-level elections are conducted by INEC, while local government elections are conducted by the SIECs. For administrative purposes, the country is divided into six geo-political zones; these administrative divisions are central to Nigeria's politics.

INEC has offices in all 36 states and the FCT, and has a presence in the 774 local government areas of the federation (either in separate offices or shared with the local government authority). Though the commission has a decentralized structure, policymaking is centralized at the national level through a committee system, while policy implementation is decentralized. The INEC chair is the chief executive officer at the national level, while at the state level the REC serves as the chief executive officer, supported by an administrative secretary who is a permanent staff member as chief accounting officer and head of administration. At the local government level, an electoral officer serves as the representative of the commission.

The commission consists of the chair, who is the chief electoral commissioner, and 12 members, the national electoral commissioners. The commission has offices in the 36 states and the FCT, which are headed by RECs, who are also appointed by the president and subject to senate confirmation. While two national commissioners are appointed from each geo-political zone, one REC is appointed from each state of the federation and deployed to INEC offices outside their states of origin. For presidential elections, the chair of the commission is the returning officer, while RECs are the returning officers for governorship and state assembly elections. Members of the commission and the RECs are appointed to serve a five-year term, which is renewable.

It is important to note that prior to the passage of the 2006 Electoral Act and the 2010 amendment to the 1999 constitution, the chain of command between the commission and the RECs was ambiguous, and the legal framework was silent on the procedures for their removal from office. This was viewed as a challenge because RECs were not answerable to the commission, but rather to the president who appointed them.[9] This issue was addressed in the reform process by providing for the tenure of RECs and their accountability to the commission. The amendment of the constitution also took into account the need to stipulate procedures for removing RECs from office.[10]

The secretary of the commission is the head of the commission secretariat and head of administration. Prior to the 2006 Electoral Act, the secretary of the commission was seconded to the commission from the pool of permanent secretaries by the head of the civil service. As part of the structural reforms of the commission that took place before the 2007 elections, the power to appoint the secretary was transferred to the commission. By virtue of its establishment as a federal executive body, the commission has the status of an agency of government, which is independent of the federal civil service. It has the power to appoint and exercise disciplinary control over its staff.

The heads of administration in INEC state offices are the administrative secretaries, who are senior staff of the commission. At the local government level, electoral officers who are permanent employees of INES are responsible for the operations of INEC offices, and they report to the RECs.

INEC is the second-largest government agency, in terms of its staff strength, it is ranked second to the Nigerian Police Force. As at December 2013, the commission's staff strength was approximately 14,000 full time staff members across the country.[11] The commission also appoints ad hoc staff for election duty (about 300,000 were recruited during the 2011 elections).[12] The size of the commission's permanent and ad hoc staff base has raised concerns about the efficiency of its administrative system and the professionalisation of its staff. It is important to mention that permanent INEC staff are recruited in line with civil service rules. In June 2005, the Electoral Institute was established as part of the commission's efforts to develop the capacity of its staff and professionalize the administration of elections in Nigeria. The institute is headquarted in Abuja and has learning centres that offer diploma and certificate courses in election administration. These trainings have contributed to the development of a pool of election administration professional across the country and ad hoc staff are drawn from this pool during election periods.

For the purpose of efficiency, the commission's administrative structure has been restructured several times since 1999, in line with the leadership policy at different times. At its inception in 1999, the commission had eight departments and three units.[13] At some point, the leadership decided to streamline the number of departments to six departments, three directorates and three units.[14] After the 2003 elections it was restructured to create more departments and a longer reporting chain. As of July 2010, when there was change of leadership at the commission, it had 16 departments and an Electoral Institute that comprised four departments.[15] A more recent restructuring took place under new leadership that took office in June 2010. The process took place in April 2013; the commission currently has 20 departments and an Electoral Institute with three departments.[16]

Powers and Functions of the Commission

The 1999 constitution mandates the commission to organize elections into executive and legislative offices at the federal and state levels; to register, monitor and regulate political party operations; to monitor party finance and campaigns; to create and maintain a register of qualified voters; to delimit constituencies for representation in the National Assembly according to the number of seats provided in the constitution; to delegate its powers to RECs; and to carry out other functions conferred on it by an act of the National Assembly. The Electoral Act adds the conduct of voter education and the prosecution of electoral offences to the INEC's responsibilities. The commission is also empowered to recruit its staff and issue guidelines and regulations to guide the conduct of elections.

Independence of the Electoral Commission

The mode of appointment of the commission remains an issue of concern for its independence, as many believe it may be biased toward the appointing authority. The amendment of the 1999 constitution strengthened the commission's independence by guaranteeing its financial autonomy. It is funded from the Consolidated Revenue Fund, which ensures that it is not hindered in its operations by the many bureaucratic processes of budgeting and disbursement of funds.

Beyond its financial independence, the constitution also provides security of tenure for the commission by providing for the removal of its members and RECs (on the basis of misconduct or an inability to perform the duties of office) by the president, supported by a two-thirds majority of the senate.

The amendment also addressed the concerns raised by the previous qualifications for membership of the commission. Prior to the amendment, members of the commission were required to hold the same qualifications as members of the House of Representatives. This could be interpreted to mean that they were expected to be members of a political party. The amendment of the constitution clarified this issue by stating that persons appointed into the commission should not be members of political parties.

The Electoral Act also protects the commission from undue influence from the executive by making RECs accountable to the commission and empowering the commission to appoint and discipline its staff and secretary.

Relationship with Political Parties, CSOs, the Media and Other Government Agencies

The conduct of elections in Nigeria is an enormous task that requires efforts from all stakeholders and agencies of government. Considering the country's long history of fraudulent and violent elections, security agencies play an important role in the conduct of elections. Since its inception, the commission has worked closely with the police and armed forces to guarantee the security of the electoral process. While the military is not deployed around voting areas, it plays a role in securing interstate borders during elections. The naval and air forces also provide support for the distribution of election materials to locations with difficult terrains.

An Inter-Agency Consultative Committee on Elections Security was set up to coordinate the efforts of the different security agencies involved in securing the 2011 elections. These contributed to the success of the 2011 elections and the containment of the post-election violence that broke out in the northern part of the country.[17]

During election periods, INEC establishes a dialogue mechanism through which it meets with political parties and civil society groups to update them on preparations for the elections. The relationship between INEC and political parties has not been particularly cordial, as there has been a high level of distrust and the commission is not perceived as independent. The 2011 elections, however, proved to be different as the new leadership of the commission increased its efforts to improve the transparency of the commission's work. Fifty-two political parties signed the code of conduct ahead of the elections, and the commission reassured stakeholders of its commitment to sanitize the electoral process by prosecuting offenders, including election personnel.[18] The current commission enjoys a high level of public trust, as evidenced by the acceptance of the results of the 2011 elections.

The success of the 2011 elections can be attributed to the openness and transparency of the current commission. This transparency came into play when the decision to postpone the National Assembly elections by a week was taken after polling had started in some places. This decision did not degenerate into violence because the stakeholders had come to trust the commission, and they were made aware of the logistical challenges involved. The Inter-Party Advisory Council was also established, which further improved the dialogue between the commission and political parties.

The commission's relationship with the media is another important aspect of its interactions. The responsibility for regulating the media is assigned to the Broadcasting Organisation of Nigeria (BON). Section 100 of the 2010 Electoral Act, however, stipulates regulations on media coverage of candidates during an election. The BON and INEC therefore work together to ensure that the media complies with the general broadcasting and election-related codes.

The commission also works with the National Youth Service Corps Scheme to recruit youth corps members as ad hoc staff in the electoral process. In 2007 and 2011 this proved to be a success.

International donor agencies and technical assistance groups play an important role in the conduct of elections in Nigeria. INEC therefore has a long-standing relationship with these groups. Over the years, technical assistance groups such as IFES and UNDP have been involved in recruiting experts to work in the commission. Donor agencies also engage with the commission to provide funds for specific aspects of the elections for which support is recruited.

INEC Funding

INEC is now funded directly by a federation account. This was not always the case before the amendment of the 1999 constitution, when INEC was funded like any other government agency—i.e. it was expected to submit its budget for approval by the National Assembly, and it would await the bureaucratic processes of fund disbursement. During the 1999, 2003 and 2007 elections, disbursement of funds for the conduct of elections was a major challenge that led to substantial delays in the electoral process. For instance, voter registration was delayed in 2003 and 2007 because of the delayed disbursement of funds.

Under the current procedure of funding the commission directly from the Consolidated Revenue Fund, the commission is able to prepare its budget for approval, and thereafter it is disbursed directly to the commission through the Independent National Electoral commission Fund (INEC fund), which was introduced in the 2006 and 2010 Electoral Acts. The establishment of the fund enables the Commission to directly manage the disbursement of its funds.

INEC Accountability

The National Assembly has oversight functions over the commission in the performance of its mandate. While there is no mandatory reporting chain between the commission and the relevant committees of the National Assembly, it reports to these committees when it is requested to do so. As part of its public accountability procedures, the commission also issues periodic reports of its activities to the public.

In terms of financial accountability, the commission's budget is presented to the relevant committees of the National Assembly. It is also mandated to report to the office of the auditor general at the end of the year.[19] In the procurement of election materials, it is expected to comply with due process requirements through the Bureau of Monitoring, Prices and Intelligence Unit (BMPIU).[20]

INEC's Role in Electoral Reform Management

INEC has been very vocal and involved in the national discourse on constitutional and electoral reforms. It is important to mention that the 2004 Electoral Bill was drafted by the commission and submitted to the National Assembly, and was later passed as the Electoral Act of 2006. This approach was criticized because it was not submitted in line with the prescribed procedure.[21] The commission also conducts post-election review exercises at which issues for reform are identified.

Opportunities and Constraints

The tenure and stability of the commission have been a challenge in previous years, because every chair of INEC has conducted only one election. However, the timing of the commission in charge of the 2011 elections created an opportunity for continuity as it allowed the commission to conduct two elections. This will be the first in the history of the commission. It is also important to note that the renewal of the tenure of some national commissioners, and the appointment of some RECs and national commissioners, also provides an increased opportunity for stability and continuity of policies.

The large size of the commission's manpower could serve as both an opportunity and a constraint. The commission is able to deploy more permanent staff while depending on ad hoc staff for the conduct of national elections, yet its large staff numbers can be considered a constraint given the level of supervision required. In the absence of effective modernized administrative structures, the large staff could be inefficient.

The establishment of the Electoral Institute and the support of technical partners such as International IDEA, UNDP and IFES create an opportunity to professionalize the commission and develop the capacity of its staff, for example via BRIDGE trainings. The very high level of trust that the current commission enjoys also creates an opportunity for it to plan toward future elections in an atmosphere of trust and transparency.

Notes

[1] Jinadu, Adele, 'Nigeria', in Ismaila M. Fall, Mathias Hounkpe, Adele L. Jinadu and Pascal Kambele (eds), *Election Management Bodies in West Africa* (OSIWA, 2011).
[2] Ibrahim, Jibrin and Garuba, D. *Governance and Institution-Building in Nigeria: A Study of the Independent National Electoral Commission* (Abuja: Center for Democracy and Development, 2008), p. 27.
[3] Section 197 of the 1999 constitution.
[4] Third schedule (Section 153) of the 1999 constitution.
[5] Electoral (amendment) Act 2010.
[6] Jinadu 2011, p. 153.
[7] Constitution (first alteration) Act 2010
[8] Constitution (second alteration) Act 2010
[9] Guobadia, Abel I., *Reflections of a Nigerian Electoral Umpire* (Benin City: Mindex Publishing Co, 2009).
[10] Section 7 of the 2006 Electoral Act and Section 6 of the 2010 Electoral Act provide for the tenure of RECs and the chain of command between the commission and the RECs.
[11] Interviews with commissioners and senior staff of the commission, 1–16 August 2010 and 28 June 2014 in Abuja.
[12] Jega, Attahiru, *Improving Elections in Nigeria: Lessons from 2011 and Looking to 2015* (London: Chatham House, 2012).
[13] Independent National Electoral Commission [INEC], *Report of Activities, August 1998–December 1999* (Abuja: INEC, 1999).
[14] Independent National Electoral Commission [INEC], *Report of Activities 2000–2003* (Abuja: INEC, 2003), pp 35–39.

[15] Interviews with commissioners and senior staff.
[16] Interview with senior officials of the commission and the Electoral Institute. See list of directorates <http://www.inecnigeria.org/wp-content/uploads/2013/09/INDEPENDENT-NATIONAL-ELECTORAL-COMMISSION-LIST-OF-DIRECTORS11.pdf>
[17] Jega 2012.
[18] International Crisis Group [ICG], *Lessons from Nigeria's 2011 Elections*, Policy Brief No. 81 (ICG, 2011), p. 2; Jega, p. 6.
[19] Sections 3–5 of the 2010 Electoral Act as amended.
[20] Jinadu 2011, p. 134.
[21] The 2004 Electoral Bill was neither a private member bill nor an executive bill.

Bibliography

Africa Programme Meeting Summary (London: Chatham House, 2012)

Commonwealth Secretariat, *Report of the Commonwealth Observer Group on the Nigeria National Assembly and Presidential Elections*, 2011

Constitution of the Federal Republic of Nigeria (first alternation) Act 2010

Constitution of the Federal Republic of Nigeria (second alteration) Act 2010

Constitution of the Federal Republic of Nigeria 1999

Electoral (amendment) Act 2010

Electoral Act 2010

Electoral Act 2006

Guobadia, Abel I., *Reflections of a Nigerian Electoral Umpire*. (Benin City: Mindex Publishing Co., 2009)

Ibrahim, Jibrin and Garuba, D., *Governance and Institution-Building in Nigeria: A Study of the Independent National Electoral Commission* (Abuja: Center for Democracy and Development, 2008), p. 27

Independent National Electoral Commission (INEC), *Report of Activities, August 1998–December 1999* (Abuja: INEC, 2003)

Independent National Electoral Commission, *Report of Activities 2000–2003* (Abuja: INEC, 2003)

International Crisis Group, *Lessons from Nigeria's 2011 Elections*, Policy Brief No. 81, 2011

Jega, Attahiru, 'Improving Elections in Nigeria: Lessons from 2011 and Looking to 2015', *Africa Programme Meeting Summary*, 4 July 2012, Chatham House London

Jinadu Adele, 'Nigeria' in Ismaila M. Fall, Mathias Hounkpe, Adele L. Jinadu and Pascal Kambele, *Election Management Bodies in West Africa* (OSIWA, 2011)

CASE STUDY

Norway: Governmental, Decentralized and Trusted

Kåre Vollan

There is no single, unified EMB in Norway. The administrative and legal responsibility for elections is divided, both in terms of decentralization from the national to the local level and between bodies at the central level. A single unified structure with a central body from which the local bodies take their powers does not exist. At the central level, the Ministry of Local Government and Regional Development (hereinafter called the Ministry) fulfils most of the core tasks of an EMB. However, there is also a National Electoral Board (Riksvalgstyret, NEB) with limited authorities, and Parliament has the final say in certifying—approving the election of—its own elected members.

The NEB and Parliament have roles only at parliamentary elections. Local elections are managed by the local authorities, under the supervision and partial instruction of the Ministry.

Elections in Norway

Elections are held to assemblies at three levels of administration:

- Parliament (Stortinget) at the national level;
- 18 County Assemblies (fylkesting); and
- 429 Municipal Councils (kommunestyrer).

The capital, Oslo, is both a county and a municipality, and the Municipal Council assumes the authority of both levels. (Elections to the Same Parliament (Sametinget), which is a representative assembly elected by the indigenous Same people according to a law of 1987 (Sameloven), fall outside the scope of this study.)

Of the 169 members of Parliament, 150 are elected as county representatives under a List PR system, while 19 are elected as members at large to compensatory seats that compensate for any deviation from a nationwide proportional result. The term of office for all elected assemblies is four years. The periods of office are staggered; county and municipal elections are held simultaneously two years after the parliamentary elections. None of the bodies can be dissolved, and there are no by-elections. Elections can therefore be planned a long time in advance.

Background

Norway has had an elected Parliament since 1814, which has been directly elected by voters since 1906. Suffrage has included all men from 1898 and women from 1913. Directly elected Municipal Councils were introduced in 1836 (with a limited voting right).

Election administration has never been regarded as anything different from other public services, and the conduct of elections has therefore been left to the regular administrative and elected bodies. Local and parliamentary elections have been conducted by the elected local authorities, assisted by the local administration.

Until 1985, the election authorities were the executive Boards of the Municipal Councils, elected under a PR system by the councils and consisted of Council members. They were the highest political board of the municipality, and were led by the mayor. The boards would in turn appoint polling station staff, using the municipal administration to assist them. They managed polling for all kinds of elections. For municipal elections, the boards issued the certificates confirming their election to the successful candidates.

County Electoral Boards were selected by proportional election by the County Council Assemblies. These would collect the protocols of the election results from the municipal executive boards for elections to the County Assemblies and Parliament, and issue certificates to the elected members of the County Assembly and Parliament.

At its first meeting, Parliament would approve the validity of the elections. Any complaints about the election would be adjudicated by the executive board for municipal elections, by the county electoral board for county assembly elections and by Parliament itself for parliamentary elections. For all elections, the Ministry would issue directives and instructions and supervise when needed.

In 1985 a new election law was adopted, which consolidated the provisions for elections at all three levels for the first time. Previously, there had been one law for parliamentary elections and one for the two local levels. The main change to the election administration was the introduction of a National Electoral Board (NEB). This body is appointed by the government, and by common practice (not law) has representatives from all parties that are represented in Parliament. The introduction of the NEB was not prompted by any identified need for an independent EMB. Rather, it arose from the need for a body to allocate the compensatory seats at the national level, which were introduced by this law. After this, the NEB certified the elected members of Parliament, even though Parliament maintained the final say over the validity of the elections in part or as a whole. The NEB was not given any overall authority to oversee or supervise the elections.

A further new election law was adopted in 2002. Despite proposals for drastic changes to the election administration, this law essentially represented a streamlining of the legal texts, although it introduced some important modifications to the system of representation and the conduct of elections. The most important change to the administration of elections was that the NEB was given the authority to adjudicate appeals on parliamentary elections raised at any level. For appeals regarding the right to vote, the Parliament is the final authority, but in any other case the NEB has final adjudicating powers (apart from any criminal proceedings against individuals). Parliament still makes the final decision on the validity of the election as such, and decides whether a repeat election is merited. At the municipal level, the Municipal Council can now either decide that the executive board should administer elections itself, or elect a separate Municipal Electoral Board. In the latter case, the political composition of the Electoral Board reflects the composition of the Municipal Council in the same way the composition of other commissions of the council does. Candidates for election might be serving as Electoral Board members, even if the municipality appointed a separate board.

The Legislative and Institutional Framework

Elections are regulated by the constitution and by the Election Law of 2002. The constitutional provisions relate only to parliamentary elections. They give the responsibility for conducting elections to the municipalities, and state that the keeping of electoral registers and the manner in which the polls are conducted shall be regulated by law. The constitution stipulates Parliament's role in approving the credentials of its elected members, and gives it the power to determine appeals against decisions related to disputes regarding the right to vote.

Following further amendment in 2005, the Election Law defines the following election bodies:

- the Election Boards, elected by the Municipal Councils;
- the Polling Station Committees, appointed by the Municipal Councils or on their decision by the Election Board;
- the County Election Boards, elected by the County Assemblies; and
- the National Electoral Board, appointed by the government in years when there is a parliamentary election.

The first two bodies have a role in all elections, the County Election Board has a role in elections to the County Assemblies and Parliament, and the NEB has a role in parliamentary elections only.

There is a separate Party Law from 2005 that regulates, among other issues, the registration of candidates for elections. Administrative responsibility for party registration is given to the national administrative body that registers companies. The government appoints a Party Law Complaints Commission, led by a judge, to adjudicate complaints regarding party registration and financing.

The administrative authority for conducting elections is thus highly decentralized. At the central level there is one multiparty body (the NEB) with limited formal authority. Most other tasks at the national level are carried out by the Ministry. However, other administrative bodies are involved in elections. Electoral registers are extracts of the civil registers, which are administered by a unit under the national tax authorities. Appeals may be filed with a committee appointed by the Ministry.

The Ministry of Local Government and Regional Development

The Ministry's responsibility for elections falls into three areas:

1. *Laws, rules and regulations.* This area includes the preparation of any changes to the laws regulating elections, the issuing of detailed instructions within the legal framework, and support for election administrators and the public in interpreting the law and the instructions.

2. *The conduct of elections.* The Ministry's functions include the provision of detailed instructions, including the definition of electoral procedures; the production of election material, including forms and the design of the ballot paper; the provision of information to election personnel; advice to local administrators, including the provision of report templates; voter education campaigns; approving e-voting arrangements; coordinating the information flow of election results with the media and private IT companies; serving as the secretariat for the NEB; preparing any complaints relating to parliamentary elections for a final decision by Parliament; and adjudicating complaints for local elections (as a final instance). The Ministry may order a repeat election, if necessary, if a fault has affected the results.

3. *Budget and budget control.* The Ministry administers and controls the budget for elections only at the central level, whereas the main costs are carried at the local level and there is no overview of the total election costs. The budget for the Ministry's own costs was approximately EUR 6 million for 2013. The Ministry has 16 persons working on elections, which is a significant increase from earlier years; this was necessitated by the development of a centrally operated information and communications technology (ICT) system for election administration. The election boards at the municipal level are the main authorities responsible for keeping skilled election staff.

The National Electoral Board

The NEB is not a permanent body; its term ends when the parliamentary elections are certified. It has at least five members. Each party with representatives in Parliament proposes one man and one woman, and the government appoints one as a member and one as an alternate. The authority of the NEB is limited to:

- distributing the national compensatory seats;

- issuing certificates to all elected members of Parliament and informing the County Electoral Boards about the results; and

- adjudicating complaints. For issues regarding the right to vote or the validity of a parliamentary election, Parliament is the final instance, after having heard the NEB; in other issues the NEB is the final adjudicator.

Electoral Management Reform

The new election laws of 1985 and 2002 followed a political debate on issues regarding the system of representation; in both cases, the government had appointed commissions with both expert and political representation, which had the mandate of proposing reforms. The structure of electoral management was assessed by the Election Reform Commission, which submitted its report in 2001. The structure was inspired by the UK model, thus an independent election commission was proposed with mainly policy tasks and few direct administrative duties. This proposal arose from the perceived advantages of having a body to concentrate mainly on election reform, leaving electoral administration to the regular parts of the government administration, rather than from a call for greater independence in the administration of elections. Such a commission would, however, bring Norway closer to international trends and to standards being recommended in new democracies. The proposal did not win much support, mostly because the current arrangements work well. Nor was a second proposal, to transfer the administrative work on elections from the Ministry to the department of the tax authorities which maintains the civic register, adopted.

In 2010 the Ministry took two initiatives, one on reforming the central administration of election support and one on making a few changes to the election law. On the administrative side, a government directorate had issued a report suggesting that a new central election unit should be established with the status of a directorate, which would secure a degree of independence from the politically led Ministry and take over most of the tasks covered by the Ministry. It was also foreseen that in the future, a more intensive development and testing of new election technology would be needed. It was further suggested to remove the authority to settle disputes, which today rests with the Ministry, to a separate complaints committee. The Ministry requested stakeholders' opinions on the suggestions, but they have not yet passed any formal proposal to Parliament.

Partly based on comments made by the OSCE/ODIHR mission to assess the parliamentary elections of 2009, the Ministry suggested some amendments to the law that were passed by Parliament in 2012. The most relevant amendment was that candidates can no longer be members of election boards or serve as polling committee staff.

New Technology

Three municipalities and Spitsbergen conducted tests for e-voting in polling stations during the 2003 local elections. Then a government commission issued a report proposing a strategy on e-voting in February 2006. Among the commission's recommendations was a trial of Internet voting; the Ministry initiated a large ICT project, including an election administration system and piloting of Internet voting, in ten municipalities during the 2011 local elections. There are political disagreements regarding the principle of allowing Internet voting in uncontrolled environments, and a decision on whether that will be continued in full scale remains to be taken.

Opportunities and Constraints

The Norwegian approach to electoral management has never been seriously challenged by the political contestants. Generally speaking, the government administration enjoys a high level of trust in its integrity and independence, despite being subordinate to politically appointed ministers. Elections have not been seen as requiring independent administration. On the rare occasions when serious mistakes have occurred (for example, when the IT system for marking the electoral registers broke down in Oslo during the 1993 parliamentary elections), these have been seen as incidental lapses. Fundamental questions regarding the organization of elections have not been raised.

The principle of 'if it ain't broke, don't fix it' has so far proved decisive in the decision-making process about Norway's electoral administration.

CHAPTER 5

Planning and Implementing EMB Activities

The EMB Secretariat

The EMB secretariat is the policy implementation component in all EMB models. In EMBs under the Governmental Model, the secretariat is almost always the EMB, and may also assist in making policy under the direction of the executive branch of government. In EMBs under the Independent Model, the EMB secretariat is the structure below the policymaking/supervisory EMB member level, and encompasses the officials in the EMB who are responsible for electoral implementation. Where the Mixed Model is used, the component governmental EMB is the secretariat, which has responsibility for implementation. The component independent EMB will also have a secretariat to service its own administrative needs.

Where the Independent Model is used, both the membership and the secretariat of the EMB are institutionally independent. Equally, where the Governmental Model is used, the membership (where it exists) and the secretariat are both part of the executive branch. Where the Mixed Model is used, the policymaking level is usually independent from the executive, while the implementation level is part of the executive branch, and usually lies under the Ministry of Interior or the Ministry of Justice.

Table 11: The Policymaking and Implementation Components of the Three Models of Electoral Management

	Independent Model	Mixed Model	Governmental Model
Policymaking component	Independent of the executive branch of the government.	Independent of the executive branch of the government.	Institutionally part of/arranged/set up under the executive branch.
Electoral implementation component	Independent of the executive branch of the government.	Institutionally part of/arranged/set up under the executive branch.	Institutionally part of/arranged/set up under the executive branch.

Electoral Management Design

The staff of the secretariat in EMBs under the Governmental Model and component governmental EMBs under the Mixed Model may be temporary appointments, undertaking other duties when there is no electoral activity. In EMBs under the Independent Model, the secretariat is generally headed by a full-time administrator, who has a title such as director of elections (Tanzania and Zambia), secretary-general (Burkina Faso, FYROM and Thailand), chief electoral officer (Afghanistan) or electoral commissioner (Australia). In some countries, for example Australia and Tonga, the head of the secretariat is also a member of the EMB.

The EMB Secretariat and the Public Service

Procedures for appointing EMB secretariats vary. In countries that use the Governmental or Mixed Model, elections are implemented by the executive through a ministry or local authorities. EMB secretariat staff are normally public servants, appointed by the executive through the same rules and regulations that apply to all public service appointments, and subject to public service policies on rotation, training and dismissal. There is commonly no mention in the electoral law of these issues.

Such public servants may be engaged in electoral administration full time, as in the Czech Republic, Greece, Morocco and Norway, or have other duties during electoral off seasons and only be engaged in electoral work during elections. They are then deployed or seconded to the electoral office to assist with various tasks, such as boundary delimitation, voter registration, voter education and information, political party and candidate registration, voting and counting. Ideally, such staff will have had previous relevant electoral experience, though turnover of personnel is likely to mean that this cannot be guaranteed. Similar arrangements are used in countries such as Bermuda, Cyprus and the Republic of Ireland.

In some countries that use the Independent Model, the EMB secretariat staff are directly appointed by the EMB under staffing structures and conditions that are determined by the EMB (as in Cambodia), while in other countries they are public servants and their salaries and conditions of service are linked to those of the public service. Even where secretariat staff are public servants, they may hold statutory appointments under electoral law.

External control of EMB staffing by a government department or body such as a Ministry of Administration (Indonesia) or a Public Service Commission (Nepal) can give rise to a range of challenges. The EMB may have little or no control over secretariat staff selection. Policies requiring rotation of staff at fixed intervals, or specifying limits on how long a public servant may remain at a senior level before compulsory retirement, may constrain the development of institutional capacity and memory—and in the most extreme cases could prevent senior staff from managing more than one election. Deadlines associated with such policies may well fail to take into account the electoral cycle, which could lead to the departure of key staff at critical times.

The extent to which an EMB is empowered to hire and fire its public servant staff can be an indication of its independence from the government. EMBs have this power in India, Mexico, South Africa and Uruguay. In other countries, such as Antigua and Barbuda, Botswana, Tanzania and Yemen, the president appoints the head of the secretariat.

In Georgia, the EMB staff are all public servants. Except for the head of the secretariat, the staff of the Namibian EMB are also all public servants. The government approves the creation of EMB positions, and all EMB appointments are linked to public service salaries and conditions of service. The EMB determines the conditions of service for temporary election staff, such as polling station staff, but the treasury must first approve their remuneration.

In Canada and Kenya, the EMB's returning officers (managers) at the electoral district level for national elections were, until comparatively recently, appointed by the government rather than the EMB. That practice was regarded as a weak link in electoral administration, since it had the potential to compromise the EMB's overall authority in the conduct of elections, and to call the neutrality of the returning officers into question. For federal elections in Canada, returning officers have been appointed on merit by the chief electoral officer since 2007, while in Kenya such appointments have been made by the EMB since 2011.

Table 12: Possible Advantages and Disadvantages of Using Public Servants as EMB Secretariat Staff

Advantages	Disadvantages
• Where the public service has tradition of neutrality, it may provide professional, loyal service. • Knowledge of general public administration issues may reduce EMB training needs. • May have networks within the public service that assist electoral activities (e.g. in procurement of materials, use of state facilities). • Offers a clear career path, even if not in the EMB. • May be cost-effective and provide a pool of staff that can be used flexibly to meet staffing needs. • Job security may promote continuity of staffing and organizational learning.	• May not be regarded as neutral or impartial, thus reducing the credibility of the electoral process. • May lack specific electoral skills. • May not be accustomed to the time-critical nature of electoral tasks. • May transfer/be transferred out of the EMB with little notice, resulting in critical skill losses. • Pay scales may be insufficient to motivate performance or loyalty. • May be working second jobs due to low pay, thus affecting commitment at critical times.

Critical issues to consider when determining whether to use public servants as EMB secretariat staff are those of political neutrality and 'job fit' or skill levels. Public servants may be publicly regarded as associated with or easily influenced by the government—on which they depend for their appointment, promotions and salaries—which may jeopardize the EMB's credibility. Strong independent EMBs under the Independent or Mixed Model can overcome this perception.

In many countries, public servants may not be highly trained or, because they only work infrequently on electoral matters or due to public service rotation policies, not technically skilled in electoral tasks. Blending skills that are available within the public service with outside appointments and the use of consultants or advisers can help raise skill levels. In a number of countries, including Indonesia, Tonga and Timor-Leste, the EMB has successfully employed or worked with consultants and/or contractors for voter information and information technology (IT) tasks, and transferred skills to the EMB's public service staff.

Structuring the Secretariat

Regardless of the model of EMB used, budgetary restrictions provide an overall constraint on the number and types of positions that an EMB can afford to fund. EMBs following the Independent Model that have the authority to hire and fire staff may be best placed to determine their own structure. Even in such cases, however, the law or government regulation may have already determined key elements of the organizational structure, such as senior executive positions and required functional divisions.

All EMBs that rely on public service staffing for their secretariat may face constraints on their ability to determine their organizational structure. General laws and practices for the public service may require approval for all organizational structures from a central supervisory body; set rigid standards for how departments, sections, subsections and other work units must be structured; or restrict the use of non-public service contractors or experts. The staff of governmental EMBs under either the Governmental or Mixed Models, all or most of whom work within public service departments, may have even greater constraints, as they may have to fit not only the structure of a temporary electoral organization but also the continuing work structure for their department or authority's other tasks. EMBs under the Independent Model that have control over their staffing may have more structural flexibility.

'Developing' is a key term for EMB organizational structures. Devising an initial structure is the first step, but maintaining a structure that continues to meet the evolving legal framework, the rapid advances in electoral information and communications technology, and stakeholder expectations is a real challenge. It is harder to be flexible enough to meet these demands when the organizational structure is partially or wholly defined by law or regulations of bodies other than the EMB, or where the EMB's structure and staffing are subject to general public service rules. While constant organizational change is unsettling, including structural reviews in major evaluations and giving the EMB powers to make changes or additions to organizational structures can enhance the effectiveness of electoral management.

Temporary task forces or project teams drawn from different parts of an EMB can be a more effective short-term response to evolving challenges than major changes to organizational structures, especially when rapid action is required and when the disruption of major restructuring may outweigh any immediate benefits.

Organizational Structure Charts

Determining the internal working relationships of the EMB entails creating an organizational structure chart (organigram) that facilitates effective integrated planning, service delivery and management control. Examples of organigrams from South Africa, Afghanistan, New Zealand, Costa Rica and Tonga are provided in Figures 3 to 7 on pages 153–57.

The EMB may design its own organizational structure if it has in-house expertise, or it could hire an expert consultant or organization or another EMB to help. It is important for an EMB or its agents to consult broadly on the development of its organizational chart in order to promote stakeholder involvement in its operations. Stakeholder involvement can ensure that the EMB considers external service delivery expectations, rather than merely internal management needs, when developing or reviewing the organizational structure.

The number of staff positions to be created, their levels of seniority and their management relationships will be determined by what is required to effectively fulfil the EMB's mandate. Ideally, the structure will wholly reflect the EMB's objectives and functions rather than be tailored to the staff skills available, although this approach may be more difficult in EMBs that are completely reliant on more inflexible frameworks of public service staffing.

Maintaining the continuity of electoral work is a major consideration when developing an organizational chart. The timing of EMB functions may be as important as the functions themselves. There are basic administrative, review and evaluation, and electoral event planning and preparation tasks that are almost always thought to require a base level of permanent staff. The EMB may also have other powers and functions that require ongoing implementation, such as voter and party registration, oversight of funding, and voter education and information. Even if there are relatively few continuous tasks, the EMB may benefit from maintaining a strong and broadly based permanent management team across all functions to effectively handle peaks of activity.

Creating too many positions on the EMB organizational chart is likely to promote public criticism, especially during the period between elections, when it is difficult for the public to visualize what, if anything, EMB staff are doing. Equally, maintaining too lean a structure may increase efficiency during periods of low activity but may undermine progress and continuity. Before implementing a 'lean' staffing plan, the potential availability of additional staff for peak workload periods and the in-house capacity to train new staff have to be carefully assessed. In this respect, EMBs that can draw on additional public service resources to handle peak workloads, particularly Governmental and Mixed Model EMBs, may be better placed to operate continuously at peak efficiency.

The quantity and quality of EMB staff appointments should match the outcomes and outputs required by the EMB's strategic plan.

How to Develop an Organizational Chart

The task of developing an organizational chart requires an EMB to identify:

- the powers, functions and tasks that the electoral legal framework gives to the EMB;
- the timing of implementation of those tasks;
- the number of permanent staff required to perform each function or task;
- the number and types of consultants and temporary staff required to deal with peak period activities;
- the level of qualifications and experience required to perform each identified function and task;
- who is answerable to whom in the EMB's management hierarchy; and
- the relationships among various EMB layers, including the need to create permanent or temporary positions at regional locations, and the hierarchy and structure of accountability within and between EMB locations.

Model Secretariat Structures

EMB structures have to be robust enough to deal with real-world conditions that may be disorganized or conflictual. Despite the multiplicity of possible organizational structures for an EMB, there are some general concepts worth considering when developing the secretariat's structure:

1. Flatter organizational structures (fewer management levels) can deliver services faster, often more effectively, and reduce inefficient empire building.
2. Structures are most effective when they are clearly linked to the EMB's strategic plan.
3. Outward-looking structures focused on service delivery to stakeholders are better than inward-looking ones focused on management or support functions.
4. Structures need to facilitate both vertical and horizontal communication within the EMB.
5. Clear work output expectations and accountability for services should be designed for each organizational unit.
6. Structures should promote support of operational areas by corporate service (e.g. finance and personnel) areas.

7. Given the prominence in the electoral cycle of the functions of monitoring, evaluation, review and reform, it is appropriate that they are reflected in and supported by the EMB's structure.

8. In conjunction with that, an independent internal audit function that bypasses the secretariat structure and reports directly to the head of the secretariat or EMB members can help ensure integrity and probity.

Decentralized EMBs need to determine the accountability structure for regional offices. Do they report directly to the EMB members, or to the chief of the national secretariat, which is the more usual route? The situation becomes more complex if the legal framework defines a structure in which there are appointed members of regional EMBs and EMB secretariats at both regional and lower levels. This has been the case in Indonesia, where the appointed regional EMB members report hierarchically to the EMB members at the next-highest geographical-level EMB, and the regional-level secretariat reports to the head of the EMB secretariat at the next-highest level. Such complex and divided reporting arrangements may confuse staff about who ultimately directs them.

Where Independent or Mixed Models are used, there must be clarity regarding the way in which individual members of the policymaking/supervisory EMB are to deal with the secretariat and its staff. If the policymaking body reaches collective decisions that are communicated to the head of the secretariat for action, this minimizes the risk of confused lines of authority. If, however, members of the policymaking body are given separate responsibility for particular key activities, there is a danger that their roles will overlap with those of the heads of components of the secretariat. Such a situation can be especially problematic if the policymaking body consists of or includes political party representatives.

Some EMBs are structured into two main divisions:

1. electoral operations: covering subdivisions such as voter registration, boundary delimitation, organization of voting and vote counting, party and candidate registration, electoral training and development, research, information services and publications, and legal affairs; and

2. corporate services: covering subdivisions such as financial management, human resources management, knowledge management and IT infrastructure management.

However, some functions that do not fit easily into either of these two divisions—such as stakeholder relations, international relations and support for EMB members—may be attached directly to the head of the secretariat's office. It is preferable that audit and evaluation functions report directly to the chair or members of the EMB for independent EMBs under the Independent Model and component independent EMBs under the Mixed Model, and to the EMB's chief executive officer for governmental EMBs under either the Governmental or Mixed Model.

Electoral Management Design

This two-division structure may not, however, necessarily fit specific electoral environments. There is great variety in structures deemed appropriate by EMBs, some of which are presented in the case studies. Judgement on an appropriate structure has to be made by each EMB, bearing in mind its environment, functions, priorities and strategy.

Strategic Planning

Developing a strategic plan is a basic step in focusing an EMB's efforts on achieving a set of agreed objectives based on its legally defined responsibilities. The strategic plan is the management tool from which fundamental decisions on EMB activity flow—operational planning and prioritizing, resource allocation and service standards. The strategic plan provides the EMB with a blueprint for service and organizational strengthening, integration and improvement. It helps the EMB operate in and understand its changing environment.

The strategic plan is also a public document that serves as a record of what the EMB stands for, what it does and why, and what it intends to achieve. It is a road map that guides and motivates the EMB for a defined period of years, and plays an important role as a marker against which stakeholders can measure its performance.

An EMB without a strategic plan is like a pilot without a compass.

An effective EMB strategic plan sets out a vision of an open, democratic and accountable institution. It is also consistent with the EMB's mandate and implemented within the framework of the constitution and the electoral law. It takes into account all known factors that could affect the EMB's performance, such as the regulatory environment, technology, the likelihood of conflict, stakeholder participation or voter apathy, and EMB-government relations.

It would be unusual for an EMB's strategic plan to cover more than one national electoral cycle, as post-electoral event reviews may result in significant changes to the electoral administration environment. A strategic plan is not set in concrete: it is a practical, strategic guide, and must evolve if significant changes in the external or internal environment require a revised strategy.

Yet it is also important for a strategic plan to take account of environmental factors such as the increasing use of the Internet worldwide or rising demands for out-of-country voting, which over several election cycles can significantly alter the context in which elections are conducted. Figure 8 on page 160 is an example of a succinct summary strategic plan, developed by the Australian EMB.

Figure 3: Organizational Structure of the South African Independent Electoral Commission

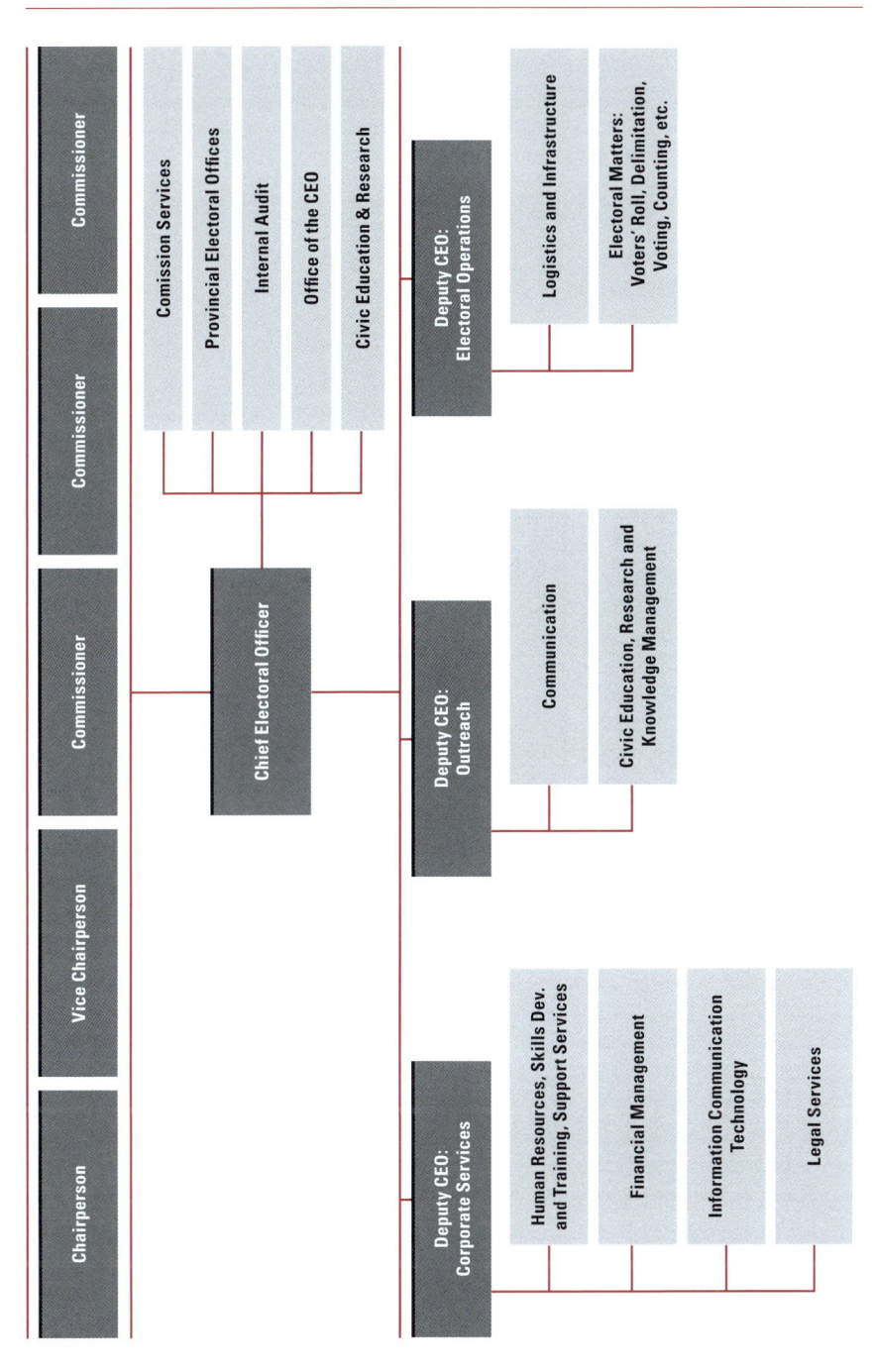

Source: Website of the Independent Electoral Commission of South Africa <http://www.elections.org.za/content/Dynamic.aspx?id=391&LeftMenuId=79&name=About%20Us&BreadCrumbId=212>, accessed on 12 August 2014.

Figure 4: Organizational Structure of the Afghan EMB

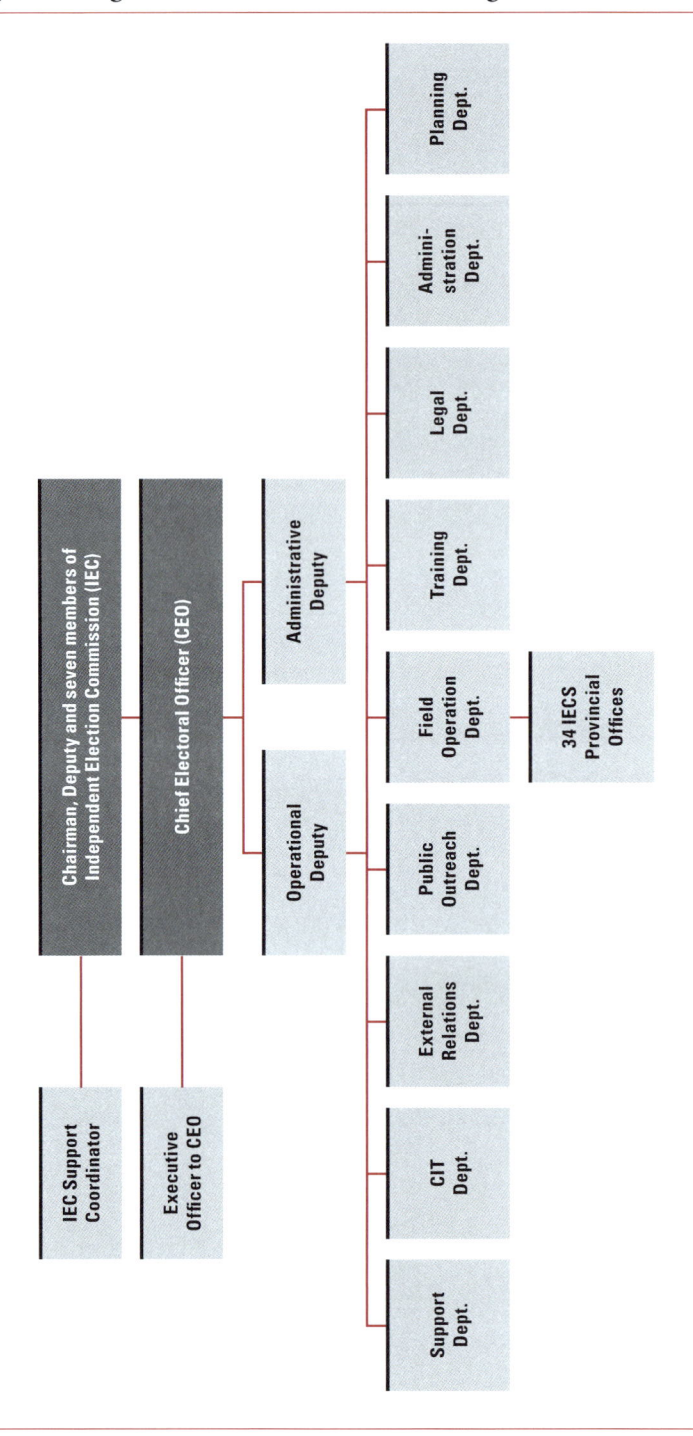

Source: Website of the Independent Election Commission of Afghanistan, <http://iec.org.af/2012-05-29-07-06-38/iec-structure>, accessed 12 August 2014.

Figure 5: Organizational Structure of the New Zealand Electoral Commission

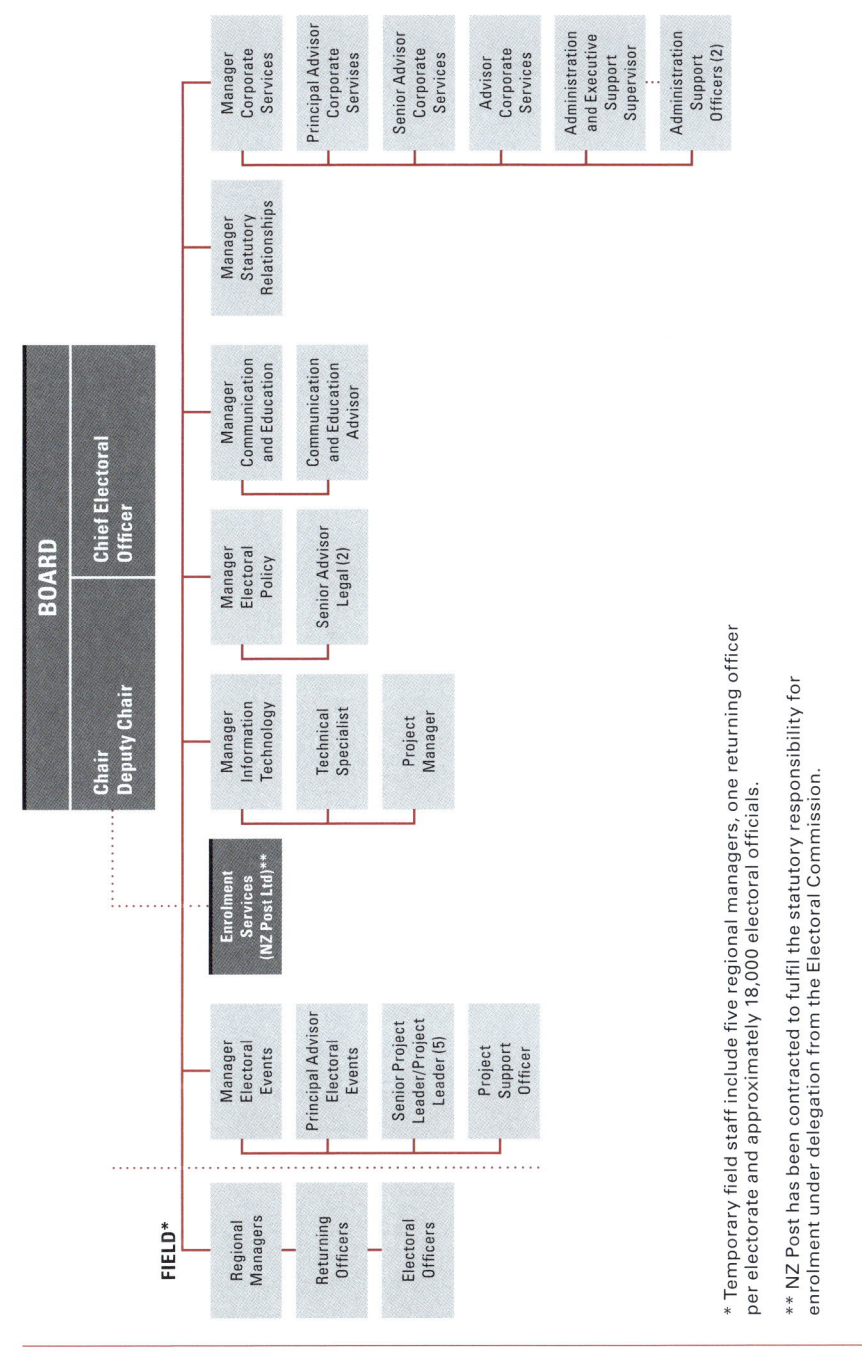

BOARD
- Chair
- Deputy Chair

Chief Electoral Officer

Reporting to the Chief Electoral Officer:
- Manager Corporate Services
  - Principal Advisor Corporate Services
  - Senior Advisor Corporate Services
  - Advisor Corporate Services
  - Administration and Executive Support Supervisor
  - Administration Support Officers (2)
- Manager Statutory Relationships
- Manager Communication and Education
  - Communication and Education Advisor
- Manager Electoral Policy
  - Senior Advisor Legal (2)
- Manager Information Technology
  - Technical Specialist
  - Project Manager
- Enrolment Services (NZ Post Ltd)**
- Manager Electoral Events
  - Principal Advisor Electoral Events
  - Senior Project Leader/Project Leader (5)
  - Project Support Officer

FIELD*
- Regional Managers
- Returning Officers
- Electoral Officers

* Temporary field staff include five regional managers, one returning officer per electorate and approximately 18,000 electoral officials.

** NZ Post has been contracted to fulfil the statutory responsibility for enrolment under delegation from the Electoral Commission.

Source: New Zealand Electoral Commission, 2013. <http://www.elections.org.nz/sites/default/files/bulk-upload/documents/electoral_commission_annual_report_2013.pdf>, accessed 12 August 2014.

Figure 6: Organizational Structure of Electoral Management in Costa Rica

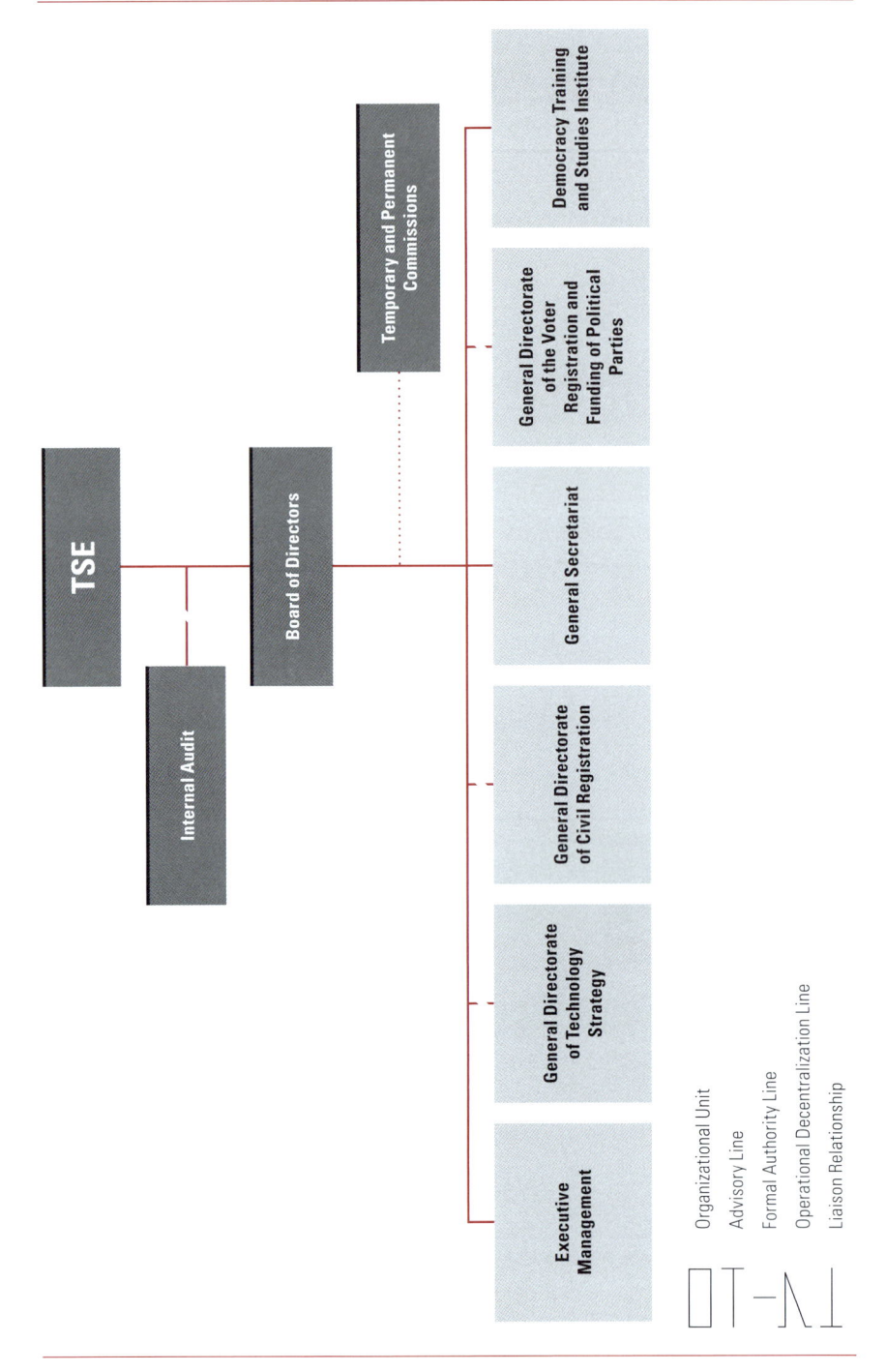

- Organizational Unit
- Advisory Line
- Formal Authority Line
- Operational Decentralization Line
- Liaison Relationship

Boxes: TSE; Internal Audit; Board of Directors; Temporary and Permanent Commissions; Democracy Training and Studies Institute; General Directorate of the Voter Registration and Funding of Political Parties; General Secretariat; General Directorate of Civil Registration; General Directorate of Technology Strategy; Executive Management.

Source: Website of the Tribunal Supremo de Elecciones (TSE), <http://www.tse.go.cr/organigrama.htm>, accessed 12 August 2014.

Figure 7: Organizational Structure of Electoral Management in Tonga

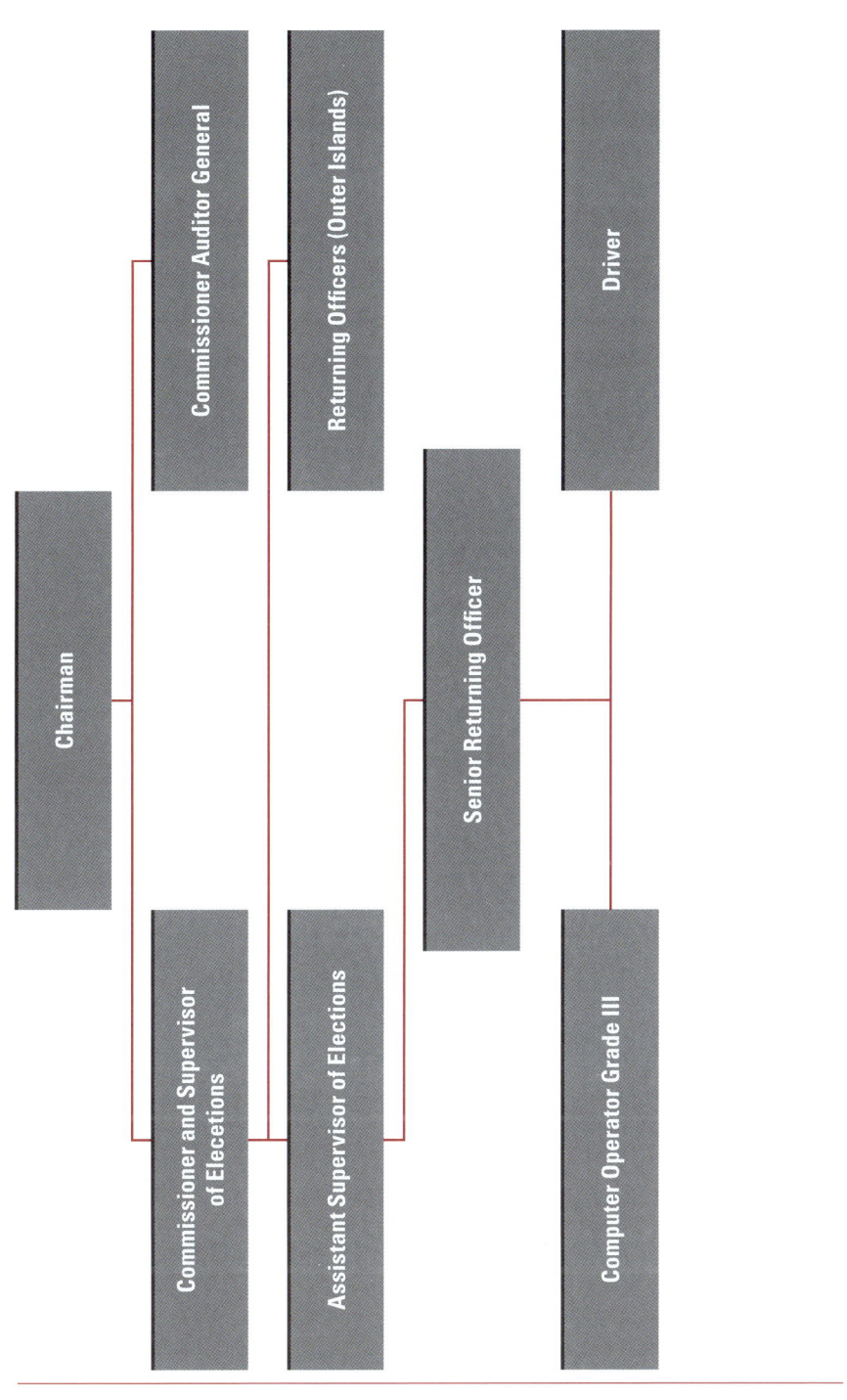

Source: ACE Project, <http://aceproject.org/ace-en/topics/em/eme/eme02/eme02d>, accessed 12 August 2014.

Basic elements of the strategic plan are:

1. Vision: what the EMB aspires to be;
2. Purpose, objective or mission: the fundamental focus of the EMB;
3. Values: the ethical concepts on which the EMB's activities are based, such as impartiality, accountability, independence, professionalism, effectiveness, equity and service-mindedness;
4. Outcomes and focus areas: what the EMB aims to achieve;
5. Key results: the effects that the EMB wants to have on its environment;
6. Indicators: measurable targets that help determine how well the EMB has achieved its intended results;
7. EMB data: the establishment, structure and composition of the EMB; and
8. Performance management strategy: how the EMB will promote the improvement of individual, team and organizational performance in a holistic, systematic and sustainable way.

An analysis by the EMB of its strengths, weaknesses, opportunities and threats may be an important tool in facilitating the development of a strategic plan. Identifying the contextual elements on which the intended outcomes of the strategic plan are based is necessary in order to make valid evaluations of achievements. The assumed context could include specific levels of stakeholders' participation, adequate infrastructure to support the strategic plan, and the recruitment and retention of qualified and experienced staff. Each country is likely to have a unique context, such as the EMB's efforts to deal with, for example, inter-ethnic conflict or the effects of HIV/AIDS on its employees.

It is important that the EMB consult with its stakeholders in the development, monitoring and review of its strategic plan. This promotes stakeholders' awareness and appreciation of the EMB's challenges and strengths, and may boost their confidence in the electoral process in general. It also promotes the EMB's awareness of its stakeholders' expectations and priorities.

Operational Planning

The operational concept provides the framework for operational planning under the strategic plan. It is important to integrate the operational concept with the electoral cycle, and to link operational planning with each phase of the cycle. The operational concept takes account of the establishment of a proper legal framework, and the nature and scope of the electoral processes. It needs to acknowledge any constraints on the EMB's planning, and be realistic in its assumptions about issues such as security and stability, and any unforeseen circumstances that could affect electoral management and the preparation and conduct of elections. The importance of stakeholders' full participation should be stressed in the operational concept.

For the purposes of detailed planning and effective administration, the operational concept may divide an electoral process into several phases, for example, the establishment of the legal and administrative framework; the preparations for voter registration; the conduct of voter registration; preparations for polling and counting; candidate registration; the political campaign; polling; the counting and announcement of results; and post-election activities. Each operational activity needs to be targeted at the objectives stated in the strategic plan.

Operational planning is most effective when the staff implementing the activities are involved in their planning. Operational plans may set yearly or longer-term operational targets and be broken down into half-yearly, quarterly, monthly and weekly segments, taking into account the availability of resources and the legal and operational deadlines for effective electoral service delivery. Operational plans for each EMB activity need to be split into divisional workloads, and may be harmonized through a committee of senior secretariat staff, possibly with EMB member involvement. The EMB membership's formal approval of operational plans emphasizes the significance of the plan. Divisional plans need to be broken down to the work unit and individual level, to reinforce the importance of each EMB staff member meeting the organization's objectives and performance targets, and to provide a monitoring mechanism for staff and work unit performance.

The Electoral Calendar

The primary purpose of an electoral calendar is to help an EMB keep its planning and preparation on schedule in order to meet its statutory or administrative deadlines. The calendar will also inform the public, political parties and the media about key dates, thus enhancing transparency and the EMB's public image.

Electoral calendars convey the range and sequence of EMB activities. An EMB may produce calendars with different levels of detail for internal use (e.g. dates for receiving election forms from printers) and for different stakeholders. A political party may only be interested in dates for voter and candidate registration, campaigns and campaign funding, voting, vote counting and determination of the results.

A simple summary calendar, such as those shown in Figures 9 and 10 (on pages 162 and 163), can enhance media and public understanding of electoral processes, whereas publicly distributing a highly detailed document may be confusing. However, in the absence of security concerns, there is no reason why the EMB could not give stakeholders, such as political parties, candidates, election staff, NGOs and donor agencies, access to copies of its internal administrative calendar, if requested.

Project management software can help an EMB develop a comprehensive election calendar that functions as a sophisticated electoral operations plan with clear milestones, time frames, individual staff responsibilities and interdependences of activities. This type of calendar can be shared with stakeholders and among staff as the basis for managing their progress and completing tasks.

Figure 8: Extract from the Australian Electoral Commission (AEC) Strategic Plan, 2009–14

Why we are here	To deliver the franchise: that is, an Australian citizen's right to vote, as established by the *Commonwealth Electoral Act 1918*.
What we do	We implement the Parliament's directives on electoral policy as embodied in the legislation. We have three primary outcomes for which we are funded, namely: 1. Voter entitlement for Australians and support for electoral events and redistributions through maintaining an accurate and up-to-date electoral roll. 2. Access to an impartial and independent electoral system for Australians through the provision of election services. 3. Informed Australians through the provision of information services on electoral matters.
This means we	• manage the federal electoral roll • conduct elections, referendums, including fee-for-service and industrial elections • educate and inform the community about electoral rights and responsibilities • provide research, advice and assistance on electoral matters to the Parliament, other government agencies and recognised bodies • provide assistance in overseas elections and referendums in support of wider government initiatives • administer election funding, financial disclosure and party registration requirements, and • support electoral redistributions.
For whom we do it	Our services are used by a wide range of customers including electors, political parties, the Parliament, the Government and organisations requiring electoral services. The pursuit of high standards in each of these areas ensures all Australians have a say in the government of the country.
What we value	As an independent statutory body we embrace the values of the Australian Public Service in the high standards of behaviour we display on a day-to-day basis. In particular, we: • conduct our business in a non-partisan manner with **fairness** and **impartiality** • maintain high standards of **integrity and ethical behaviour** • respect and **uphold the law** • are **tolerant of difference,** sensitive to special needs and show respect for one another • are **open, transparent** and **accountable** in what we do, and • **respect** and **listen** to our clients and stakeholders and each other.
We abide by the following principles	• We act to serve the Australian people and the Federal Parliament. • We strive for excellence. • We never knowingly mislead anyone.

The environment in which we operate	The AEC operates in a complex environment with many stakeholders. We constantly scan for opportunities and threats so we can act accordingly to ensure we continue to provide a world class electoral service.
	Key issues expected to influence the AEC's operations in the next five years are:
	• Australia's changing demographic profile
	  – age profile, ethnic mix, generational mix
	• changing community expectations
	  – need to keep the elector central to service delivery
	  – nationally consistent service delivery through standard processes and systems
	  – interactive means of communicating with the elector
	  – legislation revised to enable enhanced service delivery
	• spread and acceptance of the Internet and online access to services
	  – continuing drive for efficiency in delivery of Government services
	• increasing need to embrace a whole-of-government approach to policy development and service delivery
	• a changing work force, both inside the AEC and the pool from which we recruit
	• the continuing reviews conducted by the government and the Joint Standing Committee on Electoral Matters which could significantly reshape the way we do our business.

(cont.)

Our strategic focus	There is evidence of a decline by Australians in electoral matters, as measured by the number of eligible Australians not enrolled to vote and the number of enrolled voters who choose not to cast a ballot during elections. To address these trends the work of the AEC over the next five years will be shaped by a number of activities centred around three strategic themes: modernisation, collaboration and investing in our people. By focussing on these areas the AEC will improve how it does business and best position itself to meet future challenges.

	Modernise our products and services, and our organisation:
	• legislation, governance, policies, systems, and processes:
	  – consider how electoral law may be amended to facilitate modernisation and assist with informing lawmakers
	  – improve our methods of accountability
	  – ensure our policies and processes are aligned
	  – review and improve our committee structure
	  – ensure our organisational structure is optimised for our outputs and allows us to achieve efficiency and effectiveness
	• review our methods for interacting with electors to increase accessibility:
	  – adopt modern technology to streamline processes and increase accessibility
	• other aspects of the way we do business in the AEC:
	  – our selection and promotion processes will be based on merit using selection procedures that encourage wider participation
	  – our default approach will be *elector centric*.

	Collaborate with stakeholders:
	• identify and pursue efficiencies through collaborating with other electoral bodies on:
	  – roll management
	  – national standards for elections and electoral officers
	• give greater emphasis to the Electoral Council of Australia
	• share best practice with electoral bodies in other western democracies, for example Canada, United Kingdom and New Zealand.

	Invest in and develop **our people:** So that we remain competitive in the labour market and recruit and retain high quality people, we will: • embrace APS best practice in all human resource activities • commit to addressing concerns expressed by staff in the State of the Service survey and improving the overall health of the organisation • develop the professional, managerial and leadership qualities of our staff • institute a new performance management program to inform staff development and career planning by July 2010 • recognise good leadership skills as an essential capability for all managerial staff.

Source: Extracted from Australian Electoral Commission, Strategic Plan 2009–14 (<http://www.aec.gov.au/About_AEC/Publications/Corporate_Publications/index.htm>).

An electoral calendar is especially helpful for ensuring the timely procurement of voter registration and polling supplies and materials. It is also a useful guide to political parties in countries such as Kenya and Nigeria, where political party primaries or other internal candidate selection processes have to be undertaken before nominating candidates for election, and where such political party events have a bearing on the election timetable.

A thorough review of the electoral calendar after each election or other electoral event will help identify where changes to the organizational structure, resource allocations, or the legislative or regulatory frameworks would improve electoral operations.

Figure 9: The Elections Calendar for the 2011 Presidential, Parliamentary and Local Elections in Zambia

No.	Activity	Start Date	End Date
1	**Certification of the 2011 register of voters**	31 July	31 July
2	**Campaign period**	29 July	06:00 18 September
3	**Notices of nomination centres and returning officers**		
	Gazetting of statutory instrument	29 July	29 July
	Gazetting of nomination centres and returning officers	2 August	6 August
4	**Briefings**		
	Briefing of Political Party Liaison Committee	2 August	2 August
	Briefing of aspiring presidential candidates and party secretaries general	3 August	3 August
	Briefing ambassadors and high commissioners accredited to Zambia	3 August	3 August
	Briefing civil society organizations	4 August	4 August
5	**Accreditation**		
	Accreditation: international observers (Electoral Commission of Zambia HQ)	2 August	16 September
	Accreditation: local monitors (district councils)	3 August	16 September
	Accreditation: elections results centre	10 September	19 September
	Accreditation of election and polling agents—district councils	8 August	16 September
6	**Nominations**		
	Presidential nominations (09:00–16:00)	7 August	10 August
	Briefing of election agents/observers and monitors for NAE/LGE	10 August	10 August
	Parliamentary and local government nominations (08:00–16:00)	12 August	12 August
	Publication of validly nominated candidates	13 August	19 August
7	**Polls**		
	Briefing of elections/polling agents, monitors and observers	17 September	17 September
	Election day	20 September	20 September
8	**Verification of ballot paper accounts' forms**	26 September	26 September

Source: Electoral Commission of Zambia
(<http://www.elections.org.zm/news/press_release_-_2011_elections_100043.php>).

Figure 10: National Assembly Elections Calendar, Bhutan, 2013

No.	Event	Date
1	Issue of royal decree calling the National Assembly elections and setting the process in motion.	28 April
2	Election Commission of Bhutan (ECB) notification on the National Assembly election schedule.	29 April
3	Registered political parties to commence submission of letter of intent to contest primary round.	29 April
4	Eligible postal voters to start submitting application for postal ballot to respective returning officer.	29 April
5	Last date for submission of the letter of intent by registered political parties.	5 May
6	Scrutiny of letter of intent by the Election Commission.	6 May
7	Start of application for election campaign fund by political parties.	6 May
8	Commencement of the election campaign.	6 May
9	Release of the election campaign fund.	7 May
10	Last date for withdrawal from the elections.	17:00, 8 May
11	Returning officer to start sending/mailing postal ballots.	17:00, 8 May
12	Last date/time for receipt of application for postal ballots by returning officer.	17:00, 8 May
13	First public debate for the primary round: ideology.	17:00, 8 May
14	Second public debate for the primary round: issue based.	10 May
15	Start of the common forum in all 47 *demkhongs*.	11 May
16	End of election campaign.	9:00, 29 May
17	Last day/time for receiving postal ballots.	17:00, 30 May
18	**Primary round poll day.**	31 May
19	Counting of results.	31 May
20	Declaration of results and submission of the results to His Majesty the Druk Gyalpo.	1 June
21	Start filing of nominations by candidates of the two parties that secured the highest and second-highest total votes in the primary round.	1 June
22	Last date for filing nominations by candidates of the two parties that secured the highest and second-highest total votes in the primary round.	11 June
23	Scrutiny of nominations of candidates.	12 June
24	Candidates start submitting application for election campaign fund.	12 June
25	Commencement of the election campaign.	12 June
26	Release of the election campaign fund by ECB.	13 June
27	Last date for withdrawal of candidature.	14 June
28	Returning officer to start sending postal ballot to postal voters.	14 June
29	Last date of receipt of application for postal ballots by returning officer (in case of change in postal address from the application submitted for the primary round).	14 June
30	End of election campaign.	9:00, 11 July
31	Last day/time for receiving postal ballots.	17:00, 12 July
32	**General elections poll day.**	13 July
33	Counting of results.	13 July
34	Declaration of results and submission of the results to His Majesty the Druk Gyalpo.	14 July
35	Start of election petition period.	14 July
36	Issuance of the certificate of election.	19 July
37	Completion of election petition period.	26 July

Source: Election Commission of Bhutan, *Strategy for the Conduct of The Second Parliamentary Elections 2013: National Assembly* (<http://www.election-bhutan.org.bt/wp-content/uploads/2013/04/StrategyforNAElections2013.pdf>)

Chapter Summary

- EMBs may have more effective control over electoral activities if they are empowered to directly hire and fire, and set the conditions of service for, their secretariats. Yet many EMB secretariats are drawn from public service staff and are subject, to a greater or lesser degree, to common public service rules that may limit both the EMB's human resource flexibility and its ability to develop continuity in the professional electoral service.

- Each EMB needs to develop an organizational structure that facilitates cost-effective achievement of its strategic objectives by designating the necessary numbers of skilled staff at appropriate locations and levels of seniority who are subject to effective lines of accountability.

- An EMB's strategic plan is the basis for all of its activities, defining for a fixed period the EMB's vision, purpose, values, target outcomes, result outputs and performance indicators. Stakeholder involvement in the development, monitoring and review of an EMB's strategic plans focuses the planning on service delivery, and can boost confidence in the EMB.

- An EMB also needs operational work plans, based on the strategic plan, which detail individual work processes and their integration, deadlines and responsibilities. These are usefully developed into a detailed electoral calendar, a simplified version of which is an important source of information and transparency-enhancing tool for public distribution.

CASE STUDY

Senegal: Sub-Saharan Multiparty Elections*

Vincent Tohbi

Background

Senegal is a Sub-Saharan democracy that has been holding elections regularly since gaining independence in 1960. Though the 1963 constitution acknowledged multi-partism, the 1976 and 1978 constitutional reforms put an end to the single-party system and opened the political space to competitive elections with the participation of several political parties.

However, the 1983 and 1988 elections were marked by widespread violence. Then-President Abdou Diouf put in place a National Commission for the Reform of the Electoral Act that produced recommendations in 1992 that were passed into law by the National Assembly:

- the voting age was lowered from 21 to 18;
- the use of voting booths to cast ballots was made compulsory ;
- presentation of the voter's card before voting was made compulsory;
- the use of indelible ink became mandatory;
- new national voters' lists under the supervision of political parties were established;
- party agents to monitor the voting process in the polling stations were authorized;
- it became required to distribute voters' cards in the presence of the party representatives;
- a national (and provincial) commission in charge of tallying the votes were established—headed by a magistrate and composed of party representatives;

---

* A case study on Senegal also appeared in the original edition of the Handbook: Claude Kabemba and Andrew Ellis, 'Senegal: Independence Strengthened in a Mixed Model of Electoral Managment', *Electoral Management Design: The International IDEA Handbook* (Stockholm: International IDEA, 2006), pp. 110–12.

- it was mandated to hold presidential and parliamentary elections on different dates;
- the Court of Appeal was tasked to handle electoral disputes; and
- the FPTP electoral system at the departmental level and the PR system at the national level in the parliamentary elections were combined to favour the representation of smaller parties.

However, this new Electoral Act did not prevent the country from experiencing new contestations of the presidential and parliamentary elections in 1993 and local elections in 1996. New reforms were discussed and adopted, and a National Elections Observatory was established in 1998, which subsequently became a National Autonomous Electoral Commission in 2005.

EMBs

Unlike many other African countries, several different institutions are responsible for various aspects of the management of elections in Senegal.

Ministry of Interior

The ministry has always been the backbone of elections management in the country. This was inherited from the French administrative tradition, as Senegal is a former French colony. The Ministry of Interior works with the governors and local authorities (i.e. *préfets* and *sous-préfets*). In 1997, the responsibility for elections management was transferred to the Direction General of Elections within the Ministry of Interior. Decree N° 2003–292 of 8 May 2003 reoriented the missions of the Direction General of Elections and gave it the following functions:

- the establishment and revision of voters' lists;
- conception and maintenance of all elections documents and archives;
- organization and follow-up of the distribution of voters' cards;
- supervision of the printing of ballot papers;
- support to the security services in ensuring safe electoral operations;
- training of the institutional administrations in charge of various aspects of the electoral process, such as the judiciary;
- voter education;
- the use of new IT; and
- analysis of elections.

The Ministry of Foreign Affairs

This ministry works under the supervision of the Ministry of Interior in matters related to the election of Senegalese from the diaspora, and enjoys the same mission as above.

The National Autonomous Electoral Commission

To increase parties' confidence in the management of elections by the Ministry of Interior and by civil servants who may not be impartial, consensus was reached among political parties to ensure the supervision of the ministry's electoral work by the National Autonomous Electoral Commission (*Commission Electorale Nationale Autonome*, CENA). As per law N°3 2005–07 of 11 May 2005, the CENA's role is to:

- supervise and control the establishment of the voters' rolls;
- supervise and control the purchase, printing and distribution of voters' cards;
- avail the voters' lists to parties;
- supervise voting operations and all election-related activities;
- supervise the collection, tallying and centralization of results; and
- make recommendations to improve the electoral process.

CENA is composed of 12 neutral and independent members appointed by presidential decree after consultations with various institutions. They have a six-year term and one-third of the membership is renewed every three years. CENA has representatives at the regional and departmental levels, and has members in every polling station on voting days. Currently it has 48 technical staff members.

The National Commission for the Tallying of the Votes

The National Commission for the Tallying of the Votes (*Commission Nationale de Recensement des Votes*, CNRV) was created in the 1992 reforms mentioned above. There are 14 regional commissions and 45 departmental commissions. The National Commission is headed by the president of the Court of Appeal and two judges. Each party, party list or candidate has a representative in the National Commission. Each of the 14 regional commissions is led by the president of the regional tribunal. The regional commissions are composed of two judges and a representative of each party and candidate. Each of the 45 departmental commissions is composed of three magistrates appointed by the Court of Appeal and a representative of each party or candidate.

According to sections 134, 182, 217, 218 and 219 of the 1992 Electoral Act, the CNRV manages the tallying of the votes on the basis of the results sheets transmitted by the polling staffs. Unlike the departmental commissions, the national and regional commissions can declare the results null and void or order the review of each result sheet from the polling stations. The National Commission announces the provisional results of the presidential and parliamentary elections.

National Council for the Regulation of TV and Radio

The National Council for the Regulation of TV and Radio (*Conseil National de Régulation de l'Audiovisuel*, CNRA) was established by law N°2006–04 of 4 January 2006. It is composed of nine independent members chosen among academics, media professionals, NGO activists and artists, among others. Its mission is to regulate private and public TV and radio stations during electoral processes and ensure equal access to the media for political parties and candidates.

EMB Funding and Accountability

All the institutions above receive their funding from the government. Senegal has no external financial dependence for electoral management. The government fully covers the cost of elections. However, there are some complementary or bilateral projects that receive support from donors (e.g. voter education and security). The Ministry of Interior accounts financially and administratively to the government.

CENA refused to have its budget included in that of the Ministry of Interior. It now has financial autonomy and accounts to the National Assembly. The CNRV is accountable to the judiciary. All other institutions are accountable to the government.

Electoral Dispute Resolution

There is no systematic alternative electoral dispute resolution mechanism in Senegal. All disputes are dealt with either administratively by CENA and CNRA, or legally by the courts. The Court of Appeal in Dakar plays an important role in the resolution of disputes resulting from parliamentary and local elections, whereas the Constitutional Council deals with disputes related to presidential elections.

Legal Framework of Elections

Different laws regulate the holding of elections. Political parties are free as per law N°89–36 of 12 October 1989. However they should not be formed on the basis of race, ethnic group, sex, religion, language or region.

As for media regulation, law N°96–04 of 22 February 1996 governs the freedom of the press. This has led to the creation of many media companies or press agencies: five national commercial radio stations, several local commercial radio stations, more than 70 community radio stations and nine TV channels with national coverage. As for the printed media, there are 20 dailies and more than 12 weeklies. All public and private TV and radio stations fall under the scrutiny of CNRA during elections.

A new Electoral Act was passed in January 2012. The last general elections were governed by Electoral Act No 2012–01 of 3 January 2012, which replaced Electoral Act No 92–16 of 7 February 1992.

Relations with Civil Society, Political Parties and Observers

Political parties are an integral part of the electoral process, and have representatives in all EMBs, with the exception of the Ministry of Interior. They are also the major actors in the process of electoral reforms through Parliament.

Civil society is also involved in CENA and CNRA, but is less engaged in EMB consultations. During the 2012 elections, civil society was involved in voter education activities, as well as conflict prevention initiatives, since those elections took place in a volatile atmosphere.

Political parties and CSOs are formally involved in and consulted on all electoral issues in the steering committee called the *Comité de Suivi et de Veille* (Monitoring and Follow-up Committee).

Thanks to its relatively stable democracy, Senegal is not used to the deployment of large numbers of international observers. However, given the tense atmosphere that prevailed in the months prior to the 2012 presidential elections, the country recorded its highest ever number of international observers: 3,000. As for citizen observers, who have always monitored elections in the country, the figure amounted to more than 6,000 in 2012. The accreditation of observers by the Ministry of Interior is a fast and easy process.

Relations with Other Institutions and Agencies

It is important to mention that although several institutions are involved in conducting elections, the relationships and collaboration between them is smooth and harmonized overall—as is the relationship between the EMBs and the police, despite the serious incidents that occurred in the weeks before the elections.

Electoral Review and Evaluation

There is, unfortunately, no formal and collective electoral review involving the various EMBs. Each EMB drafts periodic reports, points out achievements and weaknesses, and makes recommendations for improvement. Some of those reports are not disclosed to the public, and the recommendations are not followed up. For instance, CENA proposed reforms in 2009 for implementation before the 2012 election that were never passed into law. Among those recommendations was the suggestion to decentralize dispute resolution from the Court of Appeal to the regional and provincial Courts of Appeal. Other suggestions included increasing CENA's powers to include appointing polling staff members, tallying the votes and transmitting the results sheets to the CNRV; and the introduction of the unique ballot paper. Senegal still uses multiple ballot papers, which are costly, damaging to the environment and susceptible to manipulation.

The Monitoring and Follow-up Committee—comprised of all EMBS, political parties, civil society and observers—was established in 2010. It was created in response to the increasing crisis in confidence among electoral stakeholders regarding the reliability of the voters' rolls. The committee meets when the need arises to discuss all electoral issues, and directs its recommendations to the government and Parliament. It can also propose reforms, laws and amendments.

Training and Professionalism of EMB Staff

The EMB staff do not have regular refresher training. Training events are mostly organized in the run-up to elections or during election time. But because there is an election almost every two years in Senegal (local or national), the EMBs have the opportunity to keep their staffs updated about electoral procedures, new regulations and new technologies.

The professionalism of the polling staff is commendable; they perform their duties in a remarkable manner and generally enjoy the confidence of the voters. The country's long tradition of elections has greatly contributed to the professional handling of electoral matters.

The Use of New Technologies

Since 2007, the Ministry of Interior has introduced new technologies to improve its performance. Digital and biometric technologies were used to create the national voters' rolls and produce IDs and voter cards. All registration centres are equipped with computers and the equipment required to capture fingerprints and photographs. In 2011, political parties acquired new technologies to track fraudulent registrations, which uncovered 55,856 fictitious voters.

CENA put an IT unit in place in 2012 that can collect any information about voting in the polling stations.

Opportunities and Constraints

The 2012 presidential and parliamentary elections have proven the maturity of Senegalese democracy. Apart from some discussions about the voters' list that produced a consensus in the political arena, the electoral operations did not suffer major flaws. There is general confidence in the electoral process. However, Senegal should review its system and decide whether the current EMBs can still operate independently and enjoy the same confidence.

The use of a unique ballot paper may be a matter for further discussion. The predominant role of the Ministry of Interior may become a matter of concern if civil servants are more inclined to obey their hierarchy than to work impartially. But for now, the EMBs are relatively trusted and have contributed to peace in Senegal by performing their duties professionally.

CASE STUDY

Republic of Korea: An Independent and Neutral Electoral Management Body

Jeong-Gon Kim

Providing all qualified voters with an equal opportunity to cast a direct and secret ballot, the democratic electoral system was first introduced in Korea for the election of Constitutional National Assembly members in 1948. When the Korean government was founded, the Election Commission was part of the executive branch, and its impartiality was difficult to secure. Consequently the Election Commission was re-established by the fifth revision of the country's constitution as an independent constitutional agency in 1963, during the Third Republic of Korea.

Background

In the beginning, the Election Commission focused on the fair management of elections and referendums in accordance with election laws, as well as the promotion of voter sovereignty. In 1973 the Election Commission, then bureau level, was expanded and raised to the status of vice minister level.

With the introduction of direct elections in the 13th presidential election in 1987 and progress toward democracy, the freedom of election activities was greatly increased. Yet illegal campaign activities skyrocketed as well. In order to ensure free, fair and credible elections, the Election Commission strictly enforced election laws, and these efforts received public support. Its authority to control illegal campaign activities was expanded and stipulated in writing in 1992. The commission continued its strict enforcement of election laws and strengthened its investigative authorities. In 1987, a constitutional revision gave the commission the right to enact internal regulations. In 1992, the Election commission Act was revised to allow the commission to submit a bill to the National Assembly when it is necessary to enact a new law or amend an existing law concerning elections. The revised act also upgraded the status of the Commission to the ministry level, and it was restructured accordingly.

In 1996 the National Election Commission (NEC)—the top tier of the Election Commission—established the Korean Civic Education Institute for Democracy and has offered civic education programmes for political parties, candidates and the general public since then. The Election Commission has managed and supervised elections for members of the Education Committee as well as the superintendent of education.

The 2004 election for the 17th National Assembly members was a turning point for free, fair and credible elections; it abolished costly local party branches and some of the campaign methods. In order to prevent illegal campaigns, cash rewards were given to those who reported election law violations. Administrative fines were imposed on those who received illegal contributions (e.g. money, food) from candidates. These efforts helped ensure free, fair and credible elections.

The NEC also established the Election Broadcasting Debate Commission (EBDC) and the Internet Election News Deliberation Commission (IENDC). The EBDC encouraged active discussion and debates among political parties, while the IENDC monitored Internet media to ensure accurate reporting of facts. The Election Commission's authority was further strengthened to investigate the illegal use of political funds and to request the inspection and submission of communication documents. The commission also introduced a cyber election surveillance unit for election law violations.

Beginning with the management of a residents' referendum in 2004, the commission has been entrusted with managing elections for the heads of local agricultural, livestock, fisheries and forestry cooperatives as well as the presidents of national universities since 2005. In 2006, the commission started to manage residents' recall votes concerning the heads of local governments and council members.

With the 2010 revision of the Act on the Maintenance and Improvement of Urban Area and Dwelling Conditions for Residents, the Election Commission's responsibilities now include management of elections for non-public offices, such as board members of housing-related organizations.

The Election Commission has expanded its role in international cooperation by joining the Association of Asian Election Authorities (AAEA) in 2008 and became the chair in 2011. It also signed memoranda of understanding with electoral management bodies in other countries to establish mutually cooperative relationships in the field of elections. The commission has also hosted seminars and training sessions for foreign election officials to share the views and experiences of different electoral practices.

With the amendments made to the Public Official Election Act in 2009, Korean citizens visiting or residing in foreign countries (including those with a permanent residency visa) can vote in the presidential and National Assembly elections.

The Legislative Framework

In accordance with the provision of Article 114, paragraph 1 of the country's constitution, the NEC was established in the Election Commission Act of 1992 as an independent constitutional agency compatible with the National Assembly, the government, the courts and the Constitutional Court of Korea for the purpose of managing fair elections and national referendums, and dealing with administrative affairs concerning political parties and political funds. The Election Commission Act states regulations on the establishment and duties of Election Commissions at each level, appointment procedures and qualifications of election commissioners, and the chairperson's and full-time commissioner's authority and roles.

The NEC, after self-examination regarding the illegal election of 15 March 1960, became a constitutional agency following the enactment of the Fifth Constitutional Amendment in 1963. The term and status of each election commissioner is strictly guaranteed, as prescribed in the constitution and act, to guarantee the fair execution of duties without any external interference.

Institutional Structure and Professionalism

The Election Commission of Korea is an electoral management body with permanent nationwide organizations. The Election Commission has a four-tier structure consisting of the NEC at the top, Si (special metropolitan, metropolitan city)/Do (province) election commissions (ECs), Gu (district)/Si (city)/Gun (county) ECs, and Eup/Myeon/Dong (township) ECs. Overseas Voting Committees are set up at Korean overseas missions for presidential and National Assembly elections. Currently, there are 16 Si/Do ECs, 251 Gu/Si/Gun ECs and 3,470 Eup/Myeon/Dong ECs.

The NEC is composed of nine commissioners, including one chairperson and one full-time commissioner. Since the chairperson, who is a current Supreme Court justice, does not serve full time, a minister-level commissioner serves full time to assist the chairperson and oversee the secretariat.

The secretariat, including a minister-level secretary general and a vice minister-level deputy secretary general, is composed of two offices, one bureau, six departments and 27 divisions, and the Korean Civic Education Institute for Democracy for democratic civic and political education. The IENDC and EBDC are subordinate to the NEC. The 16 Si/Do ECs have one full-time commissioner who is a ranking public official, commissioners who do not serve full time, a secretariat and the EBDC. The secretariat is headed by a director general, and has four divisions. The 251 Gu/Si/Gun ECs are members of the commission and have a secretariat. The members of Gu/Si/Gun commissions do not serve full time.

With the exception of the full-time NEC commissioner, the election commissioners do not serve full time. Therefore, each election commission at all levels has a secretariat that deals with electoral affairs. All employees of the EC secretariats are public servants who have passed the civil service exam. The full-time commissioner of the NEC and the head of the secretariat and secretary general are all minister-level officials. While commissioners have a short term of office of six years and do not serve full time, public servants at the secretariat have both expertise and many years of experience in electoral management, which gives them a certain degree of independence from the commissioners in terms of their duties at work. Moreover, except for matters requiring a decision of the commission (e.g. rules and regulations of duties of the election commission, rules on delegation and arbitration, candidate registration, announcement of the election results, decision of the elected, revision and enactment of the rules, changes in precedents), its powers and duties are delegated to the secretariats, which can handle the responsibilities with autonomy and independence.

The secretariats' autonomy is fundamental to carrying out their duties impartially, and helps provide independence from the legislative, judicial or executive branches as well as political parties or factions.

Powers and Functions

The NEC may issue regulations relating to the management of elections, referendums, administrative affairs concerning political parties within the limit of acts relating to the management of elections, and internal disciplines that are compatible with the Electoral Act (article 114, paragraph 6 of the constitution).

While guaranteeing equal opportunities to parties and candidates and complying with proper election processes, the ECs are engaged in prevention activities that help people comply with the election laws and strictly monitor and control the activities that impede fair elections.

In particular, the commissioners and employees of an EC are given the authority to investigate any violation of the Public Official Election Act or Political Funds Act, to collect evidence of such violations, and to ask the person in question to present him/herself at the EC office. When they suspect a violation, the election officials may request relevant institutions to submit financial transaction and communication records. Administrative fines may be imposed as a result of election law violations, and a halt or correction order or warning may be issued. When a halt or correction order or warning is not carried out, or when there are election law violations that are deemed to greatly harm the integrity of an election, the case will be brought to the prosecutor's office.

In addition, democratic civic and political education programmes are offered to encourage voters' participation in the electoral process and to help them exercise the right to vote, and to help realize democracy in everyday life.

There have been frequent enactments and amendments of the Public Official Election Act, Political Parties Act and Political Fund Act according to political interest and policies or political compromise. The NEC submits bills about laws and amendments that run counter to the interests of political parties in the National Assembly after paying careful attention to public opinion trends.

Financing

When preparing budgets for independent agencies including the NEC, National Assembly, the Supreme Court and the Constitutional Court, in accordance with article 40 of the National Financing Act, the monetary authority shall ask for the opinions of the heads of independent agencies on the budget and respect their opinions to the greatest extent possible.

When preparing budgets, monetary authorities tend to reduce budgets to only the essential expenses. However, expenses for public official elections are not excessively adjusted, since they are usually for procedural administrative work set by law. Also, as discussions and coordination between the monetary authority and the NEC take place during the process of deliberation, the expenses required to conduct fair elections are usually reflected in the budget without reduction.

The monetary authority submits a budget proposal to the National Assembly after consultation with the NEC. The Assembly votes on the budget proposal and makes a final decision after deliberating on (and increasing/decreasing) the budget. The monetary authority or the National Assembly is not allowed to reduce the finalized budget.

Relations with Other Institutions and Agencies

According to article 115 of the constitution and article 5 of the Public Official Election Act, the ECs at all levels may request assistance from relevant administration agencies such as the government, local governments and public agencies concerning the management of elections, including personnel/equipment support, promotion of elections, crackdown on electoral offenders, etc. The agencies, if asked for support, shall prioritize its provision.

Electoral Reform Management

Under article 17, paragraph 2 of the Election Commission Act, the NEC has progressively contributed to improving legislation in order to guarantee the public convenient and fair elections, improve the electoral system and resolve inconveniences by putting forward propositions on the Public Official Election Act.

The NEC submitted an amendment bill on the Public Official Election Act to the National Assembly in 2008, and the act was revised. The purpose was to promote free elections by guaranteeing overseas voters' rights and expanding the range of Internet election campaigns and preliminary candidates' election campaigns. The amendment bill also included the establishment and operation of the Broadcasting Deliberation Committee and stipulated more rigorous regulations against negative campaigning, including defamation and false propaganda.

In 2009, the NEC submitted another amendment bill to the National Assembly to further revise the Public Official Election Act. This amendment bill was proposed in order to enhance the freedom of election campaigning by easing regulations on political party activities and candidates' election campaigns.

The Constitutional Court ruled in 2011 that banning the Internet in election campaigns was a violation of the constitution. In 2012, the NEC decided to allow the use of social networking services in election campaigns at any time, and the National Assembly referred to this decision when revising the Public Official Election Act in favour of the NEC's determination. Allowing online campaigning year-round (except on election day) has expanded the range of voters' free expression on politics. Under the new guideline, candidates and their supporters can stage campaign activities using Internet portal sites, blogs, emails, mobile messages and social networking sites.

CHAPTER 6

The Development of Professional Electoral Management

Compliance with the legislative framework, including electoral regulations, procedures and manuals, is a prerequisite for the achievement of professionalism by an EMB. The term 'professional electoral administrator' demands a range of skills beyond those associated with technical or management qualifications in other specific fields. He or she also needs:

- an understanding of strategies for strengthening democratic development;
- a commitment to the fundamental principles of electoral good practice; and
- a strong commitment to high-quality electoral service to all stakeholders.

Specialist professional credentials and relevant management and technical experience help EMB members and staff become professional electoral administrators. They are also committed to the principles of electoral good practice, which include:

- *integrity:* the ability to carry out duties in a non-partisan and independent manner by not acting to benefit political interests and/or corruptly, and by ensuring that the electoral law, rules and codes of conduct are followed;
- *impartiality:* the ability to be fair and to afford stakeholders equitable and honest treatment on a level playing field, and to treat all stakeholders in an even-handed, non-partisan manner;
- *independence:* the ability to work without influence from or being under the control of an external force, such as the government or the ruling party;
- *transparency:* the ability of the EMB to be open and truthful, and to make timely information and access to EMB records available to stakeholders;
- *efficiency:* the optimal use of all resources—electoral funds are used wisely, and activities are designed and conducted in a sustainable and cost-effective manner;

- *service-mindedness:* ensuring that all activity is aimed toward delivering high-quality services to all stakeholders, and in particular voters; and
- *professionalism:* the meticulous and accurate implementation of electoral procedures, which is a key element of delivering credible elections. EMBs need to ensure that all election officials, whether core staff or temporary workers, are well trained and have the necessary skills to apply high professional standards. Professional training prompts public trust that the entire process is 'in good hands'.

No matter how great their commitment to their work, the bulk of EMB members are not experienced in the full range of responsibilities associated with leading and managing electoral processes. Professional development for EMB members is as essential as the development of EMB secretariat staff for attaining and maintaining high-quality EMB performance.

As the former chief electoral officer of Ghana has observed, people in the community do not know how the election administration works, and are just as likely to seek information from EMB secretaries, drivers or security staff as they are from operational staff. The EMB therefore ensures in its training that all staff have a basic understanding of its mission and principles.

An EMB's capacity to perform all of its electoral functions and responsibilities effectively depends very much on the capacities and performance of its secretariat staff. The capacities of both temporary and permanent secretariat staff can be enhanced by implementing appropriate recruitment strategies and vigorous training and development programmes. Most of the issues faced will be similar for all three models of electoral management, although they may manifest themselves in different ways.

Public concerns about an EMB's professionalism can lead to calls for institutional reform (see the case studies on Mexico and Kenya). However, EMBs with a strong set of values can deliver elections whose results are accepted by stakeholders even though they are still in the process of developing professional staff (for example, in Bhutan).

Use of Public Service Staff for EMB Secretariats

Many EMBs rely on public service staffing for their secretariats. This may be required in governmental EMBs and in other models where this is government policy. Independent EMBs that have their own employment rules may find it difficult to offer their staff good career prospects, due to the small number and specialized nature of many secretariat positions, and thus may find it more effective to rely on public service staff. Such a reliance does not by itself inhibit the development of professionalism. An example is the Election Commission of India, which co-opts large numbers of public servants to assist with election preparation, and runs a professional electoral management system. Allowing an

EMB to set its own rules for secretariat staff who are public servants is beneficial. These rules could prohibit transfers from the EMB during specified periods, and could provide conditions of service appropriate to the high-pressure environment of electoral events.

In any case, EMBs will at some point have to deal with the mobility of any public service staff assigned to the EMB. Staff who have gained electoral experience move on to other government positions, leaving a skill and experience gap. For those public service staff in governmental EMBs under the Governmental and Mixed Models who remain available for electoral tasks, there is a long period between elections when they do work that can be of a completely different nature. Regular development measures, such as refresher courses and archiving electoral materials so that they are easily accessible, can assist in maintaining electoral skill levels.

Permanent and Temporary Staff

No EMB can justify or afford to permanently maintain the number of staff needed for all polling stations (which in a country such as Indonesia require over 4 million staff). Efficiency considerations may also preclude the permanent maintenance of secretariats or subsidiary EMBs at regional and local levels, or the full permanent staffing of functions that are only needed during an electoral period. For governmental EMBs under the Governmental and Mixed Models, much of the management structure for major electoral events may be based on temporary appointments or made up of staff seconded from other areas of the public service. Temporary EMB secretariat staff are often not recruited long enough before elections, or stay long enough after elections, to be trained thoroughly for their work.

Each EMB needs to devise appropriate strategies to promote the effective use of temporary staff. These strategies could include timely recruitment processes; measures to ensure the availability of experienced temporary staff for each electoral event, such as the payment of availability retainers; and measures to maintain contact with temporary staff between electoral events, such as databases of contact information, newsletters, reunion meetings or refresher courses. Such measures can be particularly appropriate for EMBs in countries without fixed intervals for elections.

This type of approach is not possible, however, for an EMB such as that of Mexico, where temporary polling officials for each election are chosen using a lottery system. Significant lead times, and a very well-funded recruitment and training effort, are then essential.

Employment Conditions: EMB-Specific or Public Service Staff

Staff of governmental EMBs under the Governmental and Mixed Models, and of independent EMBs that use public servants as staff under the Independent and Mixed Models, are usually employed under conditions broadly equivalent to those of public servants of similar rank and seniority. In Australia, the public service regulations allow the EMB (in common with other public agencies) considerable flexibility in its employment practices. Special allowances for electoral work, particularly to compensate for the long hours involved during electoral periods, may also be available.

In independent EMBs that are responsible for their own staffing, the salaries and conditions of senior secretariat staff are often pegged to those of senior public servants. In Romania, EMB staff are employed on contract with conditions equivalent to those of legislature staff. Salaries and conditions that are better than the public service standard may be offered to attract the highest-quality permanent and temporary staff, and as compensation for the long hours of electoral period work. However, the continued payment of higher salaries to officials of independent EMBs between elections has been criticized as inefficient.

Where government policies aim to reduce or constrain staffing levels of public agencies, or where in-house skills are not available or cannot easily be maintained, EMBs (as in South Africa in 1994 and Indonesia on a number of occasions since 1998) have often used external individual or corporate contractors, especially for technical development and support tasks, often at higher basic costs than public service rates, but without pension and allowance payments. Such an approach must be carefully managed, and may cause disquiet among EMB staff who fear for the permanency of their own positions and are aware that their base rate of pay is inferior. It may also affect the sustainability of the EMB's operations.

Staff Pensions

Many EMBs link their staff pension to that offered by the public service, and it is natural to do so in EMBs where secretariat staff are public servants. It is cost effective and convenient for these EMBs to maintain the pension link to the public service, and it may provide more secure or higher retirement benefits for EMB staff. In Australia, the EMB's pension package is by law linked to the public service pension, without compromising its independence.

Career Patterns of Professional Electoral Officers

An EMB may seek to create career opportunities that are open to electoral professionals by favouring internal applicants who have specified professional electoral management qualifications to fill some vacant posts. In larger EMBs, as in India, Mexico or Nigeria, there may be career opportunities at both the regional and central levels.

Procedures for Recruiting EMB Staff

EMBs use various methods for recruiting secretariat staff. Governmental EMBs and other EMBs that rely on public service staff may not be free to implement their own recruiting practices. In Indonesia, the EMB may have to take whatever secretariat staff are allocated to it by the civil service. In some countries, public service staff rotation policies are seen as an anti-corruption mechanism, which can help prevent a unit from becoming dominated by corrupt officials. Yet rotating staff may compromise institutional memory, and the skills accumulated by honest officials can be lost.

Good practice is to hold an open selection process, as in Georgia, advertising widely for candidates and clearly specifying the skills, qualifications and personal attributes required for each position to be filled. This is possible even where EMB staff are public servants, as the Australian example shows. It is more difficult where governmental EMB secretariats have part-time or fixed-period electoral tasks, and electoral skills may not be prominent in the profile required of staff, or where public service recruitment practices require prioritization of generic selection criteria rather than specialized technical skills.

Since EMBs must set an example of acting equitably, they need to implement recruitment and staffing policies that are conducive to gender balance in EMB staff and that promote the employment of women. Women and men need to be afforded equal opportunities for employment, training, promotion and benefits for all permanent and temporary EMB positions. This may require the EMB to introduce gender-sensitive employment practices and training. Enforceable requirements to appoint women to electoral management positions, from EMB membership through all levels of the organization to polling station staff, may assist in this regard. In Timor-Leste, for example, the law provides that at least three women, in addition to a representative of women's organizations, must be appointed to the National Commission on Elections. Some customary traditions, such as separate polling stations for women and men, may affect the details of implementing gender balance.

The implementation of gender balance in an established EMB permanent secretariat may take time and involve the careful consideration of policies for filling vacancies. While this constraint does not apply when a new EMB secretariat is being established, the issue of gender balance may be lost in the hurry to find suitable people when recruiting for all levels of a complete EMB secretariat at one time—a lesson identified in retrospect in South Africa.

Some countries use political parties to help identify suitable EMB secretariat staff. In the USA, it is common for party nominees to participate in election administration, especially at the local or county levels.

One of the biggest recruitment tasks is finding short-term electoral staff, particularly polling station staff. In Hungary, local governments recruit polling station staff. Other avenues for recruiting temporary polling station staff include corporations and voluntary organizations.

One of the key choices that any EMB faces is whether, when recruiting polling station staff, to favour those with previous electoral experience or to conduct a more open recruitment process for each event. Having experienced and effective staff can help to ensure the smooth conduct of polling, but a systematic staff evaluation process needs to be put in place to ensure that less competent staff are not employed election after election merely on the strength of having done the job before. A more open recruitment process can help increase the number of people that have worked on elections, and involve a more representative cross-section of the community in election work. In South Africa, the EMB has been notably successful in efforts to engage women, young people and the unemployed to serve as polling officials.

As Internet use increases worldwide, online recruitment and staff management systems will increasingly be an option for EMBs to consider. In Australia, the EMB uses such systems extensively to recruit and train polling staff.

In Uruguay, any civil servant may be compelled to undertake election work; in Mexico and Spain, this compulsion may extend to any voter. In Mexico, the electoral law requires the EMB to conduct a multiple-stage process, including a lottery of all eligible citizens, to make an initial selection of temporary staff for polling stations. Those selected are trained, after which a final selection is made, and staff are allocated to specific roles at polling stations.

Screening candidates for permanent or temporary EMB staff appointment is a necessary component of the recruitment and appointment process, which enhances its transparency. This process aims to ensure that staff have the specified qualifications, are of good character, and are not likely to be politically active or otherwise unsuitable. It is best kept simple, quick and under the control of the EMB rather than political parties (as in the USA) or other organizations. As the number of temporary polling staff at most elections will vastly exceed the number of EMB staff managing the recruitment process, screening and recruitment should not be left to the last minute. Contingency plans for responding to staff drop-outs (even on polling day) are also needed.

Procedures for the Appointment of EMB Secretariat Staff

The overriding consideration when appointing EMB secretariat staff is a fair selection procedure that chooses the most suitable candidates. An EMB may often delegate the power of appointment to the head of the secretariat or one of its members, who may then delegate the appointment of lower-ranking officials to other secretariat staff. The appointment of temporary staff for voter registration and polling station work is often done by election committees or returning officers, or their equivalents, at the electoral district or local level.

It is good practice to require EMB staff to sign the EMB's code of conduct as a condition of appointment. It is also good practice to inform the public about senior appointments to the EMB and its secretariat by placing this information on the EMB website, and in newspapers and other media. To speed the integration of new staff into the EMB, it is important that the organization develops a comprehensive orientation programme that is compulsory for all new staff within the first weeks of their appointment.

In some countries, such as Mexico, the EMB has full hiring and firing powers over its secretariat staff. The law requires that all management, supervisory and technical officials of the EMB are members of the Professional Electoral Service, which is essentially a specialized civil service devoted entirely to electoral work. Citizens may gain provisional access to the service by taking training courses, winning a contest for membership or passing an examination. Full membership can only be obtained after passing required annual performance evaluations, undertaking further training and being involved in managing an election. Initial recruits in 1992 were obtained through responses to a national media campaign.

Staff Training and Development

One pillar of professionalism in electoral administration is the ongoing proper training and development of core permanent EMB staff (if any); temporary management staff appointed for specific electoral events; and the large numbers of field staff that may be temporarily employed for large-scale events such as elections, referendums or census-style voter registration. The principles of good electoral practice—such as impartiality, transparency, voting secrecy, equality of access, accountability and efficiency—form the basis of all EMB staff training. Staff training and development is a continuous activity. Changes in electoral procedures and technology, and the time that elapses between elections, mean that even the most experienced staff cannot rely entirely on their experience.

Because staff training and development is not immediately tangible, as ballot boxes or voter education and information materials are, there can be difficulties in persuading governments to approve sufficient funds for this task. Training and development also needs to be managed by a sufficiently senior individual to ensure that it is an organizational priority, including in the budget.

As the chief electoral officer of Canada has observed, voters expect the same high standard of service from every one of his 190,000 staff, whether they are long-term electoral professional employees or temporary staff who have only received two hours of training.

EMB Organizational and Staff Development for Permanent Staff

Organizational and staff development (OSD) for EMBs addresses their long-term capacity-building and skills requirements, and takes into account staff career development. OSD aims to unify the EMB's strategic objectives and the skills required to attain them and its staff's career and personal development goals. An active OSD element will contribute to the EMB's sustainability.

It is important for an EMB to develop both short- and long-term strategies to address its OSD requirements. OSD requires a substantial, and preferably separate, dedicated budget, so the EMB will need to prioritize its training and development needs. For example, the Russian EMB has decided that training of core staff (rather than polling station staff) is its priority.

OSD is based on a needs assessment, which may be conducted in house or by outside contractors or management consultants. This needs assessment identifies all EMB tasks, compares the skill levels of staff with these tasks and identifies the gaps—from which specific organizational and individual staff training needs, and the appropriate training methodologies, can be determined. OSD programmes aim to train each EMB staff member to perform his or her tasks with maximum efficiency and professionalism.

When assessing needs and developing OSD plans, EMBs may sense a need to choose between (1) training staff to ensure they have the skills to do their current jobs and (2) providing them with a broader set of skills, firmly based on the core principles of sound electoral administration, which they may not need immediately, but which will improve their ability to perform a range of different functions over time. EMBs that ensure staff are diversely skilled may be better placed to cope with change in the long run—and more able to respond with agility to evolving demands of the electoral environment—than those that have focused predominantly on current needs.

Depending on the needs analysis, OSD can include:

- general skills development, for example in:
  - written and verbal communication;
  - creativity, innovation and enterprise;
  - team building;
  - critical and strategic thinking and problem solving;
  - self-management;
  - dispute resolution skills;
  - project management;
  - using technology;
  - leadership, management, coaching and supervisory skills; and/or
- the development of technical skills relevant to the specific EMB division.

Staff development may take a number of basic forms, such as customized short-term informal training in the form of staff meetings and reviews, retreats and seminars; the formal or informal mentoring of staff by senior EMB or another organization's officials; and long-term formal training such as courses or academic development programmes. Continuous horizontal and vertical communication within the EMB not only contributes to development objectives but also greatly helps maintain organizational focus and improve staff performance. Open internal communication also reinforces the importance of transparency, and helps staff build knowledge of the organization and its activities on a continuous basis, outside the framework of formal training or mentoring.

Some EMBs have had an institutionalized separation of responsibility for the training and development of core EMB staff on the one hand, and polling staff on the other; the latter has often involved areas specializing in polling operations rather than longer-term staff development per se. Such an approach may be suboptimal in countries where polling staff might be a potential source of core EMB staff.

Using International Experience

Through bilateral and multilateral cooperation, many EMBs have sent their staff to observe electoral management in other countries, or seconded them to other EMBs for training and exposure to different approaches to electoral organization. This is a quick and relatively inexpensive way of gaining new ideas and exposure to good practices in electoral administration. A number of large EMBs, like INE in Mexico and NEC in South Korea, organize international visitor programmes for their elections. Regional electoral associations can also facilitate the exchange of information and the secondment and training of electoral administrators (see also Chapter 11).

International advisers and consultants have the potential to help EMBs solve difficult specific problems, to advise EMB members and staff on how to ensure that their operations meet international standards, and to enhance the EMB's internal problem-solving capacities.

International advisers may be specialists in particular electoral and technical fields or skilled electoral managers, but EMB projects that use advisers and consultants with experience in other countries need to be structured to ensure skills transfer and capacity building through formal or informal one-to-one mentoring of EMB staff so that the project's achievements do not depart with the advisers. When substantial teams of advisers are deployed to an EMB, it is particularly important to ensure that they avoid becoming a discrete clique within the organization, dealing with each other rather than with their counterparts.

Mentoring

The one-to-one mentoring approach to the professional development of selected permanent staff is not limited to projects with international consultants, but can be used to good effect internally by an EMB. Formal mentoring typically involves clearly establishing the conditions and goals of the mentoring programme at the outset. Informal mentoring, which ought to be part of any supervisor/subordinate relationship, can be less structured. Mentoring programmes can also help an EMB achieve some of its equity goals—for example, increasing the number of women or other targeted social or ethnic groups holding more senior management or technical positions. In addition to internal mentoring programmes, it may be possible to arrange short-term secondments of EMB staff to work with a mentor in another public sector agency or private sector organization.

Education and Development Courses for EMB Staff

There is a strong case for EMB staff gaining graduate or postgraduate qualifications in electoral management and governance to increased their actual and perceived professionalism. More institutions of higher learning are offering courses on aspects of governance and electoral administration, including American University (USA), Griffith University (Australia) and the University of Paris II (France). International IDEA developed a Model Curriculum for Master Programmes in Electoral Policy and Administration to encourage post-graduate professional education in electoral management.

The best-known professional development course available for electoral administrators is the Building Resources in Democracy, Governance and Elections (BRIDGE) course, which is supported by a partnership of the Australian Electoral Commission (AEC), International IDEA, IFES, UNDP and the United Nations Electoral Assistance Division (UNEAD). BRIDGE courses are presented by accredited BRIDGE facilitators, to whom the curriculum materials are made freely available as a global good. BRIDGE consists of 24 stand-alone modules in three main streams (Foundation Modules, Electoral Operations and Working with Electoral Stakeholders), so that any course can be tailored to an EMB's specific professional development needs. All BRIDGE modules are available in English. Some are also available in Arabic, Armenian, Dari and Pashto (Persian), French, Georgian, Indonesian, Portuguese, Romanian, Russian, Spanish and Tetum. As of July 2014, some 900 BRIDGE courses had been hosted in 93 countries, with the number being held increasing exponentially each year.

In the UK, the Association of Electoral Administrators (AEA) conducts regular training and education for election administrators. EMBs (local authorities) in the UK usually require candidates for election-related positions to have the relevant AEA qualifications. The South African EMB has been developing a formal training and education curriculum for election practitioners and an accreditation mechanism for qualified election managers. The Bangladeshi EMB has set up the Electoral Training Institute in Dhaka, which conducts intensive training for electoral staff at all levels, both face to face and electronically. There are strict entrance, accreditation and continuing professional development requirements for membership of the Professional Electoral Service of the EMB in Mexico.

> **Box 3: Some Important Steps toward Developing Electoral Administration as a Profession**
>
> - the introduction of formal training and qualifications;
> - the establishment of a professional and sustainable EMB to safeguard and promote the professional interests of electoral administrators and regulate their ethical conduct;
> - the creation of a pool of resources and a network of expertise electoral practitioners can refer to and consult while performing their professional duties; and
> - the development of a career path and opportunities for electoral administrators.

Operational Training

For an electoral event to proceed smoothly, it is essential that both permanent and temporary EMB staff receive appropriate operational training so that they fully understand the tasks required of them, especially when they are interacting with voters or other stakeholders, handling ballots or other accountable materials, or dealing with sensitive issues. At a minimum, such training needs to reinforce the importance of key requirements—such as respect for the law, neutrality and transparency—and to give participants a full understanding of the tasks they will be performing. For temporary staff, this will be the main emphasis, and manuals and checklists will be key tools. For permanent staff, training should also include an emphasis on the underlying systems and processes for which they will be responsible, with particular attention to contingency planning, backup mechanisms and problem solving.

Training Methods

Intensive training of temporary staff before every electoral event is a critical element of electoral service delivery and staff performance. The provision of a high-quality service, based on the principles of integrity and good electoral practice, is the underlying message of all temporary staff training. It is important for an EMB to develop a database of temporary staff who have been trained and worked satisfactorily during electoral events so they can be contacted to work in future electoral events.

Experience has shown that it is more effective to focus training for temporary staff on the specific operational elements of their responsibilities. Training in tasks such as voter registration, polling and counting is invariably more effective if supplemented with simulation exercises, such as role playing or mock exercises. Evaluation of each training session by the participants is essential for improved training performance.

Cascade Training

Cascade training entails the training of a core group of trainers in both electoral technical matters and training techniques—the 'training of trainers' who in turn train others at a lower level. The second level trains the third level and so on, until all targeted staff are trained. Cascade training's relative cost effectiveness and the ability to train large numbers of people in a short period of time mean that it is widely used in both new and established EMBs. It is especially useful for tasks undertaken by large numbers of staff, or where training has to be delivered simultaneously or almost simultaneously over large geographical areas—for example, for voter registration and polling staff. Trainers at each level may be EMB members or staff, or may include external professional trainers, academics or respected members of CSOs. Using a mix of EMB staff and external trainers can have advantages for stakeholder buy-in and sustainability.

Cascade training is effective if the training at different levels is sequenced within relatively short time periods, and if the training at the final level of the cascade (e.g. polling station staff) is conducted just a few days before the electoral event. This method requires that a large number of trainers fully understand the contents of the training sessions and the training methodology. Any failure or misunderstanding at the top of the chain will be passed on to the lower levels and may damage the whole exercise. Quality control measures—such as limiting the number of levels in the cascade and spot-check monitoring of training sessions—help to ensure that all training sessions are conducted accurately and consistently.

Training by Mobile Teams

A small number of mobile teams of trainers can conduct training for all election staff at all levels. This method has the advantage that the information is imparted accurately by competent teams of trainers. However, it requires more time, since a small number of teams are responsible for training all electoral staff across the country. While this may be an effective solution for electoral events held in very small geographical areas, it is not generally feasible elsewhere. If a large number of staff need to be trained and the mobile team starts training long before polling day, there is also a risk that the groups trained early will forget what they have learned.

Simultaneous Training

Simultaneous training involve training all temporary staff on a single day or series of days. This approach could be used if there is very little time to prepare for an electoral event, or where a large-scale training event is useful to an EMB as an image-building exercise or to stimulate interest in or education about an electoral event, as in Cambodia in 1993. However, it requires a very large number of competent trainers who would generally need to be externally recruited and trained in the technical content. It is also costly and requires very intensive planning to implement. Using video technology to brief temporary staff with previous experience on the changes that have been made to procedures since their last election might be another way to carry out simultaneous training.

Training Materials

Instructions

Instructions in the form of easy-to-read sheets or checklists have long been used to complement cascade training of some tiers of electoral staff, for example polling station security officials, polling station staff and counting staff. An example of such a checklist was used in Tonga in 2010. Materials of this type can be made available in electronic format where such facilities exist.

Training Manuals

Most EMBs rely on training manuals to impart skills to election officials. Manuals that are accurate, user friendly, well written, and easy to interpret and apply are an indispensable training aid. It is effective to develop separate components of a manual to cover categories of staff with different duties, and to include simple checklists of their essential tasks and a set of questions to verify their knowledge. Hard copy manuals can be supplemented by soft copies from which additional materials can be printed. Sufficient copies of manuals can be printed to allow election officials to take them home after training, either for further reading or for reference while they are working. In Hungary, electronic training facilities are used, including an electronic manual and a test on its contents.

EMBs can also consider producing manuals on electoral processes for their various stakeholders, such as political parties and candidates, party agents, the media and election observers. The better the stakeholders' understanding of the electoral processes, the easier a competent EMB's work is likely to be.

Simulations and Videos

Simulating electoral processes, such as voter registration, polling and counting processes, is a popular training method. Simulations and similar hands-on and interactive training experiences are generally regarded as the most effective method of training temporary EMB staff, and are worthy of being included in every training session.

The use of videos and graphics to illustrate and reinforce training texts and messages, and make presentations to smaller groups, is growing in popularity with trainers. These materials are useful to support, rather than serve as the basis of, electoral training. Video materials can be most effective when developed as short, focused segments that can be used to illustrate specific work activities and guide simulations. Before developing training sessions that rely on video content, an EMB needs to be sure that appropriate video facilities are available and affordable at all training locations.

Factors that May Inhibit EMB Professionalism

An EMB may have to overcome numerous problems to achieve an acceptable level of professionalism. Some may be within the EMB itself, such as behavioural, planning or resource prioritization issues. Others may be the product of factors in its external environment, including:

- *The political climate* within which elections take place largely determines the credibility and legitimacy of elections. It is difficult to manage credible elections in environments of political fear, intimidation and violence; societies with no respect for the rule of law; or where governments have no transparency or accountability. Nevertheless, a professionally oriented EMB can still work hard under such circumstances to demonstrate a commitment to ethical principles, which will help build confidence in the electoral process. Examples of EMBs that delivered acceptable results under the most trying circumstances include Afghanistan (2004), Iraq (January 2005), Mozambique (1994), Nepal (2008), Nicaragua (1990), Palestine (2006), South Africa (1994) and Timor-Leste (1999).

- *A sound electoral legal framework* is essential for the successful planning and conduct of electoral events, and for the professionalization of the EMB. Where the legal framework falls short of acceptable norms, the EMB may have difficulty delivering electoral events that are acceptable to all stakeholders, and may thus appear to be unprofessional. In order to avoid political disruptions and other uncertainties that may undermine the electoral process, changes to the legal framework should be finalized long before an electoral event. This gives the EMB sufficient time to educate its stakeholders about the changes, make the necessary modifications to its procedures and train its staff. It also allows the parties and candidates time to adjust their plans if necessary. Yet the experience of many EMBs, particularly in emerging democracies, is that last-minute changes to the legal framework are common.

- *A lack of continuity* undermines professional development where EMBs are temporary bodies. While a permanent EMB tends to have the time and resources to train its staff between elections, a temporary EMB has limited time in office—in many cases less than 90 days—which makes long-term training and capacity building very difficult. Temporary EMBs' heavy reliance on temporarily seconded public servants may also undermine their professionalism, especially because the office from which they are seconded may not be able to release the same staff to the EMB for every electoral event.

- *Lack of adequate or timely funding* can also undermine an EMB's professional development programmes. Some EMBs, especially in fledgling democracies, struggle to get enough funds for electoral events. When funds are eventually made available, it may be too late to conduct meaningful staff training, especially of temporary staff. Funding may also include conditions that inappropriately limit the EMB's choice of types of staff training or development.

Chapter Summary

- Professional EMB members and staff need appropriate skills and, most importantly, a commitment to the principles of electoral management, including integrity, impartiality, independence, transparency, efficiency and service-mindedness.

- The use of public service staff in EMB secretariats can provide the benefits of public sector experience, but can create challenges for EMB professionalization, especially in governmental EMBs, where electoral work may not be the vocation of EMB staff. EMBs that can hire their own staff and are not subject to public service rules may be able to use other incentives to attract higher-quality staff. The existence of attractive career paths in EMBs will help professionalize and retain staff.

- EMB staff requirements are cyclical, with very high peaks that cannot justify the maintenance of sufficient permanent staff throughout the entire electoral cycle. Each EMB needs to devise appropriate strategies to promote the effective use of temporary staff, which may include timely recruitment processes, availability of incentives and training opportunities, and mechanisms for regular contact.

- Equitable recruitment and employment practices—including open, merit-based selection processes, gender balance, and a fair and safe working environment—fulfil an EMB's internal responsibility as an institution that promotes equity in public life.

- Investment in staff training and development is critical for improving overall EMB effectiveness. This could be through internal courses, professional associations, academic qualifications, or mentoring and skills transfer by consultants and senior managers, or through the use of an electoral management curriculum such as the BRIDGE course.

- Operational training for temporary staff has been found to be most effective if it concentrates on specific technical processes and includes simulations, backed by good-quality materials such as manuals and checklists, instructions, appropriate audiovisual aids and rigorous training evaluation. Such training for permanent EMB staff needs a greater emphasis on systems, contingency planning and problem solving.

- EMBs typically need to provide operational training quickly for large numbers of electoral event staff. Mobile team training requires a relatively long training timetable, and simultaneous training a relatively large number of trainers. Cascade training is commonly used, although it requires strict timing and quality controls to ensure that accurate and complete information reaches the lower levels in a timely manner.

- EMBs may have to overcome negative influences on their professionalization, such as conflict environments, flawed legal frameworks, the temporary nature of EMBs, or insufficient or late release of funds.

CASE STUDY

Liberia: The National Elections Commission

Jebeh Kawa

Background

The formation of the National Elections Commission (NEC) of Liberia was part of the 2003 Comprehensive Peace Agreement that ended 14 years of civil war in the country. The NEC replaced the 1986 Elections Commission.[1] It is one of three autonomous public commissions established by the country's 1986 constitution.[2]

Legislative Framework

In Liberia, the legal framework for the conduct of the 2011 elections included the constitution, the Elections Law as amended by the Electoral Reform Law of 2004, organic laws of the courts, the law on political parties, as well as NEC regulations and decisions.[3]

As an autonomous government agency that is independent of any branch of government, the commission's powers and duties include:

- administering and enforcing all laws related to the conduct of elections throughout the Republic of Liberia;
- organizing the office of the commission as necessary and practicable for the effective operation of the commission; and
- proposing to the National Legislature the enactment, amendment or repeal of any provision of the Election Law.

The NEC itself incorporated amendments to the 1986 Elections Law in 2003 and 2004 and instituted several guidelines for the conduct of elections, including:

- NEC Code of Conduct;
- Code of Conduct for Political Parties;
- Code of Conduct for Media;

- Code of Conduct for NEC Personnel; and
- Guidelines for NGOs involved in Civic Education.

Institutional Structure

The seven-member governing board of commissioners of the NEC comprises a chairperson, co-chairperson and five commissioners; each has oversight of assigned political subdivisions with the chairperson having oversight of the most populous region. The criteria for becoming a commissioner are not extensive. They require only that the person is a Liberian citizen, at least 35 years of age, of good moral character, unaffiliated with any political party and not from the same county as another commissioner.

The commission has an executive director, as well as a legal section that is responsible for performing all legal duties related to the administration of the Elections Law. Election magistrates are assigned to each of Liberia's 15 political subdivisions, and in heavily populated regions more than one magistrate may be designated. The magistrates serve as liaisons between the commission and the county or district they represent on election matters.

Supporting staff at both the central office and in political subdivisions—including civic education directors, political party liaisons, technical support personnel, registrars, presiding officers and other poll workers—are appointed by the commission.[4]

Powers and Functions

In addition to the primary functions of the NEC, the following comprise the essential duties of the commission:

1. give accreditation to and register all political parties and independent candidates who meet the minimum requirements laid down by the commission;

2. reject, and if already registered, revoke the certificate of accreditation of any political party or independent candidate based on specific objectionable criteria outlined in the commission's guidelines in accordance with due process;

3. conduct elections for all elective public offices including the chieftaincy election and referendums;

4. formulate and enforce guidelines consistent with provisions of the constitution and the Elections Law that control the conduct of all elections for elective public offices;

5. appoint all officials and employees necessary for the effective performance of the duties and functions of the commission in consultation with the president of Liberia and other appropriate government officials;

6. in consultation with the appropriate local officials, appoint election officers in the political subdivisions of the country who perform their duties under the direction and supervision of the commission;

7. maintain a register of all qualified voters;

8. establish constituencies in every political subdivision, reapportioning them when necessary and expedient based on population figures (for example, following boundary delimitation in 2011, electoral districts for the House of Representatives were redrawn and increased from 64 to 73);
9. maintain a register of the constitution, article of incorporation and rules of all political parties and independent candidates and their organizations;
10. assess whether candidates for elective public office are qualified to run based on commission guidelines;
11. prescribe the kinds of records that must be kept by all political parties and independent candidates and their organizations;
12. examine and audit (or order the auditing of) the financial transactions of political parties and independent candidates and their organizations by an independently chartered public accountant (not a member of any political party or the organization of any independent candidate);
13. judge contests relating to election results (commission decisions are appealed to the Supreme Court);
14. perform accreditation of successful members who have been duly elected as president, vice president, members of the National Legislature, paramount, clan and town chiefs and city mayors with their common councilmen;
15. submit annual reports to the National Legislature and the president of Liberia on the general operation of the commission;
16. issue citations for the appearance before it of political parties or their leaders in connection with complaints; issue subpoenas for the purpose of obtaining witnesses in hearings;
17. revoke the certificate of accreditation of any political party, alliance or coalition, impose punitive fines, or punish for contempt any obstruction or disobedience of its orders; and
18. perform other duties and functions as provided by law, including civic education activities carried out by both NEC and external organizations, such as non-governmental, community-based and CSOs.[5]

The Composition and Appointment Methods of EMB Members

Seven NEC commissioners are appointed by the president of Liberia, with the advice and consent of the senate, to govern the affairs of the commission for a period of seven years as long as they do not engage in misconduct. With the consent of the senate, the president nominates an executive director, who serves at the pleasure of the president.

Upon consultation with the chief justice of the Supreme Court of Liberia and the minister of justice, the commission nominates and, with the consent of the president of Liberia, appoints legal counsels and research officers who serve at the pleasure of the commission. Other employees of the Legal Section are appointed by the commission on the basis of their civil service qualifications and serve at the pleasure of the commission.

The commission appoints within each county or district as many magistrates of elections as necessary, as well as local district workers who are usually recommended by the district magistrate. The Board of Commissioners appoints the supporting staff of the central office.

Financing

The NEC submits an annual budget to Liberia's Budget Bureau for consideration and approval. Upon approval of the budget, funds are paid in a timely manner, according to the planned expenditure, into an account established by the NEC. International donor support was critical in both the 2005 and 2011 national elections, although less so during the 2011 elections. While the NEC has not published its 2011 elections report, the estimated 2010–11 budget was over USD 38 million, of which over USD 27 million (70 per cent) came from international donors.[6]

During the 2010–11 electoral cycle, funds from gender mainstreaming projects were intermittently redirected to processes regarded as more critical to the success of the national elections, such as voter registration, poll worker training and technology acquisitions.

Accountability

The NEC is required to publish an annual updated strategy, together with an annual plan and the funding provision for that year, as agreed with the Budget Bureau. It is also required to submit annual reports to the National Legislature and the president of Liberia on its general operations.

The commission is also required to publish an annual report and an externally audited set of accounts related to its achievements and activities compared to the annual plan. The report must reflect sources and usage of Liberian government and external funds and other resources.

Electoral Justice Processes

Challenges and complaints are assessed, investigated and determined according to regulations and procedures issued by the NEC. Critical issues are heard by a chief hearing officer in Monrovia, who makes recommendations to the NEC's Board of Commissioners. Other issues are investigated, heard and determined by the magistrate, who is assisted by a local hearing officer. An NEC or magistrate decision is published on the premises of the NEC or the magistrate's office, respectively. A magistrate's decision can be appealed to the NEC Board of Commissioners within 72 hours.

A determination by the NEC Board of Commissioners on a complaint can be appealed to the Supreme Court of Liberia no later than 48 hours after the determination is issued. After the final results are announced, complaints may be filed with the NEC; NEC decisions may be appealed to the Supreme Court. The judiciary hears and adjudicates any complaint cases against the electoral process that have been appealed to the Supreme Court.[7]

Professional Capacity Development Training

Through continuous training, electoral officers are typically well versed in the conduct of their duties, with the exception of the gender sensitivity component (discussed below).

Media Relationship

The media operates under the Press Union of Liberia (PUL) Code of Conduct for elections coverage. Liberian journalists continue to work with the NEC and its partners by engaging in capacity-building workshops.[8] The only specific provision regarding the NEC's media access during election campaign periods is Article 10.21 of the Election Law, which states, 'Political parties are also privileged to use, and shall not be denied the right to use any public building or such facilities necessary and appropriate for their purpose', as long as a 'timely request' is made.[9] The NEC has no direct ability to regulate political parties' free access to publicly owned media.

Relationship with Other Institutions and Agencies

The NEC deals extensively with stakeholders in the electoral process through its liaison officers, including political parties and candidates, executive government entities, the legislature, the judicial system, election monitors and citizen and international election observers, the media, the electorate, non-governmental and community organizations, and donor and electoral assistance agencies. The NEC fosters numerous partnerships, agreements and understandings that are critical to the successful conduct of elections, including training and information dissemination workshops, codes of conduct and memoranda of understanding.

During election exercises, the relationship between the NEC and political parties and the media has become strained on a number of occasions due to perceived biases in the commission's conduct. The NEC chairperson resigned in October 2011 following intense pressure from the main opposition party over the chairperson's alleged partiality to the incumbent candidate.

EMB Sustainability

Financial and logistical support remains a critical challenge to the successful operation of the commission, including staff capacity building and civic education.

New Technologies

The central and satellite structures of the NEC include both a technology and a telecommunications division. The technology division normally operates with a skeletal team that is augmented during the election phase.

Technologies such as solar panels for remote power supplies, satellite dishes for data transmission and mobile phones were critical in the 2011 elections to ensure the timely reporting of election results.

Opportunities and Constraints

The NEC's structure facilitates the successful conduct of national elections and the maintenance of political (and thereby social and economic) stability based on the public's (and parties') perception of its trustworthiness. The Carter Center states that 'Throughout the 2011 elections, the NEC demonstrated its technical competence and effectiveness administering credible elections that met international standards.'[10] Nevertheless, electoral reform to address flaws that resulted in major disputes, continuous and consistent training of NEC staff, and disseminating information to the general and voting public as well as political parties, media and other stakeholders are essential to sustaining the current achievements.

Gender

The NEC formally instituted its gender mainstreaming efforts with the creation of a Gender Office in 2010. Because this coincided with the height of the electoral cycle, the commission's efforts were focused externally on increasing female participation in all aspects of the elections—particularly candidacy, registration and voting.

During the 2011 national electoral cycle, the work culture of the NEC was still heavily male dominated at all levels of the organization, with the exception of the Board of Commissioners. A breakdown of NEC staff showed that the Board of Commissioners was 47 per cent female (three out of seven), and the executive and deputy executive directors (five members) included no females. Of the 14 directors, two were females (14 per cent), and women constituted 27 per cent (21 out of 78) of officers and supervisors and 11 per cent (27 out of 239) of non-officers.[11] Data on poll workers was not disaggregated by sex.

As of December 2013, the NEC does not have a formal gender policy. However, a draft gender policy has been crafted and is under review by the commission's board of directors. The draft policy proposes to:

1. strengthen the NEC's organizational capacity to address gender inequalities and promote the empowerment of women in electoral processes;
2. establish institutional practices and policies that promote gender equality and women's empowerment in the workplace; and
3. develop programming to promote gender equality and the empowerment of women in all areas of the electoral process.

Operational planning for the 2011 elections discounted the unique needs of women working in the field. For example, a number of locations where female staff worked during election exercises (registration, polling) were not equipped with adequate toilets.

The NEC's leadership demonstrated an extensive commitment to promoting gender equality in the conduct of its external elections operations. Modest budgetary and logistical assistance was extended to support various projects to promote the equal participation of women and men in the election despite the stiff competition with other elections processes for resources. In just over a year, the Gender Office conducted at least five major exercises advancing gender equality, in addition to information campaigns, capacity-building training for potential candidates and Gender Office staff, and consultations with other stakeholders, such as the media and political parties, which heavily influenced the level of female participation in electoral exercises.

Through the Gender Office programmes, the NEC developed and deployed various materials to promote gender sensitivity and equality, including the use of billboards, flyers, t-shirts, and radio and TV jingles and specials.

Up to 2011, only the Gender Office staff were actively and continuously trained in gender mainstreaming principles, including BRIDGE Gender and Elections training and UNDP Transformative and Gender-sensitive Elections Management workshops, although proposals for organization-wide training were repeatedly submitted. Due to ongoing election activities (voter registration, referendum, polling), gender mainstreaming training for NEC staff in general was assigned non-priority status.

At a certain point during the 2010–11 electoral cycle, magistrates were required to record the male-female ratio of registrants and voters. However, no such data is recorded for temporary NEC staff at polling centres. Regardless, the data collected was not used to account for gender mainstreaming in the organization's operational planning.

The NEC Gender Office engaged in several information dissemination campaigns and consultations and workshops with political parties and CSOs to enhance women's political participation in the 2010–11 electoral process, including:

- NEC–International IDEA media conference with political parties on gender equality in political parties' nominations;
- NEC–International IDEA radio drama series project for the 2011 national elections in Liberia;
- NEC–ECOWAS project with CSOs on a gender-sensitive awareness campaign for the 2011 national elections in Liberia;
- NEC–International IDEA briefing with CSOs on a gender-sensitive awareness campaign for the 2011 national elections in Liberia;
- NEC one-day women's consolidation forum in preparation for the 2011 electoral process, particularly the voter registration exercise; and
- Campaign tour of three counties by the NEC Gender Office to augment women's political participation in the 2011 referendum and electoral process.

The NEC strongly supported the introduction of a gender quota bill to Liberia's national legislature in May 2011. The NEC Gender Office supported women's civil society and community organizations by joining demonstrations on the senate grounds and observing the senate floor during the introduction of the bill. The bill and its modified successor were both struck down in the senate, without ever reaching the House of Representatives. Without a gender quota law, the NEC faces the usual challenges of implementing voluntary quotas and the objections it invites tokenism and discriminates against men.

Notes

1. Republic of Liberia, *New Elections Law* (September 1986, updated 2003, 2004).
2. National Constitution Committee, *Constitution of the Republic of Liberia* (Monrovia: Republic of Liberia, 1986).
3. The Carter Center, *National Elections in Liberia Final Report*, 2011.
4. New Elections Law, Section 2.9: Powers and Duties.
5. Ibid.
6. UNDP Liberia, *Project Document Support to the 2010–2012 Liberian Electoral Cycle*, (Monrovia: UNDP, 2010).
7. International Foundation for Electoral Systems, *Elections in Liberia 8 November Presidential Run-off Election Frequently Asked Questions* (Monrovia: IFES, 2011).
8. NEC website, available at <http://www.necliberia.org/other.php?&7d5f44532cbfc489b8db9e12e44eb820=NTI0>, accessed 31 October 2013.
9. Republic of Liberia, *New Elections Law*, S. 10.21: Freedom of Travel Throughout the Country and the Use of Public Facilities by Political Parties (September 1986, updated 2003, 2004).
10. Carter Center 2011.
11. Data collected from NEC Human Resource Office, May 2011.

CASE STUDY

Timor-Leste: Election Administration

Michael Maley

The people of Timor-Leste, in a plebiscite dubbed (for diplomatic reasons) a 'popular consultation', voted in 1999 by an overwhelming margin for the restoration of their country's independence after almost 24 years of occupation by Indonesia. Since then, they have gone to the polls ten more times: in 2001 to elect a Constituent Assembly (which subsequently adopted a constitution and became the nation's first National Parliament); in 2002 to elect a president; in 2004–05 and 2009 to elect local representative bodies; and three times each in 2007 and 2012, to vote for a president in a first-round poll and a subsequent run-off, and to choose a new National Parliament.

Timorese involvement in the organization and conduct of the popular consultation was very limited. International staff of the UN Mission in Timor-Leste, including UN volunteers, occupied all senior positions of responsibility, and local staff served only as language assistants and polling officials under close supervision. For most of the period between the popular consultation and the restoration of independence in May 2002, Timor-Leste was under UN transitional administration. In March 2001, the transitional administrator created by regulation an Independent Electoral Commission (IEC), which ultimately conducted the 2001 and 2002 elections. In that body, Timorese officials played a much more prominent role—including as members of the Board of Commissioners—and by the time it had run a second election, it was a relatively well-consolidated institution. However, in a move that can with the benefit of hindsight be questioned, the transitional administrator abolished the IEC when his mandate was about to expire and replaced it with an identically named but much smaller body that had only a limited advisory role.

Subsequent Timorese government decisions on the future shape of election administration were significantly shaped by article 65, no. 6 of the country's constitution, which states that 'Supervision of voters' registration and electoral acts shall be incumbent upon an independent organ, the competences, composition, organization and functioning of which shall be established by law.'

Implicit in this notion of 'supervision' was that the country would adopt a mixed model of electoral management with two electoral bodies: one that organized and conducted elections, and one that supervised the process. The first of those bodies, the Technical Secretariat for Electoral Administration (*Secretariado Técnico de Administração Eleitoral*, STAE), was created by government decree in July 2003 as an organ of the Ministry of State Administration, replacing, but also incorporating the staff of, the advisory IEC left behind by the UN. Two separate supervisory bodies, each designated the National Elections Commission (*Comissão Nacional De Eleições*, CNE), have been created. The first was set up only for the purposes of the local representative elections of 2004–05, and was disbanded after fulfilling its mandate. The second, and permanent, CNE was appointed in early 2007.

While STAE and CNE are the primary EMBs, the Court of Appeal (pending the appointment of a Supreme Court of Justice) has a number of electoral roles to play, especially in relation to the registration of political parties, the receipt and validation of presidential nominations, and the final certification of election results.

The Legislative Framework

The primary document governing the operations of STAE and CNE is Law No. 5/2006 of 28 December 2006, entitled Electoral Administration Bodies (to which a number of amendments were made by Law No. 6/2011 of 22 June 2011). This formally established both organizations, and specifies their powers and functions in detail.

The law defines CNE as being independent from any bodies of central or local political power, and as enjoying financial, administrative and organizational autonomy. It defines STAE as 'a service of indirect state administration (Administração Indirecta do Estado), under the aegis of and supervised by the government, with its own budget and enjoying technical and administrative autonomy', but also states explicitly that 'Decisions made and procedures undertaken by STAE relating to operations of voter registration, elections and referendums shall be supervised by CNE.'

STAE's functions and methods of operation are further addressed in Decree Law No. 01/2007 of 18 January 2007, entitled the Organic Statute of the Technical Secretariat of Electoral Administration, which, among other things, makes STAE subject to the authority and oversight of the Minister of State Administration, and confers a wide range of powers on the minister. These include: defining STAE's strategic and policy guidelines; approving its budget, management reports, accounts, financial plans, internal regulations and staffing; and appointing and dismissing members of STAE bodies.

Separate laws dealing specifically with the election of the president and the National Parliament also detailed further duties, powers and functions of the CNE and STAE.

Composition and Appointment

CNE consists of 15 commissioners:

- three appointed by the president of the republic;
- three elected by the National Parliament;

- three appointed by the government;
- one judicial magistrate, one public prosecution magistrate and one public defender, each elected by his or her peers;
- one nominee of the Catholic Church;
- one nominee of the remaining religious faiths; and
- one representative of women's organizations.

Commissioners are appointed for a six-year term, which may only be renewed once. The director-general of STAE is entitled to participate in CNE meetings, though without voting rights.

Institutional Structures

CNE has a president chosen by the commissioners from within their own ranks, and has sub-commissions on political parties and candidacies, voter registration and the registration database, civic education, legal affairs and litigation, and public relations and liaison. The commission's work is supported by a secretariat based in Dili, headed by a director-general, which includes key functional areas such as planning, administration, finance, information technology, communications, documentation and legal support. CNE also has field staff located in each of the 13 districts.

STAE is also headed by a director-general, and has around 120 staff, the majority of whom are located in district offices. Key functional areas of STAE cover training, electoral education, information technology, voter database management, finance and logistics. Additional STAE staff are recruited to serve at election time.

Powers and Functions

CNE's legislated functions include:
- supervising the electoral process;
- ensuring the enforcement of related constitutional and legal provisions;
- approving regulations for which legal provision is made, as well as codes of conduct for candidates, observers, monitors and media professionals;
- promoting information about the electoral process through the media;
- ensuring equality of treatment for citizens in voter registration and electoral operations;
- ensuring equality of opportunities and freedom of campaign propaganda for the candidates during the electoral campaign;
- notifying the Office of the Public Prosecution about suspected electoral offences;
- preparing and submitting to the Court of Appeal provisional documents setting out national election results, so that the final results of the general elections can be validated and proclaimed; and
- verifying the STAE database of registered voters.

STAE's legislated functions include:

- carrying out the actions needed to complete electoral processes, referendums and electoral register updates in a timely manner;
- proposing appropriate clarifying, educational and informative measures for citizen involvement in electoral processes, referendums and electoral registration;
- planning, carrying out and providing technical support for elections, referendums and electoral register updates, both nationally and locally, through cooperation with existing administrative structures;
- compiling and publishing statistics involving the electoral register, electoral processes and referendums;
- supporting and cooperating with CNE; and
- organizing and updating the electoral register, under CNE's supervision, by proposing and carrying out technical procedures and organizing, maintaining and managing the central database of registered voters.

Neither CNE nor STAE is mandated to register political parties (which is a function of the Court of Appeal), set election dates (that is done by the president of the republic) or engage in boundary delimitation (all elections in Timor-Leste thus far have been held either on a nationwide basis or using pre-existing administrative boundaries).

There is a degree of overlap and ambiguity in the functions of CNE and STAE, which has made their ongoing relationship challenging in a number of ways. A lack of clarity in legal provisions relating to the development of regulations led to a significant disagreement in the run-up to the 2007 elections, which was only resolved when CNE sent regulations directly to the Official Gazette, insisting that they be published. There have, indeed, been times when the STAE and CNE have appeared to be working competitively rather than cooperatively. Most of these sorts of challenges have, however, been resolved over time through the adoption of mechanisms that, if not ideal, have at least proven to be workable.

Finances and Accountability

STAE and CNE are both funded from the state budget. For 2012, CNE received a budget allocation of USD 5,85 million, USD 3 million of which was to fund the political parties represented in the National Parliament. STAE was allocated USD 8 million to cover the costs of the presidential and parliamentary elections. Neither of these amounts included the normal administrative expenses for both institutions.

STAE and CNE have also benefited from programmes funded by donors and the UN, which they might otherwise have had to forgo or fund themselves. Generally speaking, both organizations have been relatively well resourced, and Timor-Leste has more electoral officers per capita than many comparable countries.

CNE, though independent, is required to be accountable by filing an annual report with the National Parliament. For its part, STAE has faced the difficulty, in performing its functions, of being accountable (in some sense) to both CNE and to a minister.

Professionalism of Electoral Officers

The core staff of both CNE and STAE are, in general, relatively experienced, professionally competent and politically neutral. Most of the senior staff of STAE were originally selected by the UN to work with the IEC in 2001–02. While so employed, they benefited from a substantial capacity-building programme jointly implemented by the IEC and the Australian Electoral Commission, based on the earliest version of what became the internationally recognized BRIDGE curriculum. Throughout its history, STAE has actively encouraged and prioritized staff development, not least through the fostering of contacts with other EMBs, including those of Australia, Portugal and Indonesia. STAE staff have also frequently taken part in election observation, workshops and network meetings outside Timor-Leste.

CNE, though a younger organization, has also given priority to staff development. It has benefited from the relative stability of its membership since 2007, and from the fact that a number of the commissioners served on the first CNE in 2004–05. CNE has also displayed a good degree of professional unity, which is no mean achievement in an organization designed to draw people from a range of different backgrounds.

Both bodies have benefited greatly from support from the UN, bilateral donors, and other EMBs in the region and in the wider Lusophone community.

Relations with the Media and Other Institutions

CNE and STAE have generally managed to maintain relatively transparent relationships with the media and with a range of other institutions. Except in relation to electoral offences and CNE's promulgation of codes of conduct for the media, they are not explicitly empowered to engage in media regulation. Both organizations actively publish useful material, including on their websites. They also appear to have earned a relatively high degree of public trust, and there has been little significant public questioning of their neutrality or effectiveness. A nationwide opinion poll commissioned by the International Republican Institute and conducted in November/December 2008 found that 80 per cent of those surveyed judged STAE to be doing either a 'good' or 'very good' job.

The Future

The prospects of well-sustained election administration in Timor-Leste look promising. Successive governments have shown a willingness to invest in the development of the country's EMBs, and the major growth in the state budget flowing from oil and gas revenues suggests that the required resources will be available for the foreseeable future. STAE and CNE have demonstrated sound judgement in the selection of workable technologies, and the STAE voter registration database, and voter registration more generally, have been perceived as credible and effective. STAE and CNE have also been greatly helped in their work by the fact that political elites and the broader population are mainly respectful and supportive of proper electoral processes.

As is the case in most countries, it is inevitable that a rapidly changing electoral environment worldwide will pose challenges for Timor-Leste's EMBs. An attempt to introduce out-of-country voting for the 2012 elections had to be abandoned on the grounds of administrative difficulty, but the demand for such a service is unlikely to go away. The skill base now present within the CNE and STAE should enable them to analyse such proposals effectively, and advise the National Parliament professionally.

The greatest challenge that CNE and STAE may have to face in the future is likely to flow from the peculiarity of the Mixed Model of administration, which seeks to reconcile a need for cooperation with the institutionalization of an intrinsically conflictual relationship. This was a real concern in 2007 and appears to have been ameliorated with the passage of time, but could at some point become a problem again.

CHAPTER 7

The Financing of EMBs

Common EMB Financing Issues

The funding of elections may appear to be costly, and has to compete with vital national services such as defence, health and education, which may yield greater immediate political returns. Inadequate or untimely funding of electoral processes may occur because governments are not able to appropriate sufficient funds or ensure the timely disbursement of approved funds.

EMB funding needs are dependent on the electoral cycle and will vary hugely between election and non-election years. Other significant factors include the range of functions and responsibilities, the model of electoral management used, the electoral procedures in place and the frequency of elections. EMBs have been regularly accused of procuring expensive goods and services, such as high-technology equipment, which is not put to effective use. Some EMBs have also been accused of printing more ballot materials and recruiting more election staff than necessary. The independence of some models of EMBs from the executive branch of government may lead to perceptions that they are not subject to the controls on spending that are applied to government agencies.

Many EMBs, such as those in Afghanistan, Cambodia, Haiti, Indonesia, Iraq and Liberia have relied on international donors for substantial amounts of budgetary support, as well as technical assistance. Apart from the sustainability issues raised (see Chapter 11 of this Handbook), the conflicting conditions that different donor agencies impose on EMBs, combined with the requirements from their own governments, may make it difficult for them to account properly and within a reasonable time for their funding.

EMBs have had to deal with the question of whether and how to fund new technologies, particularly for voter registration, voting and vote counting, such as electronic voting. The increased emphasis on access issues—such as the provision of mobile polling stations, facilities for absentee voting (within or outside the country), facilities for voters with disabilities and multilingual electoral information—has also had financing implications. In many established democracies, government policies of slimming down public sectors have reduced the certainty of funding for EMBs, particularly for staff costs.

What Electoral Costs Need to be Financed?

Electoral finance refers to the electoral budget or the costs that a country incurs as a result of the various activities undertaken by EMBs and other agencies to organize and conduct an electoral process. Some electoral costs may be easily identifiable EMB costs, while others may be difficult to quantify because they are contained within the general services budgets of other government agencies. Electoral cost comparisons between countries have proved difficult, largely because different items can be identified and quantified as electoral costs in different electoral environments using different models of electoral management. The UNDP and IFES-sponsored Cost of Registration and Elections (CORE) Project divides electoral costs into three categories:

1. *core costs* (or direct costs): routinely associated with implementing an electoral process in a stable electoral environment;

2. *diffuse costs* (or indirect costs): electoral-related services that cannot be disentangled from the general budgets of agencies that help implement an electoral process; and

3. *integrity costs:* over and above the core costs, which are necessary to provide safety, integrity, political neutrality and a level playing field for an electoral process.

In transitional and developing democracies, integrity costs are often largely sponsored outside EMBs, mainly by the donor community: for example, the sophisticated, internationally-funded electoral register data processing and production activities in the transitional elections of Afghanistan and Iraq. Such additional costs may not be included in analyses of EMB budgets, although they relate to functions within EMB mandates. According to the CORE Project, core costs are proportionally highest in stable democracies, as progress toward democratic consolidation tends to lead to a decrease in integrity costs and an increase in core costs. The increase in core costs results from demands for increased participation to be fostered through more widely accessible electoral operations, and from the use of technology to expedite voter registration, voting and the transmission of election results.

The CORE Project further shows that diffuse costs tend to be higher in stable democracies, especially in Western Europe, where electoral processes are more likely to be implemented by governmental EMBs under the Governmental or Mixed Model, and where several government agencies may be used to implement electoral services. Where, for example, a national civil registration agency is responsible for providing electoral register data, as in Hungary and Norway, it incurs costs related to electoral events that may be difficult to separate from overall civil registration costs. Even where governments have a policy of cost recovery for governmental agency electoral services, the true cost may not be charged.

EMBs under the Independent Model are more likely to have sole responsibility for electoral functions, and thus have a higher level of readily identifiable direct costs and a lower level of diffuse costs than EMBs under the Governmental or Mixed Models. A higher level of readily identifiable costs may give a false impression of higher actual costs.

Table 13: Attributes and Examples of Electoral Core, Diffuse and Integrity Costs

	Core Costs	**Diffuse Costs**	**Integrity Costs**
Attributes	• Covers the basic costs of electoral tasks. • Usually identifiable in the budget of the EMB or other authorities responsible for electoral tasks. • May be difficult to quantify and amalgamate if split between several agencies.	• Costs of support services for electoral events provided by other agencies. • May not be possible to separate election-related costs. • May be difficult to quantify, as often contained within the general budgets of several agencies.	• Additional costs to ensure the integrity of fragile electoral processes. • Usually identifiable in the budget of EMBs or other authorities responsible for electoral tasks. • May be difficult to quantify if split between several agencies. • Particularly relevant in post-conflict or emerging democracies.
Examples	• Basic costs of voter registration, voter information, printing of ballot papers, voting, counting, and transmission of results.	• Security services provided by police. • Voter data provided by civil registration agencies. • Logistical support by governments, such as provision of transport or premises. • Statistical IT system services. • Salaries for teachers seconded as polling officials.	• High-integrity voting security measures such as the use of indelible ink and tamper-proof containers, external processing of electoral registers, and special security paper for printing ballot papers. • Election-related costs of international peacekeeping missions. • Political equity costs such as funding of party campaigns, media monitoring.

Electoral Management Design

Who Finances EMBs and How?

State or Public Funding

Electoral events are a core function of a democratic state. The state thus remains the primary source of funding for the core costs of most EMBs. The electoral budget forms part of the consolidated annual national budget, yet different models of EMBs may receive their funding by different methods and routes from the budget.

Method of Disbursing State Funding

Funding for many EMBs under the Independent Model, for example in Albania, Ghana and Kosovo, is a separate line item in the national budget, released directly to the EMB by the treasury. For others, the EMB budget is released through a government ministry.

Budgets for EMBs under the Governmental Model are usually part of the budget of the government ministry responsible for implementing electoral processes, as in Cook Islands, Denmark and Singapore. Where the Mixed Model is used, the budget of the component independent EMB may be channelled through a line ministry, such as the Ministry of the Interior in France.

Integrated or Distributed Electoral Budgets

An electoral budget may be a single integrated item in the national budget, or may consist of many components that are spread across the budgets of various government agencies. National, regional and local governments' budgets may each provide funds to EMBs. In the unitary state of Indonesia, the national budget fully funds the EMB to conduct presidential elections and elections to national and regional legislatures, but regional and local authorities provide most of the funding for elections for provincial governors and local mayors. Such arrangements are more common in federal states. Funding for the EMB in Bosnia and Herzegovina is provided by all four levels of government; their respective shares vary according to the type of elections being held. In India and Mexico, the national government funds the EMB to conduct national elections, but regional governments contribute funds when their elections coincide with national ones. In the UK, the costs of elections are funded by local authorities and reimbursed by the central government according to fixed scales.

Donor Funding

Some countries emerging from conflict have relied on donor assistance, through the UN or other agencies, to fund the whole or a significant part of their electoral budget. Examples include Cambodia (1993), Mozambique (1994), Bosnia and Herzegovina (1996), Timor-Leste (2000), Sierra Leone (2002), Afghanistan (2004), Iraq (2005) and Palestine (2005–06). In post-conflict elections, donor assistance can be essential, especially if a breakdown of state institutions has destroyed their ability to collect revenue.

Donor assistance from the UN, the European Commission, the United States Agency for International Development (USAID) and other sources has made a significant contribution to funding electoral processes in many other countries. There is a growing pattern of regional donor assistance. For example, South Africa and other SADC countries offer electoral support to EMBs of other SADC member countries, and the OAS has provided regional assistance in countries such as Haiti.

In emerging democracies such as Libya, assistance may be necessary to implement electoral processes that meet international obligations. Assistance may also be necessary to allow fledgling opposition parties to contest elections in a comparatively competitive manner. In countries wishing to upgrade their electoral services, such as Papua New Guinea, general institutional capacities and awareness may not be sufficiently developed to deal with the 'intangibles' in electoral costs—such as training and education. Even in relatively consolidated democracies, flagship projects in fields such as data processing and communications may require donor assistance. Some emerging democracies rely heavily on foreign donor assistance to fund their core election budget. The resulting sustainability issues are examined in Chapter 11 of this Handbook.

The availability of donor funding will be affected by donor funding cycles, which may be difficult to coordinate with the timing of EMB needs. Donor assistance is usually channelled either directly to the EMB or through a government ministry. Channelling it directly to the EMB facilitates easier disbursement and provides a direct line of accountability. In Cambodia, the EMB has a dedicated account in the National Treasury established for electoral management funding from all sources. Different accounting requirements from multiple donors may complicate the EMB's financial reporting mechanisms. Yet, exposure to these different requirements can encourage EMBs to review and improve their own financial accountability systems.

Control of donor funds can be a contentious issue. Channelling donor funds through government ministries may lead to delays or diversions in the disbursement of funds due to government bureaucracy or corruption, but host countries may insist on this to ensure that *their* funding priorities, rather than those of the donor, are followed. Steering committee mechanisms—involving representatives of all donors, the EMB and possibly the government—can be an effective solution, and can prevent duplication of funding. Formal or informal use of an agency such as the UNDP to coordinate all donor funding for an EMB can also be effective. In Indonesia in 2004, a significant proportion of multiple donors' electoral assistance funds was disbursed through a UNDP trust fund under priorities established by the EMB.

EMBs need to be careful that donor assistance meets their priorities and is not driven by the interests of consultants provided by the donors or by equipment providers from the donor country. Technical assistance provided by donors needs to include training and skills transfer to EMB counterpart staff so that the EMB can assume full ownership of future electoral processes. Donors may prefer to directly contract suppliers of products or services for an EMB, but this can raise public questions about foreign interference. Donors may also require that systems, equipment and other tangible items they provide be purchased from their home country suppliers. Yet experience shows that externally driven equipment solutions, such as the choice of equipment for voter registration in Timor-Leste in 2000, may be inappropriate for the local environment.

Table 14: Some Key Advantages and Disadvantages of International Donor Funding for Electoral Processes

Advantages	Disadvantages
• May be necessary to ensure that an electoral event is held.	• May create dependence on foreign funding of electoral processes.
• Donor-funded technical assistance can raise electoral administration standards.	• May lead to the introduction of costly and unsustainable electoral practices.
• Assistance with implementing international standards can enhance the freedom and fairness of electoral processes.	• Unless carefully coordinated, can lead to duplication of funding.
• Skills transfer from technical assistance can create sustainable improvements in electoral processes.	• May concentrate on high-profile activities to the detriment of essential ones.
• Coordinated donor assistance can plug critical gaps in an EMB's budget.	• May not ensure that sufficient funding is received in time.
• Funding may assist an EMB to improve its service and credibility by acquiring appropriate technology.	• Ineffective or inappropriate externally driven technical solutions may be imposed on an EMB.
• May encourage EMBs to improve their budgeting and accounting processes.	• May be difficult to implement different accounting mechanisms required by multiple donors.

Other Sources of EMB Funding

Some EMBs receive income in the form of nomination fees, lost deposits, or fines imposed following breaches of electoral campaigning or other regulations. It is important that this income is fully and transparently accounted for.

EMBs may also receive funds and donations in kind from large corporations, the business community and philanthropists. EMBs need to be careful that the manner of raising funds from the corporate sector does not affect perceptions of their financial probity, impartiality or credibility.

Some EMBs, as in Australia, raise some funds through the administration of elections on behalf of bodies such as professional associations or trade unions. Others, as in Mauritius, charge a fee to recover the costs of printing copies of the electoral register that are distributed to political parties.

Budget Formulation Methods for EMBs

For permanent EMBs there are two distinct types of budgets: one for ongoing costs and one for events such as a voting registration update, a voter education campaign and an election. Different approaches may be taken to formulate the two types of budgets. An EMB's approach to budgeting tends to reflect that of the public sector in its country, especially if it is bound by general public sector financial rules.

All budget processes are, ideally, linked to the goals and projects identified in the EMB's strategic plan and related activity plan for the coming years. This linkage encourages a 'programme' or 'performance' approach to budgets, whereby EMB activities are separately costed and budgets are linked to specific output targets and objectives, as is done by the Australian EMB. Thus instead of having EMB-wide, generic budget categories such as staffing, forms printing, transport, security, regional office costs—which makes it difficult to determine the cost of any EMB service or product—relevant costs are budgeted and attributed to a specific programme or project, such as ballot paper printing and distribution, staff training, or information programmes for political parties.

Basing budgeting on the strategic plan greatly improves an EMB's accountability for its use of public and other funds, and helps it focus on delivering cost-effective services. It requires all divisions within the EMB to have individual work plans that are tailored to its strategic goals, which identify the required outcomes, contain performance objectives based on measurable output targets and specify verifiable indicators that these targets are being achieved. Each work plan aims to achieve a particular objective that contributes to the EMB's overall strategic goals, and has a specific budget structure. Linking the budget to the strategic plan in this way makes it easier to determine how effectively funds have been expended to reach each objective, and to determine where and to what extent funding requests may be cut, or need to be increased.

Within both the ongoing and election event budgets there will be many layers of detail. The budget submitted for approval often contains high levels of amalgamation; one figure will be provided for an entire functional area, such as political party registration or voter education. For internal purposes more detail will be provided, for instance showing the costs of people, office costs and materials within the budget for the functional area.

Different approaches may be taken to create these different budget levels. For instance, the EMB may be told by the finance ministry or parliament that the total budget for ongoing costs will be the same as the previous year, or will only rise in line with inflation (known as the incremental or baseline budget model). In such cases, the EMB then has to assess detailed costs related to the goals in the strategic plan and make choices that fit within the budget. In times of austerity, all state-funded bodies may be told that their budget will be cut by a certain percentage; again, the EMB has to choose between items in the strategic plan. In many stable democracies, the budget for an event such as a voter registration update or an election is calculated incrementally by increasing the previous budget to allow for inflation, and in some cases population growth. Again, the EMB then has to decide how to manage the event within that total budget while meeting goals from the strategic plan and accommodating rising costs.

An alternative budget-setting approach is the zero-base(d) model, in which each cost for an election, or election-related project, is estimated to find the total budget needed. A planning and finance section of the EMB secretariat may be responsible for these calculations, or it may be the task of each division to estimate the cost of performing its assigned tasks in the coming year. Costs for each area will then be checked for accuracy and justification against the strategic plan.

While the component costs of the previous year's work or the previous elections are often used to assist in this process, each component of the budget has to be assessed and justified in the current context. This approach is often used when there have been major changes since the previous election, or if major changes are proposed, such as the use of voting machines or a change in the electoral system. EMBs are rarely given an open money chest, and so will still have to make choices within the set budget once spending starts and actual costs are higher than estimated costs, or if unexpected costs arise. When donor funding is project based, then the budgets are often created using this model.

Budget Formulation and Approval Process

In Algeria, Botswana, Iceland, Lesotho, Niue and Tonga, the legislature determines the EMB's budget as part of the annual budget process, using past expenses and reports as the basis for setting the funding level. In the Philippines, the Department of Budget and Management determines the budget for public bodies.

It is common for EMBs to create their own budget and then submit it for approval. In some cases the budget goes to the government for approval (for instance Angola, Burkina Faso, Cameroon and Chad), while it more commonly goes to the legislature for approval (for instance Bolivia, Brazil, Gambia, Guam, Guyana, Mexico, Mongolia, Pakistan and Venezuela). The budget creation and approval process may include discussion with the finance ministry. For instance in South Korea, the EMB creates the budget, which is then adjusted by the Ministry of Planning and Budget and considered for approval by the legislature. In some countries, such as Costa Rica, the legislature has no power to alter or reject any part of the proposed EMB budget (see the case study on page 93). In other countries, only specified parts of the EMB's proposed budget (e.g. dealing with members' salaries and allowances) cannot be altered by the executive or its agencies.

In some countries, the EMB budget has two parts: the recurrent budget, which covers costs such as permanent staff and related material support; and the elections budget, which covers additional expenses directly related to an election or referendum. The recurrent budget may be altered by the government, while the elections budget may not. The EMB provides an annual estimate of its elections budget to the government, but is allowed to spend more than this estimate. Following the election, the EMB accounts for these expenditures to a legislative committee. Such dual budgets are used in Cameroon, Georgia, Liberia, Madagascar and Rwanda.

Availability of Budget Funds

In many countries the treasury releases funds to the EMB in a lump sum after legislative approval has been secured, or at the start of each financial year, as in Senegal. This applies where the EMB has autonomy over its finances, and often its own bank account, as in Gambia. In some cases, EMB funds are kept and managed by the Ministry of Finance, and the EMB makes requisitions for the ministry to pay its creditors and staff, mainly by cheque. The EMB budget is charged directly to the Consolidated Fund in some countries, for example Bhutan, Ghana, Sierra Leone, Solomon Islands, Tanzania, Uganda and Zambia, but there may be significant legal and administrative barriers to be dealt with before such an approach can be implemented in other countries. For governmental EMBs under the Governmental or Mixed Models, funds for electoral processes may be released to the host ministry and disbursed through that ministry, or directly through the treasury's bank accounts.

Control of EMB Funding

During an election, availability of funds is vital so that temporary staff can be paid and logistics are not hampered. It is not feasible to delay election day because the money to pay local staff has not been transferred to divisional banks. While it is common to have a delay of several months in settling bills, many election costs need to be covered before election day. Therefore, making sure funds are available during this crucial time must be considered as part of the logistical planning for the election. Emerging democracies often fail to fund major election processes in an adequate and timely manner. Where EMB expenditure processes and cash flow are controlled by a government ministry and subject to government rules and procedures, there may be delays in disbursing critical funds.

Delayed disbursement of funds to an EMB can create major problems in electoral administration. It can delay decisions or leave insufficient time for the EMB to use high-probity tender processes or organize the supply of acceptable quality goods for electoral purposes. Late payment to suppliers can cause disruptions to supply in the time-critical election environment. Late payments to staff, as has happened in Papua New Guinea, can also threaten electoral processes. It may be to the advantage of both an EMB and the government to agree on a memorandum of understanding regarding funding disbursement arrangements.

If a ministry controls EMB payments, the EMB may be perceived as controlled by the government, which can threaten its credibility. Even where an EMB is constitutionally independent of the government, linking it to the government financial payments system can limit its autonomy.

Giving EMBs control of their own payments procedures and systems enhances their credibility as being independent of the government, and may lead to faster payment processes. However, it also places an additional workload and a significantly greater burden of control on the EMB to ensure that all payments are made correctly, on time and to the highest standards of probity. Before assigning control of payments to an EMB, it must have sufficient resources, skills and control systems in place to manage its own payments. Robust accountability systems—including internal and external audits and reporting to stakeholders, such as a legislative committee—are essential.

EMB Procurement Policies and Procedures

Governmental EMBs under the Governmental and Mixed Models are often bound by government procurement guidelines and practices. EMBs under the Independent Model, and independent EMBs under the Mixed Model, may be bound by governmental procurement requirements (such as those targeted at enhancing probity and effectiveness in procurement), or they may be able to determine some or all of their procurement policies and procedures.

Some EMBs have to use a generic government or public sector purchasing agency for all procurement. In some circumstances, the complexity of purchasing rules means that it is often more effective for the EMB to use such an agency than to undertake this task internally. Where the EMB must use a government-wide purchasing agency, it may obtain post-purchase approval of expenses or have some purchases designated as exempt from purchasing agency rules. However, this practice is generally regarded as incompatible with the principles of good governance and efficiency.

Using government-wide purchasing agencies may not result in effective EMB procurement, as many government bureaucracies are not able to work to the very short and strict timelines that generally confront EMBs in acquiring electoral goods and services. EMBs can thus set up their own internal purchasing boards to manage their procurement independently; this increases an EMB's control over procurement decisions and timing, but makes it accountable for all procurement.

Any public or government criticism of the probity or suitability of EMB procurement decisions can very quickly reflect on the EMB's overall credibility. EMBs need to ensure that their purchasing processes are fully transparent, meet the highest standards of probity, show no favouritism, include a genuinely competitive bidding process, determine the winning bidders on objectively provable grounds and are free from any taint of corruption. Before assigning control of procurement to an EMB, it must have sufficient resources, skills and control systems in place, including an enforceable code of conduct and conflict of interest provisions.

Robust checks and review procedures are required for major procurement decisions, as are control measures that are rigorous enough to withstand the pressures of any fast-tracked purchasing required due to late operational decisions or delayed release of funding. An EMB's procurement procedures may be streamlined with no loss of integrity if it sets up pre-qualification procedures that identify earlier in the electoral cycle those suppliers that meet its specifications for supplying specific goods or services, and who are invited to tender for these before an electoral event. Pre-qualification procedures must, however, be as transparent and strict as the procurement itself. It is good practice to require bidders for contracts to accept the EMB code of conduct.

EMB Financial Control Measures

There are four standard levels of control in EMB financial management: purchase and expenditure approvals processes, internal monitoring, internal review, and external review or evaluation. These controls are necessary to ensure that errors are corrected, and that corrupt or illegal practices are prevented. The basic level of control is of the EMB's procedures for approving purchasing and authorizing expenditures. Approvals of expenditure up to defined financial limits may often be effectively delegated to secretariat staff with appropriate seniority. The important factor is diffusion of control—for example, by requiring transaction approvals from:

- the operational area that requests the financial commitment;
- the finance control area that checks that the commitment is in line with EMB strategic directions and financial policies; and
- the finance disbursement area that authorizes payment for the transaction.

Internal monitoring is conducted by the EMB staff who are responsible for managing its financial resources at all levels. This includes the heads of division, who are responsible for monitoring and reviewing staff performance and managing their divisional budgets. Overall financial monitoring is the responsibility of the division, usually the finance division, that is responsible for managing EMB expenses and financial transactions through accounting records such as general ledgers, journals and suspense accounts. This division also usually controls the entire budget and produces regular financial reports, including cash projections.

Some EMBs have a special members' subcommittee on financial matters, which advises the secretariat on financial issues and may also have the mandate to approve the proposed EMB budget and appoint its external auditors. This can be a wise method of controlling expenditure, although the EMB's work will be hampered if the limit is too low.

The EMB may also have an internal auditor, a member of the secretariat whose objective is to ensure financial regularity and the alignment of the EMB's budget and staff performance with its strategic direction. To maintain the independence of its internal auditing procedure, it usually reports directly to a member of the EMB or the head of the secretariat, rather than through a division of the secretariat. While a primary function of internal audit is to assure the EMB of the accuracy and integrity of its financial management, it can also play a broad internal development and evaluation role within the EMB. It can advise on the audit requirements of various systems, especially those based on new technology, and provide an impetus for change through the reports of internal evaluations of the EMB's operational processes.

The financial control process also includes external audits, which are usually required at least annually, and often after significant electoral events as well. Audits of electoral processes in governmental EMBs under the Governmental Model and component governmental EMBs under the Mixed Model may be part of the external audit of the host department. External audits may be conducted by a government audit agency (if one exists) or by a private contractor, which examines the EMB's financial transactions for the relevant period and reports on whether they were free of irregularities, and also identifies areas of financial management that require improvement.

The final stage of financial control includes public submission, often to the legislature, as in Guyana and Nigeria, of the EMB's election or annual reports and audited financial statements. Accountability mechanisms for EMBs are discussed in detail in Chapter 10.

Asset Management

EMB assets are public property, so the EMB has a responsibility to protect their value by controlling all assets—equipment, materials and other assets such as software—after purchase. Responsibilities for asset management need to be clearly identified in the EMB's structure and staff job descriptions. Donors may also wish to ensure that an EMB has the capacity to manage all assets they provide.

Basic controls on an EMB's assets include placing an EMB identification number on each item, maintaining comprehensive and up-to-date asset registers, ensuring that there are audit trails for transfers of assets, implementing regular inventory of assets, and investigating and enforcing appropriate sanctions if any discrepancies are found. Inventories need to be conducted at least annually. Asset registers need to record all relevant data, including asset name, serial and ID numbers, purchase date and cost, current location and location history, depreciation data, current value, current condition, last inventory date and disposal information.

When purchasing assets, EMBs need to fully understand their life cycle. Timing of asset purchases is critical for ensuring both the efficient use of funds and the availability of assets for electoral events, and needs to consider issues such as production lead times, storage costs and distribution facilities.

Records Management

Archiving of EMB materials is important to protect the institutional history and memory of an EMB, and to ensure that reference materials are available when required. Archiving policies need to include requirements for document security, for the structure and locations of current hard-copy and electronic file records (including electronic file back-up policies), for the preservation of historical records on or off site, and for the timing and manner of disposal of records that are no longer required. Clear archiving, disposal and/or destruction plans for all EMB equipment and materials are necessary, and are especially important to ensure that electoral materials that could be used in future legal proceedings or for research to improve electoral processes are appropriately preserved. Environmentally sound methods of disposing of unwanted assets—for example, the packaging for used registration kits in Cambodia in 1998—are a good practice.

Principles of EMB Financial Management

The requirements for key EMB financial processes—such as budgeting, procurement, expenditure authorizations, financial reporting and auditing—may be contained in law, accounting and financial reporting codes, or in EMB or government regulations. A clear legal framework for managing EMB finances ensures certainty, regularity and consistency, and fosters good governance within the EMB. As well as the legal framework, there are fundamental principles that are the basis of good-practice EMB financial policies and procedures.

Transparency

Financial transparency raises stakeholder and public awareness of the EMB's structures and programmes, financial policies and challenges, and can bolster stakeholders' confidence in the EMB's capacities. Financial transparency also promotes good governance and serves as a strong deterrent to corruption and fraud within the EMB. When there are allegations of bad or dishonest practices, the EMB can better protect its credibility by rigorously exposing such practices, rather than seeking to hide them, including ensuring that whistle-blowers are protected.

Transparency in the preparation, justification and approval of an electoral budget builds public confidence in the EMB's management. Rigorous public scrutiny and legislative accountability give the EMB the opportunity to publicly demonstrate its commitment to financial integrity. It is good practice for the EMB to be transparent in its procurement practices, especially where fast-track methods have to be used to meet electoral deadlines.

Prompt public disclosure of EMBs' financial audits, and of reports on the awarding of procurement contracts, guards against financial irregularity and corruption or patronage in contracting. The most fundamental way an EMB can promote financial transparency is by publishing its annual performance reports, including audited financial statements, and submitting them to the legislature and other stakeholders, including political parties and the general public.

Efficiency and Effectiveness

As a guardian of public funds, the EMB has an obligation to expend these responsibly and to be efficient and effective in managing its financial, human and material resources. An outcome-based approach to the EMB's budgets, regular monitoring of staff performance, and regular auditing of financial records help promote efficiency and effectiveness in the use of its funds, which can enhance public confidence in its management of electoral processes.

Integrity

The commitment of all EMB members and staff to integrity in their conduct is the basis of the organization's integrity. Strong codes of conduct and policies on conflicts of interest promote integrity. Integrity in financial management covers monetary transactions as well as issues such as respect for intellectual property. The development of integrated financial management systems with clear audit trails enables breaches of financial integrity standards to be discovered and reported. A strict regime of sanctions for breaches of integrity requirements, and fearlessness in using them, will enhance public confidence in the EMB.

Chapter Summary

- New technologies and demands for high integrity and widely accessible elections are placing new demands on election funding and reliance on donor funding in some emerging democracies. EMB funding needs vary significantly between years, requiring accurate budget estimations based on resource needs for planned strategic outcomes.
    - The UNDP- and IFES-sponsored CORE Project divides electoral costs into three categories:
        - core (direct) costs: 'normal' directly attributable electoral costs;
        - diffuse (indirect) costs: support costs hidden in budgets of organizations other than the EMB; and
        - integrity costs: additional costs required to secure the integrity of fragile electoral processes.
- Election costs are measured with different levels of comprehensiveness and under different circumstances in various countries, making cost-effectiveness comparisons difficult.
- State budget funding for elections may be from a single source or multiple sources or proposed by the EMB. Funding must in most cases be approved by the legislature and disbursed to the EMB through a government ministry, though this may affect perceptions of the EMB's ability to act independently and in a timely manner.
- Especially in emerging democracies, a large proportion of electoral funding may come from donor agencies. While donor assistance can have a positive impact on election technical standards and integrity, it needs to be carefully targeted at the EMB's priorities, coordinated between donors and the receiving country, promote sustainability rather than donor dependence, and be subject to appropriate controls to allow the EMB to effectively use the funds.
- EMBs variously use baseline budgeting (based on historic funds allocations) or zero-based budgeting (based on future activity required to

meet strategic objectives) to create electoral budgets. Zero-based budgeting may initially require more skill and effort, but it more effectively allocates resources and more accountably ties EMB activities and performance to its strategic plan outcomes.

- An EMB that controls its own expenditure processes and cash flows is more credibly independent and may be better able to disburse electoral funds in a timely manner. However, it requires sufficiently rigorous controls on expenditure and payments to prevent error and fraud.

- In some complex purchasing environments, it may be preferable for the EMB to use a public sector-wide procurement agency. In most cases, however, the EMB can better meet the tight deadlines for electoral procurement by managing its purchasing independently, provided it has sufficient resources, skills and internal controls to ensure integrity and value for money in procurement. Necessary controls include enforceable conflict of interest polices and codes of conduct, and measures to ensure that purchases are not vendor driven.

- EMBs need to institute graduated levels of financial controls, such as diffused approvals of procurement and disbursements, work unit and EMB-wide internal financial monitoring, and regular internal and external financial audits.

- EMBs hold public assets and are accountable for their use, safekeeping, and appropriate archiving or disposal at the end of their useful life. Professional asset management systems—including regularly checked asset registers—are necessary.

- The financial management of EMBs must be in accordance with the principles of transparency, efficiency, effectiveness, integrity and sustainability.

CASE STUDY

Tonga: A New Commission in a Small Island State

Vake Blake

Background

The Electoral Commission was established as part of Tonga's political reform by the Electoral Commission Act of 2010. It marks the first commission to be established in the kingdom to supervise general elections and to ensure that such activities are implemented in a free and fair environment. The commission was also authorized to organize and conduct local elections, and assisted on other elections as well.

In recent years, all electoral matters have been administered and managed by the Office of the Prime Minister. That responsibility has now been taken over by the Electoral Commission and in the exercise of its functions and duties, the commission shall be independent.

The Tonga Electoral Commission Office serves the people of Tonga, which has a voting population of roughly 42,000 out of a total population of just over 100,000.

Legislative Framework

The following acts and regulations provide the legal frameworks for most of the activities carried out by the commission: the Act of Constitution of Tonga, the Electoral Act, the Electoral Regulations, the Electoral Commission Act, the Legislative Assembly Act, District and Town Officers Act, the District and Town Officers (Election) Regulations, the National Retirement Benefit Scheme Act and the National Retirement Benefits Scheme (Election) Regulations.

The Electoral Commission, with the approval of the cabinet, may make regulations that are necessary or expedient for carrying out the purposes of the Electoral Act, and in particular:

1. to provide for all electoral officers to take an oath of office, and the form thereof;
2. to provide the procedure to be followed by any civil servant who wants to stand as a candidate at an election;

3. to provide rules for compiling and keeping the roll;
4. concerning the functions of various electoral officers before, during and after polling day;
5. to provide for the manner in which the ballot box shall be kept and ballot papers kept and disposed of after the election;
6. to provide for voters who are blind or who, because of some physical handicap, require special assistance at a polling station;
7. to regulate election advertising and electioneering; and
8. to provide for the use of a national identity card to assist in the identification of electors and applicants for registration.

Powers and Functions

The Electoral Commission is responsible for the general administration and management of national elections. Its primary function is to provide a free, fair and credible electoral process that is consistent with its desired mission to:

- ensure that electoral procedures are in compliance with relevant existing legislation;
- continually review and revise existing legislation and policies to suit the changing needs of society; and
- disseminate relevant electoral information to the voting public through suitable voter education programmes.

The principal roles of the commission as set out in the Electoral Commission Act of 2010 are:

- to undertake long-term planning for the proper conduct of elections and the establishment and maintenance of proper records and rolls;
- under the powers granted to it in the Electoral Act, to determine appeals, challenges and any other disputes;
- to consider the need for regulations and other rules for the proper and efficient conduct of elections and related activities;
- as authorized by law, to make and amend regulations and keep them under review;
- to recommend prosecution for election offences;
- to devise, undertake and review programmes of education for voters, candidates and others involved in elections;
- to compile and make reports on elections and related matters, and recommend changes to the law and procedures to improve the electoral system;
- to publish for general information such data and reports on elections as the commission sees fit;
- within three months after any general election, to report to the cabinet on any changes that it recommends implementing before the next general election;

- for the purpose of promoting fairness and equal opportunities for all candidates and to prevent abuses, to regulate the use of radio, television, newspapers, Internet and other political notices, reports, appeals and advertising during the election period;
- to regulate and monitor electoral expenditure by candidates in accordance with section 24 of the Electoral Act;
- to perform any of the functions that are specified for it in the Electoral Act or any other act.

Some of the commission's priorities for the near future include:
- creating a strategic plan to cover the next four years, including the next major electoral event;
- creating an annual operational plan;
- developing a by-election plan;
- developing a staff development and training plan;
- developing manuals and procedural documents for the commission's day-to-day electoral operations, covering elections and roll management;
- compiling an office procedures manual to include corporate, human resources, finance, logistics and job descriptions;
- expanding the role of public education through development and delivery of appropriate programmes and manuals;
- developing policy for media access to polling stations;
- creating a commission website;
- maintaining the voter roll: ongoing, growth, ID cards, redistribution; and
- training polling officials.

Composition and Appointment

In accordance with Section 4 of the Electoral Commission Act of 2010, members of the commission shall consist of the following:

1. a person appointed by the king for a term of five years, who will be the chairman;
2. the supervisor of elections; and
3. a person appointed by the king.

Under the direction of the chairman, the daily operation of the commission is supervised by the electoral commissioner and supervisor of elections, and supported by the staff of the chief returning officer and assistant supervisor of elections, a senior returning officer, a computer operator grade III and a driver.

Financing

Funding for the commission consists of:

- money allocated by the Legislative Assembly;
- money paid to it (or for it) by an external agency or government for general purposes, for a specific purpose, or for the remuneration and benefit of specialists.

EMB Accountability

Under Section 14 of the Electoral Commission Act of 2010, 'the Commission shall report to His Majesty the King and the Speaker of the Legislative Assembly on its activities for each calendar year by 30 March in the next year and upon the conduct of any general election and on matters arising from such experience, within 3 months of the general election'.

Responsibilities for Electoral Justice

Some of the commission's responsibilities related to electoral justice have been mentioned under its functions. Furthermore, where there is an election petition, 'the member whose election or result is complained of shall be the respondent to the petition, and if the petition complains of the conduct of any official the Chairman of the Electoral Commission shall also be a respondent' (Electoral Act of 2010, section 26(2)).

Professionalism of Electoral Officers

Tonga is an active member of the Pacific Islands, Australia, New Zealand Electoral Administrators Network (PIANZEA), of which the Australian Electoral Commission is the secretariat. The staff members of Tonga's electoral commission have participated in BRIDGE training courses.

The Commonwealth electoral network has also established a programme for junior electoral professionals to provide training for young staff of its EMBs; Tonga has taken part in this programme. These programmes and trainings have benefited individual staff in terms of upgrading their performances and skills, as well as the EMB as a whole.

Media Relations

For a small island state with smaller scattered islands, the media is an important tool for disseminating electoral information. It provides platforms for effective campaigning during electoral periods. The Electoral Act specifies a period of silence 24 hours before the start of the poll; it is illegal to make any direct or indirect reference to the poll by means of any loudspeaker or public address apparatus or cinematograph or television, video or radio apparatus.

Relationship with Other Institutions and Agencies

The commission has established closer relationships with various stakeholders such as churches, civil society organizations, local and international media outlets, government ministries, donors and private sectors in terms of voter registration, civic education, training of candidates and polling officials, and many other activities. This active participation, assistance, greater awareness and support resulted in a voter turnout of around 90 per cent in the 2010 election.

Sustainability of EMBs

There is continuous support from Australia and New Zealand to the commission in the form of funding and technical expertise whenever needed. The national government also provides assistance.

Ability to Acquire and Manage New Technologies

The commission officially launched its new website in 2012. It was designed to provide as much information as possible on electoral matters in both English and Tongan languages.

The commission hopes that the website will serve as a window into the election process in Tonga, and allow visitors to access information on constituency allocations, candidate guidelines, polling station venues, voter registration, nomination processes, voting procedures as well as relevant legislation regarding the work of the commission. The website received over 31,000 hits from all over the world in the first month of its existence, and the use continues to rise.

Electoral Reform Management

As stated under the roles and functions of the commission and legal framework, 'the Electoral Commission with the approval of Cabinet may make regulations which are necessary or expedient for carrying out the purposes of the Electoral Act'. The commission will also respond to any request/requirements from the Supreme Court whenever needed. However, it often seeks the legal opinions of the Crown Law Department to clarify any issues or legislation.

Opportunities and Constraints

The commission is currently developing a comprehensive operating manual for the tasks it conducts and is responsible for. While the existing staff are very experienced and have a well-rounded set of skills in the areas required, any loss of staff would significantly affect its ability to function.

The commission is relatively new and has been focused on creating the roll of electors and the election. As a consequence, no long-term planning has been undertaken. It needs to create a more structured planning regime, together with work plans for major events such as legislative assembly elections, roll management, and stimulus programme and public education initiatives. This may include an annual operational plan, risk management plan, by-election plan, and staff development and training plans.

CHAPTER 8

Stakeholder Relationships

Who are the Stakeholders and What Is Their Role in the Electoral Process?

The stakeholders of an EMB are those individuals, groups and organizations that have an interest or 'stake' in its operations. They can be classified as either primary stakeholders, who directly affect or are directly affected by the EMB's activities, policies and practices; or as secondary stakeholders, who have a looser connection with the EMB's activities. Genuine and open dialogue with stakeholders can build confidence in the electoral process and trust in the EMB's activities.

Primary Stakeholders

Primary stakeholders include the following groups:

- political parties and candidates;
- EMB staff;
- the executive branch of government;
- legislatures;
- electoral dispute resolution bodies;
- the judicial system;
- election monitors and citizen and international election observers;
- the media;
- the electorate: voters and prospective voters;
- CSOs; and
- the donor community and electoral assistance agencies.

Political Parties and Candidates

Political parties and candidates are key stakeholders; EMBs must consider their concerns and interests when designing and implementing policies and activities. Unless the EMB enjoys a good relationship with, and the confidence of, political parties, its policies and programmes will attract criticism that will make it difficult for it to enjoy widespread stakeholder support. Where political party nominees are appointed as full members of an EMB, as in Georgia, or as non-voting members, as in Mexico, there is a permanent structure for EMB dialogue with the political parties.

Political parties and candidates are more likely to have confidence in an EMB that maintains an open-door policy to them; treats all political parties and candidates with respect, impartiality and fairness; and considers their opinions and suggestions. It is important that all political parties believe that they are being treated equitably and are offered the same opportunities and information by the EMB. Regular meetings with political parties—possibly more frequently during an electoral period—can provide a framework for reciprocal communication and can promote acceptance of the EMB's timetables, processes and outputs.

EMBs in Canada, Lesotho and South Africa have arrangements along such lines. In Kenya, the EMB liaises with parties in a formally constituted political party liaison committee. In South Africa, the law requires the EMB to set up political party liaison committees at all levels of government, from the national to the local level, and in Mexico political parties' non-voting membership of the EMB serves a similar purpose. Other countries, such as Australia, have instituted consultative structures although they are not legally required to do so. It is preferable for the EMB to meet all the political parties at the same time (rather than separately) to discuss its decisions or policies. Minutes of these meetings need to be provided to all political parties, whether they have attended or not.

In addition to these regular meetings, an EMB may be able to improve its relationships with political parties by including their representatives in EMB-sponsored events. Examples of joint activities are familiarization visits to voter registration facilities, participation in voter education and information workshops, joint media interviews or EMB-sponsored public debates between candidates. Equal opportunity to participate should be given to all political parties/blocs and candidates.

It is important to involve political parties in consultations about setting an EMB's strategic objectives and evaluations of its performance. As key EMB customers, political parties' and candidates' opinions on the EMB's focus, priorities and service are a useful way to improve electoral management. After each electoral event, it is useful for the EMB to include political parties in general consultations with stakeholders on how to improve the electoral framework, and to consider them in any proposals for electoral reform.

EMB Staff

An organization's greatest asset is its human resources—permanent, temporary and contracted staff. Unless an EMB safeguards the interests of its staff and responds to their concerns, it may well fail to deliver successful elections. Staff that are not loyal to the EMB and its principles may frustrate the EMB's programmes or be corrupted by suppliers who want to win a tender or by politicians who want to win an election. Unhappy staff may strike, even during elections, and thus derail the electoral process.

An EMB cannot assume that its staff will be loyal and automatically share and work hard to implement the EMB's values: it needs to support and generate this loyalty and professionalism. One of the great advantages of a professional EMB is that it can honestly tell its staff that their work, and that of the organization, is intrinsically worthwhile, and can contribute greatly to the welfare of the country. This should be constantly emphasized. The EMB also needs to treat all employees with honesty and fairness; provide competitive salaries and conditions; recognize the need for career opportunities; acknowledge staff achievements; provide a safe working environment; ensure equal opportunities; foster a culture of cooperation, teamwork and trust; train and develop staff to enable them to enhance and diversify their skills; and involve staff in the organization and planning of their work.

The temporary staff employed at election time are, for most voters, the public face of the EMB. In many countries they form a cohort that works each election, and therefore represent the organization, formally or informally, in their communities, and not just at election time. If they are motivated to project a positive image of the organization, this can help consolidate public trust in and support for election processes over time. This factor needs to be taken into account by countries considering mechanisms that involve less public interaction with staff, such as universal postal voting.

EMBs need to make a determined effort to support their staff, instil in them the values of professional electoral administration and respond genuinely to their needs.

EMBs under the Governmental Model, and other EMBs that are staffed by public servants, may be bound by public service-wide regulations and policies that may restrict their ability to deal in the most appropriate manner with their staff stakeholders. In such EMBs, staff relations may depend more on the attitudes of EMB management toward staff than on the ability to provide material benefits.

The Executive Branch

There are many reasons for an EMB to promote sound relations with the executive branch of government. The treasury or Ministry of Finance is often responsible for the EMB's budget. EMBs under the Governmental Model need to work within the confines of a line ministry, and may need to maintain close relationships with local authorities that implement electoral processes. In many cases, an EMB relies on government ministries (and regional EMBs similarly rely on local authorities) for transport and other electoral logistical support, such as premises for polling stations, and on staff seconded from various government agencies to serve as election officials. Approvals from government purchasing agencies or import licensing agencies may be required for essential procurement. EMBs may be subject to audit by the state audit authority, and may also be required to respond to inquiries from the ombudsperson or the anti-corruption agency. An EMB relies on the police force for security and, in some countries, may rely on the armed forces for security and some transport services during electoral events.

Cooperation and coordination will be enhanced if an EMB strives to keep all relevant government ministries and agencies informed of its activities and to consult with them on a regular basis about the services and support it may require from them. It can be useful for there to be a permanent working group or liaison committee involving the EMB and the government agencies on which the EMB relies for the provision of resources for electoral events. For independent EMBs, a ministry, such as the Interior Ministry or Ministry of Justice, may be its 'liaison' ministry for representations to the cabinet or the legislature. In Canada, the chief electoral officer communicates with the government through a minister appointed for that purpose.

The EMB must maintain good relations with whichever department is responsible for vetting its budget requests and releasing its funding in order to ensure that this department is familiar with the EMB's programmes and the time-critical nature of its funding requirements. For a good relationship, it is important that the treasury or Ministry of Finance has confidence in the EMB's budgeting, accounting, financial control and reporting systems.

Arrangements for the EMB chair or members to make courtesy calls on government leaders, which may include the head of state, to create awareness about the EMB's programmes and challenges, such as legislative, financial or logistical constraints, will raise the EMB's profile with its executive branch stakeholders.

The Legislature

EMBs need access to the legislature to ensure that their views are considered in developing electoral legal frameworks and electoral resource allocations, and to obtain feedback on their performance from an important stakeholder. This access can be facilitated by having a formal point of contact in the legislature. In Australia for example, this is a special standing committee of the legislature, while in Namibia it is the speaker of the legislature. In the Solomon Islands, the speaker of the legislature is also the chair of the EMB.

The legislature is the body usually responsible for making laws, including electoral laws, and it may also approve the government budget and scrutinize all public accounts, including those of the EMB. In many countries, the EMB is required by law or convention to submit election reports and annual reports to the legislature. Maintaining a good relationship with the legislature lets an EMB put forward its budget proposals and reports knowing that they will be dealt with by a body that has some understanding of its activities.

In Costa Rica, the EMB is able to propose amendments to the electoral law to the legislature. In Canada and Palestine, the EMB may make recommendations for amendments to electoral laws, although this is done by a line ministry or a government office in many other countries. Recommendations regarding amendment to the electoral law are also a major part of the remit of the UK Electoral Commission, which does not have responsibility for organizing elections—although it acts as an EMB for referendums (see the case study on page 302). EMBs may play a particularly important role in developing electoral legal frameworks in emerging democracies. EMBs should liaise with the legislature to sensitize it about electoral reform needs and the importance of passing amendments to electoral laws long enough before an electoral event to allow the EMB to make appropriate preparations. There are numerous examples of delays in lawmaking that have affected electoral performance, as in Malawi in 1997 and Timor-Leste in 2006–07, which arose from procrastination or lack of understanding or cooperation between the legislature and the EMB or between the legislature and the head of state.

Electoral Dispute Resolution Bodies

An EMB may have to deal with electoral dispute resolution bodies that have powers to deal with issues such as challenges to EMB decisions, disputes between the EMB and other stakeholders, the legality of the content of EMB regulations or challenges to election results. These may be judicial, quasi-judicial or less formal conciliation bodies. Their decisions can greatly affect the activities and public perceptions of the EMB.

General openness with these bodies—including ensuring that they are well informed on all EMB activities and decisions through regular meetings, receive all EMB publications and are invited to inspect EMB operations—can help maintain a good relationship. This needs to be done in a manner that does not, and does not appear to, impinge on the independence of decision-making of either the EMB or the dispute resolution body. This is especially important if the EMB is also mandated to play a role in resolving disputes, which will often be the case (even if only in the sense that complaints might be made to the EMB in the first instance, and then escalated).

It is of critical importance that an EMB is professional and cooperative in any investigations of electoral disputes by these bodies. It will be difficult to maintain a good relationship if the EMB obstructs a dispute resolution body's access to relevant electoral materials or sites, if it lobbies to limit the powers of such bodies, or if its presentation of evidence on disputes is not professional.

Judicial Bodies

Many components of the judicial system may interact with EMB activities. EMBs may need the cooperation of the police and prosecuting authorities in investigating alleged electoral offences, and to appear before the criminal justice or administrative court systems for any resulting court action. The EMB, its members or its staff may be subject to judicial investigation or civil litigation, and EMB administrative policies and practices may be subject to challenges in tribunals. As with relationships with electoral dispute resolution bodies, it is extremely important that the EMB is professional, accessible and cooperative in its dealings with the wider judicial system.

Election Monitors/Certification Teams and Citizen and International Election Observers

It is important for an EMB to create and sustain a good relationship with election monitors, certification teams (where appointed) and observers. Election monitors (who have the power to intervene and rectify any shortcomings in the electoral process), certification teams (which play an agreed role in assessing and validating (or not) an election process, especially in a post-conflict environment), and citizen and international election observers (who do not have the power to intervene and must only gather information and report) can be critical players in the electoral process. EMBs need to put in place simple accreditation procedures and adopt effective and timely accreditation mechanisms.

An EMB can organize and/or participate in observer pre-election briefings, held some weeks before voting day, for longer-term observers and observation planning teams. A further round of briefings could be arranged some days before voting day, whenever most citizen and short-term international observers are ready for deployment. It is increasingly common for EMBs to invite political parties and representatives of civil society to attend observer briefings so that they can brief observers about their impressions of the EMB's preparedness for elections. Observer briefing packs prepared by an EMB can also help observers understand the election's framework and operational processes.

Observers, as part of their accreditation process, typically have to subscribe to a code of conduct laid down by the EMB (or in legislation), which may require them, or their sponsoring organization, to bring problems in the electoral process to the EMB's attention. Observation missions will normally also seek to define the standards of conduct they expect from their members. Formal sanctions associated with breaches of the code may include withdrawal of accreditation, though this is unlikely to be widely used in practice, because it will usually have an impact only after the event, and may have undesirable diplomatic repercussions.

Traditional Media

The traditional media, both print and electronic, public and private, can be a key ally of an EMB in informing the public about its mandate and operations as well as informing and educating voters about democracy and elections. People who read newspapers, watch television and listen to the radio regularly tend to inform others about what they have read, seen or heard.

An EMB needs a media relations strategy that promotes regular positive contact with the media and ensures that the media have access to accurate electoral information—including on EMB activities. If an EMB does not promote a transparent relationship with the media, there is a greater risk that incorrect information may undermine its credibility.

Elements of implementing a media relations strategy for any EMB include:

1. identifying the relevant media and their coverage;
2. identifying the key people in the various media who can ensure accurate and prominent reporting of the EMB's activities;
3. being proactive and transparent in releasing information to the media;
4. ensuring that the information given to the media is clear, concise and easily understandable;
5. developing a timetable for providing electoral information;
6. creating a single EMB spokesperson for the media and one point of administrative contact within the EMB for the media; and
7. setting up a media centre within the EMB.

Some specific activities that will assist an EMB in its relations with the media include:

1. facilitating training programmes for journalists;
2. issuing regular media releases on electoral issues;
3. organizing regular media conferences;
4. having a readily accessible EMB media liaison officer;
5. preparing a media information handbook for each electoral event;
6. conducting media briefings on technical electoral issues; and
7. making electoral data easily and freely accessible to the media.

Media conferences could be at least weekly during electoral periods, and as needed at other times. It is advisable for an EMB to establish a full-time unit to assume responsibility for media relations and to appoint a person, preferably someone with a solid media background and who is respected in media circles, as its spokesperson.

EMBs may also need to deal with the media on a commercial basis, in relation to electoral advertising, or on a regulatory basis, if an EMB plays a role in regulating political campaigns. Maintaining professionalism and probity in these relationships will help create a positive atmosphere for the media's reporting of electoral activities.

For a number of reasons, an EMB is likely to have to monitor information that is published by the traditional media. It will need to be aware of stories that might constitute, or point to, breaches of the law or a code of conduct. It may be required to gather data on the extent of campaign publicity by various parties or candidates in order to monitor compliance with campaign expenditure limits. The EMB will also need to take account of publicly expressed criticisms of, or concerns about, the conduct of the election. Appropriate media monitoring techniques will vary from country to country; they could be pursued in-house or through the use of commercial media monitoring services, and could include gathering press clippings, TV and radio recordings, and Internet news alerts.

Social Media

The recent vast increase in the use of social media in many countries poses significant challenges for EMBs. Rather than being published through a limited number of relatively easily monitored nodes (mainly newspapers, radio and television stations), information is conveyed almost instantaneously between social media users, in a way that makes comprehensive monitoring virtually impossible. Material may be published via Internet sites hosted in another country, making the enforcement of laws relating to content difficult if not impossible. Many EMB stakeholders use social media to gather or share information, and will expect the EMB to be represented there, and to respond rapidly and concisely to questions and emerging issues. Social media users will increasingly be accessing the Internet using mobile rather than fixed devices.

In such an environment, it is not feasible to channel all media communication through a dedicated spokesperson who represents the EMB at press conferences and issues carefully crafted media releases. The EMB will need to be prepared to have a presence in multiple media channels (e.g. Facebook, YouTube, Twitter, etc.); to provide information in the restrictive format that such channels permit; and to delegate responsibility for communicating through such channels to staff who can respond very quickly in a tone that is communicative rather than bureaucratic, without having to clear most messages through a chain of command.

The Electorate

An EMB exists primarily to render services to the electorate—not only those who regularly vote, but those who are entitled to vote. Given the many and wide-ranging tasks an EMB performs on behalf of voters, it needs to keep the electorate informed about its activities and programmes, and seek its views on EMB processes and performance. It is wrong to assume that, since political parties, CSOs, the legislature and the government are the institutions that by and large represent the electorate, an EMB need only deal with these institutions and can ignore individual voters.

An EMB can profit from creating direct channels of communication with the electorate. Potential means include telephone inquiry services; public inquiry desks and suggestions boxes at locations such as markets, shopping precincts or transport hubs; and interactive radio and television programming and 'town hall'-type meetings featuring EMB members. Publicizing a list of EMB contact persons and their contact details on a regular basis is always a valuable service. In India, the EMB publishes a directory of contact details at the national level on its website within the information published under the Right to Information Act, and senior staff at the state level are appointed as public information officers. During the 2006 general elections in Fiji, the electoral office distributed a voter satisfaction survey at a sample of polling stations to collect impressions and direct feedback from voters on the conduct of the elections. At a number of elections in Australia, the EMB has arranged a survey involving structured interviewing of voters leaving polling stations; it has also commissioned a stakeholder satisfaction survey focused on candidates, political parties, the media and state electoral offices. More generally, feedback from voters can be obtained through focus groups research and broader surveys of voters.

It is important that an EMB respond quickly and accurately to all questions and comments received from the public. A delayed response, or no response, gives the EMB a public image of an inefficient organization that is not interested in serving the electorate. An EMB may also need to make extra effort to provide electoral services, materials and information to those marginalized through disability, illiteracy or remoteness.

An EMB can use the media to inform and educate the electorate about elections, and undertake its own publicity programmes—such as print and audiovisual information products, and a regularly updated website—to keep voters in touch with its activities. It is helpful to set up a professional unit within the EMB to deal with media relations and voter information.

Civil Society Organizations

Civil society organizations dealing with a wide range of issues—such as democratic development, women's empowerment, legal reform, human rights, civic education, governance and rights for people with disabilities—have a stake in an EMB's activities. Regular consultation with these stakeholders, as is practised in the Democratic Republic of the Congo, Ghana and South Africa, directly advises the EMB of their specific needs and provides a forum for discussing and publicizing the EMB's programmes in their support. EMBs may also build positive relationships with CSOs by using them as partners to implement electoral activities, e.g. training temporary electoral staff, or voter education and information programmes. Some EMBs include civil society representatives; in Timor-Leste, for example, the membership must include three civil society representatives (see case study on page 200).

The Donor Community and Electoral Assistance Agencies

The key role played by donor agencies in democracy building and electoral assistance around the world makes them an indispensable partner of many EMBs. Donor funding may go directly to an EMB, or through an intermediary, such as a government ministry. There may be a direct bilateral electoral assistance agreement with a donor, or multiple donors' assistance may be channelled through arrangements such as a UN Trust Fund (as in Nepal in 2008 and in Timor-Leste in the period preceding the 2012 elections) or a UN Basket Fund (as in Kenya, Sudan and Yemen). In all cases, an EMB needs to ensure that all donor requirements—including budgets, project implementation reports and financial reports—and any requests for access to inspect the EMB's activities are met with maximum efficiency and timeliness. Donor round tables can be used as a mechanism for an EMB to report on its progress in electoral administration and use of donor funding. Donors may require, and certainly appreciate, an EMB acknowledging donor assistance in its public relations events, publications and media productions.

Secondary Stakeholders

The range of secondary stakeholders of an EMB is likely to be diverse, and includes the following:

1. EMB suppliers;
2. the public at large; and
3. regional and international networks.

EMB Suppliers

An EMB relies on many suppliers for products such as technology, equipment, vehicles and election materials as well as services such as consulting, cleaning, security and transport. Unless an EMB maintains good working relations with these suppliers, its performance may be adversely affected by, for example, suppliers not keeping deadlines or supplying substandard products and services.

To maintain good relations with its suppliers, an EMB should ensure transparency, professionalism and efficiency in the invitations for expressions of interest to supply goods and services; share information with suppliers and prospective suppliers on the EMB's values, such as strict adherence to integrity, dignity, professionalism and efficiency; pay suppliers within the deadlines agreed; and arrange suppliers' information forums to discuss their concerns and formulate agreed solutions.

The Public at Large

The general public is also an EMB stakeholder. As an organization promoting democratic values and improved governance, an EMB has the responsibility to be a good corporate citizen. In its activities it needs to consider the community's health and safety, and be environmentally safe. In its external and internal working relationships, an EMB has the responsibility to be a good practice model of the values it represents, such as democratic decision-making processes; respect for the rule of law; non-intimidatory practices; honesty and incorruptibility; transparency; accessibility for all societal groups, including those marginalized through disability, illiteracy or remoteness; and promotion of gender balance. An EMB can seek to develop programmes of social responsibility by ploughing back into the community the skills, knowledge and other resources at its disposal.

Regional and International Networks

An EMB has stakeholders that do not form part of its immediate environment but have a bearing on its policies and programmes. The connections between EMBs and the international community have become stronger as a result of intensified international cooperation in democracy promotion and electoral assistance. The creation of regional and international electoral networks has opened up opportunities for EMBs to meet regularly at conferences and workshops and to undertake study visits and other joint projects (see Chapter 11 of this Handbook). Regional networks present opportunities for partnerships in sharing knowledge and materials and in the processes of peer review and evaluation.

International and regional instruments are a basic yardstick for assessing the quality of elections and have been widely used by election observers. The Global Declaration of Principles and Code of Conduct for International Electoral Observation adopted by the UN and by global and regional organizations in October 2005 is an example. An EMB that seeks to maintain a good reputation needs to align its practices and policies with internationally and regionally recognized principles, and be aware of global trends in electoral management.

Maintaining Relationships With Stakeholders

It is important for an EMB to foster close cooperation with its stakeholders to ensure their support for its policies and programmes and to strengthen their confidence in the EMB's performance. While some EMBs have at times sought to distance themselves from participants in the electoral process in the belief that their 'independence' calls for such an approach, that has typically not proven to be productive. Unless the EMB works hard to create and sustain sound relations with its stakeholders, there are likely to be misunderstandings and suspicions about its activities. This may ultimately generate lack of public confidence and trust in the EMB and the electoral process.

Legal frameworks in countries such as Indonesia obligate the EMB to communicate with stakeholders. Even without such legal requirements, the

Figure 11: Stakeholder Engagement – Statement of Principles

The Australian Electoral Commission (AEC) engages with three main stakeholder groups:

Political	Political stakeholders can shape electoral policy. Stakeholders include Parliament, the Special Minister of State, candidates and political parties.
Government and Corporate	The public and private sectors help to deliver our services to the public. Stakeholders include government agencies, state electoral commissions, contractors and suppliers, and other private companies.
Community	Community stakeholders help shape elector-centric service delivery. Stakeholders include community representative bodies, non-government organisations, media, academia, education providers and the public.

Engaging with stakeholders

The AEC's approach to stakeholder engagement aligns with the goal to provide world-class electoral services.

The AEC provides accurate and clear information to stakeholders in a way that is well structured and consistent across the agency. The AEC identifies shared objectives and encourages two-way communication.

Six principles that guide the AEC's stakeholder engagement:

Inclusive and Targeted	Actively identify and engage with individuals and organisations that have a stake in, or will be affected by, our services. Stakeholder input is sought on issues that matter to them.
Transparent	Engage stakeholders openly and make clear our purpose, goals, responsibilities, expectations and constraints. The AEC is impartial and objective.
Appropriate and Adaptive	Identify issues of significance and respond appropriately. Collaborate with stakeholders and look for mutual benefit. The AEC is flexible to changing needs.
Accessible and Innovative	Provide clear and accessible information. Evaluate our engagement to encourage ongoing improvement and foster a culture of innovation.
Respectful	Keep stakeholders informed of issues that affect them and engage in a manner that encourages mutual respect and trust. Ensure the AEC is honest and timely in our dealings with stakeholders.
Supportive	Provide support to AEC staff to engage with our stakeholders professionally and consistently.

Source: AEC website (<http://www.aec.gov.au/About_AEC/Publications/engage.htm>).

Australian Electoral Commission (AEC) has published formal commitments on how it will deal with stakeholders (Figure 11).

Like any business, an EMB needs to undertake consultative activities that will help it 'know its market'—that is, what the EMB's stakeholders (its customers) expect of it. But consultation alone is not sufficient. An EMB needs to develop an operational culture that makes it responsive to the expectations and needs of its stakeholders. This will generate support for and goodwill toward the EMB's policies and practices, and enhance its credibility. For example, an EMB may organize an election that, technically speaking, is of very high integrity and flawless in implementation, but if stakeholders are not involved and kept 'in the loop' about the process, their suspicion and distrust may lead to the rejection of the election results.

The combined power, influence and interest of a stakeholder can be referred to as its stakeholder value to an EMB's policies and practices. Stakeholder value is the basis on which an EMB can develop an appropriate strategy for promoting sound relationships with each stakeholder. For example, political parties in general are a high-interest/high-power stakeholder in elections (though in a particular country parties can vary greatly in size, salience and influence). If a significant political party rejects an election result because it mistrusts the way in which an EMB conducted an election, the EMB may come under attack. Thus EMBs must take their relationships with political parties very seriously. The EMB may be less focused on its relationships with low-interest/low-power stakeholders that have only a peripheral interest in its activities.

An EMB's strategy for dealing with each individual stakeholder will also be guided by each stakeholder's attitude toward the EMB. For example, if a stakeholder supports the EMB's policies and practices, the EMB may find it useful to involve it in as many of its activities as possible. This would not be appropriate where stakeholder involvement could damage an EMB's independence of action. If a stakeholder is marginal, and has little influence on EMB policies, the EMB needs to monitor it and keep it informed of the EMB's activities, but may not need to invest too much effort in involving it. Where an EMB identifies a wholly unsupportive stakeholder, it will need to analyse that stakeholder's potential intentions and reactions to EMB activities and develop a strategy for including the stakeholder, and an appropriate defence strategy, should this be unsuccessful.

An EMB can take a number of basic actions to maintain good relationships with its stakeholders, including:

- maintaining open, two-way communication with stakeholders;
- being sensitive to stakeholder needs and concerns;
- seriously considering stakeholder views when making decisions;
- treating stakeholders equitably, so that none are unfairly advantaged or disadvantaged by EMB activities;
- acting transparently, with meetings open to scrutiny and follow-up;

- maintaining the highest standards of ethics, respect for human rights, impartiality and care in its relationships with stakeholders; and
- equitably resolving any conflicts between the needs of EMB members and staff and those of other stakeholders.

A relatively low-cost way in which an EMB can foster its stakeholders' awareness of its activities and gain their loyalty is through a sustained effort of promoting open communication and dialogue. This could be by sharing its publications such as annual reports, election reports, financial reports and newsletters with all stakeholders, and regularly organizing information meetings to which stakeholders are invited.

An EMB can also adopt a formal policy on transparency, which can reflect the rights of stakeholders and emphasize to EMB staff the importance attached to this objective (a value that is not necessarily recognized in all public service institutions), as well as clarify how it is to be achieved. A key element of such a policy can be the practice of preparing and issuing formal statements of reasons in support of major decisions. The need to prepare such statements can improve the quality of an EMB's decision-making by helping to sharpen thinking on complex or sensitive questions; their publication can facilitate stakeholders' understanding—and more ready acceptance—of the reasoning underlying difficult decisions.

How To Deal With Difficult Stakeholders

Not all stakeholders will be favourably disposed toward EMBs. Some may be difficult for reasons that are legitimate, such as an EMB's failure to treat them with fairness, respect and impartiality. Others may simply be difficult for reasons such as personality clashes, past misunderstandings or the seeking of political advantage. It is common for some candidates and political parties to threaten to boycott or withdraw from elections citing EMB incompetence or partisanship, or to blame an EMB when they lose an election. This may occur because the EMB has not fulfilled its mandate to be fair and impartial, because of actions by bodies beyond the control of the EMB, or due to lack of public support for these political parties or candidates.

When attempts at inclusion fail, an EMB may need to decide whether it is wise to deal directly or indirectly with a difficult stakeholder, or whether to be on the offensive or defensive in dealing with it. If a small political party with little following announces that it is boycotting an election, the EMB may decide to restate its position publicly and monitor the situation. If a large and influential party decides to boycott an election, the EMB may need to seek mediation by a third party. There may be an advantage to approaching the courts for a binding determination if the differences between an EMB and a stakeholder involve an interpretation of the law.

Liaison structures, such as working groups with civil society or suppliers, committees of the legislature or political party liaison committees, may be useful in reducing or resolving differences between an EMB and its stakeholders. When a large majority in the liaison group supports the EMB's views, the dissenting views of a difficult stakeholder may be muted or stifled. Yet when a large majority in the liaison group supports the difficult stakeholder, the EMB can recognize that it is dealing not with a difficult stakeholder but with common perceptions of its performance—in which case it may need to reconsider its policies and decisions.

Where differences between the EMB and a difficult stakeholder are nearly irreconcilable, an EMB can resort to a strategy of defending itself against attack. Media releases and appearances by the EMB's spokesperson on news and other programmes, and other publicity opportunities such as the EMB's website, can be used to clarify the EMB's position so that the public understands its side of the story. The EMB may seek to publicize areas of agreement, rather than emphasizing areas of difference, to demonstrate that it can work with a difficult stakeholder. In such a situation, it is especially important for the EMB to express itself in a neutral, factual, detached, dignified and conciliatory way: any perception that it is becoming a player rather than an umpire will be to its long-term (and possibly short-term) detriment.

By ensuring that it is irreproachable in all its conduct by maintaining a high level of transparency, impartiality, dignity, integrity, professionalism, service and efficiency in all of its dealings with stakeholders, an EMB can construct a good defence against detractors.

Chapter Summary

- An EMB's stakeholders are those groups that affect or are affected by its actions, and to which it is accountable. Primary stakeholders include institutions such as legislatures, political parties, the executive branch of government, EMB staff, voters, the media, the electorate, CSOs, various components of judicial systems, election observers and donors. Secondary, more loosely affiliated, stakeholders include suppliers and the general public.

- EMBs should seek to deal with stakeholders in a way that is inclusive, transparent, appropriate, accessible, respectful and supportive. An EMB needs to treat all stakeholders fairly and to maintain regular two-way communication and consultation with them. Methods may include meetings to consult or discuss policy, media briefings, including stakeholders in EMB activities and training, and the wide distribution of EMB reports.

- EMB-initiated communication and consultation with stakeholders may be on issues such as strategic plans, election timetables and processes, electoral reforms, and voter education and information needs. Transparency, professionalism and reliability in an EMB's regular communications with stakeholders promote confidence in it and the electoral process.

- An EMB's culture needs to be responsibly sensitive to stakeholder needs and expectations. Relationships with stakeholders require active management by the EMB to promote goodwill and credibility. The attention that an EMB pays to a particular stakeholder will vary depending on its importance and power.

- Despite an EMB's best efforts, it may have to deal with difficult stakeholders. EMBs need to decide whether to deal with these directly (e.g. through liaison committees with a wide membership of stakeholders) or indirectly, using other institutions such as the courts for arguments over legislative interpretations.

- An EMB may need to take defensive action to protect its reputation, using the media and other publicity opportunities to explain its side of any difference with stakeholders. An EMB's best defence is a high standard of professionalism, integrity, transparency, impartiality and service in all its conduct.

CASE STUDY

The United States Administration of Elections: Decentralized, Pre-modern and Contented

Robert A. Pastor

The United States is the oldest constitutional republic in the world, and elections have been held since the English first settled in the early 17th century more than 150 years before independence. Currently, the United States elects executive, legislative and judicial officials for more than 500,000 positions at the federal, state and local levels. Elections not only sit at the core of the American political system, but for more than a century, democracy and free elections have been an important objective of US foreign policy, as well.

It is therefore ironic that the US government has provided almost no funds and given little attention to establishing national institutions or formulating procedures to conduct elections. The United States lacks a national election commission; instead, 13,000 independent local entities manage elections without uniform procedures. The 50 states are theoretically responsible for supervising elections, but few exercise much responsibility or even oversight. Though deeply engaged in shaping public policy on a wide range of issues, the American people have accepted this state of affairs and have not insisted on election reforms. With the exception of a few cases, the public has taken for granted that elections are free and fair. This attitude, combined with the general desire for less government, may explain the absence of electoral initiatives and the failure to modernize the electoral system.

American history can be seen as a struggle to expand the franchise from the narrow base of white, male property owners. The process of managing elections was always left to the local governments. The first serious effort in the modern era to reform the electoral system occurred as a result of the perceived failure by the state of Florida in 2000 to conduct a fair or competent election. The presidential election was decided in Florida by 537 votes, and a national spotlight focused on the many flaws in the elections.

Confidence in the electoral system was shaken, and Congress was finally moved in 2002 to pass the first federal law in election administration—the Help America Vote Act of 2002 (HAVA). This law proved inadequate to the magnitude of the task, but the federal government has done little since then. Many states have acted, but the new state laws have reflected partisan concerns. In some states where the Republicans have a majority in the legislatures, they have passed laws to prevent voter fraud by requiring photo identification cards and restricting the time and manner in which registration can occur. The Democratic Party has opposed these initiatives, arguing that their true purpose was to suppress voter turnout by poor and minority voters. Thus far, the laws have not had a discernable effect on voting, but that could change in subsequent elections as the new laws grow stricter.

Historical Background of Election Administration

The US constitution of 1787 does not guarantee citizens the right to vote. Indeed, it says very little about the administration of elections except to suggest that states have the responsibility to determine the procedures for choosing electors to the Electoral College, which serves as an intermediary between the voters and the final choice for president and vice president. That was a progressive innovation for the 18th century, but it is an anachronism in the 21st.

Over time, individual states devolved responsibility for administering elections to the local level because most elections were for local offices, and national elections occurred at the same time. Counties and municipalities registered voters, designed the ballot papers, purchased the voting machines and trained polling officials. Few states had a budget to help the local election authorities, and thus they had little power over the conduct of elections.

Although Americans vote for four national offices (president, vice president, senator and member of Congress), the only national election is for the Electoral College, in which electors designated by the candidates then choose the president. All other elections are technically the responsibility of the states, though they are conducted by 13,000 counties and municipalities. The election authorities at that level are selected and replaced in many different ways. Most officials are appointed by mayors, who are themselves elected at the local level; some are appointed by political party officials; and some are civil servants. Most officials are partisan; some states require bipartisan administration; few are nonpartisan. As a result, there are numerous and diverse administrative and technical procedures.

Until the end of the 19th century, the principal means of voting was a ballot paper given by the political parties to individual voters. This procedure lent itself to vote buying, and in the 1880s states gradually adopted the 'Australian' secret ballot, which identified all the candidates on a single page, giving voters the privacy of selecting the one they supported.

Although some campaign finance reforms were implemented during the Progressive Era at the beginning of the 20th century, especially the ban on corporate financial contributions, candidates long relied—and continue to do so—on private financing for their campaigns. State laws regulate campaign finance in state and local elections, but the first major reform at the federal level was the Campaign Finance Act of 1974 after the Watergate scandal.

In the presidential election of 2000, the losing candidate, Senator Albert Gore, won the popular vote but lost the electoral vote because Governor George W. Bush was reported to have won the state of Florida by 537 votes. Gore and the Democratic Party claimed that the many flaws in the system had biased the process against him. They asked for a recount, but the Supreme Court in a 5–4 vote decided to stop the count. Largely because of this decision, many Democratic Party members believed the election was unfair. Most Republicans disagreed with that assessment.

A bipartisan commission chaired by former US Presidents Jimmy Carter and Gerald Ford issued a report with numerous recommendations on ways to improve the electoral system. Congress reviewed and incorporated some of these suggestions in the first federal law on election administration, HAVA.

Legislative Framework

The statutory requirements for most elections are defined by laws passed by each of the 50 states. HAVA is the only national law addressing the issue of election administration. It sets a few national standards and requirements for voting, but makes most of these conditional on whether the states decide to accept funding from the Election Assistance Commission (EAC), which is established by the same law. Through the distribution of funds and the requirement that states develop and publish plans for meeting the national standards and establishing statewide computer-based registration lists, the new law aimed to help states retrieve authority over the conduct of elections, and to exercise it in a way that permits some uniformity at the national level. The states were mandated to be in full compliance with the law by 1 January 2006, but there were many laggards. By 2009, however, the states had integrated their registration lists, although 41 states did so in a top-down way. Eight states, including California, New York and Illinois, allowed the counties to organize the list in a bottom-up manner; one state (Texas) combined both techniques. A comprehensive study of the list by the Pew Center estimated that approximately 24 million (1 in 8) names on the registration list were not valid or accurate, so there was still much room for improvement.

In the 2008 election, there were 206 million eligible voters, of whom 71 per cent registered to vote. About 131 million people voted (nearly 90 per cent of those registered and 63 per cent of those eligible to vote).

HAVA did not provide for uniformity of standards, and the EAC was quite weak. A Commission on Federal Election Reform, chaired by Former President Jimmy Carter and Former Secretary of State James A. Baker and organized by American University's Center for Democracy and Election Management, offered 87 recommendations to address the remaining problems in the system. Its report was published in 2005.

Institutional Structure

The EAC was established in Title II of HAVA (Public Law No. 107–252). It is composed of four members: two nominated by Republicans in Congress and two by Democrats. (The FEC is similarly constituted, but its sole responsibilities relate to the supervision of campaign finance laws.)

The EAC is not an EMB. Its main responsibility was to transfer federal funds for the state governments to invest in new voting equipment and statewide registration lists; almost all of that funding was spent within a few years.

The institutional structures responsible for administering elections remain at the state and local levels. In most states, the secretary of state is technically responsible for the conduct of elections, but the county and city election boards are the EMBs; they conduct the elections. Secretaries of state are elected and tend to be individuals who aspire to higher political office. State and local officials are usually appointed by partisan officials, although some are civil servants or are appointed by local elected officials.

The Powers and Functions of the EAC, Secretaries of State and Local Officials

The EAC oversees the testing, certification, de-certification and re-certification of voting system hardware and software, provides election assistance, and encourages states to adopt voluntary guidance. Any EAC action requires the approval of three members, but its regulatory powers are sharply limited. It cannot, for example, 'issue any rule, promulgate any regulation, or take another action' that imposes a requirement on any state or locality.

The 13,000 individual counties and municipalities continue to manage virtually every stage of the electoral process. Republican leaders in Congress have questioned the utility of the EAC, and have withheld appropriations, and commissioners have not been suggested or approved by Congress.

Funding and Accountability of Election Administration

Until HAVA, the federal government spent no money on elections, and the states spent very little. Most funding was raised and spent at the local level. With the passage of HAVA, the federal government transferred nearly USD 3 billion between 2003–05 to the states to purchase new machines and implement statewide plans, including for computer-based, statewide registration lists. When that money was exhausted within a few years, the EAC's budget declined to less than USD 20 million per year.

The EAC (like the FEC) is accountable to Congress, the executive branch and the courts. The local authorities are accountable to their communities and, secondarily, to the state officials and the courts.

Technology

In the 2000 presidential election, more than half of all voters used punch card or lever voting machines. Their flaws became obvious during the review of the election. Many of the chads in the punch cards failed to dislodge, and those votes were not counted. Many of the lever machines, which were first built a century earlier, simply broke down. As a result, substantial funds were invested in new electronic machines, and by 2008, 89 per cent of all voters used electronic machines (DRE and optical scans); fewer than 7 per cent used punch cards and lever machines.

This change toward computer-based machines, however, created new problems. Polling officials had to be better trained to demonstrate how the new machines worked and to fix them if they broke. More importantly, some of the computer-based machines lost votes. Therefore, several members of Congress and several state legislatures advocated adding a voter-verified paper audit trail (VVPAT). The machines would affix the voter's preference on a ballot paper that would be counted in the event that a machine lost votes. Polling stations would also need to audit their count and their machines after each election. These initiatives moved forward slowly, but by 2009, 35 states had adopted some variation of them.

Professionalism of Electoral Officers

For much of US history, election officials' posts were viewed as patronage jobs to be awarded by the party in power. To a great extent, this has not changed. At the local level, there are great difficulties in hiring temporary workers, and as a result most are quite old (average age of 72) and may have difficulty working a long and stressful day. For the presidential election in 2008, approximately 131 million people voted in 200,000 polling districts. This required nearly 2 million poll workers, but only about 1.5 million were recruited, and they received little training. They were supervised by 20,000 election administrators. Wide variations in electoral professionalism were—and remain—inevitable.

Strengths and Weaknesses of the US Election Administration

Both the strengths and weaknesses of the US electoral administration system stem from its decentralized nature. It allows for great autonomy and diversity, but no uniformity. Most Americans are content with the decentralization of the electoral process, and many members of Congress are reluctant to override states' authority over elections. As a result, it is difficult for Congress to consider, let alone approve, even modest reforms such as requiring a back-up paper ballot in the event that voting machines break down. In the absence of a voting crisis, the prospects for a wholesale reform of the system—e.g. establishing a national, nonpartisan, independent election commission to conduct the elections—are remote.

At the beginning of the 21st century, the polarization of American politics affected and infected the rules for a fair election. Republican-dominated state legislatures in several states passed legislation that imposed voting identification requirements and tighter restrictions on efforts to register voters. Republicans insisted that they were most concerned about electoral fraud and assuring the integrity of the ballot, while Democrats accused them of trying to disenfranchise poor and minority voters, which traditionally represent an important part of the Democratic Party's constituency. Several of these state laws were challenged in court. The US Supreme Court found that the use of voter identification is legitimate, but concerns have been raised about how the laws are being implemented.

Moreover, most Americans tend to focus on the results of elections rather than the process. It is true that close elections often lead people to examine the process more closely, and the electoral crisis of 2000 catalyzed Congress to approve some reforms, but they were inadequate to the task of modernizing a national electoral system. For the foreseeable future, the US election system will be managed at the state level.

CASE STUDY

Tunisia: The Independent High Authority for the Elections

Mohamed Chafik Sarsar

Background

Tunisia has never experienced democratic elections throughout its contemporary history. For 50 years, the Ministry of Interior Affairs was officially in charge of elections, but in practice the ruling party controlled them. The 1969 Electoral Code, despite its amendments, did not establish a framework for honest and free democratic elections.

In 2011, Decree Law Nr. 2011–27[1] established the Independent High Authority for Elections (known by its French acronym, ISIE) to supervise the election of a National Constituent Assembly. Although its mission ended after the announcement of the final results of the Assembly elections, it changed the history of electoral administration in Tunisia.

The preamble of Decree Law Nr. 2011–35 (dated 10 May 2011, relating to the election of a National Constituent Assembly) emphasized the importance of a public, free, direct and secret ballot in accordance with the principles of democracy, equality, pluralism, fairness and transparency. But given the circumstances, the legal framework for the elections of 2011 was temporary; the effect of the legal texts ended with the election of the Assembly.

And although the ISIE outlasted the October 2011 elections, despite time pressures and the lack of traditions in Tunisia, political actors chose to establish a new permanent body to manage elections. The choice of an independent electoral administration is now shared by most political actors in Tunisia and this is how Organic Law Nr. 2012–23, dated 29 December 2012, rectified by Organic Law Nr. 2013–44 dated 1 November 2013, creates a permanent EMB, also called the Independent High Authority for Elections.

The Legal Framework

After the partial suspension of Tunisia's constitution in March 2011, the country's legal framework governing elections was put forth by the High Authority for the Achievement of the Revolution Objectives,[2] created to lay the groundwork for Tunisia's democratic transition. This framework included:

- Decree Law Nr. 2011–27 dated 18 April 2011, establishing a higher independent electoral commission;
- Decree Law Nr. 2011–35 dated 10 May 2011, relating to the election of a National Constituent Assembly, modified by Decree Law Nr. 2011–72 dated 3 August 2011;
- Decree Law Nr. 2011–91 of 29 September 2011, on the procedures and methods of control of the Court of Auditors over the electoral campaign funding for the National Constituent Assembly (clarifies the nature and extent of the Court of Auditors control, the body responsible for the regularity of electoral campaign funding); and
- Application Decree Nr. 2011–1087 of 3 August 2011.

Tunisia is still in its second stage of democratic transition, which is marked by the absence of a constitution. Constituent Law Nr. 2011–6 of 16 December 2011, relating to the provisional organization of public authorities, provided for the creation of a permanent ISIE.

The choice of the ISIE is consolidated by the provisions of the draft constitution, which provides in its June 2013 version a section 123 entitled 'Instance Elections', which states that 'The electoral body is responsible for the management and the organization of elections and referendums and their supervision in their different phases. The department ensures consistency, integrity and transparency of the electoral process and announces the results. The body has regulatory authority in its field of competence.' This provision reflects the desire to establish a permanent body with constitutional status.

The Structure of the ISIE

The ISIE is composed of a council, which has decision-making authority, and an executive body. It has nine members: a judicial magistrate; an administrative magistrate; a lawyer, notary or bailiff; a university professor; an engineer specialized in IT systems and security; a communications specialist; a public finance specialist and a member representing Tunisians abroad.

Members of the ISIE Council are elected by an Assembly Plenary of the National Constituent Assembly. The president of ISIE is elected by the Assembly Plenary from among those who apply of the nine elected members.

The elected members meet at a first session to choose the vice president by consensus, and if not, by the absolute majority of members. The term for each member is six years, and is non-renewable. One-third of the ISIE Council shall be renewed every two years.

The ISIE can create, prior to elections or referendums, regional authorities responsible for assisting the ISIE in carrying out its tasks. The ISIE Council shall determine the composition of regional authorities, which shall not be more than four members in each regional authority. The candidates are selected by the ISIE Council by an absolute majority of its members in accordance with the application requirements. The ISIE Council may delegate to the regional authorities some of its prerogatives, which they shall exercise under the supervision of and in accordance with the decisions of the Council.

The ISIE shall have an executive body under the supervision of the ISIE Council that is in charge of administrative, financial and technical affairs, and it shall be headed by an executive director.

Powers and Functions

The ISIE shall be in charge of all processes related to organizing, administrating and supervising elections and referendums. It shall ensure the following functions:

1. hold the voter register and continuously update it; prepare voters' lists for each election or referendum, review them when needed, and publish them on the official ISIE website in accordance with the deadline set by the electoral law;
2. guarantee voters' right to vote, and ensure equal treatment of all voters, candidates and stakeholders during electoral or referendum processes;
3. set, publish and implement electoral calendars for elections and referendums, as stipulated by the constitution and electoral law;
4. receive and approve the nomination applications for election according to the provisions of the electoral law;
5. establish mechanisms of organization, administration and control, ensuring the integrity and transparency of elections and referendums;
6. count the ballots and announce the preliminary and final results of elections and referendums;
7. prepare the election codes of conduct, guaranteeing the principles of integrity, transparency, impartiality, proper management of public funds and no conflict of interest;
8. accredit the representatives of the candidates in the polling stations, and accredit national and international observers, guests and journalists to follow the stages of the electoral process;
9. train supervisors of the various components of the electoral process;
10. establish voter education and awareness programmes, and cooperate within this framework with all components of civil society that are active nationally and internationally in the field of elections;
11. control the commitment to the regulations and means of election campaigns as established by the Electoral Law, and require respect for the law in collaboration with public bodies;
12. control the financing of election campaigns and enforce the necessary related decisions, while ensuring equality among all candidates in public funding;
13. propose suggestions for the development of the electoral system and give opinions on all draft texts related to elections and referendums; and

14. prepare a special report on the outcome of each election or referendum process, and present it to the president of the republic, the president of the Legislative Assembly and the president of government. The report will be published in the Official Gazette and on the ISIE website.

The ISIE Council shall establish the necessary regulations for the implementation of electoral legislation and the tasks conferred on the ISIE.

Accountability

The ISIE shall submit its detailed report on the progress of the elections, which it shall publish with the announcement of the final results in the Official Gazette of the Republic of Tunisia and on the commission's website.

The president of ISIE or a member of its council may be revoked in cases of serious misconduct in the performance of his or her obligations, or if convicted by an absolute judgement for an intentional offence or a crime, or if this member no longer meets one of the requirements for membership in the ISIE Council. The revocation request shall be submitted by at least half of the members of the ISIE Council and presented to the Legislative Assembly at a plenary session for approval by an absolute majority of the members of the Legislative Assembly.

If a member has a conflict of interest, he or she must declare it to the ISIE Council and then refrain from participating in related meetings, discussions or decisions until the ISIE Council decides on the matter. If it has knowledge of a conflict of interest, the ISIE Council, after hearing the concerned member, shall investigate it. If it is proven that the member deliberately concealed a conflict of interest, he or she shall be dismissed.

The president and council members of the ISIE cannot be prosecuted or arrested for deeds related to their work or the performance of their duties within the ISIE until after their immunity is lifted by the Legislative Assembly at a plenary session by an absolute majority of its members, at the request of the concerned member, or two-thirds of the members of the ISIE Council or judicial authority. The request to lift immunity presented by the judicial authority is subject to examination, along with the file's case.

The president and members of ISIE may not be sued or arrested for deeds related to their activities or the exercise of their duties within the commission without having the authorization of a two-thirds majority of its members.

The Professionalism of Electoral Officers

The president of the ISIE and members of its council are particularly bound by the following obligations:

- at least ten years' experience;
- the obligation of neutrality;
- the obligation of reserve;
- the obligation to attend meetings of the ISIE Council; and
- to serve as a full-time ISIE Council member.

In addition, the president of the ISIE and its council members are prohibited from standing in any election during their membership in the ISIE and during the five years that follow the end of their mandate. They are expected to behave in accordance with the procedures prescribed by law on the declaration of honour on property of members of the government and certain categories of public officials.

The ISIE president and council members shall report any conflicts of interest during their mandate in the ISIE.

Relations with Political Parties, Other Institutions and the Media

The ISIE tried in 2011 to establish rules of cooperation with international organizations that offered their electoral assistance. Further, it created spaces for dialogue and consultation with political parties, the media and civil society associations. These actions led to the adoption of a code of conduct and improvements to the training programme. The ISIE also organizes voter awareness campaigns.

However, the new ISIE should conduct targeted outreach efforts to political parties and candidates to facilitate a better understanding of the complaints and appeals procedures, and legal actions against violations of the law.

Financing

ISIE's resources shall consist of annual funds from the state budget. The budgetary expenditures of the ISIE shall include:

- operating expenditures of the ISIE;
- capital expenditures; and
- elections and referendums expenditures.

The ISIE budget shall be based on a proposal from its council. It shall be submitted to the government for an opinion before its transmission to the Legislative Assembly for approval in accordance with the specific procedures for the state budget.

All public administrations are called on, to the extent possible, to provide the ISIE with all material and human resources, databases and information, including statistics and data related to the electoral process, to assist the ISIE in carrying out its missions. In case of an unjustified refusal on the part of the concerned administration, an order can be obtained for this purpose from the Administrative Court. Prior to elections or referendums, the Office of the President of the Government shall endeavour to facilitate cooperation between all public administrations and the ISIE.

ISIE procurement shall be conducted in accordance with the procedures related to the procurement of public companies, as long as they do not contradict the provisions of this law. ISIE expenditures shall be exempt from prior control of public expenditure.

The ISIE shall oversee the implementation of an internal control system of administrative, financial and accounting procedures that guarantees the safety, integrity and transparency of financial statements and their conformity with the applicable laws. An audit and internal control unit shall be created for this purpose, which shall be chaired by a chartered accountant. This unit shall exercise its functions in accordance with international professional standards of internal auditing and through monitoring of an annual plan approved by the ISIE Council in order to improve performance, risk management and control all actions of the ISIE. The unit of audit and internal control shall report directly and regularly to the ISIE Council.

ISIE financial statements shall be under the control of two auditors and appointed by the ISIE Council, in accordance with the applicable legislation related to public institutions and companies, for a term of three years, which is renewable once. Annual financial statements of the ISIE shall be approved by the ISIE Council in light of the report of the two auditors. The report shall be subject to the approval of the Legislative Assembly and shall be published in the Official Gazette and on the ISIE website by 30 June of the following year. If the financial report is not approved by the Legislative Assembly, a commission of investigation shall be created that is composed of three chartered accountants and appointed by the Legislative Assembly. The financial statements of the ISIE shall be subject to the a posteriori control of the Court of Auditors. A special report shall be issued by the Court of Auditors on the financial management of each election or referendum process. This report shall also be published in the Official Gazette.

The new ISIE must make a special effort to consider criticism from the Court of Auditors in the elections of October 2011 and best practices in financing the electoral process.

The Future of the ISIE

The decisions of the Administrative Court (4 and 7 November 2013), which declared the results of the ISIE candidature selection committee null and void, has delayed the formation of the ISIE.

The responsibility for the future election administration is great. It must build an executive body headed by an executive director, avoid gaps in the experience of 2011, and regain the confidence of politicians and voters in quite difficult conditions.

Notes

[1] Decree Law Nr. 2011–14 of 23 March 2011, on the provisional organization of the public authorities, gave the interim president of the republic the authority to legislate by decree law in some fields, including the electoral system and the funding and organization of political parties.
[2] Decree Law Nr. 2011–6, dated 18 February 2011, created the High Authority for the Achievement of the Revolution Objectives, Political Reform and Democratic Transition.

CHAPTER 9

Electoral Technology

Elections Technology in Recent Decades

In recent decades, electoral administrators have adopted several types of technology into the electoral process. While these technologies can bring great benefits in accuracy, speed, efficiency and effectiveness to the process, they also pose challenges in the fields of security, costs, sustainability, transparency and vendor dependence.

In a fully electronic electoral management system, the entire electoral process—voter, party and candidate registration; verification of candidate support signatures; ballot production; electoral logistics; voter identification; voting in polling stations or remotely; vote counting; results transmission; and presentation of preliminary and final results of data—can all be performed by electronic and digital equipment and with very limited human intervention. Currently, only a few countries, such as Norway, have achieved this level of automation of election administration. EMBs usually combine manual processes and electronic technology into a suitable hybrid system, which is influenced by a wide range of factors, and may arguably be considered unique in any given country.

Types and Main Features of Elections Technology

EMBs can use electoral technology in virtually all aspects of managing the electoral process:

- *Voter registration systems* for building and maintaining a voter register with personal details of all eligible voters in electronic format, in some cases also biometric information such as photographs or finger print scans. Voter registration data in electronic format can be used in many ways (e.g. data cross-checks, duplicate detection, issuing voter identification documents, targeting voter information, planning and electoral logistics, producing voter lists for polling stations and obtaining demographic information about the electorate).

- *Voter identification systems* (electronic poll books) for checking the eligibility of each voter at the polling station level by comparing his or her personal details to a database of all eligible voters.
- *Party and candidate registration systems,* for tracking the registration status of all political subjects for an election, checking any required support signatures and providing the data in appropriate formats for designing ballot papers and tally sheets, configuring voting machines, etc.
- *Observer registration and accreditation systems,* for tracking the accreditation process for citizen and international observers and issuing their identification documents.
- *Districting and boundary delimitation systems,* using geographical information systems to delimit political boundaries and distribute polling stations and catchment areas.
- *Electronic voting and vote-counting systems,* various systems ranging from machine counting of paper ballots to voting machines used in polling stations and Internet voting systems; these speed up the counting process and eliminates human interference.
- *Result tabulation and transmission systems,* for processing electronically captured turnout and results data, greatly speeding up related procedures and avoiding and detecting human error through automation and data cross-checks.
- *Results publishing systems,* for presenting and visualizing election results in various formats including maps, charts, detailed results databases and overviews.
- *Voter information systems* to provide voters and other electoral stakeholders with detailed data about electoral process. Such systems include polling station locators allowing voters to easily find their polling station, legal databases of regulations, information about parties and candidates running for election, databases allowing access to detailed election results and statistics, and continuously updated calendars with key events and deadlines.
- *E-learning systems,* for the professional development of EMB staff.

All of these electoral information and communications technology (ICT) solutions employ a wide range of technology, from simple mobile phones to private satellite links, from standard productivity and collaboration systems to specialized biometric databases, and from private intranet systems to public websites and social media channels.

Initially, electoral technology was often entirely custom built for each EMB, based on general-purpose ICT systems. In such systems, any specific electoral functionality had to be built from scratch. In recent years, however, election technology vendors have increased their range of products and provide ready-made solutions that only require relatively minor adjustments to local requirements and conditions.

Selected ICT Concepts with Impact on Elections Technology

ICT Innovation Cycles and their Relation to the Electoral Cycle

ICT systems evolve very quickly compared to the duration of an electoral cycle. Most ICT equipment, both hardware and software, has a useful life of about 3–5 years. After this period, equipment needs to be either replaced or significantly refurbished and upgraded. For electoral ICT applications, this can pose a significant challenge. With many electoral cycles lasting about four years, an ICT system that was successfully deployed for one election can be expected to require major upgrades or even a complete replacement for the next election.

Where the time between elections and use approaches the end of the useful life of ICT equipment, the sustainability and efficiency of purchasing, owning, storing and maintaining equipment needs to be considered. To avoid the high costs of storing unused equipment, EMBs can lease selected equipment, share it with other countries, or plan to reuse, sell or donate some of it after an election for non-electoral use.

Figure 12 (on page 260) provides a visual comparison of how operating systems, data transfer technology, mobile computing and fingerprint standards have evolved between elections, assuming a four-year electoral cycle starting in 1992.

The 'Bathtub Curve' and Electoral Cycles

Another challenge related to long electoral cycles and the comparatively short useful life of ICT systems becomes evident when considering the bathtub curve, a concept that is widely used in engineering to describe the occurrence of failures in technical systems.

The curve starts with a 'burn-in' phase in the early stages of using a system. This phase is characterized by the high failure rate of a still-immature system. As problems are detected and addressed, the failure rate decreases and the system enters the period of its useful life with a very low failure rate. Finally, as the useful life of a system comes to an end, wear and tear lead to an increased failure rate and require the eventual upgrade or replacement of the system.

While most non-election systems will be used primarily during the second phase of this curve, the sporadic nature of elections implies that electoral technology will often be used only shortly after its development and may therefore still be in the failure-prone burn-in phase. The period of useful life of election technology therefore coincides mostly with the time between elections when the system is not used. And when the next election occurs, after several years, the system may already be close to or in its wear-out phase with increasing failure rates.

Electoral Management Design

Figure 12: How ICT Equipment Has Evolved Between Elections

Election year	Operating System	Data Transfer	Mobile Computers	Biometrics Standard
2012				1-2011
2008				1-2007
2004				1-2000
2000				1a-1997
1996				1-1993
1992				1-1986

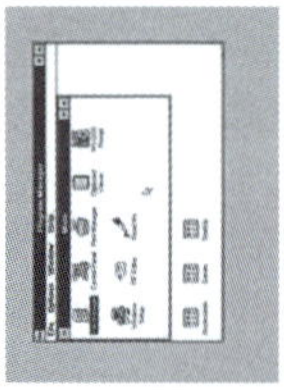

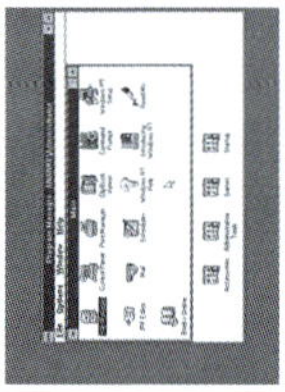

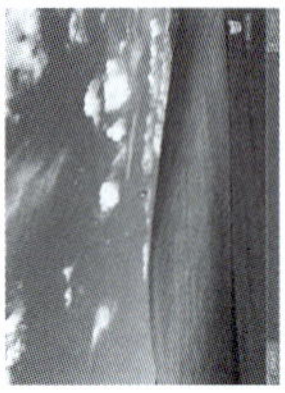

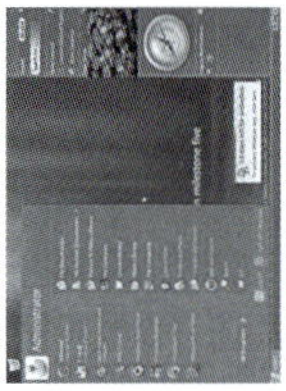

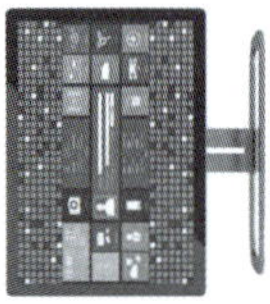

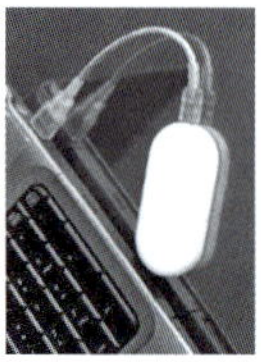

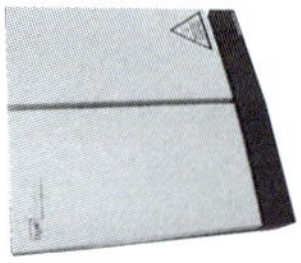

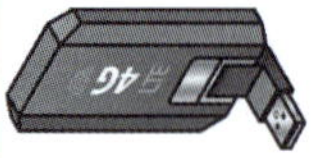

260 International IDEA

Figure 13: The Bathtub Curve

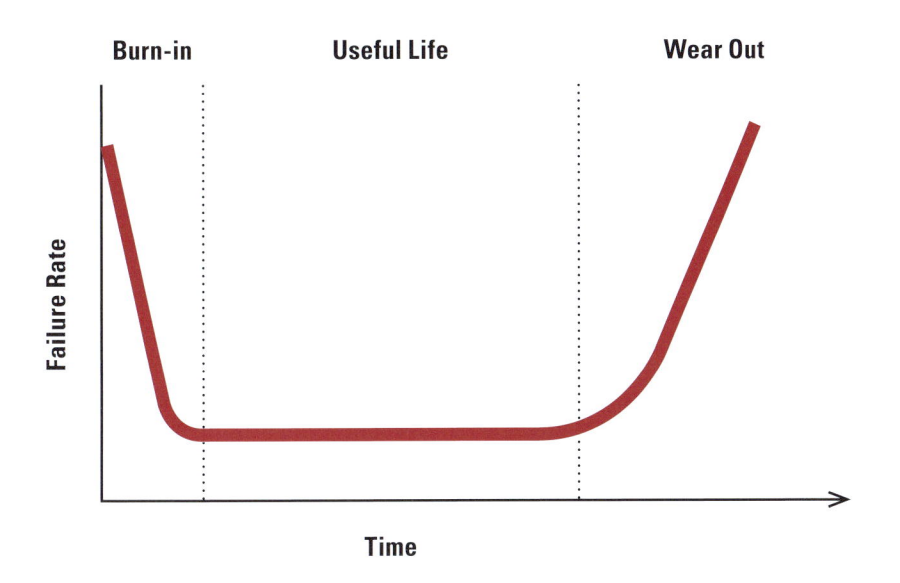

The bathtub curve demonstrates that long preparation times are required for the introduction of electoral technology to make sure the burn-in phase takes place before election day, and that the time between elections must be used to identify and implement all upgrades required for the next election period.

Total Cost of Ownership of ICT Systems

One of the main claims offered in support of elections technology is cost effectiveness. However, experience suggests that the initial capital investment required to purchase an ICT system can be as low as 25 per cent of its total cost of ownership (TCO) over its expected lifetime. The TCO is the sum of all direct and indirect costs involved in purchasing, operating and eventually disposing of the equipment. It can be easy to underestimate the TCO when only looking at the initial purchase price of ICT equipment.

The TCO of electoral ICT systems includes the costs of:
- public dialogue about the introduction of the new system;
- purchasing or developing system hardware and software licences;
- system certifications and auditing;
- securing the system physically and technically;
- preparing the infrastructure required to operate the system;
- deploying, configuring and testing the system for an election;

- training staff and operators to use the system;
- operating the equipment during the election;
- retrieving the equipment after the election;
- storing and protecting the systems between elections;
- disaster recovery: preparing for back-up planning;
- replacements or upgrades, possibly for every election; and
- disposal of outdated equipment.

Many of the costs above are difficult to quantify, which makes it difficult to establish the precise costs of using an ICT solution, to compare ICT costs between different solutions, or even to estimate any cost savings incurred by automating parts of the electoral process. While a realistic estimation of the TCO and securing the required resources is necessary to effectively control and manage the use of electoral technology, claims about savings through introducing new technologies or between different types of technologies should always be carefully examined.

ICT Security and Costs

ICT security works like preventive medicine: one does not know if it is working or how well it is working until it fails. Moreover, there is no perfect security. Securing electronic systems is an arms race between those trying to protect them and those prepared to invest in breaking into them. Electoral stakeholders often demand the highest possible security standards for election technology, since a country's democracy is at stake when election technology seriously fails or is manipulated. But the highest security levels are expensive. Each EMB must determine, in consultation with all electoral stakeholders, how at risk its ICT systems are; how likely failure or various types of attacks are; what the consequences of such events are; and how much security investment is needed, possible and justifiable.

Internet-based systems raise additional security concerns since they are connected to a public network and thus exposed to an unknown threat environment with similarly unknown threat capabilities. This environment includes not only national actors but also, by virtue of the online environment, foreign governments and hackers.

Election Technology Vendors

In recent years, election technology vendors have started to provide more and more services to EMBs around the world. By deploying their solutions in more contexts and elections than a single EMB would usually be responsible for, vendors have developed a great amount of technical, operational and sales experience. EMBs are often confronted with many offers by vendors to evaluate and eventually purchase new types of election technology. The products and services on offer can be of great help in organizing an election, but there are also several challenges related to this increased vendor involvement in elections.

Needs-driven Approach

While vendors have an interest in the smooth conduct of elections they are involved in, their primary objective is naturally to expand their business rather than to improve the electoral process. Vendors will therefore shape their proposals in order to maximize the use of their products rather than look at the electoral outcome of using their technology. The EMB's role in selecting electoral technology needs to be the opposite: its primary objective must be improving the electoral process, which may or may not be facilitated by the different technological options available.

Therefore an EMB's starting point for evaluating technology should not be which technology to choose or how to implement it. An EMB should first and foremost define which electoral problem needs to be addressed and which are the best ways to do so.

Procurement

Elections are unique in each country, and elections technology needs to provide unique solutions for the country in question. Electoral procurement is expected to be conducted with a high degree of integrity, transparency and competitiveness. Yet with high-value contracts at stake, lengthy appeals procedures need to be included in the envisaged timeframe. Technology procurement is a complex process, and tends to take longer than initially expected. With a set election date, this can come at the expense of implementing the chosen solution. Therefore, tender exercises need to be initiated well in advance of the election in which the technology will be used.

The procurement process needs to carefully determine the appropriate systems to purchase. While a full specification would ideally be developed without vendor participation, an EMB may not be able to fully specify all needs and be aware of all technical options and possibilities. In such cases, a competitive dialogue can be considered as part of the procurement process: after several suitable vendors have been identified, the EMB can conduct a structured dialogue with all of them to identify feasible alternative solutions for the EMB's requirements.

Vendor Lock

Where technology is proprietary to a vendor, where data formats are not open or when an EMB relies heavily on a vendor for its electoral operations, it risks being locked into a particular vendor. In other cases, electoral stakeholders may have strong preferences for a well-established and trusted vendor and may not want the EMB to engage any alternatives. Any such tie to one particular vendor should be avoided to make sure the EMB remains in control of the systems it uses and the costs incurred.

Open Source vs. Proprietary Systems

When the transparency of an electoral ICT application is important to stakeholders, they frequently request open source software be used, which has source code that is accessible to all and comes with a software licence that allows free usage and distribution. Access to source code is one requirement for experts to understand exactly how an ICT system works. In addition to the added level of transparency, open source software is also considered to be cheap and secure, and it limits vendor lock. At the same time, vendors tend to build their business models on proprietary software with closed source codes, mainly to protect their intellectual property and sometimes to limit access to security issues to a small internal audience.

Proponents of open source electoral management software argue that elections technology is 'mission critical' for democracy and should therefore be completely transparent and owned by the public. Initiatives such as the Open Source Digital Voting Foundation (OSDV) work on the development of fully open source electoral systems. However, open source initiatives for electoral management systems currently find it difficult to gain momentum and are increasingly confronted with a market that is already served by experienced vendors and their proprietary systems.

Vendors are increasingly recognizing the high demand for transparency by many electoral stakeholders. Norway made open source software a requirement for its Internet voting system and the selected vendor's source code was published online.

While vendors may not always be ready to switch to open source and free use of their software, they are usually willing to disclose their source code for public scrutiny. Such disclosure can either be limited to certain time frames, controlled environments or selected experts, or it can be complete and public. Increased transparency and access to proprietary codes often come with significant additional costs; depending on the application in question, an acceptable trade-off may need to be made.

Commercial Off-the-shelf Systems vs. Customized System Development

A fundamental decision for electoral administrators is whether to obtain ready-made ICT solutions or pursue the development of a custom-built system. A ready-made system can usually only be adapted to a certain extent, and may therefore require changes in the electoral process to match the system. Such changes are in some cases beneficial and reflect best practices for using electoral technology; in other cases they are required for the sole purpose of making the selected technology work in the given context. By contrast, a custom-built system may more closely fit the existing electoral process. However, customized development is a lengthy and expensive process, and poses extra challenges in managing the development process.

Voter Education and Public Information

Voters and other electoral stakeholders are exposed to various electoral technologies in very different ways. Accordingly, the need for voter education and public information campaigns varies greatly. Overall, it is important to include all prospective users in the introduction of new technologies in order to increase acceptance and the likelihood of successful implementation.

Some new technologies, such as polling station locators and other voter information systems, are mostly a convenient additional service at the voters' disposal. Public outreach for such systems only focuses on the widest possible awareness and usage of such systems.

In other cases, voters will be required to comply with certain procedures or use the technology themselves and need to know what to do. In addition to disseminating the information through its regular communication channels, the EMB can also set up demonstrations in public locations where voters can try the technology, for example cast an electronic test vote or check their registration status on an electronic poll book before the election takes place.

Any technology that plays a central role in the electoral process will be of interest to stakeholders such as political parties, the media or election observers. For them, the EMB needs to provide appropriate detailed documentation and make competent EMB staff available for enquiries.

In cases where technology is potentially disputed, for example when it seems very costly or is not welcome by all stakeholders, information campaigns need to go one step further. The EMB then needs to inform or remind stakeholders why the technology was chosen, which trade-offs and options were considered, and how expected improvements to the electoral process outweigh the potential downsides. Such an information campaign will not only be conducted around the election itself, but begin in the early stages of considering and selecting a technology, when relevant stakeholders should be given an opportunity to have their say.

Training and Expertise

Most EMBs have ICT departments that are tasked with operating at least the standard ICT solutions used by the institution. Larger ICT departments can play a leading role in the development, introduction and maintenance of specific elections technology. However, with more complex electoral solutions, private companies provide an increasing share of the development and operational work and related expertise. Therefore it is important to delineate the areas of responsibility between the EMB and the vendor, and ensure that knowledge and skill transfers to EMB staff takes place. Capacity building should be part of the vendors' deliverables.

With electoral technology being introduced down to the polling station level, EMBs' need for ICT capacity goes far beyond the ICT department. All levels of permanent and temporary election staff increasingly use technology in all aspects of their work. Efficient training for using elections technology requires at least basic computer literacy. ICT training from scratch is costly and time consuming, and the availability of a pool of computer-literate election workers is a key success and cost factor in the deployment of elections technology.

When ICT is used in crucial steps of the electoral process, there is a growing expectation that the EMB's IT expertise is not limited to its technical departments. Election commissioners, spokespersons and other high-ranking EMB staff are increasingly expected to understand and explain technical details of the electoral process with just as much confidence as any other operational or legal aspects. With the introduction of electronic voting, countries such as the Philippines recognize the need for technical expertise at the commission level and put more emphasis on ICT skills when selecting commissioners.

Administrative and Operational Objectives

Maintaining EMB Oversight

As EMBs are rarely able to develop all of the required elections technology themselves, most will need to rely on vendors to some extent. Where much of the electoral process is outsourced, the roles and responsibilities of the EMB and vendors need to be clearly delineated to ensure that the EMB has full oversight of the process. A reasonable option is that the vendor's role is to develop and maintain electoral ICT systems, while the EMB's role is to configure the system and operate it during the election.

Accountability and Integrity

The lack of any tangible evidence of transactions in computer systems and the incomprehensibility of computer programming to the bulk of the population lead to a lack of transparency. This lack of transparency—combined with the risks of interference with data and widely publicized media reports of computer viruses, hackers and system malfunctions; and an increasing awareness of online surveillance—can affect EMBs' credibility. When relying on computer systems for vital tasks such as voter registration, voting and vote counting, EMBs are expected to be openly accountable for their use of technology.

Measures that EMBs can take to ensure the integrity of their computer-based systems include:

- rigorous pre-implementation testing of computer systems and public release of the results of the tests;
- robust ICT policies that cover all aspects of technology use, including acceptable access to and use of ICT equipment and data, physical security of ICT equipment, data security, back-up, retention, archiving and disposal, appropriate of use email and social media, and disciplinary measures for cases of deliberate or serious breaches;

- regular auditing of computer systems, with particular attention paid to their security features;
- making test versions of source codes for computer systems available for public comment (for example, the Electoral Commission of the Australian Capital Territory posted proposed code for its computer-based vote recording and counting system on its website and invited comments from computer professionals);
- independent, third-party certification of computer systems based on national and international standards, guidelines, recommendations and requirements to confirm that the system complies with prescribed technical requirements and standards; and
- holding an authenticated copy of the authorized codes in an independently controlled off-site location, as has been recommended in the USA. Regular comparison of this with the code being used in the EMB can detect and remove any unauthorized changes.

Focus on the Whole Electoral Process

When new technology is used for the first time, when a significant part of the election preparations and budget is invested in technology, and when there are great expectations of the impact of technology, ICT aspects of elections tend to attract a lot of EMB and public interest. In this situation, it is important that this attention does not come at the price of neglecting other, equally important, components of the electoral process.

Inclusiveness

Technology tends to benefit the more affluent and educated citizens more than other, disadvantaged parts of society. Therefore the introduction of new technology needs to be accompanied by measures that ensure equal access for the entire electorate, including voters with special needs, voters in rural areas with less access to infrastructure, elderly voters and those who feel less confident using technology.

Sustainability of Donor-funded Technology

With high costs and short usage spans, elections technology is difficult to sustain—particularly in post-conflict settings and emerging democracies, where a challenging environment, limited and unreliable infrastructure, and possibly low trust in a newly established EMB require even more complex ICT solutions. Unfortunately, this is precisely the context in which donors may be willing to invest heavily in technology, hoping to facilitate the smooth conduct of the election. Such an investment risks delivering one well-administered election, but creating sustainability problems in the long run. With only the next election in focus, little consideration is given to maintaining the system and related expertise for future elections, especially when donor funding is no longer available. Systems, services and expertise that can be efficiently procured by an assistance provider through their procurement channels and networks may be difficult and expensive to obtain following national procurement regulations on the local market.

Selecting Appropriate Technology

The most advanced, high-tech solutions are not necessarily the most suitable technologies for use in the electoral process. Appropriate technology is designed with consideration of its economic, social and environmental impact as well as its affect on the entire electoral process. Simpler systems that still fulfil all requirements are usually more appropriate, require fewer resources and maintenance, and have a lower TCO.

Issues of Electronic Voter Registration

The use of ICT in voter registration can become controversial for several reasons. The accuracy of voter registers is often a contentious issue, and technology upgrades may be seen as a solution to that. However, voter registration is a large and costly exercise, and increased ICT use comes at a high cost. The sustainability of high-tech approaches can be questionable, especially when substantial donor funding is required or when registration mainly focuses on establishing a single register for an upcoming election rather than a permanent system for continuously maintaining a register.

The operational complexity and cost of voter registration primarily depends on how voter registers are built and maintained. If an EMB can share data with other administrative bodies and build a voter register based on existing population registers (e.g. national identification card systems, civil registry data), this will require significantly less technical effort than if it has to compile the voter data itself. For use in elections, population registers must be maintained by a widely trusted institution, use high-quality data, have a high registration rate (with many incentives and few disincentives for registering) and contain all information about eligible citizens required for the electoral process. If these conditions are met, an inexpensive and highly accurate voter register can be extracted automatically from such a system.

If data sharing with other administrative bodies is not possible and the EMB needs to conduct voter registration on its own, costs will be significantly higher, as the EMB must operate a system that can reach all citizens and capture or update the personal details of all eligible voters. The simplest solution in such a case is to only conduct a paper-based registration exercise. However, paper-only voter registration data may often be insufficient: the data quality may be poor, data cross-checks and efficient updates of the register are not possible, and it is difficult or impossible to establish or publish accumulated registers for larger regions or an entire country. Any claims about inaccuracies of the register will be hard to verify.

One step up the technology ladder, and usually the cheapest way to capture registration data electronically, is the use of machine-readable paper registration forms. Data can be collected by manually filling in optical mark recognition (OMR) forms, from which registration data can later be scanned into an electronic database. The disadvantages of such a system include a lack of data integrity checks when the data is captured, a lack of feedback about any problems at the point of registration, the difficulty of correcting or completing any wrong or missing data discovered during the scanning process, as well as mistakes due to incorrectly filled in forms.

Further technical upgrades include the use of electronic registration systems at the point of registration. In their simplest form, electronic registration systems are offline and only capture registrants' personal details. Such a system may be sufficient if voters' details can be confirmed by widespread availability of reliable personal identification documents. In such a case, local duplicate checks and data validation must be possible. Data back-up plans at the point of registration need to be extensive, as any lost data cannot be restored.

Online registration systems require data connections to all registration points. They have the potential to immediately check a registrant's data against the entire voter register, and to detect and resolve duplicate registrations. Such systems can upload data directly to central registration databases and reduce the risk of data loss at the point of registration.

The most comprehensive registration data collection will include capturing registrants' biometric details such as fingerprints and facial or iris recognition data. The costs of such a system will increase due to the need for biometric data-capturing equipment for every registration system as well as more comprehensive data-processing requirements for storing and comparing biometric data. The additional cost of setting up biometric systems is usually justified by the difficulty of establishing registrants' identity due to a lack of reliable identification documents.

A Brief Background of Electronic Voting and Vote-counting Systems

Introducing new ICT systems in elections is always challenging, and requires careful deliberation and planning. Electronic voting (e-voting) is arguably the most difficult upgrade, as this technology involves the core of the entire electoral process: the casting and counting of votes. E-voting greatly reduces direct human control and influence in this process, and provides an opportunity to solve some old electoral problems, but it also introduces a whole range of new concerns. Therefore e-voting can be expected to trigger more criticism and opposition than any other ICT application in elections.

There are a number of e-voting and vote-counting systems that are marketed as a means of improving voting methods and reducing costs. Some of the systems claim to offer a high degree of reliability and resistance to electoral malpractice.

- Direct recording electronic (DRE) voting machines can come with or without a paper trail (VVPAT, or voter-verified paper audit trail). VVPATs are intended to provide physical evidence of the votes cast.

- OMR systems are based on scanners that can recognize the voters' choice on special machine-readable ballot papers. OMR systems can be either central count optical scanning (CCOS) systems (ballot papers are scanned and counted in special counting centres) or precinct count optical scanning (PCOS) systems (ballots are scanned and counted in the polling station directly as voters feed them into the voting machine).

- Electronic ballot printers (EBPs) are similar to a DRE machine, and produce a machine-readable paper or electronic token containing the voter's choice. This token is fed into a separate ballot scanner, which conducts the automatic vote count.

- Internet voting systems transfer votes via the Internet to a central counting server. Votes can be cast either from public computers or from voting kiosks in polling stations or—more commonly—from any Internet-connected computer.

The accuracy and integrity of these machines depend not only on the companies and persons that design, programme, test and maintain them, but also on the systematic checks and balances introduced by the EMB, including system audits and certifications.

Comprehensive controls and accountability measures come at a price. More transparent and secure systems cost more. A system with the highest possible levels of transparency and security can increase costs so much that the benefits of the e-voting solution no longer justify the expenditure.

System Requirements, Certification and Audits

More than for any other electoral technology system, certifications and audits are of crucial importance for building trustworthy and credible e-voting and counting systems. Certifications and audits confirm the compliance of the e-voting system against a clearly defined set of functional and operational requirements. The exact requirements are different in each context, and need to take into account legal, technical, operational and functional aspects as well as key stakeholder needs.

System certifications provide EMB- and vendor-independent, third-party confirmation that an e-voting and counting system meets the requirements. System audits verify the proper functioning of the e-voting and counting systems through stringent testing before, during and after usage. However, thorough certification and audit can come at a significant additional cost, and can for smaller implementations come close to the technology costs of the system.

Voter Verified Paper Audit Trails

One response to concerns about the integrity, reliability and security of e-voting systems and the need to conduct transparent audits has been the use of a voter-verified paper audit trail (VVPAT) process. The voter is provided with a printout of the vote just cast, which can be checked on the spot and then placed in a ballot box, to be used if necessary to audit the validity of figures produced by the automated system. Many e-voting systems can provide audit trail facilities, including electronic voting machines (EVMs) that have been used in countries such as Belgium, the United States and Venezuela in recent years. In 2013 the Indian Supreme Court directed the Election Commission to introduce paper trails for voting machines, and the EMB has taken steps to introduce VVPAT after more than 20 years of using e-voting machines that did not provide such a facility.

The use of OMR devices to count votes, such as in the Philippines, can also provide accuracy and time effectiveness in the electoral process while producing a paper ballot that can be physically examined if necessary in post-election disputes.

VVPATs only work for e-voting in the controlled environment of a polling station (not, for example, with Internet voting). The Venice Commission has undertaken a detailed analysis of the compatibility of remote voting and e-voting with the broader electoral standards of the Council of Europe.

Beyond technical performance issues, some of the debate regarding the integrity of elections technology entails the propriety of politically aligned or foreign-influenced suppliers. Media reports of alleged integrity problems with mechanical and e-voting machines has increased pressure on EMBs to be open and accountable in their sourcing and use of technology.

Costs

Although there is no reliable cost-effectiveness analysis on the use of new technology for voting and counting, the evidence that technology such as EVMs may reduce election costs over time, especially costs associated with printing and storing ballot papers and vote counting, is controversial. India has used relatively cheap EVMs for decades and has concluded that EVM-based elections are much cheaper than paper-based ones. Yet the Netherlands abandoned old EVMs in 2007 and subsequently investigated the introduction of a modernized system. Their findings as of 2013 were that voting with new EVMs would be twice as expensive as paper-based voting.

Chapter Summary

- Key benefits of electoral technology include accuracy, speed, efficiency and effectiveness.

- Key challenges remain in the area of security, costs, sustainability, transparency and vendor dependence.

- Trends are away from custom built systems for each EMB toward specialized vendors' ready-made solutions.

- As a consequence of short ICT life cycles, most equipment needs major upgrades or complete replacement between elections.

- ICT equipment that was only put in place shortly before an election is likely still immature and has higher failure rates.

- The initial purchase price of ICT systems can be expected to be only a fraction of the total cost of ownership over the equipment's lifetime.

- Highest ICT security levels are expensive; each EMB must determine how much security investment is needed, possible and justifiable.

- Specialized election technology vendors offer an ever increasing range of services to EMBs, but also require EMBs to be aware of the challenges involved in dealing with these companies.

- Voter education, public information and EMB staff expertise are important success factors for election technology implementations.

- EMBs are expected to be accountable for the use of elections technology and need the ability to maintain ultimate oversight of the systems in place.

CASE STUDY

Kenya: The Independent Electoral and Boundaries Commission

Shumbana Karume

Background

The post-election violence in Kenya in 2007–08 triggered action by the regional and international community that resulted in successful mediation efforts led by former Secretary General Kofi Annan. An agreement that became known as the Kenyan National Accord and Reconciliation Act was brokered between various factions and political parties and signed on 28 February 2008. The accord, which aimed to address the post-election crisis, committed all parties to immediately stop the violence, restore fundamental human rights and liberties, and address long-term issues including constitutional and institutional reforms. By way of spearheading the assumed constitutional and electoral reforms, the accord provided for the formation of an Independent Review Committee (IREC). In conformity with its terms of reference, the IREC presented its findings and recommendations in January 2009 in the Kriegler Report.

The report's findings were based on its analysis of the Kenyan elections legal framework; the structure, composition and management system of the Electoral Commission of Kenya (ECK); and its organization and conduct of the 2007 electoral operations. The report concluded that 'the voter register which has been updated from time to time since 1997, is materially defective in various respects that in themselves already impair the integrity of elections results' and that 'numerous implausibly high turnout figures reported in the strongholds of both main political parties evidence extensive perversion of polling, probably ballot stuffing, organized impersonation of absent voters, vote buying and/or bribery'.[1] It also made extensive and detailed recommendations on correcting practices that were inconsistent with good practices in election organization. The report highlighted a number of measures to address some of these shortcomings, and the ECK was advised to implement these measures to improve future elections.

Following the IREC report, and consistent with the public's sentiments, the Kenyan parliament voted in 2008 to replace the ECK with a new electoral management structure. The Interim Independent Electoral Commission (IIEC) was thus established in May 2009 by amending sections 41 and 41A of the former constitution. The IIEC consisted of a chairperson and eight commissioners who were nominated through a competitive process by a parliamentary select committee, approved by the National Assembly and appointed by the president in consultation with the prime minister. As per the constitutional amendment, the IIEC's tenure was to come to an end three months after the promulgation of the new constitution, which would provide for a permanent electoral body to succeed the IIEC and take on its role of reforms. The IIEC in effect had a total of 12 months to discharge its mandate.

The functions of the IIEC were the following; however, its function of delimiting boundaries was transferred to the Interim Independent Boundaries Review Commission.[2]

- reform of the electoral process and the management of elections in order to institutionalize free and fair elections;
- the establishment of an efficient and effective secretariat;
- the promotion of free and fair elections;
- the re-registration of voters and the creation of a new voter register;
- the efficient conduct and supervision of elections and referendums;
- the development of a modern system of collection, collation, transmission and tallying of electoral data;
- the facilitation of the observation, monitoring and evaluation of elections and referendums;
- the promotion of voter education and the culture of democracy;
- the settlement of minor electoral disputes during an election, as may be provided by law; and
- the performance of other functions prescribed by law.

The IIEC's mandate was explicitly formed to carry out specific electoral reforms recommended by the IREC report, such as creating a new voter register due to serious anomalies in the existing register. The IIEC was generally able to undertake several electoral reforms; its most notable success was the management and organization of the constitutional referendum of 4 August 2010, which was commended and found to be transparent by all stakeholders.

The referendum ushered in a new constitution in 2010 that had an approval rating of 68 per cent of the votes. Article 88 of the new constitution called for the establishment of the Independent Electoral Boundaries Commission (IEBC). The IEBC is also recognized by and subject to the constitutional provisions that apply to constitutional commissions and independent offices.[3]

Like any other constitutional commission, the IEBC is expected to be subject only to the constitution and to be independent—and hence not subject to the direction or control of any person or authority.[4] This institutional independence is also enforced by article 25(2) of the Independent Electoral and Boundaries Commission Act, which stipulates that every individual member and employee of the commission shall perform the functions and exercise the powers provided for in this act independently, and without direction or interference from any state officer, public officer, government organ, political party or candidate, or any other person or organization.

Legislative Framework Governing the Kenyan Electoral Commission

The passage of the new constitution in August 2010 was a resounding landmark for Kenya's political development. It provided a framework for implementing a number of important institutional and legal reforms, many of which were non-existent and therefore were required under the new constitution, or were simply needed to ensure that other laws and acts in the relevant sectors were compliant with the new constitution.

The electoral sector was the most affected by the promulgation of the country's new constitution. The constitutional provisions relating to elections—chapter 7, articles 81-92—are considered progressive, and draw on best practices from the organization of democratic elections in other countries. Article 88 of the constitution defines the IEBC's functions and sets out the criteria for membership and the formula for appointing members. The constitution also stipulates the rights of all Kenyans to participate in elections and referendums (article 83) and includes provisions to promote the participation of traditionally excluded groups (e.g. women and people with disabilities) in the electoral process (article 81).

The constitution also includes provisions on election legislation. It stipulates that Parliament shall enact legislation to provide for the delimitation by the IEBC of electoral units for the election of members of the National Assembly and county assemblies, the nomination of candidates, registration of voters, the conduct of elections and referendums, and the progressive registration of citizens residing outside Kenya.

The new constitution also defines several guiding principles for introducing regulations and administrative decisions on the electoral system. Article 81 sets out the guiding principles for the electoral system, stipulating that citizens should have the freedom to exercise their political rights; not more than two-thirds of the members of elective bodies can be of the same gender; there should be fair representation and equality of vote; and free and fair elections should be held that are by secret ballot, free from violence and intimidation, and conducted and administered by an independent body in an impartial and neutral manner. These principles paved the way for replacing the FPTP system with a PR system.

In addition to the constitution, a number of laws have also been enacted to govern elections in Kenya. These acts directly govern different aspects of elections and the electoral process. Stakeholders emphasize that conflicting requirements among the new legislative acts must be reconciled before election day. Prior to the new constitution coming into force, many laws governing elections in Kenya were scattered among various acts, which presented a huge challenge to those tasked with implementing these laws. Several laws were revised and consolidated in 2011, including three key pieces of legislation: the IEBC Act, the Political Parties Act and the Elections Act.

The IEBC Act provides a comprehensive mechanism and framework for the appointment, effective operation and management of the commission. Part II of the act contains provisions on the administration of the commission, including its internal structures, functions, and the appointment and terms of service of its members and staff. Part III provides for the establishment and administration of the IEBC Fund and other financial procedures of the commission, and Part V comprises miscellaneous provisions on the principles that govern the commission in the fulfilment of its mandate, its independence and its management of information. The IEBC Act also contains a series of schedules: the First Schedule defines the procedure for appointing a commissioner; the Second Schedule provides for the conduct of the business and affairs of the commission; the Third Schedule prescribes the oath or affirmation of office for the members and the secretary, while the Fourth Schedule contains the code of conduct for members and staff of the commission.[5]

The code of conduct, which applies to elections and referendums, is a new development in the Kenyan electoral environment. It is a fairly comprehensive code that serves to strengthen the professionalism of IEBC employees, as well as create obligations for political parties and referendum committee officials and candidates to adhere to the values and principles of the constitution. It requires all members and employees to conduct themselves professionally, efficiently, impartially and independently, and prohibits employees from holding another public office. All members are expected to perform their duties in a manner that maintains public confidence and to respect the rights and freedoms of all persons.

Powers and Functions

The IEBC's functions were set out in article 88(4) of the constitution and the Electoral Act of 2011:

- conducting or supervising referendums;
- conducting and supervising elections to any elective body established by the constitution;
- conducting and supervising any other elections as may be prescribed by an act of Parliament;
- continuous registration of citizens as voters;
- regular revision of the voter register;
- delimitation of constituencies and wards;
- regulation of the process by which parties nominate candidates for elections;
- settlement of electoral disputes, including those relating to or arising from nominations, excluding election petitions and disputes arising after the declaration of elections results;
- registration of candidates for elections;
- voter education;
- facilitation of observation, monitoring and evaluation of elections;

- regulation of the amount that may be spent by or on behalf of a candidate or party in any election;
- development of a code of conduct for candidates and parties contesting elections;
- monitoring compliance with legislation related to parties' nomination of candidates; and
- investigation and prosecution of electoral offences by candidates, political parties or their agents.

The IEBC also has the residual power to perform such other functions as provided for by the constitution or any other written law. This has given the commission the occasion to conduct work that is outside its formal legal mandate, including advising or administering elections for institutions such as the Law Society of Kenya. The commission's broad mandate also gives it the reputation of being the primary institution with adequate authority to advise on issues relating to elections.

Composition and Appointment of Commission Members

Section 5(1) of the IEBC Act provides that the commission shall consist of a chairperson and eight other members. It has a chairperson and eight commissioners, which is much smaller than the 22 members of the former ECK. The formula for appointing the chairperson and members of the commission is set out in the First Schedule of the IEBC Act. The president is required within 14 days of a vacancy arising in the commission to appoint a selection panel comprising a chairperson and eight members drawn from distinguished professionals in the private sector or public service with relevant expertise.[6] The selection panel is required within seven days of its convening to invite applications and publish the names of all applicants. The panel is then required to consider the shortlist of applicants and conduct interviews. After the interviews, the panel is required to select three persons qualified to be appointed as chairperson and 13 persons qualified to be appointed as members of the commission and forward these names to the president, who must have his or her selections approved by the National Assembly. For the purposes of appointment, the president is required to consult with the prime minister in accordance with the constitution.

Upon consideration and approval, the National Assembly forwards the names to the president for appointment. If the National Assembly rejects any nomination, the speaker is required to notify the president as soon as possible. Within 14 days of the rejection, the president shall submit to the National Assembly new nominations from the list of nominees received from the selection panel. If the National Assembly rejects all or any subsequent nominee submitted by the parliamentary committee for approval, the selection panel shall forward to the president fresh names from the persons shortlisted and interviewed, and the procedures outlined above would be repeated.

The IEBC Act provisions on the appointment and effective operation of the IEBC also stipulate the qualifications of the chairperson and members of the commission. The chairperson must be qualified to hold the office of a Superior Court judge under the constitution, while commissioners must be citizens; hold a degree from a recognized university; have proven relevant experience in electoral matters, management finance, governance, public administration or law; and meet the requirements of leadership and integrity as set out in chapter 6 of the constitution. Anyone who has held office within the preceding five years or stood for election as a Member of Parliament and/or governing body of a political party, or who holds any state office, is ineligible for IEBC membership.

The chairperson, vice chairperson and members of the commission can serve for six years and cannot be reappointed; they must retire at the age of 70. As stipulated in section 7 of the IEBC Act, the chairperson and vice chairperson are required to serve on a full-time basis, while the seven other members serve part time. The commissioners enjoy security of tenure as governed by chapter 15 of constitution articles 248(1) and 251, and can be removed from office only for serious violation of the constitution or any other law; gross misconduct; physical or mental incapacity to perform the functions of office; incompetence and bankruptcy. Should the question of removal arise, the president is authorized to appoint a tribunal to investigate the petition for removal after consideration by the National Assembly. The tribunal is required to make a binding recommendation to the president, who shall act in accordance with the recommendation within 30 days.

The secretary to the commission and commission's secretariat—which comprises professional, technical, administrative officers and support staff—are appointed by the commission through an open, transparent and competitive process. Public officers may also be seconded to the commission upon its request. A public officer who is seconded to the commission is deemed to be an employee of the commission, and shall enjoy the same benefits and is required to comply with the constitution, the act and any other written law relating to elections. As with the chairperson and members of the commission, the secretary of the commission has a six-year term of office, but is eligible for reappointment.

Institutional Structure of the IEBC

The IEBC is structured in accordance with the provisions set out in the IEBC Act, which requires the chairperson and members to respect the delimitation of duties between the commission as the policymaking organ and its secretariat as the policy implementation and administrative organ. Commission policymaking is implemented by one of several committees.

The secretariat is headed by a chief executive officer who is responsible for executing the commission's decisions; he or she assigns duties and supervises all employees of the commission, and is responsible for facilitating, coordinating and ensuring the execution of the commission's mandate. The secretary heads a secretariat that manages the day-to-day running of the commission. The secretariat is composed of a deputy CEO, nine directors and 17 managers. The current directorates are Voter Registration and Electoral Operations, ICT, Human Resources and Administration, Voter Education and Partnerships, Finance and Procurement, Legal and Public Affairs, Research and Development, Risk and Compliance, and Registrar of Political Parties. Each directorate is supported by a team of managers, officers and junior staff. The commission also has 17 regional offices administered by regional election coordinators and 210 constituency officers administered by constituency election coordinators, who are responsible for coordinating the commission's work in the regions.

Financing of the Commission

The IEBC is funded by the government through Parliament under an independent budget that is no longer tied to the Ministry of Finance. Parliament has the duty to allocate adequate funds to enable the commission to perform its functions. The funds of the commission, however, consist of other monies such as grants, gifts, donations or other endowments given to the commission and funds that may vest in or accrue to the commission in the performance of its functions.

The process of funds acquisition begins with the IEBC preparing budget proposals for each financial year and submitting them to the treasury. The agreed budget is then presented to Parliament for consideration and approval. Once approved, the money is paid into a specialized fund in which all commission funds are held. This consolidated fund is managed by the secretary of the commission in accordance with all the laws and regulations relating to public financial management. From this fund, all operational and other expenses incurred by the commission in the performance of its functions shall be paid. Previously, salaries and allowances were the expenses of the consolidated fund; since the reforms, all IEBC expenses including recurrent expenditure and expenditure for reform and electoral exercises are now charged on the consolidated fund.

While charging the IEBC's entire election expenses to the consolidated fund has improved the commission's financial independence, the IEBC continues to experience difficulties in securing adequate funding in a timely manner from the appropriate authorities to undertake its elections processes. This has prolonged the commission's reliance on donor funding and assistance, which is generally provided through the UNDP-run Kenya Elections Assistance Programme. There are also specialized donors that give the IEBC technical assistance in various areas. Early in its term, donors pledged financial support to the IEBC to be disbursed under the Elections Sub-Group of the Democratic Governance Donor Group (DGDG). This support will need to be revisited and disbursements released, since the IEBC was unable to obtain government funding for its entire budgetary outlay.

Accountability of the Commission

The IEBC is required to observe all reporting procedures on its operations as well as financial regulations and accounting procedures in the management of its funds, as stipulated in sections 20 and 23 of the IEBC Act. The commission is required to present its annual report to the president and submit it to Parliament within three months after the end of each year. The annual report shall contain the financial statements of the commission, the activities it has undertaken and any other information the commission considers relevant. The commission is required to publish the annual report in the Gazette and in at least one national newspaper.

IEBC Act sections 20 to 22 include further provisions on the financial reporting regulations to be followed by the commission. It is required to keep proper books and records of accounts of its income, expenditures and assets. These records are to be submitted to the auditor general within three months after the end of each fiscal year, accompanied by statements of its income/expenditure and assets/liabilities.

Professionalism of Electoral Officers

The IEBC code of conduct places enormous emphasis on professionalism. It has several provisions relating to integrity, honesty, transparency and professionalism to which members and employees of the commission are required to subscribe. Every member and employee is expected to perform their duties with integrity, to treat their colleagues with respect, to respect the rights of all persons they interact with, and to discharge their duties in a professional, efficient, transparent and effective manner and in line with the rule of law.

For example, the act stipulates that a member or employee of the commission shall not make private use of or profit from any confidential information gained as a result of being a member of the commission while in office. A member or employee shall conduct their private affairs in a manner that maintains public confidence in the integrity of their office and the commission as a whole. The code of conduct therefore serves to strengthen professionalism in the performance of employees' duties and prescribes several provisions to improve professional integrity.

The IEBC Act also addresses the proper functioning of the commission's internal democracy, with rules and procedures that, if adhered to, will lead to better governance, professionalism and credibility. The Second Schedule to the act seeks to regulate the business affairs of the commission by ensuring that regular meetings are held, that proper minutes of each meeting are recorded, and that members follow clear rules and procedures if there is a conflict of interest. These provisions will ensure that the commission conducts its affairs in a democratic and transparent manner.

In practice, the IEBC has been building its staff capacity and professionalism through the provision of various internal self-improvement training programmes on different aspects of elections and devolution.

Electoral Justice Responsibility

The constitution requires Parliament to enact legislation establishing mechanisms for the timely settlement of electoral disputes. Article 88(4)(e) gives the IEBC responsibility for settling electoral disputes, including those related to or arising from nominations, but excluding election petitions and disputes subsequent to the declaration of election results. In response to the constitution's provision, the Elections Act of 2011 contains various provisions (particularly section VI) that deal with election disputes resolution; section VI also specifies the timeframe within which an election petition filed through the commission should be settled.

In accordance with the Elections Act, disputes shall be determined within seven days of their lodging with the commission; where a dispute relates to a prospective nomination or election, it shall be determined before the date of the nomination or election. The Elections Act sets a timeframe of 28 days after the declaration of results by the IEBC within which an election petition may be filed.[7] The Elections Act also empowers the

IEBC to make regulations to provide complaints resolution mechanisms and settle electoral disputes—however, it has not yet issued such guidelines.

Empowered with the legal mandate to investigate and prosecute cases of electoral malpractice, the IEBC has begun recruiting investigation and prosecution staff to improve its capacity. Despite the law, to date the IEBC has not dealt with any electoral malpractices, although some (such as vote buying and voter bribery) were witnessed during the recent by-elections.

Stakeholder and Media Relations

During the disputed 2007 election, the media came under intense criticism. The IREC report in particular faulted the media for its skewed coverage and for the role it played in making inflammatory and partisan broadcasts. The government was faulted for having a weak legal and institutional framework for media regulation. New legislation and amendments to old legislation have been enacted to strengthen these frameworks. For example, article 34 of the constitution guarantees the independence of the media and provides that all state-owned media shall be free to operate impartially and independently determine the editorial content of their broadcasts and other communication. All state media should also be afforded a fair opportunity to present divergent views and dissenting opinions. The constitution also empowers Parliament to enact legislation that provides for the establishment of an independent body responsible for setting media standards, and regulating and monitoring compliance with the set standards.

Parliament also enacted the Kenya Communications Amendment Act (2009) to address some of the challenges of media regulation. The act provided for the formation of a Broadcasting Content Advisory Council, which was inaugurated in June 2010. Other relevant legal measures include the Media Act of 2010, which provided for the establishment of the Media Council of Kenya and gave it the responsibility to regulate the conduct of the media. Parliament, however, has yet to pass a number of bills to help improve the professional conduct of the media. These include the Media Bill of 2012 and the Freedom and Information Bill of 2012.

The Media Council published guidelines to help ensure professional conduct and reporting ahead of the 2013 elections. The IEBC also established guidelines on media elections monitoring and set up a media centre to provide a central location for the official release of all information concerning the elections. These accomplishments notwithstanding, there are to date no laws guaranteeing equitable access to the media during elections. The Elections Act of 2011 does empower the IEBC to establish necessary regulations for media access, however these have yet to be created.

In addition to the Political Parties Liaison Committee (PPLC), which was established by the legal framework as a statutory body to enable structured dialogue and consultations between political parties and the IEBC at the national and county levels, the commission has undertaken other efforts to help streamline consultations with stakeholders—particularly political parties. The IEBC recently issued guidelines to help guide political party practices, and has regularly provided information to all stakeholders through structured consultations such as the IEBC's Civil Society Forum and public outreach initiatives such as the Partners' Dialogue Forum, which facilitates the participation of observers in the IEBC's work and gives donors an opportunity to interact more closely with the IEBC. Despite these efforts, there are ongoing concerns that IEBC consultations with stakeholders are insufficient; therefore larger and more frequent meetings need to be considered.

Ability to Acquire and Manage New Election Technologies

The Elections Act of 2011 provides for the integration of appropriate technology in electoral processes. As per its mandate and in response to the election challenges of 2007, the IEBC introduced several new technologies to address specific election problems. The first was electronic voter registration (EVR) and the electronic poll book. The use of biometric features such as fingerprints and photos, enables the easy tracking of multiple registrations. It also enhances efficiency and accuracy, as it allows on-the-spot checking of voters' details. The EVR has been successfully used in the 2010 national referendum and in all parliamentary and civic by-elections since then. The IEBC also introduced an electronic vote tallying and transmission system in 2012 (EVT) to address delays in declaring final results, which largely contributed to the post-election crisis. It is the IEBC's ambition to fully automate electoral processes, including e-registration, e-voting and e-transmission of results.

Notes

[1] Kriegler and Waki Report on 2007 Elections in Kenya, April 2009.
[2] Constitutional Amendment, Article 41a.
[3] Chapter 15 of the constitution of Kenya.
[4] Articles 88(5) and 249(2) of the constitution.
[5] IEBC Act of 2011.
[6] IEBC Act of 2011, Fourth Schedule—Procedure for Appointment of Chairperson and Members of the Commission.
[7] Elections Act of 2011, Section VI.

References

Ballot, The, Official Newsletter of Interim Independent Electoral Commission, 1/1 (February 2011)

Commonwealth Observer Group, *Kenya General Elections, 27 December 2007*

Dundas, Carl W., *Close Elections and Political Succession in the African Union* (Bloomington, IN: Author House, 2012)

Dundas, Carl W., *The Lag of 21st Century Democratic Elections: In the African Union Member States* (Bloomington, IN: Author House, 2011)

Litscher, Jonathan, Mediation Support Project, 'Kenya, The National Accord Reconciliation Act 2008'

Kenya National Dialogue and Reconciliation, *Reforms and Preparedness for Elections Review Report,* May 2012

National Democratic Institute, 'Statement of the Pre-election Delegation to Kenya', May 2012

Ongoza, Z. Elisha and Otieno, Willis E., *Handbook on Kenya's Electoral Laws and Systems* (Johannesburg: Electoral Institute for Sustainable Democracy In Africa, 2012)

Progress project review of the Coordination and Liaison Office of the African Union Panel of Eminent African Personalities, 2009–2010

Yard, Mike, IFES chief of party in Kenya, public seminar on Kenya's new voting technology ahead of the March 2013 general elections, June 2012

CHAPTER 10

Assessing EMB Performance

Why is EMB Accountability Important?

Accountability means that an EMB is responsible for its activities, and must periodically provide evidence to its stakeholders and the public that these activities are effective and meet its prescribed legal, ethical, service and financial standards. The principle of accountability requires EMBs to provide comprehensive public information on their policies, intended outcomes, performance and the resources they have used and intend to use, including public and other funds. This is especially important where the EMB's independence from the executive government excludes the type of accountability to ministers that is a characteristic feature of public administration in many countries.

Accountability has a number of positive effects on the operations of an EMB. It increases the transparency of the EMB and promotes good governance, which helps it gain the confidence of the public and important stakeholders, particularly political parties and government ministries. A lack of proper accountability mechanisms may lead to accusations of poor operational transparency.

Principles and Best Practices for EMB Accountability

The financial accountability principles discussed in Chapter 7 of this Handbook also apply to an EMB's general accountability. Transparency and integrity are especially important. Transparency increases public trust and confidence in the EMB's operations, and may protect it against unfounded allegations.

An EMB needs to ensure that it has sufficient integrity controls on the information it releases publicly under its accountability responsibilities. Knowingly or unknowingly disseminating incorrect or unreliable information diminishes the credibility of and public trust in the EMB. How fully can the public trust an EMB's election results if it has been found to have provided unreliable information on other critical issues?

Stakeholder Accountability

An EMB has both informal and formal accountability to stakeholders, and through them, to the public. EMB accountability takes three main forms:

1. *consultation and communication* (informal) through regular contact with primary stakeholders, transparent working methods and regular reporting procedures;

2. *performance accountability* (formal) through the submission of activity reports on an annual basis, or after every major electoral event, and performance audits and evaluations to the legislature or government and other stakeholders; and

3. *financial accountability* (formal), which entails the regular submission of financial statements and audits to the legislature or government, among others, to explain how the funds allocated to the EMB have been used.

Consultation and Communication

Regular consultation with stakeholders promotes awareness about an EMB's operations and allows stakeholders to directly advise the EMB of their assessments of its performance and suggest potential improvements. These consultations may be regular or event driven, mandatory or voluntary, structured or informal. There is a detailed discussion of EMB communications with stakeholders in Chapter 8 of this Handbook.

Performance Accountability

An EMB is responsible for developing policy decisions to give effect to its mandate and ensuring their implementation. Mechanisms for performance accountability may be internal or external. EMBs are accountable for:

- electoral administration and its functioning;
- compliance with all relevant laws and regulations; and
- delivering good-quality electoral services to voters and other stakeholders.

Internal Performance Accountability

Internal performance accountability refers to the mechanisms by which:

- an EMB's lower structures account to higher structures for their performance; and
- staff with managerial responsibilities within an EMB monitor and assess institutional performance, and take corrective action in relation to activities that do not meet the required output targets, service levels and performance standards.

The key responsibility of EMB managerial staff is to ensure that the performance of its staff is of high standard, and meets the standards and fulfils the work plans that are anchored in the organization's strategic goals. Internal performance-based accountability also requires senior EMB secretariat staff to submit regular institutional performance reports and updates for review and consequent consideration of policy initiatives. EMBs may also consider following corporate board practice in regularly reviewing the performance of the head of the secretariat.

Performance expectations should have as their foundation the expected results and associated performance indicators set out in the EMB's strategic and operational plans. These need to be elaborated for the hierarchy of distinct work units (directorates, divisions, branches, sections, etc.) in the organization's structure. Each should have a plan indicating how, and by whom, progress is to be monitored and evaluated. Such plans should ultimately form the basis of personal work plans for individual staffers.

EMBs may also use the internal audit function to foster internal accountability. Internal auditors have in the past often narrowly monitored institutional compliance with rules and policies, especially in the areas of finance and administration, but internal audit functions are increasingly being used as a performance enhancement tool, assisting senior management to identify ways to improve an EMB's operational effectiveness.

External Performance Accountability

The second level of performance accountability is external accountability, for example, requirements that an EMB report to the legislature or the executive branch of government. EMBs in countries such as Cambodia, Georgia, Honduras, Lesotho and Russia submit their reports directly to the legislature. The EMB in Zambia submits reports to the president, who is required to table the EMB's report before the legislature within seven days after receipt. In Zimbabwe, the EMB is required to submit its annual reports to the president, the president of the Senate, the speaker of the National Assembly and the relevant minister (reports on specific elections are also required to be provided to the contesting political parties).

Some countries provide for EMBs to prepare performance and audited financial reports on an annual basis, for example, Bosnia and Herzegovina, Ecuador, Namibia, South Africa and Zambia. In Bolivia, the EMB has to submit an annual report to the legislature. The South African EMB is also subject to a rigorous series of accountability mechanisms. It must submit activity reports (including audited financial statements) to the legislature, both annually and following major electoral events, and prepare publicly available readiness reports on forthcoming electoral events. The president may also request the EMB to submit written reports to him/her on specific electoral matters. In the United States (see the case study on page 245), local authority EMBs are accountable to their communities, state officials and the courts.

In countries such as Costa Rica, Uruguay and Yemen, the EMBs have no formal performance accountability requirements. Australia, Costa Rica and Nigeria have legislative committees on electoral matters that could serve as an oversight mechanism on the EMB's activities. Uruguay's EMB is financially accountable through the external audit of its financial statements, but is not otherwise accountable. In Palestine, the EMB is required to publish an administrative and financial report on its activities three months after the announcement of the final election results, and copies must be submitted to the president of the Palestinian National Authority and the Palestinian Legislative Council.

It is common for EMB performance reports to be both descriptive and analytical, highlighting challenges to its operations, including funding issues and improvements to the electoral legal framework that would enhance its effectiveness. Since these reports go to the legislature and may influence government decision-making, it is important that they are comprehensive and clear enough to capture the attention and interest of lawmakers.

EMB reports may also be proactively circulated to other stakeholders, such as political parties, government ministries, donors, CSOs, universities and educational institutes, the business community and interested members of the public. Reports can be made widely accessible through cost-effective methods such as low-cost printing/copying or publication by CD-ROM or on the EMB's website. Sending copies of reports to international electoral research and assistance organizations may help promote international awareness about the EMB's country, including the challenges it faces and its election or democracy-building assistance needs.

Financial Accountability

An EMB has the responsibility to use the financial and other resources it receives effectively, to achieve its strategic objectives. It is accountable for:

- the efficient use of its resources to achieve value for money;
- compliance with all relevant laws and regulations; and
- using ethical financial practices.

Financial accountability may be provided for in the electoral legal framework, as in Lesotho, or in general legal requirements for public sector entities. Some EMBs have in the past deemed it appropriate to treat their statutory requirements as a minimum, and offered more regular financial reporting than is formally required. Like performance accountability, financial accountability has two components, internal and external.

Internal Financial Accountability

Internal financial accountability mechanisms are an EMB's internal procedures that promote control over its financial resources. They may include measures such as:

- an EMB subcommittee that oversees its finances;
- formal financial reporting structures within the EMB's secretariat and to the EMB's members (or, for governmental EMBs, to the host government department);
- the use of performance budgeting to ensure that all expenditure is in line with the EMB's operational and strategic objectives; and
- regular internal audits to monitor and review the EMB's financial management procedures and their implementation.

If an EMB cannot demonstrate that its internal financial accountability controls are sufficient to ensure the probity and effectiveness of its financial management, there is more likely to be pressure for more onerous external financial accountability controls. This may have negative effects on the EMB's financial autonomy and its capacity for independent action.

External Financial Accountability

External financial accountability mechanisms are primarily based on the external audit of an EMB's financial activities and statements. Additional external audits may be undertaken on specific financial systems (such as salary payments), or following allegations of corrupt or irregular practices within an EMB. In the latter case, state anti-corruption bodies may also be involved in the external audit.

Many EMBs' external financial auditing is undertaken by a government audit agency, such as the State Audit Office in Bosnia and Herzegovina, the auditor-general in Australia and Canada, or the Comptroller General of the Republic in Honduras and Panama (during election periods). External audit of the EMB in Turkey is by an Audit Court that is responsible to the legislature. In Portugal, the governmental EMB may be audited by the Ministry of Finance and the Court of Auditors. In Zambia, EMB finances are audited annually by independent auditors appointed by the EMB, while in Russia, the external audit is performed by the Federal Assembly through its Accounts Chamber. In Peru, EMB finances must be audited no later than three months after elections.

An EMB normally incorporates audited financial statements into its annual or other reports for submission to the legislature and other stakeholders. For example, in Cameroon, the audited financial reports are tabled in the legislature, while the performance audit is submitted to the president.

Review of an EMB's financial accounts by a committee of the legislature, often called a Public Accounts Committee, can provide a public demonstration of the EMB's financial integrity. The framework of such reviews needs to ensure that the EMB is questioned fairly, rather than for political advantage. If auditors have identified poor financial management practices, members or senior executives of the EMB may be summoned to explain the circumstances and describe the remedial action that has been taken.

Accountability for the Use of Technology-based Systems

The increasing use of computer-based systems for electoral operations and management creates some additional challenges for EMB accountability. Apart from the issue of sustainability (discussed in Chapter 9 of this Handbook), public confidence in their accuracy and reliability needs to be assured.

A lack of any tangible evidence of transactions in many computer systems, the lack of transparency and the incomprehensibility of computer programming to the bulk of the population, and the risks of interference with data are widely publicized through media reports of computer worms, viruses and hackers. These can affect the credibility of EMBs that rely on computer systems for vital tasks such as voter registration, voting and vote counting unless they are openly accountable for their use.

There is still intense debate about the reliability and security of computer-based systems for voting and counting of votes. In the aftermath of the 2000 US presidential election, the question of standards for such systems received renewed and extensive attention. One response to concerns about the integrity of such systems has been the use of VVPAT (discussed in Chapter 9).

Beyond technical performance issues, in the United States some of this debate involves the propriety of politically aligned supplier behaviour. Media reports of alleged integrity problems with mechanical and e-voting machines in the United States, including with DRE 'touch screen' vote-recording machines (as in the state of Maryland in 2004) has increased pressure on EMBs to be open and accountable in their use of technology. These concerns featured heavily in the 2005 report of the Baker–Carter Commission on Federal Electoral Reform, and the literature on the subject is growing rapidly.

EMB Assessment Mechanisms

To meet internal and external accountability requirements, an EMB needs mechanisms that can assess its activities and assure itself and its stakeholders of the quality, effectiveness and probity of its operational and financial management. These mechanisms include internal quality controls, audits, evaluations, peer reviews and external oversight.

Internal Quality Controls

Internal quality assurance programmes are the starting point for assuring an EMB and its stakeholders that EMB activities meet service, effectiveness and appropriateness standards. EMBs may wish to follow the relevant International Organization for Standardization guidelines and standards.

Components of a quality assurance programme may include:

- stakeholder consultation on new systems and methods;

- implementation of formally reviewed, benchmarked design and development processes;
- rigorous pre-implementation testing;
- comprehensive training programmes;
- ensuring that professional staff are qualified to be members of the appropriate professional associations;
- formal post-implementation monitoring programmes; and
- robust reporting of faults and rectification processes.

In relation to quality control, a specific matter requiring attention is identifying and preventing or mitigating criminal fraud (which may take the form of financial fraud aimed at enriching the perpetrators, or electoral fraud with the objective of manipulating election outcomes or compromising public faith in their validity). To develop and implement an integrated and comprehensive fraud control plan, an EMB will likely require input from the financial, operational and legal areas of the organization. It will need to carefully consider whether parts of the plan need to be kept confidential, since there is a risk that publishing fraud control strategies may help those who wish to circumvent them. It also needs to be borne in mind that mechanisms aimed at the total elimination of the possibility of fraud may have side effects, such as the suppression of voter participation, that are so undesirable that it is preferable to accept and manage some risk of fraud.

Auditing EMBs

An audit critically examines and assesses an EMB's activities, strictly within the parameters of its stated strategic objectives. Regular auditing is an essential means of ensuring that an EMB is accountable for its operations. As noted above, auditing is increasingly used for wider purposes than testing financial compliance; audits also assess the appropriateness and effectiveness of publicly funded organizations' strategies, operational methodologies, and performance in delivering services to the public.

Just as an EMB has performance and financial accountabilities, an EMB audit can be performance based (focusing on the economy, efficiency and effectiveness of its activities) or finance based (examining an EMB's accounting records against accounting standards to assess the efficiency and probity of its handling of funds). An audit may also be a combination of performance and finance based, and may be broadly based (examining overall EMB performance or transactions) or limited to a particular activity or system operated by the EMB.

Regardless of the type of audit, it is usually conducted in accordance with professional auditing standards. Audit reports, which are usually made public, would either certify this accordance or explain why such standards could not be applied, and justify the standards or methodology used. The audit investigation and report may identify good and bad practices found; assess operational or financial management controls; identify non-compliance with the law or policies, and breaches of financial probity or integrity in operations; note improvements made since earlier audits; and assess the appropriateness of methods and systems used or the levels of service provided to achieve the EMB's objectives.

A professional audit report is always objective, factual, accurate, complete and fair, and emphasizes the EMB's positive accomplishments as well as identifying any failings. It is good practice for auditors to discuss their draft findings and recommendations with the EMB, for the EMB to be given sufficient time to respond to these, and for the EMB's responses to be carefully considered before the audit report is finalized and publicly issued.

Performance Audits

Performance audits are an objective, independent and systematic examination of an EMB's activities and management systems to assess how effectively, efficiently and economically it has used its resources. They may be conducted internally or externally, and may cover the whole range of an EMB's activities or focus on a particular function or programme. Performance audits identify strengths and weaknesses in an EMB's activities, and recommend appropriate corrective actions. A performance audit is an important mechanism for improving electoral management, instituting good practice, improving public accountability and reinforcing institutional integrity.

Methodology and Scope of a Performance Audit

Performance audits typically involve both internal examination—reviewing an EMB's relevant policies and records and conducting interviews with relevant EMB members—and external assessment—interviews with an EMB's stakeholders and a review of media and other reports on its activities so as to determine the external perception of the EMB's performance. These audits commonly undertake both cost-benefit and cost-effectiveness analyses, and use performance indicators—included in the EMB's strategic plan, where appropriate—and the standards of service either defined by the EMB or expected by its stakeholders, to assess the EMB's performance against its strategic objectives.

Components of a performance audit usually include:

- *interviewing the principal stakeholders,* such as political parties, voters, members of the legislature, CSOs, media organizations, relevant government ministries and agencies, and suppliers. This may include joint consultation with stakeholders at workshops or seminars;
- *interviewing EMB members,* secretariat staff and where relevant, temporary staff or contractors engaged for the activities under review;
- *examining the EMB's strategic plan,* management structure, relevant policies, operational plans and task assignments, and the implementation of these planned activities; and

- *reviewing relevant constitutional instruments,* laws, regulations, court or tribunal decisions, codes of conduct, and the EMB's computer and other systems, reports, procedures, manuals, guidelines and relevant records.

The specific criteria for and issues covered by a performance audit will be governed by the activity or activities to be audited. For example, a performance audit of an EMB's overall conduct of an election could use the design criteria and address the issues listed in Table 15.

Table 15: Election Performance Audit: Criteria and Issues

Election Performance Criteria	Specific Election Performance Audit Issues
• Election preparation and design: the logic and completeness of election planning. • Efficiency of election processes: cost-to-output ratios and resulting quality. • Effectiveness of election activities: the contribution made by the EMB's services to election objectives. • Impact: the effect of the EMB's conduct of the election on the wider democratic environment and state stability. • Sustainability: the ability to maintain a stream of benefits from the election.	• The appropriateness of EMB's regulations, policies, procedures, plans (including those relating to fraud control) and performance standards for its election objectives. • The appropriateness of the EMB's structure and culture for delivering election services to the expected standards of service. • The level of the EMB's compliance with the election's legal framework and its internal regulations and procedures. • The level of any conflicts and duplication within the EMB's election activities, and between election and other EMB programmes. • The impact of the electoral system on the EMB's systems procedures. • The effectiveness and sustainability of the use of technology for election purposes. • The levels of knowledge about elections among the EMB members and staff, and the effects of training and staff development on these. • The impacts of the EMB's information campaigns. • The effectiveness of relationships between the EMB and other organizations with a role in the election. • The EMB's performance in implementing the major election processes. • The EMB's accountability to its stakeholders.

Performance Audit Outputs

A performance audit's output could be expected to include information related to the activities or processes being audited and recommendations targeted at assisting the EMB and its oversight bodies to improve their services to stakeholders.

Performance audits can have a wide range of impacts, on both the EMB and stakeholders' perceptions of it. These impacts can include savings in the use of resources, higher efficiency, strengthened management policies and practices, improved service quality and a better understanding of accountability.

Table 16: Possible Performance Audit Findings and Recommendations

Performance Audit Findings	Performance Audit Recommendations
• Strengths and weaknesses of the EMB's management systems and management team.	• Methods of improving management, operational and financial systems and procedures to improve performance against EMB objectives.
• Strengths and weaknesses of methods used to implement relevant activities or processes.	• Methods of using resources more economically while achieving expected quality. • Methods of using EMB resources more efficiently, reducing the cost-to-output ratio. • Methods of improving EMB effectiveness by better achieving its planned objectives, performance standards and service levels.
• Constraints that may have affected the EMB's ability to achieve objectives related to the activities being audited.	• Changes to the EMB's external environment that will assist the EMB to achieve its objectives and improve service delivery, longer-term viability and sustainability.
• Determination of the extent to which the activities and processes reviewed have achieved the objectives, performance levels and service standards defined by the EMB and expected by its stakeholders.	• Improvements to the EMB's framework and planned results, performance standards and service levels that would allow the EMB to meet its objectives in a manner that enhances its service to its stakeholders. • Changes to improve the accountability and transparency of the EMB, and to increase public trust in the institution.

Financial Audits

The EMB's internal financial audit is its final internal checking mechanism to promote financial probity and integrity. An external financial audit of an EMB reviews the EMB's accounts to provide an independent opinion of their completeness, compliance, integrity and accuracy. Most EMBs are required to prepare and submit annual audited accounts, which are linked to achievements and activities based on the annual work plan. The report may reflect the level of financial contributions by the state and external sources, where appropriate, and the expenditure of these funds.

Electoral events generate many financial transactions related to acquiring election supplies, materials and equipment and employing large numbers of additional staff. Many EMBs have a relatively large dispersed staff, including thousands of temporary workers, and procure millions of dollars worth of electoral equipment, services and materials, often in a very short time. In this environment, corruption and misappropriation of funds may occur if adequate safeguards are not in place.

Financial audits aim to provide reasonable assurance that the financial statements of an audited EMB fairly represent the financial position, the results of operations and cash flows in conformity with generally accepted accounting principles and financial reporting standards. Such audits seek to establish whether all financial transactions have followed the financial compliance criteria, based on either the EMB's own rules and regulations or on more general public sector financial accountability laws or rules. They also assess and provide an opinion on whether the EMB's internal control structure for finance and safeguarding assets is suitably designed and implemented to ensure accuracy and integrity in financial management records and to prevent fraud.

Financial audits may cover some or all of the following areas:

- financial statements and information (such as revenue and expenses, cash receipts and disbursements, and the inventory of assets);
- budget requests and variations between estimated and actual financial performance;
- compliance with laws and regulations, especially on procurement, accounting, reporting on contracts and grants, and anti-corruption measures; and
- internal controls on funds, assets and financial reporting.

Programme Evaluation by EMBs

Programme evaluation is another widely used tool to help EMBs improve their accountability. The boundaries between performance auditing and programme evaluation are blurred. Both provide independent, objective analyses of how an EMB may use its resources better. A performance audit will generally concentrate on the economy, efficiency and effectiveness of the EMB's performance in relation to the objectives stated in its strategic plan or other legal and operational framework documents. A programme evaluation will usually start by questioning whether the electoral framework and the EMB's strategic objectives meet the needs of its stakeholders.

Key questions for a programme evaluation of an EMB's activities include:

1. Do the legal framework for the EMB's activities, and the EMB's objectives, meet the needs and objectives of its stakeholders?
2. Are the services the EMB provides necessary?
3. Could the EMB's services be provided more effectively?
4. What are the long- and short-term impacts of the services being provided?

Programme evaluations are wholly outcome focused, feeding back into the EMB's strategic planning cycle. They concentrate on how an EMB serves its stakeholders, including whether the needs assessments on which an EMB's strategies and activities are based are still valid. As they are stakeholder focused, they concentrate on obtaining stakeholders' expectations of the EMB and their views on the appropriateness and performance of its current activities. In an environment of technological advances, changing societal attitudes, and evolving political and legal frameworks, these evaluations assist the EMB to identify areas of activity that no longer effectively meet its stakeholders' needs. A programme evaluation may review whether specific EMB services are still needed, or whether other institutions are better placed than the EMB to use all or some of the public funds available for specific electoral services, for example, voter education and information.

Post-election Reviews

EMBs increasingly use post-election reviews to assess the adequacy of the legal and management structures for elections, and of their performance in delivering credible elections. These reviews are complementary to financial and performance audits. Countries that require the submission of performance reports after every major electoral event include Botswana and Georgia. The Botswana EMB engaged a team of electoral experts to conduct a review of its performance during the country's 2004 general elections. This review produced several key recommendations with far-reaching implications, including requirements for constitutional and legal amendments. In 2006–07, the certification team appointed by the UN for the 2007 elections in Timor-Leste produced a series of reports on the processes that, while not designated as performance reviews, served a similar purpose by highlighting and documenting in detail a range of issues it had identified.

A post-election review report analyses what worked well, what did not and why. It may cover every aspect of the electoral system, processes, and management structures and capabilities, and is better if it is based on the analysts' direct experiences of the electoral event, not just an examination of the records. Polling and vote-counting activities, voters' attitudes and stakeholders' responses to EMB actions can be matters for detailed examination in a post-election review. Such a review could also address how the EMB's funding processes help or hinder its sustainability. The review report can examine the strengths and weaknesses of the EMB and the electoral framework, and make suitable recommendations for remedial action. The results of the review need to feed into discussions about electoral reform and the procedural development of the EMB throughout the electoral cycle.

The twin approach of needs assessment studies prior to a general election and a post-election review of EMB performance during an electoral period can help identify the level of sustainability of free, fair and credible elections that can be achieved over the longer term.

Table 17: The Botswana Post-election Review 2004: Terms of Reference

Legal Framework	• Assess the relevance, adequacy and effectiveness of the legal framework in place to guide the Independent Electoral Commission (IEC) in the execution of its mandate (Electoral Act and Constitution). • Assess the clarity of the legal framework with particular emphasis on the nature of the Commission's mandate. • Assess the adequacy of the functions of the IEC and its Secretary as stipulated in the Constitution of Botswana. • Explore the need for a specific Act of Parliament on the IEC's persona, functions, its employees and other relevant legal matters. • Propose reform or otherwise of the existing legal framework.
Operational Framework (Execution of Mandate)	• Assess the IEC state of preparedness for the 2004 general elections. • Evaluate if the IEC in preparing for the 2004 elections observed its mandate relative to the existing legal framework. • Assess the relevance, adequacy and effectiveness of the IEC Civic and Voter Education Programmes. • Assess the effectiveness of the IEC in conducting the 2004 elections and identify real and perceived problems and weaknesses. • Assess the Commission's relationships with its major stakeholders. This assessment should give priority to the Commission's relationship with the executive in order to suggest most effective ways of IEC-Government liaison which enhances IEC accountability and transparency but preserves its independence. • Assess how best to promote good communication between the Commission and the Secretariat.
Appointment of the Commision and Related Staffing Issues	• Evaluate procedures for the appointment of the members of the Commission and the Secretary and propose improvements where necessary. • Assess the competence and adequacy of the Commission's electoral staff. • Identify weak links and propose development interventions. • Assess if the Commission should have the powers to hire, discipline and fire its staff at all levels, including the Secretary.
Financing	• Assess the adequacy of the IEC financing and also the effectiveness of the current funding mechanisms.
Independence of IEC	• Assess to what extent the IEC is and should be independent. • Propose parameters that should define the independence of the IEC. • Suggest reporting channels for the IEC.
Future Performance Evaluations	• Look into ways of institutionalising performance evaluations as part of the normal post-election routines of the IEC.
Other Issues	• Assess relevance and adequacy of IEC's current strategic plan and propose improvements. • Issues relevant to gender and elections, including gender mainstreaming in the IEC.

Source: Dundas, Carl W., Maundeni, Zibani and Balule, T., 'Final Report: Audit of the Independent Electoral Commission's (IEC) Preparedness to Conduct Legitimate and Credible Elections in October 2004. Report of a Team of Consultants Appointed to Audit the Operation of the 2004 Elections in Botswana', December 2004.

Table 18: EMB Post-election Review Cycle Checklist

Responsibility	Action
EMB Management	• Before electoral period commences, develop the scope and terms of reference of the review following consultation with stakeholders, and appoint responsible EMB manager and review team, and/or external consultants (if required). • Explain to EMB staff the nature and purpose of the review.
Review Team	• Develop plan and timetable for information collection during and after the electoral period, analysis and reporting. • Review the documentary framework for the relevant election processes—such as the legal framework, EMB policies and procedures, and relevant documents issued by other bodies. • During the electoral period, witness election processes, interview external stakeholders and EMB staff, and continuously collect relevant election performance data. • Conduct post-election interviews or roundtables of stakeholders for views on overall election performance. • Collect data after the election to cover gaps in existing data, and on issues such as election result disputes. • Analyse data and draft review report.
EMB Management	• Review and respond to draft review report.
Review Team	• Draft final review report considering EMB management response.
EMB Management	• Present review report to stakeholders. • Discuss recommended changes in review report with EMB staff. • Advocacy to stakeholders, including government and the legislature, of electoral reforms recommended in the review report. • Develop new policies and procedures based on the review findings and recommendations, and any resulting electoral law reform. • In consultation with stakeholders, develop the scope and terms of reference for review of the next election, paying particular attention to issues noted in the review of the previous election.

Peer Reviews

Peer reviews can bring the knowledge of experienced electoral practitioners to both internal and external review (audit and evaluation) mechanisms. Using EMB field staff from one geographical area to assist with financial or performance audits or post-election evaluations in another geographical area of the EMB, as was practised by the Australian EMB in the early 1990s, can be extremely beneficial. The EMB offices being audited may be more likely to take note of recommendations from peers who have had to solve similar management problems, and both the reviewer and those being reviewed can broaden their knowledge through the exchange of ideas. Similar benefits arise from including senior experienced electoral professionals, from the same country or another country, on EMB external review teams.

External Oversight Issues

External oversight of an EMB is part of its external accountability, and may be implemented through mechanisms such as external audits or evaluations, reviews of EMB activities by an ad hoc or other specially appointed body, or reviews by a committee of the legislature, such as an electoral affairs or public accounts committee.

If an entity undertaking external oversight of an EMB is not fully independent, it may be subject to interference that improperly inhibits its scope and/or methodology. There may be attempts to change or influence the content of oversight reports. Constraints on oversight bodies may include restrictions on terms of reference, the time allowed for investigations, access to information, or access to sufficient funds and other resources to carry out the task. An example is the conflict that arose between the election monitoring body Panwas and the EMB in Indonesia in 2004. While Panwas was expected to act independently in its role as the monitor of the conduct of elections and the body of first instance for most electoral disputes, it had been appointed and funded by the EMB and Panwas' challenges to EMB decisions led the EMB to issue regulations that barred Panwas' involvement in challenges or disputes involving the EMB.

Oversight bodies need the rights to examine documents and computer files; to verify services paid for and property acquired with public funds; and to interview EMB members, staff and other persons. These rights can be guaranteed if they are included in the legal framework. If not, the EMB can enhance its credibility by allowing free and unimpeded access. Official oversight agencies may be given the authority to obtain court-enforceable subpoenas to compel the EMB and other organizations to produce specific documentation, with sanctions for non-compliance. Where an oversight agency is given investigative powers, it is usually able to administer and take affidavits under oath.

To be effective, oversight must be subject to rigorous quality control so that it is professional, impartial and accurate. Adequate numbers of skilled staff with a keen appreciation of the legal, financial and operational frameworks within which election tasks are conducted will facilitate good practice in oversight duties. The findings of oversight bodies need to be objective and targeted toward improving EMB services.

Chapter Summary

- Accountability to its stakeholders promotes EMB transparency and good governance, and positively influences the general public's perception of its professionalism and impartiality.
- Informal accountability through regular communication with stakeholders and formal performance and financial accountability mechanisms are all necessary, complementary measures for ensuring that an EMB is

accountable for compliance with the law, financial probity, operational integrity and effective customer-focused activity.

- Performance accountability is both internal and external. Internal measures include management monitoring and the use of internal audits to examine performance issues. External measures include external reviews and requirements for reporting to stakeholders such as the legislature. Wide distribution of EMB reports can make a broad range of stakeholders aware of the EMB's challenges and achievements.

- Similarly, an EMB is internally and externally financially accountable. Internal measures include financial reporting and control mechanisms, and regular internal audits. External measures include external audits and the regular provision of audited financial statements to stakeholders such as legislatures and donors, and review by an appropriate body.

- The use of technology-based systems, especially for voting and counting votes, places additional accountability requirements on EMBs, as these systems may not be transparent to or easily understood by stakeholders. High levels of quality and integrity assurance, including evidence of transactions, must be maintained.

- In order to assure stakeholders of the effectiveness and probity of its performance, an EMB may use a variety of measures including pre-implementation and real-time quality assurance controls, and later audit, evaluation and external oversight mechanisms. The use of peer review processes can give added credibility to audit and evaluation findings and recommendations.

- The development of a formal, well-considered and integrated fraud mitigation and control plan, which covers both financial processes and electoral operations, can be a useful tool for improving the quality of elections and enhancing stakeholders' confidence in them.

- Evaluation is the analysis of the electoral framework as a whole, while audit is a method used to analyse/evaluate specific issues within the framework. Evaluation can encompass an audit, but an audit cannot encompass an evaluation.

- Performance and financial audits can identify good practices being used by an EMB; deter and detect fraud, corruption and malpractice; identify how an EMB can improve its methods of complying with financial requirements; and improve its operational performance and institutional integrity in order to meet the objectives of its strategic plan.

- Performance audits assess the economy, efficiency and effectiveness of an EMB's activities, and can have a significant impact on improving its quality of service, make its resource use more cost effective and strengthening electoral management. Financial audits can improve internal financial controls, and promote compliance with the relevant rules and the efficient use of financial resources.

- In addition to audits, an EMB may undertake programme evaluations of specified parts or all of its activities. Programme evaluations examine not just how well the EMB has done what it intended to do, but whether its strategic objectives are appropriate for its environment and meet its stakeholders' needs. They assess how an EMB's activities could be improved to better meet these needs in an economical, efficient and effective manner. They are an effective way of helping EMBs meet the challenges of a changing external environment.

- Well-planned post-election reviews are particularly useful to EMBs. Recommendations from these reviews can feed into internal EMB policy and procedural reform, and EMB advocacy for electoral framework reform, throughout the electoral cycle.

- Independent external oversight of an EMB may be through external audit or evaluation, by a standing committee of the legislature, or by a specially appointed ad hoc body. To be effective, the body performing the oversight needs access to all relevant materials and personnel; a strongly independent, impartial and professional culture; and rigorous quality controls.

CASE STUDY

The United Kingdom: Electoral Governance in Transition?*

Toby S. James

Introduction

Until the turn of the 21st century, there had been very few changes in the way that elections are run in the UK, or in the organizations and individuals responsible for them. The foundations of electoral practices remained rooted in the Municipal Ballots Act of 1872 and the Representation of the People Act of 1918. However, the new century brought major change. The New Labour governments from 1997–2010 introduced changes such as rolling registration, postal voting on demand and innovative electoral pilot schemes.[1] Changes have also been made to the organization and governance of elections. The Electoral Commission was established in 2000 and has quickly established itself as a source of expertise on electoral law. It has fearless independence from the government and has had an important influence on the practice of elections in the UK.

However, UK electoral governance is increasingly complex and fluid, in part because a range of organizations play a role in running elections. Ultimate responsibility for running elections remains with officers employed by local authorities; therefore the UK formally best fits the Governmental Model of electoral management. However, there are different arrangements for different jurisdictions within the UK, partly as a result of the recent creation of an elected Scottish Government, Welsh Assembly Government and Northern Irish Assembly. Scotland now has its own EMB, Wales has recently discussed the decentralization of election law, and Northern Ireland has long had unique arrangements.

The Electoral Commission is a new organization, and its role has already changed since its creation in 2000. It has been granted more power over local authorities, and wants more still. If granted, it may better approximate the Mixed Model than the Governmental Model. Yet the uncodified nature of the British constitution means that

---

* A case study on the United Kingdom also appeared in the original edition of the Handbook: Ellie Greenwod, 'The United Kingdom: Electoral Modernization', *Electoral Management Design: The International IDEA Handbook* (Stockholm: International IDEA, 2006), pp. 80–3.

the Electoral Commission, like all public organizations, can be abolished at any time by a government that has a majority in Parliament.

Running UK Elections: A Who's Who

Elections have historically been run by returning officers, who are appointed by local authorities. They are responsible for the conduct of the poll and have some discretion over the timing of the count. An electoral registration officer is responsible for compiling the electoral register. Both returning officers and electoral registration officers are local government employees, but are independent of both the central and local governments with respect to their electoral duties. They are instead accountable to the courts system as independent statutory officers, and can be prosecuted for being in breach of their duties.[2]

There are some important variations across the UK. In England and Wales, the electoral registration officer and returning officer are often the same person working within the same local authority. However in Scotland, electoral registration is organized by Valuation Joint Boards, which undertake the task of valuing properties for the purpose of local taxation. The assessor in charge of the Valuation Joint Board is therefore the electoral registration officer. In Northern Ireland, a chief electoral officer acts as both the returning officer and the electoral registration officer. (S)he is supported by the Electoral Office for Northern Ireland and appointed by the secretary of state for Northern Ireland.

Electoral registration officers and returning officers implement elections according to electoral law, which is determined by the central UK government. Prior to 2000, a small Elections Department was responsible for developing advice and information from the Home Office. In 2000 a UK Electoral Commission was set up to provide advice and guidance on election administration and to regulate the financing of political parties.

In some senses, therefore, the Electoral Commission is not an EMB according to the definition used in this Handbook. It only has the power to direct officials involved in administering referendums. However, it undoubtedly plays an important role in the governance of elections. And the trajectory is toward a growing role. The Electoral Administration Act of 2006 amended the Political Parties, Elections and Referendums Act of 2000 to give the Electoral Commission the power to set performance standards for returning officers, electoral registration officers and referendum counting officers.[3] These have been an important way through which the commission can manage electoral administrators without having formal control.[4]

A further development has been the creation of the Electoral Management Board for Scotland. This was created by the Scottish Government in the Scottish Parliament (Local Electoral Administration (Scotland) Act 2011) with the aim of supporting local authorities and promoting best practice. It is convened by a returning officer, who is appointed by ministers. The Scottish EMB has statutory power of direction over local returning officers in local government elections. The Electoral Commission has welcomed the establishment of the Scottish EMB, noting that its statutory powers are limited to local elections, but that it may help to develop methods of best practice for other elections.[5] The Scottish Government proposed that the poll and count for the independence referendum be conducted by local authorities under the direction of the Scottish EMB. The Electoral Commission would therefore provide advice and regulation of the campaign.[6]

In Wales, an Elections Planning Group (comprising the Welsh Government, the Electoral Commission, representatives of the political parties and returning officers) meets to agree on uniform approaches to local and Welsh Assembly elections, such as the timing of the count. The group has no statutory power. However, the Welsh Government is considering asking for powers to be devolved to Wales to give it legislative control over local and Assembly elections.[7]

There are four advisory, non-governmental Boundary Commissions (for England, Wales, Scotland and Northern Ireland) that conduct periodic reviews of electoral districts and provide Parliament with recommendations on any changes. Their proposals are subject to a vote in the House of Commons.

Electoral justice is primarily dealt with by the court system. Election Courts can be convened by the High Court if a petition is raised challenging the result of an election. The Electoral Commission has some powers of sanction for election finance law (see below), but this is mostly dealt with by the broader legal system.

In short, Parliament retains ultimate power in deciding electoral law, and this is implemented by employees of local authorities, with a range of other institutions playing advisory or supervisory roles. Since it is the primary EMB, the remainder of this case study will focus on the role of the UK Electoral Commission.

Legislative Framework

There is no single piece of legislation that consolidates electoral law or the responsibility for elections. The Law Commission recently expressed concern that for the May 2010 elections electoral administrators had to consult 25 different pieces of legislation, some of which were UK wide and others that only related to part of the UK.[8] Some electoral administrators find the fragmented legal framework confusing, and commonly report that this makes them more likely to make errors.[9]

The Electoral Commission's role is defined by the Political Parties, Elections and Referendums Act of 2000 as amended by the Political Parties and Elections Act of 2009. The duties of electoral registration officers and returning officers are primarily specified by the Representation of the People Act of 1983. The role of the Electoral Office for Northern Ireland is covered in various legislation dating back to the 1970s.[10] Party finance regulations are covered in the Political Parties, Elections and Referendums Act of 2000, as amended by the Electoral Administration Act of 2006 and the Political Parties and Elections Act of 2009. There is a powerful case for legal consolidation.

The Powers and Functions of the UK Electoral Commission

The Electoral Commission works in five broad areas. First, it is responsible for the regulation of election finances and party donations. There are caps on the campaign spending of political parties at both the national and constituency levels. There are also regulations on who can make donations to political parties and the size of these donations. The commission maintains public registers of political parties and the details of their donations, borrowing, campaign expenditures and annual accounts. The commission compiles this information and presents it in an intelligible format to the public. They also investigate breaches of the regulations. The Political Parties and Elections Act of 2009 provided the commission with a range of sanctions (e.g. fines) that it can impose when it is clear beyond a reasonable doubt that the law has been broken. However, some breaches remain subject to criminal prosecution only.[11] The commission is also responsible for the registration of political parties.

Second, the commission undertakes considerable policy and research work on election administration, political broadcasting and election finance. It has a statutory requirement to coordinate evaluations of all elections run in the UK. It is also required to evaluate a range of specified innovations, such as recent efforts by the UK Government to use electronic databases to improve the electoral register.[12] Finally, it must keep electoral matters under review. This latter function gives the commission some freedom to undertake research that it considers important. It therefore regularly undertakes reviews of the effectiveness of existing electoral practices and public opinion toward them. For example, it has evaluated the completeness of the electoral register[13] and has recently stated an intent to review the case for voter identification requirements at polling stations, even though no political party has called for this. These reports are then used to develop policy positions and are fed into the development of legislation.

Third, the commission advises on party election and referendum broadcasts. Policy is ultimately determined by the broadcasting authorities, but they are required to consider the commission's views.

Fourth, the commission provides support and guidance to electoral administrators, parties and candidates, and the general public. It publishes resources for staff in local authorities delivering the elections. It has a password-protected area on its website where it provides a range of key resources, but it also fields miscellaneous queries. During 2011–12 it claimed to have responded to almost 4,000 queries on matters of electoral law and practice and party and election finance.[14] Electoral law in the UK has become increasingly complex, in part because of an increase in the number of elections and the use of different electoral systems, and administrators often value this resource.[15] The commission also provides information for the general public, including a website explaining how to register to vote that was well used during the 2010 general election. The commission originally had a statutory requirement and a ring-fenced GBP 7.5 million budget to promote public participation, but this was removed after a committee that was reviewing the commission's role suggested that it focus on its regulatory functions.[16]

Fifth, the commission has recently been granted the power to set performance standards for returning officers, electoral registration officers and referendum counting officers in Britain. The commission publishes a set of standards, and election officials are required to self-assess as to whether they are 'below', 'at' or 'above' the standard. The results are then made publically available in Electoral Commission reports and an online search tool. This is an innovative approach from an international perspective, and has been an important way in which the commission can manage electoral administrators without having direct control.[17]

The Electoral Commission, however, has recently revised how the scheme works. Originally, standards were published and administrators were asked to report on their performance after an election. In May 2012 a new set of indicators was devised for returning officers, who were then asked to report in real time whether they had undertaken a specific task so that the commission could check the progress of implementation. This followed a similar approach in the Welsh Assembly and alternative vote referendums in 2011. The commission currently lacks the power to direct election officials who have not undertaken a specific task for elections, but has made the case for being granted this authority, which would be a significant development because it would grant the commission much more control, and it would more closely fit the Mixed rather than the Governmental Model.

The Electoral Commission therefore cannot initiate any changes to electoral procedures itself, and its role, apart from its involvement in referendums, is advisory. In practice, however, the role that the commission plays in keeping procedures under review and advising government and other agencies means that it has often been effective at putting or keeping certain issues on the political agenda. For example, it has long argued for the introduction of individual registration in Britain and this is now being implemented. However, governments have also ignored the commission's advice and introduced changes for partisan ends. For example, New Labour governments ignored its recommendations on individual registration and the use of postal voting in the 2004 European elections.[18]

Relationships with Other Organizations

As noted above, a vast range of other actors are involved in the delivery of elections in the UK, and the commission has active relationships with each of them. The commission is well respected by the media, and its views are usually reported when changes to the law are proposed or if there are news stories relating to elections. The Political Parties, Elections and Referendums Act of 2000 allows the commission to provide assistance to overseas organizations and governments if it is requested. Overseas delegations from Australia, Bangladesh, Korea and Taiwan have observed elections in recent years. Organizations such as the OSCE have also published reports on the quality of elections in the UK.[19]

Institutional Structure and Appointment Methods

The commission is comprised of nine or ten commissioners who are supported by a chief executive, executive team and approximately 140 staff. Originally the commissioners were required to be independent of the political parties. However, the Political Parties and Elections Act of 2009 reduced the restriction on political activity for some commissioners on the basis that they brought more recent experience from party politics. As a result of these changes, there are up to six 'ordinary' commissioners who remain subject to restrictions on political activity. These are selected by a Speakers Committee in the House of Commons. There are also up to four 'nominated' commissioners whose names are put forward by the leaders of the political parties in the House of Commons and considered by the Speakers Committee. Having considered the candidates and made a recommendation on the appointment of the commissioners, the Speakers Committee has a statutory requirement to consult with the leaders of the political parties.[20] The appointment of the commissioners has not yet been a partisan issue, but there is scope for it to be.

The commission is primarily based in its central office in London, but there are smaller regional offices in Belfast, Cardiff, Edinburgh, York and Coventry. Teams in these offices provide specialized support and training for electoral administrators working in these regions or countries.

Accountability and Funding

The commission is accountable to the UK Parliament, which funds it. This accountability functions through a committee chaired by the speaker for the House of Commons. The Speaker's Committee provides a report to the House of Commons, at least once a year, on how the Electoral Commission has carried out its functions. The commission is required to submit annual resource requirements to the Speaker's Committee, which it may modify before the final request for funding is put to the House of Commons for approval. The commission must submit its accounts to the Speaker's committee. The committee also receives reports from the comptroller and auditor general on the economy, efficiency and effectiveness with which the commission has used its resources, and appoints an accounting officer for the commission. The commission had a budget of approximately GBP 21 million in 2011–12, although an additional GBP 100 million was granted to meet the one-off costs of a referendum that year.[21]

Professionalism of Officers

The professionalism of Electoral Commission staff, like most employees of UK public institutions, has not been questioned. Staff appointments are based on experience and skill. Some staff have previously worked in the implementation of elections in local authorities and are members of the Association of Electoral Administrators (AEA). Most staff in local authorities are also members of the AEA. This organization provides training and formal qualifications for those involved in administering elections. Professionalism is also extremely high, although there have been accusations that a few election officials have not always carried out their duties effectively in some cases, such as at the 2010 general election. An Electoral Commission report on this election identified problems with queues at polling stations that denied some voters the opportunity to cast their ballot.[22]

Sustainability

The commission exists so long as Parliament wishes for it to exist. The uncodified nature of the British constitution means that a government with a majority in the House of Commons that is able to control its party can make any changes that it wishes. Thus a change of government in Westminster could bring about major changes in the role of the commission or abolish it entirely. In 2010 a coalition government was formed between the Liberal Democrat and Conservative parties, which sought to make significant cuts to public sector spending. It therefore embarked on a 'quango bonfire' in which a number of other regulatory organizations, such as the National Audit Office, were abolished and their functions passed to other organizations. Before coming to office, Prime Minister David Cameron claimed that the commission had 'overreached' its role. The commission eventually survived the bonfire, however, with the government stating that it provided 'a vital independent and impartial oversight of our democratic process'.[23] The commission's existence therefore seems to have been accepted by all of the major political parties, even if there are some disagreements about its precise role and function.

Conclusion: A Fearless, Independent Advisory Watchdog?

One of the commission's key strengths is that it is a fearless organisation. It prizes its independence from the central government and will commonly criticize current government policy. It also provides an important coordination and information role in an increasingly complex and fragmented system. However, important tasks are also played by other organizations. The AEA, for example, continues to lead on the training and professional development of local authority staff who ultimately run elections. The commission has stated that it needs further authority over the administration of elections in order to ensure that errors are not made. This might be considered a weakness, but it is unclear whether this would necessarily improve elections. The principal weakness of the organization is that Parliament can abolish it at any point and remains able to ignore its advice.

Notes

[1] James 2012a, pp. 125–68, 2012c.
[2] Gay 2010.
[3] Electoral Commission 2008, p. 1.
[4] James 2012b.
[5] Electoral Commission 2011b.
[6] Scottish Government 2012, pp. 16–22.
[7] Welsh Government 2012, pp. 18–19.
[8] Law Commission 2011, p. 14.
[9] James 2012d.
[10] Electoral Office for Northern Ireland ND, pp. 3–4.
[11] Electoral Commission 2012c.
[12] Electoral Commission 2012b.
[13] Electoral Commission 2011a.
[14] Electoral Commission 2012a, p. 1.
[15] James 2012d.
[16] Committee on Standards in Public Life 2007, p. 5.
[17] James 2012b.
[18] James 2010.
[19] Office for Democratic Institutions and Human Rights 2005.
[20] Speakers Committee 2012.
[21] Electoral Commission 2012a, p. 17.
[22] Electoral Commission 2010.
[23] Cameron 2009.

Bibliography

Cameron, D., 'Cutting the Cost of Politics', 8 September 2009, available at <http://www.conservatives.com/News/Speeches/2009/09/David_Cameron_Cutting_the_Cost_of_Politics.aspx>

Committee on Standards in Public Life, *Review of The Electoral Commission* (London: The Stationery Office, 2007)

Electoral Commission, *Performance Standards for Electoral Registration Officers in Britain* (London: UK Electoral Commission, 2008)

Electoral Commission, *Report on the Administration of the 2010 UK General Election* (London: Electoral Commission, 2010)

Electoral Commission, *Great Britain's Electoral Registers 2011* (London: Electoral Commission, 2011a)

Electoral Commission, *Report on the Scottish Parliament Election on 5 May 2011* (London: Electoral Commission, 2011b)

Electoral Commission, *Annual Report and Accounts 2011–12* (London: Electoral Commission, 2012a)

Electoral Commission, *Data Matching Schemes to Improve Accuracy and Completeness of the Electoral Registers: Evaluation Report* (London: Electoral Commission, 2012b)

Electoral Commission, *Use of New Investigatory Powers and Civil Sanctions* (London: Electoral Commission, 2012c)

Electoral Office for Northern Ireland, *Management Statement and Financial Memorandum* (undated)

Gay, O., *Responsibilities of Returning Officers* (London: House of Commons Library, 2010)

James, T. S., 'Electoral Modernisation or Elite Statecraft? Electoral Administration in the U.K. 1997–2007', *British Politics*, 5/2 (2010), pp. 179–201

James, T. S., *Elite Statecraft and Election Administration: Bending the Rules of the Game* (Basingstoke: Palgrave Macmillan, 2012a)

James, T. S., 'The Importance of Policy Instruments for Managing Principal-Agent Relationships in the Administration of Elections: The Case of Performance Benchmarking in the UK', Paper presented to the workshop on Challenges of Electoral Integrity, Universidad Complutense de Madrid, Madrid, July 2012b

James, T. S., 'The Spill-over and Displacement Effects of Implementing Election Administration Reforms: Introducing Individual Electoral Registration in Britain', *Parliamentary Affairs,* first published online June 2012c

James, T. S., 'Why has Electoral Integrity Declined in Established Democracies? The Role of New Implementation Challenges and Institutional Drift in Post-Industrial, Digital-Era Election Administration', Paper for the American Political Science Annual Meeting, New Orleans, LA September 2012d

Law Commission, *Eleventh Programme on Law Reform* (London: Law Commission, 2011)

Office for Democratic Institutions and Human Rights, *United Kingdom of Great Britain and Northern Ireland General Election 2005 Assessment Mission Report* (Warsaw: OSCE/ODIHR, 2005)

Scottish Government, *Your Scotland, Your Referendum* (Edinburgh: Scottish Government, 2012)

Speakers Committee, *The Speakers Committee on the Electoral Commission: Re-appointment of Electoral Commissioners* (London: The Stationery Office, 2012)

Welsh Government, *Promoting Local Democracy* (Cardiff: Welsh Government, 2012)

CHAPTER 11

EMB Sustainability

What Is Sustainability?

Despite the axiom that 'you can't put a price on democracy', making democratic elections more sustainable is a principle that should be embraced by all EMBs. The need for cost reductions in elections results from the rising costs of election goods and services—including the use of new technologies, dwindling public-sector budgets, the increasing frequency of elections for different levels of political institutions and the tough competition among poorer countries to access international donor funding. The euphoria surrounding a successful, well-funded transitional election needs to be tempered by the reality that similar levels of funding may not be available for future elections.

In the context of elections, sustainability refers to electoral policies and practices that are cost effective and realistic, and meet the needs of stakeholders in the electoral processes both now and in the future. Sustainability aims to minimize reliance on external inputs and resources. EMB sustainability is not defined only in financial terms; it also includes the social and political returns on its activities. For example, a post-conflict country may use expensive voting systems and procedures that may not be sustainable in economic terms, but that may be politically essential in the short term to build trust among stakeholders and lasting peace and stability in the country.

There are several elements to EMB sustainability:

1. An EMB has institutional sustainability if its structures and processes enable it to fulfil its mandate and responsibilities over a series of elections. This type of sustainability refers to the adequacy of the electoral framework—the constitution, electoral law and regulations, and administrative and other policies—to allow the EMB to carry out its work effectively and efficiently.

2. An EMB has financial and economic sustainability if the nature and level of its funding and expenditure are adequate to fulfil its institutional mandate and responsibility.

3. An EMB has human resource sustainability if it is able to engage sufficient and appropriately skilled staff to manage and implement its systems and procedures.

4. Other forms of EMB sustainability include socio-political and environmental factors, for example, the extent to which EMB policies and practices promote social equality and political inclusion, minimize conflict and promote environmental sustainability.

Why Is EMB Sustainability Important?

Gearing EMB policies and practices to promote sustainability helps an EMB enhance stakeholder confidence in the electoral process and in itself. For example, governments and donors want to see that the funds they appropriate to the EMB are used effectively, and that the EMB is developing its capacity to reduce its reliance on external interventions and inputs, especially donor support. Other stakeholders, such as political parties and the general public, also want to see sustainability of EMB policies and practices as a way to increase electoral integrity and political participation.

The challenge of sustainability is more pronounced among EMBs in emerging democracies, which often rely heavily on donor aid. Economic and political hardships may prevent these countries from being able to wholly fund their own elections themselves. In transitional elections, high integrity costs relating to confidence-building processes—such as peacekeeping, voter education and information, and election observation and monitoring—may be financially unsustainable, and are often funded through donor aid.

A high level of international assistance for second and third elections in emerging democracies may not result in greater efficiency or effectiveness, even though many of the threats to the initial democratic transition may have receded. As the international political agenda moves on, reduced donor interest may mean that such funding is not even available.

Two immediate challenges have been the transfer of authority from international EMBs to fully national EMBs, as in Cambodia and Timor-Leste, and determining how best to ensure the institutional sustainability of newly founded EMBs, as in Afghanistan, Tunisia and Libya.

Needs Assessment

The sustainability of an EMB can be addressed by a thorough needs assessment, in which a country examines its current electoral management capabilities and the financial, human and technological resources necessary to organize and conduct free, fair and credible elections. An assessment may be undertaken by the EMB itself, but may in some circumstances be more credible if it is conducted by a private audit firm or an independent NGO. Donors also usually undertake needs assessments in planning assistance programmes.

The task of identifying needs can give rise to a range of complexities, and is not always straightforward. An EMB seeking to assess its own needs may lack the breadth of experience to enable it to anticipate looming challenges that ought to be addressed, and may not have the objectivity and detachment needed to document shortcomings in its own structure or performance. External assessors, on the other hand, may have their own agendas and/or prejudices, personal or organizational, which may colour their conclusions, and donors may consciously or unconsciously identify needs that can be met by solutions they can supply. More broadly, the use of the term 'needs assessment' might be thought to imply a prior assumption that needs will be found and action required.

Furthermore, any identification of 'needs' is likely to involve value judgements and assessing the risks associated with failing to take action; these are matters on which even experts might legitimately disagree. In some situations, needs assessments run the risk of being used to advance extraneous agendas or belabour bureaucratic opponents.

A needs assessment can be used to identify the elements of EMB sustainability at three levels: systemic, organizational and individual. They are normally based on an expert analysis of the electoral environment, and identify and consider strengths and weaknesses, opportunities and threats.

A system-level needs assessment covers the broader issues of the legal and institutional environments in which elections take place in order to determine the extent to which they help or hinder EMB sustainability. It includes a review of all parts of the legal and policy framework that are relevant to elections, as well as the EMB's functions and stakeholder relationships that are derived from this framework. The main legal instruments to be reviewed are the constitution, the laws dealing directly with electoral processes, the political party laws and other laws relating to institutional frameworks, the subsidiary regulations and administrative policies. The assessment may need to cover parts of the legal framework that are indirectly relevant, such as citizenship laws, criminal codes, public sector employment laws or policies, or government procurement rules and practices. It may also address the EMB's linkages and relationships with other bodies, such as the host ministry of a governmental EMB, government ministries that provide financial and logistical support to the EMB, local and international associations, and bodies that serve as EMB networks for support and resource sharing.

At the organizational level, a needs assessment looks at an EMB's strategies and management culture and considers its processes of planning, policymaking and implementation; its management structure; the division of roles and responsibilities; communication and cooperation; and standards of financial reporting and staff performance. It helps the EMB calculate the amount of resources required to organize any specific electoral event. The EMB can then work out what portion of the amount needed can be met from the national budget and how much, if any, would be needed from other sources. The assessment may also examine the nature and level of technical assistance required.

At the individual level, a needs assessment covers issues such as staff competence, available opportunities for staff development, and staff loyalty to the EMB's objectives and mission.

Where there is a record of credible needs assessment reports over time, a comprehensive picture of an EMB's capacity begins to emerge, and it can be more accurately evaluated in terms of sustainability.

Electoral Sustainability and Donor Support

Donor support may help improve the quality of an election, and in some cases may even be necessary for it to occur. However for many EMBs, donor support has implications for the sustainable delivery of free, fair and credible elections. For example, see the case studies on Afghanistan (page 61), Bosnia and Herzegovina (page 328), Kenya (page 273) and Nigeria (page 128).

While donor support may include budgetary contributions and technical assistance, including advanced technologies, some donors avoid supporting EMBs' recurrent budgets—that is, core personnel costs and rental of buildings and furniture, as well as other non-technical items, such as motor vehicles and fuel.

Donor assistance is sometimes accompanied by a tied aid concept in which the recipient EMB is required to purchase goods and services from nationals of the donor concerned. The costs of purchasing from external vendors is often considerably higher than purchasing from suppliers in-country, which inflates overall electoral costs.

In some post-conflict situations, such as those of Bosnia and Herzegovina, the Democratic Republic of the Congo, Haiti, Liberia and Timor-Leste, donors have contributed almost the entire cost of the transitional elections. In such cases, subsequent elections are unable to achieve the same level of funding and will offer a lower level of election services, which may lead to dissatisfaction with the elections. This raises obvious issues of creating transitional structures that the local authorities can 'buy into' subsequently, and building the necessary expertise to generate the financial resources to conduct future elections. In other post-conflict situations outside support may be vital, but it may not be politically or economically desirable for outside authorities to assume ownership of organizing and conducting transitional elections: Afghanistan, Iraq and Libya may fall into this category. Failed states and failed EMBs may also require considerable outside assistance from various donors; sometimes the UN plays a coordinating role, as in Liberia in 2004–05.

Donors have responsibilities to ensure that the electoral assistance they provide to EMBs is effective and promotes sustainability. Key issues for donors to consider in this regard include:

1. coordination of assistance with the EMB and other donors;
2. working with the host government, possibly through or in cooperation with a range of agencies, to ensure that electoral assistance is provided in a way that reflects the government's development priorities;
3. planning the implementation of assistance to synchronize with the EMB's needs;
4. the appropriateness of any proposed systems/solutions for the EMB's environment;
5. the inclusion of capacity building for the EMB and its staff;
6. the inclusion of EMB staff in the management of donor-funded programmes; and
7. the long-term costs of any systems/equipment provided.

The CORE Project notes that Cambodia reduced its donor dependence to less than 50 per cent during the 2003 elections. Timor-Leste has similarly succeeded since the restoration of its independence in 2002 in covering election costs from its annual state budget, rather than relying on substantial donor funding. Although it is desirable to transfer skills to local election officials during the transitional electoral period, in practice this goal has seldom been satisfactorily achieved at the senior management level, though well-trained cadres of polling staff are often generated. Therefore, capacity building is likely to be a continuing need in post-transitional elections. In post-conflict environments, initial external assistance is vital for restoring democracy and stability, but unless considerable donor assistance continues to be available in the medium term to develop EMB capabilities, both the electoral process and democracy itself may experience reverses.

New technologies can help improve the quality of electoral processes, especially where large amounts of data have to be processed quickly, as they do in the delimitation of electoral districts, voter registration, and the voting and vote-counting process. An increasing number of EMBs are entering the field of electronic voter registration, often incorporating biometric elements. Even some self-sustaining EMBs, for example in Costa Rica, have found it necessary to rely on outside assistance to fund the introduction of new technology. However, new technologies may have significant long-term cost implications for the EMB, for example maintenance costs or software licensing fees. Introducing donor-driven technological solutions may create political demands for progressively greater dependence on externally provided technology, as was experienced with voter registration in Haiti. Opinions are therefore divided on the question of the sustainability of funding voting computerization, Internet and telecommunication services, and other electoral technology such as scanners and biometrics for voter registration. Aspects to be considered by EMBs and donors include:

1. the financial, social and political costs/benefits of using donor assistance for funding new technology compared to using it for other electoral assistance programmes;
2. the life span of the technology (i.e. will the equipment require similarly expensive replacement at the next electoral event, or will it be useful in years and elections to come?);
3. capacities for local maintenance of the technology. If there is no technical or financial capacity to maintain the hardware or software that has been internationally provided, or if the appropriate skills have not been transferred to allow local operation once the international advisers have gone, internationally provided technology can be a very expensive single-use solution;
4. the potential to make the technology available for use by other government or societal organizations after the electoral event, or to lend it to other countries for their elections; and
5. training for temporary electoral staff using internationally provided technology that can be transferred to their post-electoral work environments.

Practices Favouring Sustainability

Cost effectiveness—providing an effective service at the lowest possible cost—is the major yardstick for sustainability, rather than purely lowest cost. Savings cannot be allowed to compromise the basic requirements of legitimate elections. A particular measure to reduce electoral costs may work well in one country but not in another because of differing legal, political and socio-economic circumstances. Although the practice of having a single-member EMB is a useful cost-saving measure, in India it was rebuffed by the Supreme Court as not conducive to fair decision-making, thus paving the way for the appointment of a three-member EMB in 1993. It is therefore not possible to prescribe commonly applicable sustainability solutions, only general principles. Significant cost savings can be achieved by holding elections for all levels of representation on the same day. However, the marked political effects of having either simultaneous or staggered elections mean that political sustainability arguments may outweigh financial ones.

Staffing for Sustainability

Staffing can be a significant proportion of an EMB's costs, but also represent its greatest asset. EMB core budgets may be reduced by rationalizing structures, for example reducing the number of EMB members or secretariat positions. The EMBs in Cambodia and South Africa undertook rationalization exercises during 1999 and 2002, respectively. Maintaining a small core of permanent staff, backed by well-trained temporary field staff, can reduce costs while preserving efficiency. The examples of EMBs in a number of Pacific Island states, including Niue, Samoa and Tonga, show that core election staff can be kept to a minimum while maintaining functionality. EMBs can use management tools, such as task profiling, to determine the minimum staff members it needs to perform its functions. The EMB would then be required to justify the employment of additional staff on efficiency or effectiveness grounds. Use of temporary, rather than permanent, EMBs can also assist financial sustainability.

However, the political and operational sustainability of using personnel-related measures to promote financial sustainability must be carefully considered. For example, significant budgetary savings can be achieved in governmental EMBs, or other EMBs in which public servants or volunteers can be co-opted to serve with the EMB (as in India) during an electoral period. While assisting financial sustainability, this type of staffing profile can also have a negative effect on the performance of and public trust in the EMB, and thus the political sustainability of the electoral process. Finding a successful balance may not be easy.

An inability to retain sufficient experienced staff can have a negative effect on an EMB's sustainability. Experienced staff, including temporary polling station staff, hold the institutional memory of the EMB—the knowledge of what has and has not worked, and the experience to pass on to new staff and other stakeholders. Staff retention requires active planning by an EMB, using measures such as reward schemes, professional training and development programmes (see Chapter 6 of this Handbook), and opportunities for promotion. Exit debriefings for departing staff may help identify staff satisfaction issues that may need to be addressed. Advance planning of staff changes, including timely recruitment processes and mentoring of more junior staff, combined with accessible archiving of electoral records, will help the EMB operate sustainably when key staff leave.

Office Systems

EMBs' widespread use of the technology found in typical office automation suites—word processing, spreadsheets, databases, email, etc.—can either be a risk to, or a foundation of, sustainability. Such tools need to be supported by rigorous practices and rules for their use, the main aim of which should be to ensure that information is systematically retained and stored, and is available to current staff as well as their successors. If this is done well, large volumes of data may be able to be accessed reliably and quickly. But if it is done badly—particularly if it is left to individual staffers to manage the documents and information they produce or receive—important information may not be accessible when needed. This can be a particular problem if critical communications are being sent to the EMB in the form of emails to individual officers. There can be a high risk of a failure to put the necessary procedures in place when a new EMB is appointed to run an election under tight time constraints, and short-term priority is given to immediate operational requirements rather than to the development of appropriate office systems.

Electoral Materials

Sound design, procurement and management policies for electoral materials are based on rigorous needs analysis and thus contribute to the sustainability of an EMB's operations. Before procuring materials, EMBs need to determine the most suitable options after investigating issues including:

- need: what benefit the desired materials add to electoral processes;
- local or international sourcing: issues such as cost, control, production lead time, quality, certainty of delivery, maintenance and substitutability;
- quality: issues such as cost, the conditions under which the materials will be used, ability to support integrity standards and requirements for durability;
- single or multiple use: issues such as storage and production costs, and environmental impact, including disposal and recycling methods, and opportunities for use by other organizations;
- complexity: issues such as the knowledge levels of the users, training requirements and capacity to maintain the materials;
- quantity: issues such as unit costs, production lead time, storage requirements and needs for reserves;
- distribution: issues such as costs and distribution time/scheduling;
- storage and archiving requirements: issues such as cost, accessibility, centralized or decentralized warehousing, asset protection measures and deterioration rate; and
- disposal: issues such as environmental impact, end of life value and security requirements.

EMBs have community responsibilities to consider—not just the economic sustainability of materials purchases, but the environmental and social impacts as well. Life cycle analysis, which considers the 'cradle to grave' economic, environmental and social costs and impacts of products, can help an EMB choose suitable electoral materials. This analysis assesses all material use impacts, not only those related to materials production, but also those such as opportunities for reuse, the impacts of storage and distribution over the materials' whole life, and the costs of environmentally sound disposal or opportunities for recycling.

Rigorous determination of whether special types of materials are really needed, and maintaining tight control of the quantities produced, can assist financial sustainability. Tight audit controls on the printing of ballot papers, and other forms for which accounts need to be kept, will also help reduce costs.

Existing low-cost materials options may not be fully utilized in new and emerging democracies due to a lack of public confidence in an EMB's ability to ensure security and prevent fraud if they were used. For example, EMBs may have to print ballot papers abroad because opposition political parties object to the government printer or local private printers doing this work. On the other hand, Indonesian law requires local printing of ballot papers; the EMBs of Australia, Canada and South Africa use low-cost materials for ballot boxes and voting booths; and Nicaragua has used locally produced ballot boxes without adverse effects on ballot security. Use of such low-cost materials depends on the EMB implementing sound security management controls.

Many EMBs are reducing election costs by sharing resources such as ballot boxes and voting booths. For example, Ghana's EMB lent ballot materials to other EMBs in its region during 2003 and 2004. The South African EMB has provided professional services and shared computer equipment with other EMBs on the African continent. In Bhutan, voting machines used by the EMB at the 2013 election were gifted from India. Resources can also be shared between the EMB and other government agencies, such as ministries and municipal authorities, in areas such as transport, logistics, statistical data and related professional services. In Bangladesh, information obtained by the EMB has been used to issue provisional national ID cards, the management of which will in the future be the responsibility of a national organization.

Experience in the 1990s in countries such as Cambodia and Indonesia has shown that post-election retention of electoral materials and equipment (such as motor vehicles, mobile phones, computers and ballot boxes) may be neglected, resulting in misappropriation or damage. Considerable losses to EMBs are incurred in this way, and the EMB may lose credibility with funders. Effective continuous asset management procedures (see Chapter 7 of this Handbook) can prevent this. The use of dedicated storage space, especially for valuable but infrequently used electronic equipment, is also worthy of consideration.

Structural and Technological Sustainability Implications

When considering the possible use of technology, it is important to holistically assess what impact it will have on the overall quality of elections. This, in turn, requires a realistic examination of the nature of the problems for which solutions are being sought. For example, a voter registration system is ultimately no more than a tool that can be used by honest polling officials to determine whether a particular individual should be allowed to vote. Investment in new registration systems and processes will be a pointless waste of resources if the real problem is that the officials are dishonest, suborned or intimidated, and therefore hand out ballots without even referring to the register.

This may suggest that technological solutions are most appropriate for countries where elections are reasonably well run, but trust or efficiency would benefit from reinforcement, rather than in well-established democracies (where their impact on the overall election quality is likely to be marginal) or truly dire situations (where the elimination of fraud in one area of the electoral process will most likely displace it to another area).

Electoral Systems

Each type of electoral system raises different political, social and financial sustainability issues. The type of electoral system used will have a critical impact on boundary delimitation and voter registration processes, voter education and information requirements, ballot paper design and production, the number of polling days and the need for by-elections. These issues are examined in detail in International IDEA's *Electoral System Design: The New International IDEA Handbook* published in 2005. For example, systems based on small electoral districts, which require specific boundary delimitation processes, separate ballot papers for each district, high precision in voter registration and the prevention of electoral fraud, and an EMB administrative structure that can deal with each electoral district as a distinct unit, may be more costly. Yet large multi-member electoral districts may involve complex and expensive vote-counting systems, may be unwieldy for an EMB to manage accurately and transparently, and may incur higher transport and other logistics costs. Proponents of each type of electoral system advance social and political sustainability arguments in their favour that need to be examined carefully against specific country conditions.

Electoral Boundary Delimitation

The frequency and form of electoral boundary delimitation processes may be reviewed to improve sustainability. Using an EMB to conduct boundary delimitation can eliminate the costs of a separate body. Yet if the government maintains a mapping office for other purposes, it may not be necessary for the EMB to duplicate that capability. Simple electronic mapping and population databases for determining electoral district boundaries, and streamlined review processes and periods, can be used to reduce costs. The adoption of multi-member electoral districts based on existing administrative boundaries can drastically reduce or even eliminate boundary delimitation costs. However, boundary delimitation is a politically sensitive issue, and must be implemented in a politically sustainable manner.

Voter Registration

The cost of compiling and maintaining the voter register can be significantly affected by the system used and its components. The method of data collection can have significant effects on both the costs and the accuracy—and hence the political sustainability—of the electoral register. For example, data may be specifically collected for voter registration or extracted from an existing database; registration may be continuous, or may be done by a national census-style exercise before an election; it may involve the EMB contacting voters, or voters having to contact the EMB; special voter ID cards may or may not be issued; and different opportunities may be provided for electors to challenge alleged inaccuracies in the electoral register. The use of technology in voter registration—in recording elector identity data such as fingerprints and photographs, in the use of bar-coded documents, in database matching to update registration records, or in the production of high-integrity polling day voter lists with photographs and/or other biometric data or bar codes, for example—will also have significant cost implications.

Maintaining accurate electoral registers is a costly task. Each EMB needs to determine which voter registration checks are necessary, and which, given levels of public trust and the controls in place to prevent polling fraud, may be redundant and can be eliminated to save money. Comparing data on the electoral register with information from other government agencies can help maintain the electoral register cost effectively, although it may raise concerns over data privacy. If the electoral register can be derived from a reliable and politically acceptable national civil registration database, as is done in Senegal and Sweden, or if records of births and deaths are computerized and accessible to the EMB, costs can be cut significantly. Continuous voter registration may, in the long run, be another measure to keep down costs.

Local conditions will be the primary factors for determining the most sustainable voter registration mechanism for a country. Permanent and continuously maintained registers will be most viable where the information needed to keep them up to date can be obtained from other government agencies that have access to accurate and publicly trusted data, or where there is a strong culture of compliance with a requirement for voters to notify the government of changes in their circumstances, such as new addresses. In the absence of both of these factors, the register will quickly become obsolete, and a periodic update process, involving major efforts to capture information, may be required.

The ease with which such intensive update operations can be mounted will be influenced by a wide range of factors, including climate; the size and geography of the country; population size, distribution and movements; language; transport, logistical, postal, communication, power supply, financial and public outreach infrastructure; availability of staff with requisite skills; availability of financial and technical resources, in both the short and long term; the political atmosphere in a country, particularly the degree of trust in electoral processes and institutions; local factors that may encourage fraudulent registration, including political or financial motivations for creating false identities; security concerns; procurement timelines; storage and distribution constraints; and constraints of any kind that could compromise participation by women or members of minority groups. If election dates are fixed and far apart, the effort required to keep registers continuously accurate may be unnecessary. If, however, a constituency-based electoral system is used, and frequent by-elections are required between general elections to fill casual vacancies, it might be deemed appropriate to maintain a continuous register.

The Polling Process

The preparation for and conduct of polling at a general election or referendum in any country is a significant national event, requiring a considerable budget to be implemented effectively. Careful assessment of how many polling stations, how many staff and what associated materials are necessary for each election can help reduce costs. If security, integrity and effective levels of service can be assured, polling stations in higher population density areas could be amalgamated, providing significant cost savings. Improved allocations of duties to staff, polling station layouts and staff training may make it possible to reduce the ratio of polling station staff to voters without reducing service levels. Countries that conduct polling over two or more days may also consider whether keeping the polling stations open for longer on a single day would cut costs. Any proposed reductions in voting days or hours need to be considered against patterns of working hours so as not to exclude any class of electors from voting.

Improving voter access and extending common facilities to voters, such as postal voting (as in Australia and Spain), external voting, and the provision of special services for voting in prisons, ships and hospitals, has obliged EMBs to offer relatively higher-cost services to electors. These activities, particularly if they involve large-scale or geographically dispersed absentee voting for refugees or others—as in Afghanistan, Bosnia and Herzegovina, Egypt, Iraq and Tunisia—may be a burden on the financial sustainability of electoral processes. However, increases in election costs need to be weighed against the EMB's social responsibilities and the additional political legitimacy gained from enabling these voters to exercise their franchise. In any operation of this type, there is a risk that low take-up rates will enable critics to point to extremely high costs per voter, which can make support for such processes difficult to sustain. In Australia, electronic voting systems implemented in 2007 for the benefit of the blind and sight impaired, and for military forces overseas, were ultimately abandoned on cost grounds.

The worldwide growth of the Internet has raised the question of whether remote Internet voting could better meet the needs of wide classes of voters. On the whole, the extent of use of the Internet in the act of voting has not matched its rise in most other fields of human endeavour; Estonia is the only country in which national electoral processes have been essentially Internet based. This reflects considerable ongoing controversy, driven by both technical and sociological concerns, over whether remote Internet voting meets the basic tests of secrecy, security and integrity.

A perceived requirement to support a range of different voting modalities for voters with varying needs can place a particular burden on the area of an EMB responsible for the development and implementation of policies relating to polling and counting: each different modality is likely to require a discrete set of procedures, instructions and training materials, for example, and the work involved will be essentially independent of the number of voters that is likely to use a particular modality.

Training EMB staff can be expensive, and is often a cost that governments or EMBs see as a relatively painless cut when reviewing election budgets. Inadequate training, however, is likely to result in greater financial and political costs through poor staff performance—perhaps affecting the credibility of the electoral process—and to have a long-term effect on the reputation and sustainability of the EMB.

Automated Voting and Counting Processes

A number of automated devices are marketed as a means of improving voting methods and reducing costs, especially staffing costs. Some of the machines claim to offer a high degree of reliability and resistance to electoral malpractice. Many are now capable of providing audit trail facilities. These include EVMs, which have been used in countries such as Australia, Belgium, Bhutan, Brazil, India, the United States and Venezuela. Although there is no reliable cost-effectiveness analysis on the use of new technology for voting and counting, there is evidence that technology such as EVMs may reduce election costs over time, especially costs associated with the printing and storage of ballot papers and counting votes. The use of OMR devices to count votes can also provide accuracy and time effectiveness in the electoral process while still ensuring the existence of a paper ballot that can be physically examined if necessary in the course of post-election disputes.

It is important to weigh the use of new electoral technology against the level of public trust and confidence in the electoral process, to involve stakeholders in pilot testing new electronic systems, and to obtain major stakeholders' agreement on the introduction of new technology. Due to the potential lack of transparency of e-voting and counting, the use of EVMs may generate distrust among detractors, who can argue that such technology can easily be manipulated. This is not surprising, given the security deficiencies and the omissions and errors in recording votes that are regularly reported in the use of DRE machines and other EVMs in the United States.

The accuracy and integrity of these machines are only as good as those of the companies and persons that design, programme, test and maintain them. There are ways of introducing EVMs that can provide integrity, cost and time benefits to the election process—provided that clear controls and accountability measures, such as those described in Chapter 9 of this Handbook, have been implemented. The Council of Europe's 2010 e-voting handbook provides useful background for such controls.

It is not wise for a poor country to go high tech while failing to feed and develop its own people. The use of electoral high technology such as biometric voter registration cards, computerized electoral registers, and electronic voting and counting should be weighed against other pressing national priorities such as health and education. Electoral technology may be more sustainable where it can be used for other ongoing functions. Its introduction needs to be compared not only to the immediate costs and alternative uses of funds, but also to the future costs and human skills required for its maintenance. Assessing sustainability needs to consider the longer-term consequences.

The counting process is a prime target for automation and cost reduction in many countries, and many automated machines both record votes and tally them. Unless paper audit trails are recorded for each vote, transparency may be lacking in these automated counts. The counting process is considered to be a vulnerable part of an election, and always needs to be conducted in a transparent and verifiable manner by well-trained staff.

The requirement for openness at all stages of the counting and tabulation of votes may also limit the cost-saving measures that can be introduced into manual vote counts. Stakeholders in the Union elections in Zanzibar in 1995 and 2000 and Kenya in 2007 complained that events that took place during the tallying phase of the count adversely affected the election results and underlined the importance of transparency in the entire counting process. These cases involved changes made by unknown persons to some of the count results subsequent to figures being issued from polling stations. Opposition parties believed that the interference affected the outcome of the elections.

Chapter Summary

- There is continuous pressure on EMBs to increase their capacities and performance in order to promote effectiveness and efficiency.
- Sustainability refers to electoral policies and practices that are cost effective and realistic, and meet the needs of all stakeholders in the electoral processes, both now and in the future. It is a greater challenge in new and emerging democracies.
- EMBs need to aim for financial and economic, institutional, socio-political and environmental sustainability in their activities, to enhance stakeholder confidence in the electoral process and to ensure their own survival, but do not necessarily need a permanent structure.
- The main elements of sustainability are institutional, financial and economic, and human resource sustainability.
- A comprehensive picture of an EMB's sustainability and capacity is only feasible if accurate evaluations of all the main elements are combined.
- Systemic, organizational and individual needs assessments can help an EMB identify sustainability issues.
- Especially in new and emerging democracies, donor support levels and commitment have a major impact on EMB sustainability. Donor support may have positive and negative effects: it may improve the quality of a specific election, but its influence and any dependence by an EMB on it may have a negative impact on its sustainability.
- Donors have a responsibility to ensure that their support promotes EMB sustainability, for example through coordination on EMB needs and support for skills transfer.
- New technologies are seductive to EMBs, and often attractive to donors, but EMBs need to make objective decisions based on their long-term usefulness and impact on EMB sustainability. The extent to which new

technologies are used by an EMB should be determined by the level of the country's resource endowment and the benefits to be derived from their use over time.

- Aiming for sustainability affects choices of electoral systems, and frameworks and procedures for costly, complex and integrity-demanding electoral processes such as boundary delimitation, voter registration, voting, and vote counting and tabulation. EMBs need to carefully consider the necessary levels of integrity required and the technology used for these processes, and their effects on financial and socio-political sustainability.

- Human resources, and their knowledge and experience, are an EMB's greatest asset. Investment in developing and retaining human resources, and in ensuring that institutional memory survives the loss of experienced staff, is an essential ingredient of EMB sustainability.

- Effective materials design, procurement and management policies—based on rigorous needs and cost-effectiveness analyses, and tools such as life cycle assessments—contribute significantly to EMB sustainability.

CASE STUDY

Bosnia and Herzegovina: The Challenges of an Independent EMB Model*

Irena Hadžiabdić

Background

The General Framework Agreement, known as the Dayton Peace Agreement, was signed in December 1995. It ended the war in Bosnia and Herzegovina, which had started in 1992. This agreement established Bosnia and Herzegovina as a complex state, consisting of two entities—the Federation of BiH (F BiH) and Republika Srpska (RS). The Federation of BiH consists of ten cantons, and the Brčko District enjoys a special status as a unit of local self-government. In addition, the Office of the High Representative was established as the leading representative of the international community in BiH; it has significant powers.

Annex 4 of the Dayton Agreement, the constitution of BiH, recognizes Bosniaks, Croats and Serbs as 'constitutive' people, whereas the citizens of BiH who do not declare themselves in regard to their nationality are named others. Annex 3 provided the framework for the preparation, monitoring and administration of the first post-war elections for the Organization for Security and Co-operation in Europe (OSCE).

The OSCE in BiH administered a total of six elections from 1996–2000, establishing the following institutions in the process: Provisional Election Commission (PEC), Election Appellate Sub-Commission (EASC) and Media Expert Commission (MEC), as well as OSCE field offices across BiH. Municipal Election Commissions were established at the level of the municipalities.

The PEC adopted rules and regulations that shaped the electoral process, from voter registration to the implementation of election results. The BiH Election Law was finally adopted in 2001. The BiH Central Election Commission is in charge of election

---

* A case study on Bosnia and Herzegovina also appeared in the original edition of the Handbook: Domenico Tuccinardi, 'Bosnia and Herzegovina: A Success Story for the Independent Model', *Electoral Management Design: The International IDEA Handbook* (Stockholm: International IDEA, 2006), pp. 196–99.

administration. It is an independent body that reports to the Parliamentary Assembly of BiH.

The Legislative Framework

Annex 3 and the PEC's rules and regulations are the precursors of the election legislation as it is today. The BiH Election Law (BiH EL) was adopted in 2001. It represented a great success and was the result of efforts of the international community, negotiations among the political parties, and the patience of BiH citizens.

The BiH election system is defined by certain provisions of the BiH constitution and constitutions of the lower levels of government, as well as by the BiH Election Law and 13 additional laws at the state and entity levels.

Certain provisions of the canton constitutions and municipality statutes can also be considered part of the BiH election system. The most important acts regulating the election legislation are:

1. Annex 3: Agreement on elections, provisions of the BiH constitution and amendments to the constitution;
2. BiH constitution;
3. RS constitution;
4. Statute of the Brčko District of BiH, as part of the BiH election system;
5. BiH Election Law, which has undergone 16 changes and addenda;
6. The law on filling a vacant position of a member of the BiH presidency during the mandate;
7. RS Election Law;
8. The Law on Election, Termination and Replacement of the Municipal Mayor in BiH; and
9. Election Law of Brčko District of BiH.

Institutional Structure

Immediately after the adoption of the BiH Election Law, the first BiH Election Commission, representing the top of the pyramid of election administration, was established in November 2001. A secretary general was appointed, and part of the OSCE's staff, which had significant experience in election administration, comprised the core of the newly established secretariat.

The BiH Election Commission (now the BiH Central Election Commission, CEC) has seven members, some of whom were international until 2006. The next level of election administration are the Election Commissions and the Commission of the Brčko District of BiH, followed by the Municipal Election Commission. At the bottom of the pyramid are the polling station committees, which are appointed for every election upon the proposal of the political parties.

The composition of the Municipal Election Commission in BiH has to be multi-ethnic and reflect the national structure of the constituency for which it was formed, taking into account the last census from 1991 and equal gender representation.

EMB Responsibilities

The BiH CEC has significant and wide competences, and therefore represents a unique model. In addition to its electoral responsibilities, the BiH CEC is authorized to implement the Law on Conflict of Interests (at the state level, in FBiH and in the Brčko District of BiH) and the Law on Political Party Financing. In accordance with the Law on the Council of Ministers, the BiH CEC also assesses, based on the submitted information, whether the candidates for the chairman, ministers and deputy ministers in the BiH Council of Ministers meet the conditions to be appointed. According to the Law on Agency for the Prevention of Corruption and Coordination of the Fight against Corruption, the BiH CEC checks the candidates for the director and deputy directors of the agency.

The BiH CEC's most important election-related tasks are: adopting regulations for implementation of the Election Law; accountability for accuracy; update and total integrity of the central voter register; verification of the political subjects; verification of candidates' lists; determining the content and form of the ballots; determining, verifying and publishing the election results at all levels; coordinating, monitoring and regulating the legality of the work of all election commissions and polling station committees; issuing certificates to persons who won the mandate; and maintaining statistics on elections and voters' education and information.

Composition and Appointment

The BiH CEC has seven members. The commission is composed of two representatives of each constitutive people (Bosniak, Croat and Serb) and one representative of the others. The BiH CEC's members are appointed by Parliament for a period of seven years, using a list of candidates drawn up by a special parliamentary commission upon completion of the public vacancy process. The BiH CEC's members can be re-elected, and its presidency rotates among the members every 21 months. The entity commission has been established in the RS, but not in the Federation of BiH.

Municipal Election Commissions consist of three, five or seven members, and the number of members is determined according to the number of voters registered in the central voters' register. These commissions are appointed or dismissed by the Municipal Council, subject to the approval of the BiH CEC, based on a vacancy advertisement.

The polling station committee consists of three or five members, and is appointed for every election upon the proposal of the political parties.

The BiH CEC secretariat has over 70 permanent employees, mostly civil servants, who provide logistical and administrative support.

EMB Financing

The BiH CEC's funds are ensured in the budget of the BiH institutions and international obligations. The funds for the lower commissions are ensured in the budgets of the entities, cantons and municipalities.

Even though the BiH Election Law stipulates that the BiH CEC independently manages the funds for the exercise of its competences and administration of the elections within the approved budget, the administration of elections has been endangered several times because the funds for its administration were not ensured on time. Namely, the legislative deadline for ensuring the necessary funds for the elections 15 days following the announcement of the elections was not respected on several occasions, which endangered the organization of the elections (e.g. Travnik in August 2011 and Novi Grad Sarajevo in March 2012).

In addition to the funds provided in the budget, the CEC has worked on improving elections using donors' funds (e.g. USAID, Council of Europe (COE), OSCE, International IDEA, certain embassies in Sarajevo). New electoral technologies have been introduced, such as electronic summary of the results, assessing the risk to the electoral process and building up an Integrated Election Information System (IEIS BiH). Over time, the efforts of the BiH CEC have resulted in the provision of funds from the budget of BiH institutions aimed at improving the electoral process.

The Accountability of the EMB

The annual report on implementation of the laws under competence of the BiH CEC is submitted to the BiH Parliamentary Assembly. This report contains concluding remarks and numerous recommendations for improving the elections and related laws. All previous annual reports and recommendations of the BiH CEC have been upheld in Parliament, and were the starting point of every debate on the next changes and addenda to the laws under competence of the BiH CEC.

The State Audit Office also regularly monitors the BiH CEC's management activities. It has so far received a positive assessment every year for respecting tendering, procurement and disbursement procedures, which is rare in audits of BiH government institutions.

Electoral Justice Process

Protecting electoral rights is ensured by the Election Commissions and the Appellate Division of the BiH Court. A voter whose rights (as defined in the Election Law) have been violated can submit a complaint to the Election Commission within 48 hours following a violation. The Municipal Election Commission is a first-instance body for deciding on complaints regarding violations of the rules of conduct in the election campaign, except if these violations are under the competence of the BiH CEC as the first-instance body: preventing a journalist from completing his/her work, using language that could induce or influence a person to violence or hatred, false representation on behalf of a political subject, violation of the election silence, or use of domestic or international means of communications aimed at influencing the voters.

The work of the BiH CEC in relation to appeals and complaints can be assessed as very regular and legal. Of all the appeals filed in the BiH Court, as the second-instance body, 97 per cent of the decisions related to the 2010 general elections were confirmed.

The Professionalism of Electoral Officers

In accordance with the BiH Election Law, every year the BiH CEC adopts a plan and programme of education for election administration, elected and appointed officials, and political subjects. Planned training of the election administration is usually fully realized, even though certain segments are not always completely implemented due to lack of funding.

In election years, the regular training of members of the Municipal Election Commissions is conducted, as well as training of Municipal Election Commission members in all municipalities in which early elections for the municipal mayor are conducted.

A training programme of the BiH CEC's secretariat staff is undertaken in order to maintain a high level of professionalism among civil servants and employees; the staff attends seminars organized by the Civil Service Agency of BiH.

Election officials' professional development is supported by conferences and similar events conducted in cooperation with the non-governmental sector in BiH. The most important partner is the Association of Election Officials in BiH (AEOBiH). As the result of a joint project, a code of conduct for members of the polling station committees and their deputies was adopted in 2011. The work, challenges and perspectives of the election administration are also analysed at joint conferences after every election.

Media Relations

Publicity of the work and freedom of access to information is conducted using generally accepted formal means such as Internet, press conferences, statements and press releases. The BiH CEC has not had any complaints filed by the media regarding the issue of access to information. In accordance with the BiH Election Law, the BiH CEC adopted a rulebook on media representation of political subjects during the period from the announcement of elections until election day. The basic rule is fair and equal representation of political subjects. The electronic media's respect of the rulebook is monitored by the Regulatory Communication Agency of BiH, and there have been no serious violations to date. The BiH Press Council monitors printed and online media, and mediates between readers and these media.

Relations with Other Institutions and Agencies

The BiH CEC has established numerous contacts aimed at sharing experiences with the delegations of other countries on the latest trends in the development of electoral systems. The BiH CEC has also established excellent cooperation with the non-governmental sector in BiH and Europe.

Significant parts of the BiH CEC's activities are directed at establishing international cooperation as well as cooperation with domestic agencies and ministries that are responsible for maintaining the official records for the election process.

Sustainability

In order to build up its legally set competencies, the BiH CEC would need further support in terms of provision of funds and enhancement of human resource capacities.

New Technologies

Since 2001 the BiH CEC has laboured to improve its work and introduce new technologies. One of the most important steps in this regard was the transfer to passive voter registration in 2006 and the launch of the IEIS BiH. The BiH CEC has to continue the process of building the information structure and complete the third and the final phase of the IEIS BiH project, and ensure there are necessary funds for its maintenance in the budget of the BiH institutions.

Electoral Reform Management

The BiH CEC has the right to initiate appropriate recommendations to the BiH Parliamentary Assembly, and it does so through its work in the inter-sectoral parliamentary working groups for changes and addenda of the laws under its jurisdiction. It is therefore in the position to contribute to improving the electoral legislation, but Parliament makes the final decisions, thus everything depends on the will and agreement among the political parties.

Opportunities and Constraints

During its development, this institution has made significant improvement in several areas: professional development of its staff, education of the lower election commissions, improvement of education and informing the voters (with a focus on out-of-country voters and special categories such as first-time voters, women and special needs voters), timely preparation of by-laws, reform of the registration process and application of new technologies. It has therefore made a successful transition from an international to a domestic institution, and set an example for the whole region.

Nonetheless, some constraints hinder the work of the BiH CEC. As the election law does not regulate sanctions for the violation of deadlines related to the establishment of the government, the BiH CEC faces the situation that preparing for new elections overlaps with uncompleted obligations from the last election.

An issue that requires additional attention is the financing of elections where Municipal Election Commissions lack financial means. Therefore, it is necessary to define ways to ensure the funds are available in order to have smoothly conducted the elections.

Bibliography

BiH Central Election Commission, *Report on Implementation of the Laws under Jurisdiction of the BiH CEC for 2004–2011*, available at <http://www.izbori.ba>

General Framework Peace Agreement in BiH—the Dayton Peace Agreement, USAID

Election Law of Bosnia and Herzegovina

Law on Election, Termination, Recall and Replacement of Municipal Mayors in the Federation of BiH

Election Law of RS

Election Law on Brčko District of BiH

Law on Conflict of Interest in Governmental Institutions of Bosnia and Herzegovina

Law on Conflict of Interest in Government Institutions in Brčko District of BiH

Law on Council of Ministers BiH

Law on Political Party Financing

CASE STUDY

Ukraine: The Long Road to Politically Independent Election Administration

Vasil Vashchanka

Background

The establishment of a national EMB in newly independent Ukraine acquired importance with the organization of the first competitive legislative and presidential elections in the early 1990s. The Central Election Commission (CEC) was formed in 1997 and gradually strengthened its capacity to manage national electoral processes. In the 1998, 1999 and 2002 elections, international observers assessed the CEC's performance as positive overall. Concerns were expressed, however, about its political independence and limited powers. In the 2004 presidential election, credible allegations of electoral fraud in what became known as the Orange Revolution led to the cancellation of results by the Supreme Court and a repeat of the second round of the vote. The CEC was implicated in tampering with election results and dismissed by Parliament, which appointed a new commission to administer the repeat vote. Since then the CEC has administered several election.

Legislative Framework

The 1997 constitution gives Parliament (Verhovna Rada) the power to appoint commissioners to the CEC, but does not give any details about its status and functions, which are described in the 2004 Law on Central Election Commission, which establishes the CEC as a 'permanent collegial state body'. The law stipulates the main principles of CEC operation: rule of law, legality, independence, objectivity, competence, professionalism, collegial and reasoned in decision-making, openness and publicity. It also regulates CEC formation and work processes, as well as its powers and the status of the commissioners. The CEC has adopted its rules of procedure, which detail its internal organization and work procedures. Electoral legislation in Ukraine is not codified, so the CEC's specific powers in national and local elections and referendums are further specified in the respective laws. The CEC adopts resolutions on matters within its competence that are legally binding for all participants in electoral processes.

Institutional Structure

CEC members elect a chairperson, two deputy chairpersons and a secretary from among themselves by a majority of votes. The chair heads the commission and the secretariat. The secretary prepares CEC meetings, manages its records and provides information to the mass media.

The commission's work is supported by the secretariat, which employs around 250 permanent staff. The secretariat is divided into departments and units charged with different areas of CEC support, including the Organizational Department, Legal Department, IT Department, Procurement Department, Documentation Department and others. The State Voter Register (SVR) administered by the CEC is maintained by a separate support service. The CEC is located in the capital (Kyiv) and does not have regional structures, although it is entitled by law to establish regional representative offices within its budget if it deems it necessary.

The CEC is the only permanent election administration body. Lower-level district and precinct electoral commissions are formed for each election from the nominees of political contestants.

Powers and Responsibilities

The commission is required by law to ensure the realization and protection of citizens' electoral rights and compliance with the legal framework for elections and referendums. This includes compliance by political parties and candidates with campaign finance regulations. The CEC is responsible for creating electoral districts and maintaining the SVR. It is also tasked with distributing information on electoral processes and has the authority to review petitions and complaints on all matters within its competence.

For national presidential and parliamentary elections, the CEC is responsible for organizing and managing the entire process, including establishing and controlling lower-level election commissions, registering candidates, monitoring campaign finance and announcing the results. For national referendums, the CEC likewise organizes the entire process, while for local referendums the commission approves the ballot format and performs an advisory role. For local elections the CEC performs primarily supervisory functions.

Composition and Appointment of Members

The commission consists of 15 members appointed for a seven-year term by Parliament upon nomination by the president. When nominating commissioners, the law requires the president to take into account the proposals of parliamentary factions and groups in Parliament.

Commissioners must be at least 25 years of age, know the state language and have resided in Ukraine for at least five years prior to their appointment. The chairperson, deputy chairpersons and at least five other CEC members must possess a university degree in law. Commissioners are not allowed to engage in political or business activities, and must suspend any party memberships. Commissioners are sworn in Parliament to uphold the law, maintain a non-partisan stance, and perform their duties fairly, objectively and impartially. Commissioners and staff of the CEC have the status of civil servants.

Financing and Accountability

The CEC, its secretariat and support services are financed directly from the state budget. The commission submits a yearly report on its expenses to the State Audit Chamber.

Complaints and Dispute Resolution

The commission is authorized by law to receive two kinds of applications: (1) petitions requesting CEC assistance in exercising electoral rights, clarifying electoral legislation or recommending improvements to the law; and (2) complaints alleging violations of electoral legislation and the rights of election participants. Election commissions and courts both have jurisdiction over complaints against the decisions or actions of lower-level commissions and election contestants. This overlapping jurisdiction has been criticized by international observers for its potential to result in unduly rejected claims and inconsistent decisions. Complaints that contain indications of electoral offences are forwarded by the CEC for investigation by law enforcement authorities.

Professionalism

The CEC is generally regarded as a competent body. A survey carried out prior to the 2012 parliamentary elections found that 64 per cent of respondents agreed with the statement that elections in Ukraine are competently administered. Yet international experts noted that the CEC was challenged by some issues, including the formation of lower-level commissions and the determination of boundaries for single-mandate electoral districts. They suggested that some operational shortcomings may result from the CEC's practice of giving individual commissioners operational responsibility for particular issues and particular regions.

Observers from OSCE/ODIHR assessed the CEC's performance in the 2012 parliamentary elections as adequate, but criticized it for not taking sufficient steps to regulate important aspects of the elections, specifically in ensuring transparency during the tabulation process, enforcing campaign rules, deterring indirect vote buying, addressing media-related violations and providing complainants with an efficient remedy. In the 2014 early presidential election, OSCE/ODIHR observers noted that the CEC operated independently, impartially, collegially and generally efficiently, despite the challenging environment and limited time for preparing the election.

Media Relations

The CEC is making some effort to be open in its activities and maintain ongoing contact with the media. It maintains a relatively well-developed website (http://www.cvk.gov.ua) but has not been active in social media. The current chairman has given regular interviews since his appointment in July 2013, including online Q&A sessions. After the 2012 parliamentary elections, observers criticized the CEC for insufficient transparency and for making decisions behind closed doors prior to the official sessions. These criticisms were not repeated in the 2014 early presidential election. The CEC was given credit for holding open sessions and for publishing its decisions, as well as thousands of lower-level district commission decisions, on its website.

The electoral laws contain guarantees of balanced media coverage during election campaigns and task the CEC with the allocation of mandatory coverage for election contestants in the public media. International observers in the 2012 parliamentary elections pointed out that the CEC rejected media-related complaints and disputes as falling outside its jurisdiction and referred the complainants to courts.

Relationships with Stakeholders

The commission maintains constructive engagement with the stakeholders in electoral processes. One of the persistent challenges facing the commission is overcoming the perception of partisan influences in its activities. These perceptions are influenced inter alia by the selection and appointment procedure, which leaves much room for political appointments based on partisan loyalty. The current CEC chairman repeatedly criticized the process in which political factions compete for their nominees to be appointed, and called for non-partisan nominations based on professional experience in election administration and civil society activities. In the 2014 early presidential election, partisan interferences were much less prominent due to more pressing security and political concerns, giving the CEC more space to strengthen its position as an impartial and politically independent authority.

Sustainability

The commission appears to be adequately funded and has not voiced concerns about the sustainability of its activities. Parliament has also made sufficient funding available for the recent elections, including repeat elections in five majoritarian districts after the CEC declared it was unable to determine their results in the October 2012 parliamentary elections. The commission reportedly carries out 'lessons learned' exercises after major electoral events, however their results are not published on the CEC website. For the 2014 early presidential election, the most pronounced challenges to the sustainability of election administration came from threats to the country's territorial integrity and the deteriorating security situation in several regions.

Use of New Technologies

The law authorizes the CEC to use an 'automated information system' but stipulates that the information obtained from the system is provisional and does not entail legal consequences. The use of the *Vybory* system for vote tabulation has generally contributed to increased transparency in the electoral process. At the same time, international observers have expressed concerns about the tabulation process. In the 2010 presidential election, OSCE/ODIHR observers assessed the tabulation process positively in general, while noting the lack of full access to observe the entry of data into the *Vybory* system. In the 2012 parliamentary elections, OSCE/ODIHR assessed the tabulation process negatively in nearly half of the District Election Commissions (DEC) observed. In addition to the restricted transparency of data entry and overcrowding, the observers noted irregularities in the tabulation process including discrepancies between results protocols from polling stations and the data entered into the system. The CEC ended up ordering a repeat election in five districts, but serious irregularities were alleged in more constituencies. Observers recommended greater transparency and increased capacity for results processing at the DEC level. In the 2014 early presidential election the *Vybory* system collapsed due to cyber attacks, causing disruptions to the receipt and processing of election material and a delay in the announcement of preliminary results. Domestic observers urged the CEC to strengthen its system security.

The second major area of technology use by the CEC is voter registration. In 2009 it launched a unified, centralized and computerized SVR, addressing a long-standing need to improve voter registration. The SVR was successfully used for the first time in the 2010 presidential election and earned compliments from observers in the 2012 parliamentary elections. The CEC chairman described the SVR as one of the most accurate voter registration systems in the world. The personal information of voters included in the SVR is updated monthly by over 750 local register maintenance bodies.

The 2012 parliamentary elections also saw another use of new technologies: web cameras were installed in all polling stations to increase the transparency of the voting and counting processes. This initiative came from Parliament and involved significant financial implications (around EUR 100 million was reportedly allocated). Observers questioned the usefulness of this undertaking, which did not appear to significantly increase the integrity of the electoral process. The effectiveness of this single-use investment was also subsequently questioned by the Audit Chamber. A survey found that a significant number of voters regarded web camera surveillance with suspicion. The CEC chairman commented that the system did not enjoy the demand apparently expected by Parliament, and the CEC received only about two dozen requests to review video footage from the polling stations after the elections.

Electoral Reform Management

The commission is authorized by law to put forward proposals to improve electoral legislation, and it has made use of this mandate. The CEC has emphasized the need for stability and social consensus on electoral rules, and has urged political parties to avoid unnecessary changes. This position did not prevent it from working with Parliament to ensure the conduct of the 2014 early presidential election, which required amendments to the legal framework to address significant political and security challenges to the electoral process.

Gender

In 2014, five CEC members are women, including one of the two deputy chairpersons and the secretary. Some international observers previously noted that women were over-represented at the lowest-level Precinct Election Commissions, which they attributed to the low rates of pay for this work. The CEC does not have a publicly available gender policy. Women's representation in Parliament remains low (10 per cent), and some analysts believe the CEC could do more to encourage political parties to nominate female candidates.

Challenges and Opportunities

Two sets of challenges are readily apparent for the CEC and electoral administration in Ukraine. The first set relates to the events that brought about the 2014 early presidential election. At the time of writing, security concerns and threats to the country's territorial integrity pose immediate and grave challenges for the future of Ukrainian democracy. The conduct of the 2014 early presidential election was effectively impossible in Crimea due to its annexation by Russia, as well as in a number of constituencies in eastern Ukraine, where the electoral process was disrupted by armed guerrillas.

The second set of long-term challenges facing the CEC relates to the politization of election administration at all levels. Arguably, this may be an inevitable by-product of some of the most competitive elections held in post-Soviet countries. However, the worrying propensity of political contestants, especially incumbents, to seek electoral advantage through legally questionable or fraudulent activities has not created a favourable environment for overcoming partisanship in election administration.

Elections in independent Ukraine have generally been characterized by low levels of trust. A survey before the 2012 elections found that over half the voters expected the results to be falsified. While only about 34 per cent of respondents expressed confidence in the CEC, the commission still fared better than Parliament (23 per cent), the president (32 per cent) and the cabinet of ministers (28 per cent). As noted earlier, the CEC chairman has spoken against partisan-based nominations for the next commission and argued that the nominees should be chosen from the pool of experienced election administrators and civil society actors.

While the CEC is increasingly regarded as a professional and impartial authority, the professionalization of lower-level commissions remains difficult. Political contestants traditionally fiercely battle over their representation on lower-level election commissions, often resorting to ethically and legally dubious methods. In the words of IFES experts: 'Any discussion of the formation of the election commissions should recognize the extent to which election commissions are politicized. All electoral participants seem to believe that their best defense against potential fraud committed by their competitors is to have representation on the committees.' As a result, election commissions have tended to be large and prone to partisan conflict. Political contestants routinely manipulate and withdraw their nominees from election commissions, which jeopardizes efficient election administration. Proposals for improvements have included mandatory training for commission appointees prior to their appointment and increased incentives (including financial) for their autonomy from the nominating political actors. However, change in the partisan formation of election commissions is unlikely as long as the deficit of trust permeates political and social life.

Bibliography

International Foundation for Electoral Systems [IFES], *Pre-Election Technical Assessment: 2012 Parliamentary Elections in Ukraine* (Washington, D.C.: IFES, 2012)

International Foundation for Electoral Systems [IFES], *Pre-Election Public Opinion in Ukraine: Survey Results* (Washington, D.C.: IFES, 2013)

Mission Canada, *Ukraine Parliamentary Elections,* 2012

OSCE/ODIHR election observation reports from the 1998, 1999, 2002, 2004, 2006, 2007, 2010 and 2012 elections, available at <http://www.osce.org/odihr/elections/ukraine>

OSCE/ODIHR, 'Statement of Preliminary Findings and Conclusions', 26 May 2014, available at <http://www.osce.org/odihr/elections/ukraine/119078?download=true>

CHAPTER 12

EMB Networks

What Are Electoral Networks and Why Do They Matter?

Globalization has brought rapid and dynamic changes to organizational management, including electoral administration, and such changes are encouraging EMBs to move away from the hierarchical structures and routines of the past. At both the regional and national levels, an increasing number of electoral practitioners are also working together through well-established networks to find solutions to common problems and build innovations through the sustained sharing of ideas, information and experience.

> Electoral networks are important for helping electoral managers around the world cope with the pace of change in the environments in which elections take place.

Electoral networks foster capacity development among electoral managers and serve as useful forums to address common concerns such as EMB independence, EMB funding or the use of technology in elections. Electoral managers need no longer operate in isolation from each other and without any external support to improve their knowledge and skills.

National Electoral Networks

In the UK, all senior electoral administrators (returning officers) belong to the Association of Electoral Administrators (AEA). The AEA conducts regular training and education for electoral administrators, acts to safeguard their interests, and serves as a network of resources and expertise for its members. It offers professional qualification courses, which are mandatory for appointment to electoral-related positions in UK local authorities, which are governmental EMBs.

In the United States, the National Association of State Election Directors and the National Association of Secretaries of State serve as useful forums for electoral managers to exchange views and improve their capacities and performance. The International Association of Clerks, Recorders, Election Officials and Treasurers (IACREOT) holds regular electoral professional development courses for its members, and annual trade shows for electoral-related equipment and supplies. The National Association of Clerks and County Recorders (NACRC), the Election Center and the National Association of Counties also organize events for local election officials.

The Electoral Council of Australia, a consultative forum comprising national and state electoral commissioners and chief electoral officers, meets regularly. Its main objectives are to ensure the quality of the electoral registers for all elections in Australia and to improve Australian electoral administration in general. The Association of Bosnia and Herzegovina Election Officials (AEOBiH) consists of electoral officials from the three entities of Bosnia and Herzegovina and holds conferences, seminars and other consultations to promote democratic, open, transparent elections. Similar activities are carried out by the Federal Forum of Provincial Electoral Bodies of Argentina, which brings together subnational EMBs to exchange experiences, legislation and case law in electoral matters.

Regional EMB Networks

During the 1980s and 1990s, regional cooperation between EMBs intensified, and a number of regional associations were established to facilitate and sustain cooperation. The objectives of the early regional electoral associations that were formed in the 1980s, however, were so general as to be little more than a framework pointing to desirable goals with little specific commitment. The Association of Electoral Bodies of Central America and the Caribbean (known as the Tikal Protocol), established in Guatemala in 1985, was a representative body of electoral organizations designed to achieve cooperation, exchange information and facilitate consultation. Its recommendations were not binding on its member organizations. The Association of South American Electoral Organizations (the Quito Protocol) was formed in 1989 along similar lines.

The Inter-American Union of Electoral Organizations (UNIORE) was established in 1991 to promote cooperation between the electoral organizations and associations created under the Tikal and Quito protocols. It extended the potential scope of cooperation to provide support and assistance, as far as practicable, to member organizations that requested it. The Costa Rica-based Center for Electoral Promotion and Assistance (CAPEL), established in 1983, acts as the executive secretariat of these networks.

Although the elements of information exchange, cooperation and consultation still featured prominently in the objectives of associations formed in the 1990s, there was greater focus on broad common goals such as the promotion of free, fair and credible elections, independent and impartial EMBs, and transparent electoral procedures. Specific common regional goals were emphasized, such as cooperation in the improvement of electoral laws and practices; the promotion of participation by citizens, political contestants and non-partisan NGOs in electoral processes; and the establishment of resource centres for research and information. These associations also stressed the development of professional electoral officials with high integrity, a strong sense of public service, knowledge and experience of electoral processes, and a commitment to democratic elections.

Some of the associations that typify these dimensions are:

- the Association of European Election Officials (ACEEEO), established in 1991;
- the Association of African Election Authorities, established in 1997;
- the Association of Asian Election Authorities, established in 1998; and
- the Association of Caribbean Electoral Organizations, established in 1998.

Although the mandates of these networks differ in detail, they all aim to promote the free flow of information among election practitioners and to provide electoral assistance to their member EMBs. For example, the objectives of the ACEEEO include the following:

- promoting open and transparent elections through an exchange of experiences and information relating to election law and procedure, technology, administrative practice and voter education;
- promoting training and further education of election officials and international observers;
- promoting the principle of independent and impartial election authorities and administrators;
- developing professional election officials with high integrity, a strong sense of public service, knowledge of electoral practice and commitment to democratic elections;
- promoting the principle of participation in electoral processes by citizens, political contestants and non-partisan civic organizations; and
- developing resources for election-related information and research.

Other regional networks were created around the same time, including the Pacific Islands, Australia, New Zealand Electoral Administrators Network (PIANZEA) and the ECF of the SADC. The following decade saw the establishment of more regional networks such as the Andean Electoral Council of the Andean community, the Commonwealth Electoral Network (CEN), the Electoral Council of the Union of South American Nations (UNASUR), the Forum of Election Management Bodies of South Asia (FEMBoSA), the Forum of National Electoral Commissions of the East African Community, the ECOWAS Network of Electoral Commissions (ECONEC), and the Network of Francophone Electoral Authorities (RECEF).

The potential benefits of regional cooperation through associations of electoral organizations are considerable. New EMBs can draw on the support and experience of more established electoral authorities, accelerate their capacity building by exchanging personnel, and may even be able to borrow electoral materials at relatively short notice.

The development of EMB networks is constrained in practice by two issues that affect individual EMBs: lack of resources to participate in the association's activities and fear of compromising their perceived independence. Some EMBs shy away from active participation because they fear that depending on the government for resources for travel, research or other programme activities might compromise their independence. Resource constraints also restrict the activities of the associations themselves, which have to depend mainly on outside funding.

Global Electoral Networks

The development of regional associations of electoral organizations and the increasing internationalization of elections through advocacy of international standards for democratic elections led to the establishment of a global forum for discussion of EMB collaboration. The conference of the Global Electoral Organization (GEO) Network, which was first convened in Ottawa in April 1999, is a worldwide meeting of regional associations of electoral officers. Subsequent conferences were held in Mexico (2003), Hungary (2005), the United States (2007), Botswana (2011) and South Korea (2013). GEO conferences provide an opportunity for associations of electoral officials to meet in a global professional network and serve as a forum for identifying areas of need in electoral governance, and programmes that can be developed to respond to those needs.

The National Election Commission of the Republic of Korea initiated and led the launch of the Association of World Election Bodies (A-WEB), which held its inaugural assembly during the sixth GEO conference in October 2013. A-WEB is an international organization created with a vision to foster efficiency and effectiveness in conducting free, fair, transparent and participative elections worldwide. Membership in A-WEB is open to national EMBs. Regional associations of EMBs may join A-WEB as associate members, while international election-related organizations may become partners.

The ACE Electoral Knowledge Network (<http://www.aceproject.org>), which is a continuation and transformation of the original Administration and Cost of Elections (ACE) Project, is the result of a collaborative effort between International IDEA, EISA, Elections Canada, the INE of Mexico, IFES, the United Nations Department of Economic and Social Affairs (UNDESA), UNEAD, The Carter Center and UNDP. The ACE Electoral Knowledge Network is a dynamic, online knowledge service that provides comprehensive and authoritative information on elections, promotes networking among election-related professionals and offers capacity development services. It features information on nearly every aspect of elections, with an emphasis on cost, sustainability, professionalism and trust in the electoral process. Its networking component, the ACE Practitioners' Network, provides online access to a network of election professionals from all over the world to professional advisory services. It encourages election practitioners to collaborate on common issues and challenges and to generate, share and apply knowledge; help build common methods; and improve the professionalism of those engaged in activities related to credible, sustainable, peaceful and cost-effective elections.

The growing use of social networks has also facilitated contacts between election professionals, and numerous groups and forums dedicated to elections have sprung up on Facebook, LinkedIn and similar social media. Such networking creates additional opportunities for sharing experiences, identifying expertise and promoting election-related resources.

There is an advantage to examining certain electoral issues at the global level, and setting the stage for adaptation at the regional or national levels. These issues could include improved cost effectiveness in electoral administration, principles and good practices in electoral management, the effectiveness and affordability of new electoral technologies, legislative frameworks for elections and referendums, and mechanisms for strengthening electoral justice.

Electoral Support Networks

In many parts of the world, national or regional electoral support networks have been formed that comprise CSOs such as democracy promotion organizations, media organizations, human rights organizations, women's organizations, religious-based groups and other community-based organizations. Examples include the Zimbabwe Election Support Network (ZESN) and the faith-based People's Voter Education Network (JPPR) in Indonesia at the national level, and the Asian Network for Free Elections (ANFREL) and the SADC Electoral Support Network at the regional level. While some electoral support networks specialize in election monitoring or observation, many support EMBs in areas such as research on electoral matters, training, and voter education and information. Electoral support networks can be effective partners for EMBs, using links to local communities and access to funds—particularly donor funds in emerging democracies—to augment their skills base and enhance information flows to and from them.

Chapter Summary

- Electoral networks promote information exchange and improvement in electoral processes, providing opportunities for EMBs to share experiences and good practices.
- National associations of electoral administrators, such as those in Bosnia and Herzegovina, the UK and the USA, can play a significant role in

professional development, information exchange and as a lobby group for electoral reforms.

- Regional EMB networks provide opportunities for EMBs to assist each other by drawing on the experience of longer-established EMBs, personnel exchanges, pooling of research and information, and equipment sharing.

- Global electoral networks, such as the ACE Electoral Knowledge Network, the GEO Network and A-WEB, offer collaborative opportunities for EMBs and electoral associations to share knowledge and improve electoral governance.

- Community-based electoral support networks can help EMBs disseminate information and provide additional resources for activities such as training and voter education.

CASE STUDY

Haiti: A Crisis of Credibility

Gabrielle Bardall

Haitian elections face a profound crisis of public credibility and confidence. Although Haitians consider elections to be an important instrument of political and social change, there is a widespread belief that neither the electoral process nor the political leaders are conducive to voter participation.[1]

On 12 January 2010, one month before the scheduled legislative, presidential and municipal elections, a devastating 7.0 magnitude earthquake struck Haiti, killing an estimated 220,000 people and leaving 1.5 million homeless. The catastrophe added to the political crisis and destroyed or badly damaged parts of the electoral infrastructure, including the EMB headquarters office and annex, and a number of the decentralized offices in the West and Southeast departments. Members of the EMB and its local and international partners also suffered significant personal injury and loss of life. The first round of the presidential and legislative elections was ultimately held on 28 November 2010 amid confusion, allegations of fraud, violence and intimidation. The second round was delayed until 20 March 2011 following widespread violence, which was reflective of Haitian elections for over two decades. Despite significant improvements over the first round and encouraging recent legal reforms, the Haitian EMB lacks public credibility; thus the crisis of electoral management persists.

The Electoral Institution and Legal Framework

Haiti's electoral administration system was introduced in the 1987 constitution, which mandated that transitional elections be administered by a provisional council, the *Conseil Electoral Provisoire* (CEP), until a permanent electoral council (*Conseil Electoral Permanent*) could be established.

Over 25 years later, Haiti's EMB remains transitional. A new electoral law to create a permanent commission was introduced in December 2013, and was substantively revised before being passed by the lower house of Parliament in March 2014; as of July 2014 it was stalled in Senate negotiations. The enduring challenge of electoral administration in Haiti is intimately connected to the institutional crisis of the past two and a half decades, which is embodied in the paradoxical name of its EMB: the Transitional College of the Permanent Electoral Council (CTCEP).

The electoral body is governed by three legislative documents: the constitution, the Electoral Law of July 2008 and the general regulations of the CEP as issued by presidential decree. According to the revised constitution, the three branches of government each appoint three members of the EMB. In addition to its central office, CTCEP has 11 offices at the department level (*Bureau Electoral Départemental,* BED) and 142 communal-level offices (*Bureau Electoral Communal,* BEC). In 2011, the CTCEP employed 410 employees in its national office. The BEDs and the BECs employed 99 and 994 employees, respectively, and were only operational during the electoral period.[2]

According to the 2008 Electoral Law, the CEP is an independent and impartial public institution responsible for the organization and oversight of elections throughout the Haitian territory. To date, the CTCEP has been responsible for drafting electoral legislation and proposing electoral legal reform to submit to the president, in consultation with political parties and civil society. It has also been responsible for implementing adopted electoral reforms, such as the recent introduction of the 30 per cent gender quota (under article 17.1 of the constitution). Other powers and functions include requesting the president of the republic to convoke the elections, determining the opening and closing dates of the electoral campaign period, and publishing electoral results. Although granting political parties the authorization to operate is the prerogative of the Ministry of Justice, the CTCEP registers political parties during each electoral period. The CTCEP is also responsible for electoral dispute resolution and for the decision to annul electoral votes in legally warranted circumstances.[3] These functions are expected to be assumed by the CEP under the new legislation.

To date, electoral administration has been severely hampered by two elements of the electoral legal framework. The first challenge is the poor definition of the institutional hierarchy, particularly a lack of reporting relationships and differentiation between respective roles in the management of elections between the director general and the members of the CEP. This has proven to impede effective decision-making during the electoral period.[4] While the creation of the position of director general during the 2006 elections represents an improvement, in practice the director general does not delegate sufficient authority, and the members of the secretariat have remained directly involved in the day-to-day operations of electoral management in recent years.[5] Rather than serve as a board of advisors, the nine members are involved in routine activities such as the recruitment of polling supervisors. This has contributed to the lack of public trust in the institution and slowed administration activities to the extent that in some places during the last elections, lists of poll workers were received so close to the elections that poll worker training took place either the night before or the morning of polling.

Electoral dispute management is at the heart of the second major legislative challenge. The constitution (article 197) and the Electoral Law confer exclusive authority for all issues of electoral dispute resolution on the CEP. The electoral dispute resolution process is handled within the CEP structure by a National Office of Electoral Disputes

(BCEN) and departmental and communal offices. At the departmental and communal levels, the dispute resolution bodies are composed of two members of the BED and BEC, respectively, and one lawyer named by the CEP. Housed within the CEP, the BCEN is composed of three sections, each consisting of three CEP members and two lawyers designated by the CEP (Electoral Law, section D, articles 14–18). According to the constitution, the BCEN is the court of final appeal for all disputes arising during elections or in the application or violation of the electoral law. This system undermines the neutrality of electoral justice and creates a fundamental conflict of interest for the CEP, which is both the judge and jury.[6]

The 2014 draft Electoral Law addresses both of these issues to a limited extent. Under the proposed law, the director general would be replaced by an executive director, who would be named by the CEP to implement its decisions and coordinate the activities of the other departments, thereby clarifying if not correcting the hierarchy issue. The draft law would introduce magistrates and lawyers delegated by the Haitian Bar Association into each section of the BCEN. While the CEP would continue to play an integral role in electoral dispute resolution, the introduction of these members is intended to diffuse the conflict of interest inherent in the present system.

The Implications of Failing to Respect the Electoral Calendar

Haitian elections are constantly postponed. No national or local election has been held according to the constitutionally mandated calendar since the constitution was ratified.

In the past, these delays have resulted in constitutional crises on multiple occasions. One-third of Haiti's senatorial seats are up for election every two years. The postponement of elections has exceeded the Senate term limits and placed the Senate in an unconstitutional status multiple times in recent years, opening the door for the president to govern by decree. Article 232 of the 2008 Electoral Law was revised in 2009 to address the issue of term limits for the executive, parliamentary and local councils and assemblies elected in 2006–07; however the ongoing delays in the process threw the country into constitutional crisis once again in 2012 and 2013. The systematic postponement of electoral dates has contributed significantly to the negative public perception of the electoral process.

The failure to respect constitutional provisions on the elections has created a self-perpetuating downward spiral in the ongoing problem of electoral management. The CTCEP was established according to the amended constitution, however the executive is unable to establish a permanent commission because Parliament cannot choose its three members, as per the constitution, because elections are not held on time and one-third of the Senate's term limit has expired. Without a full sitting Senate, the permanent CEP cannot be created and the country is left with the transitional council.

Electoral Operations

The fundamental conflict over the creation of a permanent body has implications in all areas of electoral operations, notably voter registration, electoral logistics and financial management.

Voter registration constitutes a major operational challenge for the CTCEP.[7] The CTCEP is responsible for maintaining a verified voter registry and publishing a voter list on the basis of civil registry information received from the National Identification Office (ONI). The ONI maintains a continuous civil registry and provides a national identification card to new registrants and already-registered voters who have lost their card. The ID card must be presented on election day in order to vote. Since 2005, the OAS has provided substantial assistance to help modernize the civil registry, including supporting the registration of over 5 million Haitians, updating card technologies to feature security measures such as biometric features and a unique identification number, and seeking to professionalize the ONI (a permanent institution) through staff training and the provision of office technology and equipment in the 141 ONI offices countrywide.[8] Yet significant legal, procedural and economic challenges continue to deprive many Haitians from obtaining civil identity documents at the ONI level.[9] Legally, discrepancy between the Electoral Law and the constitution regarding the voter registry severely limits the options for recourse.[10] There are two major persistent, practical problems with the civil registry, and therefore, the electoral lists. First, since there has never been a link between the ONI/civil registry and the issuance of death certificates, the deceased have never been removed from the list.[11] Compounding the problem, existing death certificate forms are not well adapted to electoral needs, because they do not include information that would help find a voter's name on the list, confirm their correct identity and delete the entry. Second, the replacement of documentation and reallocation of polling centres to the population displaced by the earthquake remains a substantial challenge.[12]

Electoral logistics are another major challenge. Following years of coups d'état and intervention in politics, which led to the death of an estimated 3,000–5,000 Haitians and the exile of tens of thousands, the Haitian military was disbanded in 1995 by then-President Aristide. Ever since, civilian law enforcement under the National Police and Coast Guard has relied heavily on the UN, which has been present in Haiti since 1990, for electoral security and logistics.[13]

The United Nations Stabilization Mission in Haiti (MINUSTAH) and the UNDP have played an all-important role in Haitian elections. In 1994, the UN adopted Resolution 940 under Chapter VII, which authorized the creation of a multinational force and the use of 'all necessary means to facilitate the departure from Haiti of the military leadership' and to return the elected president to Haiti (S/RES/940/1994). UN peacekeepers have remained in Haiti ever since. The current mission, MINUSTAH, is the sixth UN mission to operate in Haiti since 1993 and plays a central role in electoral operations.[14] Since its creation in 2004, MINUSTAH has been mandated to help the Haitian electoral management body organize, monitor and carry out free and fair local, municipal, parliamentary and presidential elections. Several successes have been recorded, notably the introduction of vote tabulation centres (CTV) in the 2006 and 2009 elections, full control of which were gradually transferred to CEP in the 2010 elections following a strategy of increased national ownership led by the UNDP. International support has also contributed to improved use of ICT in the electoral process.[15] Although significant implementation challenges remain, other recent initiatives—such as the increased number of polling stations (minimum of two per commune), the introduction of random selection for poll worker placement, and competitive recruitment for members of the BED and BEC—have the potential to make positive contributions in future elections. Likewise, MINUSTAH support to logistics and electoral security has been critical to protecting voters in Haiti's notoriously violent elections.

The UN presence has been critical in mitigating conflict over the financial management of elections in the absence of a permanent electoral body. The Haitian state is mandated to ensure the financial resources of the CEP,[16] including operating costs and staff salaries. Funding for electoral activities comes from special funds allocated by the Ministry of Economy and Finance and the contributions of international donors. The Haitian government is committed to funding up to one-third of the electoral budget, whether for capital expenditures, acquisition of equipment or personnel costs.[17] In terms of financial management, the CEP is accountable to the Ministry of Finance and is liable for its management before the Superior Court of Auditors and Administrative Disputes. Since 2005 the UNDP has managed the electoral basket fund, which includes procuring electoral materials, managing the electoral staff payroll, strengthening institutional capacities and providing technical advisors to the CEP. Since the 2010 elections, the UNDP's basket fund has incorporated a large part of election-related international assistance programmes operating in the country, in addition to the CEP's budget. The UNDP's role in the financial administration of Haitian elections was made necessary by a crisis in confidence in the EMB's financial management and the temporary nature of the institution.

Sustainability and Dependence on Outside Assistance

The ongoing failure to create a permanent commission has resulted in a severe deficit of institutional memory and retention of experienced staff. Between elections, the administrative personnel and management-level employees are retained at the central level of the CTCEP. All others, including all of the regional offices, are dismissed because the annual budget does not support their payroll. Almost all CTCEP staff are recruited on a contractual basis, and with each turnover of leadership or expiration of an election-period budget, almost the entire staff is dismissed. This has made institutional memory and development of staff professionalism a serious problem for election administration.[18] The absence of career development resources or minimal job security have made it nearly impossible for the CTCEP to recruit and retain experienced professionals or develop an institutional memory. Planned training and professional development programmes have been stifled by this problem. Staff frequently leave before the end of their contracts, in search of more secure employment opportunities.

The temporary nature of the institution and Haiti's relationship with international donors have had a profound impact on sustainability. The UN, OAS and other bilateral assistance providers have been involved in the organization of Haitian elections since 1990. Over the years, dependence on international funding and expertise has become entrenched. The highly sensitive task of ensuring electoral security is virtually entirely under MINUSTAH's control. There have been no systematic plans to transfer skills and capacity in technical areas such as the use of GPS systems for materials and personnel deployment.[19] As the electoral crisis continues, there is no exit strategy or long-term vision to alter the reliance on internationals for operational support in all areas.[20] Institutional sustainability is not possible until a permanent institution is created. The problem may be further complicated by the limited definition of MINUSTAH's mandate, which focuses on providing assistance to electoral events and crisis management rather than building the process and the electoral institution, which remains temporary.

Gender and Electoral Management

Haiti is one of the worst countries in the world for women's participation in elected office and electoral management. Alarmingly, the trend is worsening under the revised draft Electoral Law. Women's representation in parliament is only 4.2 per cent, one of the ten lowest scores worldwide.[21] This number has fallen even lower as the mandates of a number of elected women deputies and senators have now expired. A constitutional amendment in 2011 (published in June 2012) introduced a 30 per cent minimum quota for women's representation at all levels of public life. The original version of the new Electoral Law included this measure and extended it to municipalities and other local boards (article 90); however the quota measure was withdrawn from the later version of the law in March 2014.

The CTCEP, which is responsible for implementing the constitutional measure, has not assumed its responsibility; instead, it has passed the burden to political parties to field women candidates. The parties have no legal requirement to do so, no enforcement mechanisms have been proposed and, with most candidate-level quotas, the outcomes of women elected to office generally fall far short of the target quota level. The minimal financial incentive for meeting the 30 per cent target is open to misuse. Under Haiti's majoritarian electoral system, and given its historic gender imbalance in government, the quota is unlikely to be attained without the introduction of reserved seats.

In 2013, four of the nine members of the CTCEP were women. The EMB does not keep data on internal staffing equality, therefore it is not known how many women participate in the electoral processes as CTCEP personnel or poll workers. Data available for the CTVs in 2010 shows positive participation of women in the CTV, however women's roles are concentrated in some areas and virtually non-existent in others such as technology (0), CEP security agents (0) and lawyers (10 per cent).[22] The CTCEP has not disaggregated voter registration or turnout information by sex, thus there is no data on women's participation in these areas. Under the new 2014 law, the BED and BEC are required to include at least one woman, in any position (article 9).

While the failure to implement the constitutional quota is a primary concern for the CTCEP, electoral authorities have other important roles to play in addressing some of the most pressing factors that discourage Haitian women's participation as voters and candidates. Women candidates are often victims of gender-based smear campaigns.[23] The EMB is responsible for preventing and prosecuting acts of gender-based electoral intimidation and violence. The lack of confidence in the process and supposed corruption also contribute to a perception that electoral management and politics are not women's domains.[24]

Relations with Other Stakeholders

In terms of media relations and external communications, the CTCEP has a director of communications but no public relations services as such. Apart from weekly press briefings and press releases published during the electoral period, there are no specifically designated programmes or outreach to the media.[25] External communications have been problematic, notably due to the poorly defined management hierarchy and the involvement of CTCEP members in daily operations. A lack of message consistency, uneven relations with media outlets and erratic access for interviews has contributed to a lack of transparency, confusion and mistrust.[26] Reform of the CTCEP's external communications is critical, both to enhance the credibility and transparency of the process among political parties and transform the media into an ally to inform the public about its mandate and activities, and to inform and educate voters about the electoral process and voting operations.[27]

The CTCEP does not have a defined relationship with Haitian civil society, although it relies heavily on domestic and international organizations to provide civic and voter information and education. CTCEP voter education has tended to be last minute and limited to get-out-the-vote posters with the election date. However, there is a great need for more adapted voter education, because the lack of understanding of the electoral process fuels rumours and mistrust.[28] International organizations such as IFES have sought to address this by adapting messaging approaches to voter information needs. Nonetheless, voter turnout is exceptionally low, only 27 per cent voted in the 2010 presidential elections. This is a record low for the Western hemisphere, including Haiti, for more than 60 years.[29] Even fewer (22.9 per cent) had their votes counted. Rates of disenfranchisement (estimated at 50 per cent) were highest among populations more affected by the earthquake.[30] Haitians cite numerous barriers to participating in elections, ranging from insecurity and intimidation to fraud and corruption, lack of information and transparency, poor communication with stakeholders, controversial management of the electoral process, organizational and technical problems, poor or no voter access to information, and insufficiency of the voter awareness campaign.[31]

Conclusion

Haitian electoral administration faces significant obstacles to bringing credibility to the election process. The first step toward emerging from the ongoing crisis will be the creation of the constitutionally mandated, permanent CEP with financial and administrative autonomy. Neutrality of electoral dispute resolution must be guaranteed, and an exit strategy and transfer of professional capacity is necessary to end the long-standing dependence on external actors for electoral activities. To meet its constitutional requirements and international obligations, the permanent CEP must reverse its course on women's political participation. Improved management of external communications and responsive voter education can help improve transparency and faith in the process. As Haiti emerges from the challenges of recent years, credible electoral administration will be a key factor in building a better future.

Notes

1. Lagueny 2011.
2. Opont 2013.
3. Rioux and Lagueny 2009; Rioux 2013.
4. Opont 2013; Lagueny 2013; Kingsley 2013.
5. Ibid.
6. Rioux 2013; Descartes 2013; Opont 2013; Lagueny 2013.
7. Richards 2013; Opont 2013.
8. Sentinel 2012.
9. Ibid.; Lagueny 2013.
10. Rioux 2013.
11. Lagueny and Dérose 2010.
12. Ibid.
13. Mobekk 2001; MINUSTAH; Lagueny 2013.
14. The distinction should be noted between the CEP (institution) and the CTCEP (transitional college currently in charge of the institution).
15. Opont 2013.
16. Since 1993, the only period when no UN mission was in place was from March 2001 to February 2004. No elections were being organized during this period (Lagueny 2013).
17. Opont 2013.
18. Richards 2013; Lagueny 2013; Gonzalez, Davila and Opont 2013.
19. Opont 2013.
20. Lagueny 2013.
21. IPU no date.
22. UNDP 2013.
23. Ibid.
24. Ibid.
25. Opont 2013.
26. Lagueny 2011, 2013.
27. Ibid. It should be noted that the CTCEP is not involved in political party access to state media; this is managed by the National Telecommunications Council.
28. Ibid.; Kingsley 2013.
29. Weisbrot and Johnson 2011.
30. Ibid.
31. Lagueny 2011.

References

Descartes, Jean-Jacques, attorney, interview with author, 29 October 2013

Gonzalez, Lourdes, Davila, Roly and Opont, Pierre-Louis, UNDP Haiti, interview with author, 7 November 2013

Inter-Parliamentary Union [IPU], *Parliaments at a Glance: Women Parliamentarians* (Geneva and New York: IPU), available at <http://www.ipu.org/parline-e/WomenInParliament.asp>

Kingsley, Jean Pierre, former chief electoral officer of Canada and chair, International Mission for Monitoring Haitian Elections 2006, interview with author, 30 October 2013

Lagueny, Sophie, *How to Develop and Execute an Effective and Efficient Communications and Outreach Strategy Capable of Gaining the Trust of Voters in Transparent and Honest Elections in Haiti* (Washington, D.C.: International Foundation for Electoral Systems and US Agency for International Development, 2011)

Lagueny, Sophie, electoral expert and former IFES chief of party, Haiti, interview with author, 29 October 2013

Lagueny, Sophie and Dérose, Rudolf, *Post Disaster Assessment on the Feasibility of Organizing Free and Fair Elections in Haiti* (Washington, D.C.: International Foundation for Electoral Systems, 2010)

Mobekk, E., 'Enforcement of Democracy in Haiti', *Democratization*, 8/3 (2001), pp. 173–88

Opont, Pierre-Louis, former director general of the Provisional Electoral Council of Haiti, personal communication with author, 6 November 2013

Organization of American States [OAS], *Expert Verification Mission of the Vote Tabulation of the 28 November 2010 Presidential Election in the Republic of Haiti* (Port-au-Prince: OAS, 2013)

Richards, Lesley, electoral expert, interview with author, 23 November 2013

Rioux, Claude, attorney, interview with author, 5 November 2013

Rioux, Claude and Lagueny, Sophie, *Legal and Technical Analysis of the Haitian Elections Law of July 18, 2008* (Washington, D.C.: International Foundation for Electoral Systems, 2009)

Sentinel, The, 'OAS Issues 5 Million ID Cards in Haiti Civil Registry Project', 29 June 2012.

UNDP-Haiti, 'Fiches Thématiques Genre et Elections', unpublished manuscript (Port-au-Prince, Haiti: 2013)

UN Security Council, *Resolution 940 (1994) Adopted by the Security Council at its 3413th meeting, on 31 July 1994*, S/RES/940 (1994), available at <http://www.refworld.org/docid/3b00f15f63.html>

United Nations Stabilization Mission in Haiti [MINUSTAH] website, available at <http://www.un.org/en/peacekeeping/missions/minustah/>

Weisbrot, Mark and Johnston, Jake, *Analysis of the OAS Mission's Draft Final Report on Haiti's Election* (Washington, D.C.: Center for Economic and Policy Research, 2011)

CASE STUDY

India: The Embodiment of EMB Independence*

The Election Commission of India (ECI) is widely regarded as a model of an independent EMB. It may be even more appropriate to describe it as a 'fiercely independent' EMB. In 1948–49, the founding fathers of the Indian constitution, while debating the position of the Election Commission in the Constituent Assembly, ensured that the body responsible for conducting elections in independent India was a distinct one, separate from the government of the day, and that it should have ample financial and administrative autonomy to conduct its affairs.

The combination of the well thought-out, broadly worded provisions contained in article 324 of the Indian constitution, a supportive judiciary, an active media and Indian public opinion, and the stature and independent attitude of some of the individuals who have headed the ECI has given it the independence and reputation it enjoys today.

The Legislative Framework Governing Elections and EMBs

In addition to the fundamental constitutional provisions, two important statutes provide the legal framework for elections: the Representation of the People Acts of 1950 and 1951. The first provides for the basic requisites for elections, such as the allocation of seats for the national and state-level legislatures, the delimitation of electoral boundaries and the preparation of the electoral registers. The second stipulates detailed provisions for the conduct of elections, including the qualifications for standing as a candidate for different public offices, the rules for registering political parties and the procedure for dealing with electoral disputes.

Once the election machinery is set in motion, the electoral process is subject to the administrative supervision of the ECI, and no court of law can stop the process. Only

---

* This case study is an edited and updated version of the original case study by Vijay Patidar and Ajay Jha, 'India: The Embodiment of EMB Independence', *Electoral Management Design: The International IDEA Handbook* (Stockholm: International IDEA, 2006), pp. 192–95. The edit and update was done by Dr. S.Y. Quraishi.

after an election is concluded can an election petition be presented to the High Court. The ECI itself enquires into any allegations of procedural irregularity or violations of the Electoral Law. This procedure has ensured that the electoral process can be completed on schedule, without getting bogged down in judicial hearings.

To supplement the various provisions of these two statutes, detailed procedures are contained in the Registration of Electors Rules of 1960 and the Conduct of Elections Rules of 1961, including the instructions and forms to be used on polling and counting days.

The ECI, after consultations with all the political parties, has published a model code of conduct. This code has no legal basis, and derives its legitimacy from the consensus of the parties. It is an attempt to level the playing field and prevent the governing party from misusing the state machinery to the disadvantage of opposition parties. The ECI has done an excellent job of enforcing its provisions and reining in the governing parties during election periods. At times it has postponed elections in certain disputed electoral districts in the face of gross violations of the code of conduct.

Institutional Structure

India is a federal polity of 29 states and seven union territories. At the national level, the Union Parliament has a lower and an upper house, Lok Sabha and Rajya Sabha, respectively. Each state also has at least one elected house, the Legislative Assembly, and some of the larger states also have a second house, the Legislative Council.

The Indian constitution gives the ECI the responsibility for conducting elections for all these legislative bodies, at both the federal and state levels. In 1992, through the 73rd amendment to the constitution, a third tier of governance was introduced—district-level bodies *(panchayats),* which are India's institutions of local self-government. Elections to panchayats are entrusted to the state election commissions, which are separate entities.

Initially, there was a single chief election commissioner. However, the size, complexity and responsibility of the task led to the introduction briefly in 1989 and then from 1993 onwards of a three-member ECI. The president appoints the chief election commissioner and election commissioners to a term of six years, or up to the age of 65, whichever comes first. They enjoy the same status and receive the same salary and other benefits as judges of the Supreme Court of India. The chief election commissioner can be removed from office only through impeachment by Parliament. Impeachment can take place on two grounds only—proven misbehaviour or incapacity—and requires the same elaborate procedure that is used to remove judges of the Supreme Court and the high courts.

Other election commissioners cannot be removed from office except on the recommendation of the chief election commissioner. The ECI exercises total control over the entire election machinery, even though the members of the electoral machinery are not its employees. India has the tradition of a neutral civil service.

The key officials at the state level are the state chief electoral officers, who are selected by the ECI from a shortlist drawn up by the state government of federal civil servants posted to the state. State chief electoral officers may not be dismissed without the approval of the ECI at the national level.

However, the main electoral activity takes place in the 672 districts, with an average of 1.1 million registered voters in each district. By 2014, India has an electorate with 814 million voters, the largest in the world, of whom 550 million exercised their franchise (a voter turnout rate of 66.7 per cent). Of these, more than 130 million were new voters. The office of the district magistrate (also known as the district collector or deputy commissioner in some parts of India)—an office created by the British—plays the pivotal role for the ECI. As the district election officer, the district magistrate performs key electoral duties as the team leader of all district and subdistrict-level officials. All these officials are legally deemed to be on secondment to the ECI and come under its supervision, discipline and control for the duration of an election.

In addition to about 11 million polling staff for approximately 930,000 polling stations, senior government officials who have previously worked as district election officers and returning officers serve as electoral observers on the ECI's behalf. The ECI thus has immediate access to a large number of impartial and experienced observers without having to either employ them permanently or pay them. The observers are provided for in the Representation of the People Act of 1951 by an amendment inserted in 1989. By law they are to be officers of the government (federal or state), and they are vested with the power to stop the count if they believe malpractice has taken place. However, they have to report any such suspicion to the ECI immediately and then follow the directions given.

In practice, the ECI has also empowered observers to intervene in several matters, especially the deployment of police forces on voting day; locating polling stations in areas inhabited by weaker and poorer sections of the populace; and deciding on re-polls in cases of violence, alleged rigging and so on. Over time, the observers have become a formidable tool, acting as the eyes and ears of the commission and proving to be another important institution in ensuring the independence of the election machinery in India.

Powers and Functions

The ECI performs routine functions such as voter registration, deploying and training election officials, printing ballot papers, conducting the voting, counting the ballot papers and declaring the election results. It also allocates free time on the state-owned electronic media to national and state parties during the campaign period.

The ECI is not responsible for the delimitation of electoral boundaries: the constitution provides for a separate Delimitation Commission, headed by a sitting or retired judge of the Supreme Court. One of the election commissioners is nominated to be a member of this body. However, because the ECI has the institutional memory and provides secretarial support, it plays an important role in the delimitation process.

The ECI is also the watchdog of election expenditure. Through its appointed financial observers, it very closely monitors candidates' expenditures during the election campaign period. This has successfully reduced illegal expenditure at election time in India. The

ECI has the power to order a re-poll at polling stations (or a whole electoral district) where irregularities have been observed. It may also adjourn any poll for a few days.

Provisions to regulate political parties were originally absent from the Electoral Law, and were introduced only in 1989, giving the ECI the responsibility for registering political parties. Initially, the procedure for registering a party was quite liberal. Any association or group of persons seeking to form a political party had to apply on a prescribed form and provide certain information. This simplified procedure prompted many people to register parties that then existed only in the records of the ECI. To curb this tendency, and to facilitate the formation of serious parties, the regulations were tightened to require at least 100 members of a proposed party to give details of their voter registration and swear individual affidavits that they are not members of any other party. The ECI has also prescribed a fee of INR 10,000 for registering a new party.

Financing

It is a mark of the ECI's independence that it has not faced any major funding problems. With a staff of about 350 officials at the federal level, it is funded by the government budget through the Consolidated Fund. This pays for staff, technical operations and various office expenses, including the cost of acquiring EVMs. However, the greater part of the expense is borne by the state governments—for example, staff at the state headquarters and in the districts, the printing and transport of ballot papers, preparing and printing the electoral registers, procuring materials for the conduct of elections, training, the salaries of election officials and security forces deployed for elections, and the expenses of central election supervisors.

The cost of time on the state-owned media is borne by the government, as the parties are given this time free of charge. The broad powers given to the ECI by the constitution have been liberally and boldly interpreted to make the government pay for any necessary expenses. The ECI's accounts are subject to audit by the comptroller and auditor general, and its report is tabled in Parliament. This ensures the ECI's financial accountability, which has worked smoothly.

Electoral Reforms

Although there is no formal procedure for proposing electoral (and consequent legislative) reforms, the ECI does play a role in this regard. It has put forward a number of proposals for electoral reform that are sent to the Law and Legislative Affairs Ministry and to the prime minister directly. Such proposals are often simultaneously discussed in the media in order to bring pressure on the government and encourage public debate.

Calling a meeting of all political parties to create consensus—for example on the development of the model code of conduct—is another effective method used by the ECI. Some important reforms have recently been instigated through the mechanism of public interest litigation, through which an NGO or public-spirited person raises issues before the Supreme Court or the high courts.

Modernization of the Electoral Procedures

The ECI, after initial hesitancy, has actively and successfully promoted the application of information technology to elections as a way of handling the mammoth scale of elections in India. Each registered voter is issued with a photographic ID card to enable him/her to vote freely, and to prevent fraudulent and multiple voting. Copies of the electoral registers are made available to the political parties on CD-ROM for checking and for use on election day.

Through the use of computers at over 989 vote-counting centres, the results of the count are processed instantly and made available. Another technological innovation has been the use of EVMs at all polling stations. Although initially reluctant because of political parties' apprehensions about possible tampering, and suspicion among voters resulting from widespread illiteracy, the ECI has actively promoted the use of EVMs. Their use at all polling stations in 2014 meant that the results were available within hours of the count starting.

Capacity Building

In order to promote professional management of elections, in 2011 the ECI set up a training and resource centre called India International Institute of Democracy and Election Management (IIIDEM) with four operational wings: training and capacity building, voter education and participation, research and documentation, and international co-operation. The IIIDEM has developed a series of training modules and curricula for both domestic and international participants. Within the first three years of its existence, the institute has trained election managers from more than 40 countries.

CHAPTER 13

Reforming Electoral Processes

What Is Electoral Reform?

Electoral reform is a broad term that covers, among other things, improving the responsiveness of electoral processes to public desires and expectations. However, not all electoral change can be considered electoral reform. Electoral change can only be referred to as reform if its primary goal is to improve electoral processes, for example, through fostering enhanced impartiality, inclusiveness, transparency, integrity or accuracy. However, this distinction is not always clear in practice: some changes (e.g. US proposals to require voters to produce identity documents at polling stations) may be characterized as desirable or even necessary 'reforms' by their proponents, but as improper 'manipulation' by their opponents. Random and/or frequent electoral change, while it may be reformist, can also be confusing to voters, and thus defeat its purpose. Frequent change may also negatively affect the sustainability of an EMB's operations.

Purported electoral reforms have also often had unanticipated consequences, either in the short or long terms, which have wholly or partially negated their anticipated benefits. Such a situation may arise due to poor design or implementation, or because the reforms give rise to opportunities for parties or candidates to manipulate the system to their advantage.

Electoral reform often only catches the public eye when it involves changes to representational arrangements, such as electoral systems, but it is a much broader concept than this. There are three distinct areas of electoral reform; an EMB and its stakeholders may play different roles in each.

1. *Legal:* involving the amendment of the constitution, electoral law, and/or related rules and regulations to enhance the integrity, relevance and adequacy of the legal framework within which the EMB delivers its services. This may include institutional reform of the EMB itself.

2. *Administrative:* the introduction within an EMB of new strategies, structures, policies, procedures and technical innovations to enable it to implement its legal responsibilities and deliver its services more efficiently, effectively and sustainably. These could include policies and practices on issues such as procurement, financial integrity or employment (such as gender balance in the recruitment of EMB staff); making informed voting accessible to groups such as women, those living in remote areas and the physically impaired; or introducing new technology for services such as voting, voter registration or electoral logistics.

3. *Political:* changes that take place in the political environment within which an EMB operates, such as giving it more autonomy or creating a more effective and transparent framework for its funding and accountability.

The most dramatic examples of reform involve a previously non-democratic country introducing democratic electoral processes (e.g. Indonesia's transition to open, multiparty electoral democracy in 1998–99). In such situations, reform in all three areas (legal, administrative and political) tends to take place at the same time, often under tight time constraints, and with no single player driving, and taking a holistic view of, the overall reform process.

Since the mid-1980s, there have been substantial structural and procedural changes in the way elections are conducted around the world, such as the growing numbers of independent and permanent EMBs and the increasing use of new technologies to deliver electoral services. Electoral reform has often been part of a package of general democratization initiatives. However, many countries that previously enjoyed general satisfaction with their long-standing framework and style of electoral administration have also undertaken substantial reforms. Examples include the introduction of an independent EMB and significantly wider access to voting in Australia in 1984; the introduction of a new independent body with electoral functions, and a radically different electoral system, in New Zealand in 1993 (followed by a further consolidation and enhancement of the EMB's functions, completed in 2012); changes in Sweden in 2001 to create a more independent electoral administration; and the establishment of an independent electoral commission in Tonga in 2010.

The internationalization of electoral frameworks and administration continues to place countries under pressure to introduce electoral reform measures. The relatively recent development of generally acknowledged principles for free, fair and credible elections, and of global and regional obligations for electoral administration, have created yardsticks by which each country's electoral processes and administration can be assessed.

More problematically, countries are sometimes encouraged or even pressured to introduce processes, such as a civil register, which are not rooted in basic principles of freedom and fairness, but rather in the preferences of external advisers or election observers.

Reforms to electoral processes may be triggered by a failure to deliver acceptable elections or by conflict resulting from disputed elections. Where countries are dependent on international donor contributions, funds may be linked to the implementation of electoral reforms, as in Liberia. Even where there is no such explicit linkage, the injection of donor funds may tend to make arguments for electoral reform more compelling. Financial constraints requiring electoral resources to be used more sustainably and effectively have had a significant bearing on administrative electoral reforms.

The increasingly widespread and expert independent and political party observation of elections has produced many well-documented assessments of electoral performance and recommended reforms—for example, in connection with Nigeria's post-2003 elections and with numerous elections observed by ANFREL. Civil society and the media have become more aware of electoral rights and related international obligations. International observation of and technical assistance to elections in emerging democracies can also have an effect in the mature democracies.

While governments have initiated many electoral reforms, at times in response to societal or external pressures, EMBs themselves have often been powerful motivators of such changes. More widespread public accountability and transparency of EMBs—a significant reform in itself—has had a multiplier effect on further electoral reform. Materials supporting electoral reforms have emerged from EMBs' increasing use of election audits and the advocacy activities of CSOs and other stakeholders.

Failing EMBs

Many EMBs fail to discharge their mandate in line with accepted regional or international obligations. While there are no comprehensive data on the reasons for EMB failure, studies of individual EMBs have noted a number of internal causes, including:

1. lack of stakeholder confidence in the EMB;
2. government and/or political influence on EMB decisions;
3. a partisan approach by the EMB or its members;
4. a lack of EMB professionalism, or a loss over time of certain critical skills; and
5. EMB incompetence or financial impropriety.

In other cases, the reasons for an EMB's failure are outside its control, for example, having to implement an electoral system that produces results that are not acceptable to major stakeholders, as in Lesotho in the 1990s. Alternatively, there may be deficiencies in the legal framework. In Papua New Guinea since 2002, the extensive shortcomings of the electoral process have mainly been due to the broader political environment, in particular a culture of impunity in relation to electoral offences.

Except where the entire political system is failing, electoral reform—of the EMB itself and/or of the broader electoral framework—may be able to save future electoral processes from failure. Notable examples of this are Mexico and South Africa in the 1990s.

The EMB's Role in Electoral Reforms

While the EMB has a key role to play in all electoral reform, it may not be in a position to implement reform without the support of its key stakeholders—particularly the government, legislature and political parties. This is a significant reason for EMBs to maintain a strong relationship with their stakeholders (see Chapter 8 of this Handbook).

An EMB can only implement legal reform within the established legal framework agreed by the government and legislature. However, an EMB may have a key research, review and advocacy role in promoting electoral legal reform, which can be guided by the criteria detailed in International IDEA's publication *International Obligations for Elections: Guidelines for Legal Frameworks*. Electoral legal reform can be assisted by establishing an appropriate permanent body of the legislature to monitor electoral activities and recommend electoral reforms to the government. Effective legal electoral reform depends on a multiparty approach in the legislature that subordinates political advantage to ethical electoral principles and good practice.

An EMB has more control over the implementation of administrative reforms, and can implement them more effectively, if it formally adopts a continuous review and reform process within its management policies. However, legal and administrative reforms often need to be synchronized to optimize their effectiveness. In Australia, for example, while the EMB has modernized its election procedures extensively, reform of the election machinery has not kept pace.

Unless an EMB maintains a process for reviewing its administrative strategies, policies, procedures and practices, it will become less effective, as it will have no mechanism to deal with change in its legal, stakeholder, technological, financial and social environments.

Political and legal reform issues related to electoral processes are often strongly associated. As with legal reform, EMBs do not control political reform, although again they can play a research and advocacy role, and cultivate support among key stakeholders.

Key steps for an EMB to consider in proposing and implementing electoral reforms include:
- assigning responsibilities to specific members or staff, including at the senior level, for the development, advocacy and implementation of electoral reforms;

- implementing effective processes, including post-electoral audits and evaluations, for reviewing the electoral framework and implementing electoral processes;
- consulting with stakeholders to ascertain their views on required reforms and to enlist their support for the EMB's reform programme;
- making submissions to the government and legislature on desired electoral reforms;
- publicizing desired electoral reforms through the media and use of stakeholder networks;
- developing an electoral reform implementation strategy; and
- evaluating the effects of electoral reforms.

One challenge for EMBs is building up the skill base needed to drive electoral reforms. Well-established bodies typically have staff with a strong understanding of their existing processes. While they may be equipped to propose useful incremental improvements, unless they also have a sound knowledge of electoral fundamentals, they may be less well placed to imagine and elaborate the more radical reforms that are sometimes needed.

The Scope of Electoral Reform

A significant area of electoral reform is the nature and structure of the institutions engaged in electoral management or delivering electoral services. Reforms in this area may enhance the independence of the EMB—for example, by adopting Independent Model electoral management in countries such as Bhutan and Tonga, or a Mixed Model as in Timor-Leste. Electoral responsibilities may be reassigned among existing and/or new bodies to promote better service delivery—as in New Zealand, Sweden and the UK. In Sweden, the EMB itself initiated the reform of electoral management. In Indonesia in 1998–99 and in the UK, the government initiated the reforms. Pressure from local civil society or international groups may also instigate the reform of electoral management arrangements, as in Georgia and Liberia.

Reforms of electoral processes, such as the introduction of a new electoral system, may have a broad effect on an EMB's strategies, policies and procedures. They may target key electoral issues such as electoral participation and representation, the delimitation of electoral districts, voter registration, the registration and oversight of political parties, and improving electoral integrity. They may also target specific technical or technological aspects of the electoral process, such as introducing new procurement or employment processes, voter registration systems, or voting and vote-counting methods or systems. They may involve social policies, such as reducing a gender imbalance in representation, improving access to electoral processes for marginalized sectors of society or improving the representativeness of the EMB's staff.

Electoral system reform, as in Indonesia, Papua New Guinea and New Zealand, is one of the most far-reaching reforms in election administration. It is often the result of a functional need, for example, of perceptions of an 'unfairness' in representation or of government ineffectiveness or lack of responsiveness. In 2003 Indonesia changed its electoral system from closed-list proportional representation (PR) in very large electoral districts to open-list PR in small electoral districts in order to address perceived deficiencies in the links between voters and representatives, while maintaining the consensus nature of Indonesian governance. Electoral system reform places a substantial information responsibility on the EMB, and may require it to implement new methods of electoral district boundary delimitation, voting and vote counting.

EMBs can play a significant role in reform of electoral district boundary delimitation, for example as advocates of more transparent and equitable boundary delimitation processes; by providing expert opinions on boundary delimitation issues; and by ensuring that they exercise any responsibilities for boundary delimitation impartially, equitably and with integrity. Some electoral reforms have introduced multi-member districts, as this type of system, usually based on PR, can decrease the influence of electoral boundaries on election results. Other reforms have required boundary delimitations based on 'one person, one vote, one value'. Some reforms have attempted to make boundary delimitation processes more transparent and objective, for example by excluding the legislature from the delimitation process, placing an independent body in charge of delimitation, and requiring open hearings and independent review of proposed boundaries.

The process of registering electors has attracted many efforts at modernization in both emerging and established democracies. Voter registration determines the ability of eligible voters to participate in an election, and thus is a key element of the fairness of an election. As it generally occurs well before election day, and often outside the direct scrutiny of observers (especially where electoral registers are derived from civil or population registers), the internal integrity of voter registration systems needs to be very high. Reforms have increasingly targeted the efficiency, as well as the integrity, of voter registration processes. They have often included the introduction of biometric data capture and processing, with the stated aim of decreasing the scope for multiple registration, voter impersonation and/or multiple voting.

Many EMBs have implemented systems to improve the inclusiveness, fairness, accuracy and transparency of voter registration, for example, by providing for continuously updated voter registration, special registration provisions for transient voters, and safeguards against the wrongful rejection of a registration or removal from the electoral register. EMBs and other agencies responsible for maintaining data from which electoral registers are derived are improving the integrity of electoral registers by using better methods to check the identity of qualified persons and reducing data processing times, often using modern technological solutions. EMBs need to ensure that technological solutions for voter registration enjoy citizens' trust and are sustainable, especially in emerging democracies where EMBs may have uncertain levels of future financial support.

There have been significant reforms in the role played by EMBs in monitoring and regulating the activities of political parties. Some are the consequences of legal reforms targeted at levelling the playing field for political competition—for example, reforms in the administration of state funding of political parties and candidates' election campaigns, and the qualifications for registering parties and candidates to contest elections. Others have been targeted at improving oversight of campaign contributions and expenditures, and the internal democracy of political parties—such as oversight of candidate selection processes. Reforms to promote a level playing field for elections have also given some EMBs the responsibility of administering or monitoring arrangements that require the media to allocate campaign advertising opportunities equitably.

A growing number of EMBs are introducing new voting methods. Brazil, India, Bhutan and Venezuela have replaced manual voting with EVMs, while Estonia has introduced Internet voting. Many of the issues that need to be considered in reforming electoral processes by introducing electronic voting are discussed in Chapter 9 of this Handbook.

There have been significant efforts to make electoral participation more accessible. Access to voter registration has sometimes been opened to those who are out of the country, of no fixed abode or in prison. Access to polling has been widened for many people through the introduction of in-person absentee, postal or pre-poll (early) voting, including for voters who are out of the country, and by providing special voting and voter information facilities for refugees, internally displaced persons, the disabled, the aged and those in remote areas, in prison or in hospital. EMBs have had to respond to all these reforms by introducing procedures and systems that enable the additional access while maintaining high integrity in the voter registration, voting and counting processes. Internet voting is the subject of much current research, and poses a challenge to EMBs that might be contemplating its adoption, since the skill sets required to manage such a process are radically different from those typically found in EMBs that manage traditional voting methods.

It should be noted that reforms that give rise to a proliferation of different voting methods, or more generally to a range of different modalities for performing a particular function, tend to be more challenging for an EMB than ones that simply update a single mechanism to a different single mechanism.

Reform of electoral access has attempted in some countries to provide equal access for specific societal groups and for women. Such reforms may well have to be pursued in a complementary way in the legal, administrative and political areas. EMBs can promote equitable access by insisting on it in their own staffing, for example by requiring gender balance in temporary staffing for polling stations, and using internal professional development programmes to ensure that women advance into EMB management positions.

Electoral Management Design

Managing Electoral Change

Electoral change management requirements will depend on the extent of the reform and the specific electoral processes involved. Changes to the model of the EMB—for example, from a Governmental to an Independent Model—require particularly careful planning to ensure a smooth transition and the retention of skills and institutional memory. It is crucial that changes to electoral structures and frameworks are agreed long enough before electoral events to allow for the preparation of new materials and the effective implementation of training.

Especially where the process of change applies to the nature or structure and staff of an EMB, it is essential to appoint a skilled manager and communicator to oversee and implement the changes. Changing organizational structures and individual roles within structures will inevitably create tension. Transparency, honesty, serious consultation, communication and adequate forewarning are essential elements of managing personnel through electoral change. Timing is also critical. EMB staff have skills and knowledge that may be difficult to replace, especially close to an election date. Involving EMB members in change management demonstrates the EMB's commitment to reforms.

Reforming electoral technical processes may require the help of experts who specialize in particular technical areas. In implementing technical reforms, an EMB needs to ensure that the right procedural and system specifications have been chosen and correctly implemented. Thorough development review processes and pre-implementation testing are essential. The change management process also needs to include measurable indicators to evaluate the implementation of the electoral reforms, and clear responsibilities for reporting on indicators and improving performance if any indicator is not achieved.

Risks Associated with Electoral Reform

Where a country's electoral processes are proceeding reasonably well, risk generally tends to be minimized by the incremental pursuit of electoral reform, making small changes over a period of several elections. The simultaneous implementation of major reforms in a range of different areas can place a great burden on an EMB, and will increase the risk of suboptimal implementation, especially when deadlines are tight. While sound implementation has the potential to meet intended targets, and hopefully to build confidence and trust in the effectiveness of elections and the EMB, failed implementation can have the opposite effect. This will be especially problematic if reforms are pursued without strong political support across the board; opponents of a particular initiative are likely be looking for opportunities to characterize it as a failure, and to push for its abandonment.

There are three main risks inherent in reform processes. The first is that of trying to solve the wrong problem. For example, there will be little benefit for a country to invest heavily in a technologically sophisticated voter registration system if the real problem is that the polling officials are intimidated, suborned, or corrupted by parties or candidates, making the quality of the register itself largely irrelevant. Where a country's electoral culture is truly dire, there may be little to gain from massive investment in technology, since even if it works it may simply displace fraud from one area of the system to another. Major reforms, especially those involving technological innovation, can be very expensive, particularly when factors such as long-term maintenance costs and depreciation are taken into account. The task of setting up such systems can easily overwhelm even a well-established and resourced organization, placing massive demands on the time of senior management and potentially drawing attention away from other problem areas that, judged objectively, may be more deserving of priority attention.

A second risk is that of making unrealistic assumptions about non-technical matters on which the success of a system depends. For example, a database intended to be used to maintain a continuously updated register of voters may fail to live up to expectations if there is no way of ensuring the constant flow of data required to keep the database up to date.

A third risk is a loss of agility. A decision to adopt a specific technological approach may well lock a country or organization into maintaining a way of dealing with a problem that will be difficult, or increasingly expensive, to sustain in the long run. For example, organizations that invested heavily in Internet-based processes, not just in the electoral field, are now finding that they are having to retool their PC-based systems to make them readily accessible from smartphones and tablets, as consumers' preferred ways of accessing the Internet change.

Chapter Summary

- Electoral reforms are changes targeted at improving implementation of the guiding principles of electoral administration described in Chapter 1 of this Handbook.

- Electoral reforms may be directed at the electoral legal framework—including the EMB—the administrative and technical processes of electoral management, or the political context for electoral activities.

- No aspect of electoral frameworks, systems, institutions, planning, management or operations is immune from reform or modernization. EMBs need to have a clear strategy for developing or responding to and implementing electoral reforms.

- EMBs have vital roles as advocates of electoral reforms in general, as implementers of institutional reforms, and as initiators and implementers of administrative reforms, including technical reforms.

- Electoral reform needs to be carefully managed to ensure that it fulfils its purpose without confusing electors and with minimal disruption to electoral administration.

Annex A

World Survey: Electoral Management Bodies in 217 Countries and Territories

Country	Model of electoral management	Name of EMB	Number of EMB members
Afghanistan	Independent	Independent Election Commission	9
Albania	Independent	Central Election Commission	7
Algeria	Governmental	Ministry of Interior	N/A
Andorra	Mixed	Central government and communes	N/A
		Electoral Board	6
Angola	Independent	National Electoral Commission	11
Anguilla	Governmental	Supervisor of Elections	N/A
Antigua and Barbuda	Independent	Electoral Commission	5
Argentina	Mixed	National Elections Direction of the Ministry of the Interior	N/A
		National Electoral Chamber	3
Armenia	Independent	Central Electoral Commission	7
Aruba	Governmental	Head Electoral Council	N/A
Australia	Independent	Electoral Commission	3
Austria	Governmental	Federal Ministry for the Interior	N/A
Azerbaijan	Independent	Central Election Commission	18
Bahamas	Independent	Parliamentary Commissioner	1
Bahrain	Governmental	Ministry of Justice and Islamic Affairs	N/A

Annex A. World Survey: Electoral Management Bodies in 217 countries

The classification in this annex is based on the legal form and institutional arrangements of each country and territory at the time of publication. It does not express any judgment of an EMB's performance or independence of action in practice. The number of EMB members does not include substitute members where these exist. More information, including sources and comments, is available in the International IDEA Electoral Management Design database <http://www.idea.int/elections/emd/electoral-management-design-database.cfm>.

Term of office	EMB members selected by	Chair appointed/ elected by	Party or expert-based membership
6 years	President	EMB	Expert
4 years	Legislature	Legislature	Expert
N/A	N/A	N/A	N/A
N/A	N/A	N/A	N/A
4 years	High Council of Justice; legislature	High Council of Justice	Expert
4 years	President; legislature; Supreme Court; Ministry of Territorial Administration; National Council of Social Communication	National Assembly	Expert
N/A	N/A	N/A	N/A
7 years	Governor-General	Governor-General	Expert
N/A	N/A	N/A	N/A
Not specified	Judiciary	Judiciary	Expert
6 years	President	EMB	Expert
N/A	N/A	N/A	N/A
Maximum 7 years	Chief justice of the Federal Court, government	Governor-General	Expert
N/A	N/A	N/A	N/A
5 years	Political parties	Majority party in legislature	Combined
Unspecified	Governor-General	Governor-General	Expert
N/A	N/A	N/A	N/A

Country	Model of electoral management	Name of EMB	Number of EMB members
Bangladesh	Independent	Election Commission	5
Barbados	Independent	Electoral and Boundaries Commission	5
Belarus	Independent	Central Commission on Elections and Holding Republican Referenda	12
Belgium	Governmental	Federal Public Service Interior	N/A
Belize	Mixed	Chief Elections Officer	N/A
		Elections and Boundaries Commission	5
Benin	Independent	National Autonomous Electoral Commission	11
Bermuda	Governmental	Parliamentary Registrar	N/A
Bhutan	Independent	Election Commission	3
Bolivia	Independent	Plurinational Electoral Body – Supreme Electoral Tribunal	7
Bosnia and Herzegovina	Independent	Central Election Commission	7
Botswana	Independent	Independent Electoral Commission	7
Brazil	Independent	High Electoral Tribunal	Minimum 7
Brunei	No national elections	N/A	N/A
Bulgaria	Independent	Central Election Commission	Minimum 19
Burkina Faso	Independent	Independent National Electoral Commission	15
Burundi	Independent	Independent National Electoral Commission	5
Cambodia	Independent	National Election Committee	9
Cameroon	Independent	Elections Cameroon	18
Canada	Independent	Chief Electoral Officer	1
Cape Verde	Mixed	Central Support Service for Elections	N/A
		National Elections Commission	5
Cayman Islands	Governmental	Supervisor of Elections	N/A

Term of office	EMB members selected by	Chair appointed/ elected by	Party or expert-based membership
5 years	President	President	Expert
5 years	Governor-General	Governor-General	Expert
5 years	President, legislature	President in agreement with the legislature	Expert
N/A	N/A	N/A	N/A
N/A	N/A	N/A	N/A
5 years	Governor-General	Governor-General	Expert
For election period only	President, legislature, civil society	EMB	Expert
N/A	N/A	N/A	N/A
5 years or until attaining age of 65	Monarch	Monarch	Expert
6 years	President, legislature	EMB	Expert
7 years	Legislature	EMB	Expert
10 years	Judicial Service Commission	Judicial Service Commission	Combined
2 years	Supreme Court; Superior Court; President	EMB	Expert
N/A	N/A	N/A	N/A
5 years	President	President	Combined
5 years	Civil society, political parties (ruling and opposition)	Civil society	Combined
3 years	National Assembly and Senate	Not specified	Expert
For election period only	Legislature	Legislature	Expert
Electoral Council: 4 years, General Directorate of Elections: 5 years	Electoral Council: President; General Directorate of Elections: President	Electoral Council: President; General Directorate of Elections: President	Expert
Unlimited	House of Commons	Not applicable	Expert
N/A	N/A	N/A	N/A
6 years	Legislature	EMB	Expert
N/A	N/A	N/A	N/A

Annex A. World Survey: Electoral Management Bodies in 217 countries

Country	Model of electoral management	Name of EMB	Number of EMB members
Central African Republic	Mixed	Ministry of Territorial Administration and Decentralization	N/A
		Independent Electoral Commission	31
Chad	Mixed	Independent National Electoral Commission	31
		Permanent Bureau of Elections	N/A
Chile	Independent	Electoral Service Board	5
China	No national elections	N/A	N/A
Colombia	Independent	National Electoral Council	9
Comoros	Independent	Independent National Electoral Commission	10
Congo	Mixed	Ministry of Interior	N/A
		National Commission for the Organization of Elections	9
Congo, Democratic Republic of the	Independent	Independent National Electoral Commission	7
Cook Islands	Governmental	Ministry of Justice	N/A
Costa Rica	Independent	Supreme Electoral Tribunal	3-5
Côte d'Ivoire	Independent	Independent Electoral Commission	13
Croatia	Independent	State Election Commission	9
Cuba	Independent	National Electoral Commission	17
Curaçao	Governmental	Ministry of Government Policy, Planning and Public Services	N/A
Cyprus	Governmental	Ministry of Interior	N/A
Cyprus (North)	Independent	High Electoral Board	4
Czech Republic	Governmental	State Electoral Commission	19
Denmark	Governmental	Ministry for Economic Affairs and the Interior	N/A
Djibouti	Independent	Independent National Electoral Commission	Minimum 17
Dominica	Independent	Electoral Commission	5
Dominican Republic	Independent	Central Electoral Board	5

Term of office	EMB members selected by	Chair appointed/ elected by	Party or expert-based membership
N/A	N/A	N/A	N/A
For election period only	Not specified	EMB	Expert
For election period only	Political parties	Political parties	Combined
N/A	N/A	N/A	N/A
8 years	President, in accordance with Senate	EMB	Expert
N/A	N/A	N/A	N/A
4 years	Legislature	EMB	Expert
Not specified	President	EMB	Expert
N/A	N/A	N/A	N/A
Not specified	Government, political parties, civil society	Not specified	Combined
6 years	Political parties	Not specified	Expert
N/A	N/A	N/A	N/A
6 years	Supreme Court of Justice	EMB	Expert
6 years	Council of Ministers	Not specified by legislation	Combined
8 years	Supreme Court and legislature	The president of the Supreme Court is the ex officio chair	Expert
For election period only	State Council	State Council	Not specified
N/A	N/A	N/A	N/A
N/A	N/A	N/A	N/A
5 years	Supreme Court	Supreme Court	Expert
N/A	N/A	Ministry of Interior	N/A
N/A	N/A	N/A	N/A
For election period only	Executive, legislature, judicial, civil society, independent presidential candidates and political parties	EMB	Combined
5 years	President	President	Combined
4 years	Senate	Senate	Not specified

Annex A. World Survey: Electoral Management Bodies in 217 countries

379

Country	Model of electoral management	Name of EMB	Number of EMB members
Ecuador	Independent	National Electoral Council	5
Egypt	Independent	National Elections Commission	10
El Salvador	Independent	Supreme Electoral Tribunal	5
Equatorial Guinea	Mixed	Ministry of Interior	N/A
		Central Elections Board	No less than 13
Eritrea	Independent	Electoral Commission	5
Estonia	Independent	National Electoral Committee	7
Ethiopia	Independent	National Electoral Board	9
Falkland Islands	Governmental	Returning Officer(s)	N/A
Fiji	Independent	Electoral Commission	7
Finland	Governmental	Ministry of Justice	N/A
France	Mixed	Ministry of Interior	N/A
		Constitutional Council	9
Gabon	Mixed	Ministry of Interior	N/A
		Autonomous and Permanent National Electoral Commission	8
Gambia, The	Independent	Independent Electoral Commission	5
Georgia	Independent	Central Election Commission	13
Germany	Governmental	Federal Ministry of Interior	N/A
Ghana	Independent	Electoral Commission	7
Gibraltar	Governmental	Returning Officer	N/A
Greece	Governmental	Ministry of the Interior	N/A
Grenada	Governmental	Supervisor of Elections	N/A
Guatemala	Independent	Supreme Electoral Tribunal	5
Guernsey	Governmental	Presiding Officer/Registrar-General of Electors/Returning Officers	N/A
Guinea	Independent	Independent National Electoral Commission	25
Guinea-Bissau	Independent	National Election Commission	8
Guyana	Independent	Elections Commission	7

Term of office	EMB members selected by	Chair appointed/ elected by	Party or expert-based membership
6 years	Council of Civic Participation and Social Control	EMB	Expert
6 years	Supreme Judicial Council and special councils	Chair is the most senior member from the Court of Cassation	Expert
5 years	Legislature	Legislature	Combined
N/A	N/A	N/A	N/A
For election period only	Political parties, government, judiciary	EMB	Combined
Not specified	President, legislature	President	Party
4 years	Judiciary, Auditor General, Chief Public Prosecutor, Secretary General of Riigikogu, State Secretary.	EMB	Expert
5 years	Legislature	Legislature	Expert
N/A	N/A	N/A	N/A
Not specified	President	President	Expert
N/A	N/A	N/A	N/A
N/A	N/A	N/A	N/A
9 years	President; National Assembly; Senate	President	Expert
N/A	N/A	N/A	N/A
30 months	Political parties, Ministry of Interior	Constitutional Court	Combined
7 years	President	President	Expert
5 years	Legislature, political parties	EMB	Not specified
N/A	N/A	N/A	N/A
Unlimited	President	President	Expert
N/A	N/A	N/A	N/A
N/A	N/A	N/A	N/A
N/A	N/A	N/A	N/A
6 years	Legislature	EMB	Expert
N/A	N/A	N/A	N/A
7 years	Political parties, civil society, administration	EMB	Combined
4 years	President	President	Expert
Not specified	President	President	Expert

Annex A. World Survey: Electoral Management Bodies in 217 countries

Country	Model of electoral management	Name of EMB	Number of EMB members
Haiti	Independent	Provisional Electoral Council	9
Holy See (Vatican City State)	No national elections	N/A	N/A
Honduras	Independent	Supreme Electoral Tribunal	3
Hungary	Mixed	Ministry of Interior	N/A
		National Electoral Committee	Minimum 5
Iceland	Mixed	Ministry of the Interior	N/A
		National Electoral Board	5
India	Independent	Election Commission	3
Indonesia	Independent	General Elections Commission	7
Iran	Mixed	Ministry of Interior	N/A
		Guardian Council	12
Iraq	Independent	Independent High Electoral Commission	9
Ireland	Governmental	Department of the Environment, Community and Local Government	N/A
Israel	Independent	Central Elections Committee	Minimum 31
Italy	Governmental	Ministry of Interior	N/A
Jamaica	Independent	Electoral Commission	9
		Director of Elections	1
Japan	Mixed	Ministry of Internal Affairs and Communications	N/A
		Central Election Management Council	5
Jersey	Independent	Returning Officer	One per electoral district
Jordan	Independent	Independent Election Commission	6
Kazakhstan	Independent	Central Election Commission	7
Kenya	Independent	Independent Electoral and Boundaries Commission	9
Kiribati	Independent	Electoral Commission	3-5
Kosovo	Independent	Central Election Commission	11
Kuwait	Governmental	Ministry of Interior	N/A

Term of office	EMB members selected by	Chair appointed/ elected by	Party or expert-based membership
9 years	Executive; judiciary; legislature	EMB	Expert
N/A	N/A	N/A	N/A
5 years	Legislature	EMB	Expert
N/A	N/A	N/A	N/A
For election period only	Legislature	EMB	Combined
N/A	N/A	N/A	N/A
4 years	Legislature	EMB	Expert
6 years (or to age 65, whichever is the earlier)	President	President	Expert
5 years	Legislature	EMB	Expert
N/A	N/A	N/A	N/A
6 years	Religious leader; Islamic Consultative Assembly, on nomination by head of the judicial power	EMB	Expert
5 years	Legislature	EMB	Expert
N/A	N/A	N/A	N/A
4 years	Political parties	Supreme Court	Party
N/A	N/A	N/A	N/A
4 or 7	Governor-General	Half EMB	Expert
7 years	Governor-General	N/A	Expert
N/A	N/A	N/A	N/A
3 years	Legislature	EMB	Expert
For election period only	Royal Court	N/A	Expert
6 years	A special committee	EMB	Expert
5 years	President, Senate, legislature	President	Not specified
6 years	Legislature, President	President	Expert
5 years	President	President	Expert
7 years	Legislature	President	Expert
N/A	N/A	N/A	N/A

Annex A. World Survey: Electoral Management Bodies in 217 countries

383

Country	Model of electoral management	Name of EMB	Number of EMB members
Kyrgyzstan	Independent	Central Commission on Elections and the Conducting of Referenda	12
Laos	Mixed	Ministry of the Interior	N/A
		National Election Committee	15-17
Latvia	Independent	Central Election Commission	9
Lebanon	Governmental	The Supervisory Commission on the Electoral Campaign	N/A
Lesotho	Independent	Independent Electoral Commission	3
Liberia	Independent	National Elections Commission	7
Libya	Independent	High National Elections Commission	11
Liechtenstein	Independent	Election Commission	11
Lithuania	Independent	Central Electoral Commission	15
Luxembourg	Governmental	Central Government Office	N/A
Macedonia, Former Yugoslav Republic of	Independent	State Election Commission	7
Madagascar	Independent	Independent National Electoral Commission	19
Malawi	Independent	Electoral Commission	Minimum 7
Malaysia	Independent	Electoral Commission	7
Maldives	Independent	Elections Commission	5
Mali	Mixed	Ministry of Territorial Administration and Local Collectives	N/A
		Independent National Electoral Commission	15
		General Delegation to Elections	Not specified
Malta	Independent	Electoral Commission	9
Man, Isle of	Governmental	Chief Secretary's Office	N/A
Marshall Islands	Governmental	Ministry of Internal Affairs	N/A
Mauritania	Independent	Independent National Electoral Commission	15
Mauritius	Independent	Electoral Commissioner	1
		Electoral Supervisory Commission	3-8

Term of office	EMB members selected by	Chair appointed/ elected by	Party or expert-based membership
5 years	Legislature, President	EMB	Expert
N/A	N/A	N/A	N/A
For election period only	National Assembly	Not specified	Expert
4 years	Legislature, Supreme Court	Legislature	Expert
N/A	N/A	N/A	N/A
5 years	Monarch	Monarch	Expert
7 years	President with consent of Senate	President with consent of Senate	Expert
Not specified	Legislature	Legislature	Not specified
4 years	Political parties	Government	Party
4 years	Minister of ustice, bar association, political parties	Legislature	Combined
N/A	N/A	N/A	N/A
4 years	Legislature	Legislature	Combined
5-7	Civil society, government, political parties	EMB	Combined
4 years	Legislature	Judicial Service Commission	Expert
Until the age of 65	Monarch	Monarch	Expert
5 years	President, upon approval of legislature	EMB	Expert
N/A	N/A	N/A	N/A
For election period only	Political parties, religious leaders, judicial, human rights associations, women's association (FACO)	Not specified	Combined
Not specified	Not specified	President	Not specified
3 years	President	President	Expert
N/A	N/A	N/A	N/A
N/A	N/A	N/A	N/A
6 months	Decree by the Council of Ministers	Decree by the Council of Ministers	Expert
Not specified	Judicial and Legal Services Commission	Not applicable	Expert
5 years	President	President	Expert

Annex A. World Survey: Electoral Management Bodies in 217 countries

385

Country	Model of electoral management	Name of EMB	Number of EMB members
Mexico	Independent	National Electoral Institute	11
Micronesia	Governmental	National Election Director	N/A
Moldova	Independent	Central Electoral Commission	9
Monaco	Governmental	Electoral Commission	N/A
Mongolia	Independent	General Election Commission	9
Montenegro	Independent	Republic Election Commission	11 (plus one authorized representative of each of the submitters of electoral lists)
Montserrat	Independent	Electoral Commission	4
Morocco	Governmental	Ministry of Interior	N/A
Mozambique	Independent	Technical Secretariat for Election Administration	N/A
		National Election Commission	13
Myanmar	Independent	Union Election Commission	Minimum of 5
Namibia	Independent	Electoral Commission	5
Nauru	Governmental	Electoral Registrar	N/A
Nepal	Independent	Election Commission	5
Netherlands	Mixed	Ministry of Interior and Kingdom Relations	N/A
		Electoral Council	7
New Zealand	Independent	Electoral Commission	3
Nicaragua	Independent	Supreme Electoral Council	7
Niger	Independent	Independent National Electoral Commission	30
Nigeria	Independent	Independent National Electoral Commission	13
Niue	Governmental	Chief Electoral Officer	N/A
North Korea	Governmental	No data	N/A
Norway	Governmental	Ministry for Local Government and Regional Development	N/A
Oman	Governmental	Ministry of Interior	N/A
Pakistan	Independent	Election Commission	5

Term of office	EMB members selected by	Chair appointed/ elected by	Party or expert-based membership
6-9 years	Legislature	Legislature	Expert
N/A	N/A	N/A	N/A
5 years	President, legislature	EMB	Combined
N/A	N/A	N/A	N/A
6 years	Legislature, judiciary, president	Legislature	Expert
4 years	Legislature, political parties	EMB	Combined
5 years	Governor	Governor	Expert
N/A	N/A	N/A	N/A
N/A	N/A	N/A	N/A
5 years	Political parties, civil society	EMB	Expert
Not specified	President	President	Expert
5 years	President	EMB	Expert
N/A	N/A	N/A	N/A
6 years (or to age 65, whichever is the earlier)	Constitutional Council	Prime Minister	Not specified
N/A	N/A	N/A	N/A
4 years	Monarch	Monarch	Expert
Maximum 5 years	Governor-General	Governor-General	Expert
5 years	Legislature	EMB	Expert
For election period only	Various groups and institutions	Judiciary or President	Combined
Unlimited	President	President	Expert
N/A	N/A	N/A	N/A
N/A	N/A	N/A	N/A
N/A	N/A	N/A	N/A
N/A	N/A	N/A	N/A
5 years	President, Prime Minister, legislature	President, Prime Minister, legislature	Expert

Annex A. World Survey: Electoral Management Bodies in 217 countries

Country	Model of electoral management	Name of EMB	Number of EMB members
Palau	Independent	Election Commission	5
Palestine	Independent	Central Elections Commission	9
Panama	Independent	Electoral Tribunal	3
Papua New Guinea	Independent	Electoral Commission	1
Paraguay	Independent	Supreme Electoral Justice Tribunal	3
Peru	Independent	National Jury of Elections	5
		National Office of Electoral Process	1
Philippines	Independent	Commission on Elections	7
Pitcairn Islands	Governmental	Mayor and island secretary	N/A
Poland	Independent	National Electoral Commission	9
Portugal	Mixed	Ministry of Internal Administration	N/A
		National Election Commission	Minimum 6
Qatar	No national elections	N/A	N/A
Romania	Independent	Permanent Electoral Authority	3
		Central Electoral Bureau	23
Russia	Independent	Central Election Commission	15
Rwanda	Independent	National Electoral Commission	7
Saint Helena, Ascension and Tristan da Cunha	Governmental	Office of the Chief Secretary	N/A
Saint Kitts and Nevis	Mixed	Electoral Commission	3
		Supervisor of Elections	1
Saint Lucia	Independent	Electoral Commission	3
Saint Vincent and The Grenadines	Governmental	Supervisor of Elections	1
Samoa	Independent	Electoral Commissioner	1
San Marino	Governmental	Ministry of Interior	N/A
São Tomé and Príncipe	Governmental	Electoral Technical Cabinet	N/A

Term of office	EMB members selected by	Chair appointed/ elected by	Party or expert-based membership
4 years	President	EMB	Not specified
4 years	President	President	Expert
10 years	Legislature, government, Supreme Court	EMB	Expert
6 years	Governor-General	N/A	Expert
5 years	Supreme Court	EMB	Expert
4 years	Supreme Court; Prosecutors Board; Lima Bar Association; deans of public and private schools of law	Supreme Court	Expert
4 years	National Council of the Magistracy	N/A	Expert
7 years	President	President	Expert
N/A	N/A	N/A	N/A
Not specified	Judiciary, President	EMB	Expert
N/A	N/A	N/A	N/A
4 years	Supreme Counsel of Magistrates; legislature; government departments responsible for internal administration, foreign affairs and mass media	Supreme Counsel of Magistrates	Expert
N/A	N/A	N/A	N/A
8 years	Legislature, President, Prime Minister	Legislature	Expert
For election period only	High Court of Cassation, permanent electoral authority, political parties	EMB	Combined
5 years	Political parties, legislature, President	EMB	Combined
3 years	President, Senate	President, Senate	Expert
N/A	N/A	N/A	N/A
Not specified	Governor-General	Governor-General	Expert
Not specified	Governor-General	Not applicable	Expert
5 years	Governor-General	Governor-General	Not specified
Not specified	Public Service Commission	Not applicable	Not specified
3 years	Head of State	Not applicable	Expert
N/A	N/A	N/A	N/A
N/A	N/A	N/A	N/A

Annex A. World Survey: Electoral Management Bodies in 217 countries

389

Country	Model of electoral management	Name of EMB	Number of EMB members
Saudi Arabia	No national elections	N/A	N/A
Senegal	Mixed	Ministry of the Interior	N/A
		Autonomous National Electoral Commission	12
Serbia	Independent	Republic Electoral Commission	17
Seychelles	Independent	Electoral Commission	5
Sierra Leone	Independent	National Electoral Commission	5
Sint Maarten	Independent	Central Electoral Committee	5
Singapore	Governmental	Prime Minister's Office	N/A
Slovakia	Mixed	Ministry of Interior	N/A
		Central Electoral Commission	Equal number of representatives from each political party
Slovenia	Independent	Republic Electoral Commission	11
Solomon Islands	Independent	Electoral Commission	3
Somalia	Independent	Independent National Electoral Commission	Maximum 9
South Africa	Independent	Independent Electoral Commission	5
South Korea	Independent	National Election Commission	9
South Sudan	Independent	National Elections Commission	9
Spain	Mixed	Ministry of Interior	N/A
		Central Electoral Board	13
Sri Lanka	Independent	Department of Elections	2
Sudan	Independent	National Election Commission	9
Suriname	Independent	Independent Electoral Council	Minimum 7
Swaziland	Independent	Elections and Boundaries Commission	5

Term of office	EMB members selected by	Chair appointed/elected by	Party or expert-based membership
N/A	N/A	N/A	N/A
N/A	N/A	N/A	N/A
6 years	Various groups and institutions	Various groups and institutions	Expert
4 years	Legislature and political parties	Legislature	Combined
7 years	President	President	Expert
5 years	President, by approval of legislature	President, by approval of legislature	Expert
7 years	Appointment Committee (president of the Common Court of Justice, vice chairman of the Council of Advice and the chairman of the General Audit Chamber)	Appointment Committee	Expert
N/A	N/A	N/A	N/A
N/A	N/A	N/A	N/A
For election period only	Political parties	EMB	Party
4 years	Legislature	Legislature	Combined
Not specified	Governor-General	Speaker of legislature is the ex officio chair	Expert
No data	No data	No data	No data
7 years	President	President	Expert
6 years	President, National Assembly, Supreme Court	EMB	Expert
Unlimited	President, with the approval of legislature	President, with the approval of legislature	Expert
N/A	N/A	N/A	N/A
4 years	Supreme Council of the Judiciary, political parties	EMB	Expert
Until the age of 60	President	President	No data
6 years	President, with the approval of legislature	President, with the consent of the First Vice President	Expert
6 years	President	President	Expert
Maximum 12	Monarch	Monarch	Expert

Annex A. World Survey: Electoral Management Bodies in 217 countries

Country	Model of electoral management	Name of EMB	Number of EMB members
Sweden	Governmental	Election Authority	N/A
Switzerland	Governmental	Federal Chancellery	N/A
Syria	Independent	High Electoral Commission	5
Taiwan	Independent	Central Election Commission	11
Tajikistan	Independent	Central Commission on Elections and Referenda	15
Tanzania	Independent	National Electoral Commission	7
Thailand	Independent	Election Commission	5
Timor-Leste	Mixed	Technical Secretariat for Election Administration	N/A
		National Election Commission	15
Togo	Independent	Independent National Electoral Commission	17
Tokelau	Mixed	Director of Support Services, Tokelau Public Service	N/A
		Referendum Commission	9
Tonga	Independent	Electoral Commission	3
Trinidad and Tobago	Independent	Elections and Boundaries Commission	3-5
Tunisia	Independent	Independent High Authority for Elections	9
Turkey	Independent	Supreme Electoral Council	7
Turkmenistan	Independent	Central Commission for Elections and the Conduct of Referendums	15
Turks and Caicos Islands	Governmental	Supervisor of Elections	N/A
Tuvalu	Governmental	Ministry of Home Affairs	N/A
Uganda	Independent	Electoral Commission	7
Ukraine	Independent	Central Election Commission	15
United Arab Emirates	Governmental	National Election Commission	N/A
United Kingdom	Governmental	Local Returning Officers	N/A
United States	Governmental	Local authorities	N/A
Uruguay	Independent	Electoral Court	9
Uzbekistan	Independent	Central Election Commission	Minimum 15

Term of office	EMB members selected by	Chair appointed/ elected by	Party or expert-based membership
N/A	N/A	N/A	N/A
N/A	N/A	N/A	N/A
4 years	The Supreme Judicial Council	EMB	Expert
4 years	Prime minister, legislature	Prime Minister, legislature	Expert
5 years	President	Legislature	Expert
5 years	President	President	Expert
7 years	Senate	EMB	Expert
N/A	N/A	N/A	N/A
6 years	President; legislature; judiciary; other organisations	EMB	Expert
One year (renewable)	Legislature	Council of Ministers	Combined
N/A	N/A	N/A	N/A
No data	Faipule (head) and 2 others from each village	not specified	Expert
5 years	King; EMB	King	Not specified
5 years	President	President	Not specified
6 years	Legislature	Legislature	Expert
6 years	Supreme Court of Appeals; Supreme Council of State	EMB	Expert
5 years	President, political parties, public associations	Legislature	Expert
N/A	N/A	N/A	N/A
N/A	N/A	N/A	N/A
7 years	President, with the approval of legislature	President, with the approval of legislature	Expert
7 years	President	EMB	Expert
N/A	N/A	N/A	N/A
N/A	N/A	N/A	N/A
N/A	N/A	N/A	N/A
5 years	Legislature	Legislature	Combined
Unlimited	Legislature	EMB	Expert

Country	Model of electoral management	Name of EMB	Number of EMB members
Vanuatu	Mixed	Electoral Commission	3
		Principal Electoral Officer	1
Venezuela	Independent	National Electoral Council	5
Vietnam	Governmental	Central Election Council	N/A
Virgin Islands, British	Governmental	Office of the Supervisor of Elections	N/A
Yemen	Independent	Supreme Commission for Elections and Referendum	9
Zambia	Independent	Electoral Commission	Maximum 5
Zimbabwe	Independent	Electoral Commission	9

Term of office	EMB members selected by	Chair appointed/ elected by	Party or expert-based membership
5 years	President	President	Expert
Unlimited	N/A	N/A	N/A
7 years	Legislature	EMB	Expert
N/A	N/A	N/A	N/A
N/A	N/A	N/A	N/A
6 years	President	EMB	Expert
Maximum 7 years	President	President	Expert
5 years	President	President	Expert

Annex B

Electoral Management Glossary

Absentee voting	A mechanism voters can use to cast a vote without going to a polling station on the day(s) fixed for voting.
Amalgamation of results	The incorporation of the votes into a unified result. Also known as *Tabulation*.
Announcement of results	See *Declaration of results*.
Arbitrary dismissal	Removal of a person from an official or staff position without due cause and due procedure.
Audit trail	A sequence of verifiable records that is maintained to track activities, for example, movement and numbers of electoral materials, tabulation of electoral results, changes to computerized records, maintenance of financial records and determination of policies.
Baseline budget	A budget formulation method in which the funding allocation by the financing authority for the previous funding period is adjusted to create the estimate for the next period. Also called *Incremental budget*.
Boundary delimitation	The process of determining how constituency or electoral area boundaries are drawn; it divides a country into electoral districts and allocates electors to electoral districts and polling sites. Sometimes called *districting* or *boundary demarcation*.
Budget (electoral)	A document containing an itemized summary of proposed electoral incomes and expenditures related to specified activities by a specific organization or part of an organization, for a defined future period.
By-election	An election to fill a vacant seat in an elected assembly held at any time other than at a general election.

Calendar (electoral)	A document containing a sequence of tasks, and the dates and deadlines for their performance, during the planning, implementation and completion of an electoral event.
Campaign (electoral)	Political activity, including meetings, rallies, speeches, parades, broadcasts, debates and other media events designed to inform the electorate of or gather support for the platform of a particular candidate or political party in an election or to promote a choice available to voters in a direct democracy instrument.
Candidate	A person who is nominated to compete in an election either as a political party representative or independent of any party's support.
Candidate nomination	The process by which political parties/organizations and/or individual candidates submit their intention to compete in an election, often subject to meeting qualification criteria defined by law.
Cascade training	A method of training in which a core group of people is trained in both technical electoral matters and training techniques; that group in turn train others 'face to face' at a lower level. The second level trains the third level and so on, until all targeted staff are trained.
Centralized EMB	An organizational structure for an EMB, most often found in countries with unitary constitutions, in which the powers to conduct and implement all aspects of electoral processes at all levels are vested in the national-level EMB.
Certification of results	The formal endorsement and confirmation of election results.
Chair	The head of an independent EMB under the Independent or Mixed Model of electoral management. Formal titles may include chief electoral commissioner or EMB president.
Chief electoral commissioner	See *Chair*.
Chief electoral officer	A title that may be used for the head of an EMB secretariat. Other titles that may be used include chief executive officer, director of elections, secretary general and EMB secretary. Where the EMB is independent, the chief electoral officer can in some cases also be a member of the EMB.
Citizens' initiative	A direct democracy instrument that allows a certain number of citizens to initiate a vote of the electorate on a proposal outlined by those citizens. The proposal may, for example, amend the constitution or adopt, repeal or amend an existing law.
Citizen observer	See *Observer*.
Civic education	An informational and/or educational programme that is designed to increase comprehension and knowledge of citizens' rights and responsibilities.

Civil registry	A centrally held master database containing information generated by a country's administrative infrastructure involving the mandatory collection of information from many sources and containing information such as the name, gender, nationality, age, marital status and address of all citizens. Electoral registers and other documents may be drawn from it when required.
Civil servant	An employee of a central or local government ministry or department, who is sometimes subject to a single common set of employment procedures, terms and conditions laid down by government.
Claims (electoral)	Complaints presented by different electoral actors to dispute resolution procedures in the course of the electoral process regarding decisions, actions, or lack of action by electoral administrators or other participants in the electoral process. See also *Electoral dispute resolution*.
Closed list	A form of list proportional representation in which electors are restricted to voting only for a party or political grouping, and cannot express a preference for any candidate within the list presented by a party or grouping.
Code of conduct	A set of general rules of behaviour, for example for members and/or staff of an EMB or political parties, with respect to participation in an electoral process.
Combined EMB	An independent EMB under the Independent or Mixed Model of electoral management, some of whose members are non-partisan experts and some of whom represent political parties or interests. See *Expert-based EMB* and *Multiparty-based EMB*.
Commissioner	A term used for a member of an electoral commission. Sometimes the term is limited to the EMB chair, and in rare cases the term is used inconsistently to refer to specific senior staff of the secretariat. See *Member (of an EMB)*.
Consolidated electoral law	A single piece of legislation that gathers together all laws related to a country's electoral processes; it is sometimes referred to as the electoral code.
Consolidated fund	A country's reserved revenue funds, which are managed by the national treasury. Expenses that are charged directly to the fund are not subject to change or ministerial delays.
Constituency	A synonym for electoral district used predominantly in some Anglophone countries. See *Electoral district*.
Constitutional council	A term for the supreme body concerned with constitutional and other issues, which may be either part of the judicial branch or a separate body entrusted with adjudicating the constitutionality of laws and in some cases other tasks, including those related to electoral processes.

Core costs	Costs routinely associated with implementing an electoral process in a stable electoral environment. They include the basic costs of voter registration, boundary delimitation, voting operations, the counting and transmission of results, and voter information. Sometimes called *Direct costs*.
Decentralized EMB	A model of electoral administration in which the powers to conduct and implement different electoral processes and/or different aspects of electoral processes have been delegated by the national EMB to subnational EMBs or subnational branches of the national EMB.
Declaration of results	Oral or written formal public communication of the result of an electoral event. This may consist of the number of votes received by each candidate or political party competing in an election, and of the candidate(s) and/or party(ies) entitled to sit as/seat an elected member(s) under the provisions of the electoral law; or of the number of votes recorded for each of two or more options presented in the use of a direct democracy instrument.
Diffuse costs	The costs of electoral-related services that cannot be disentangled from the general budgets of agencies that assist with the implementation of an electoral process. Sometimes referred to as *indirect costs*.
Direct costs	See *Core costs*.
Direct democracy instrument	An instrument that gives citizens the right to be directly involved in the political decision-making process. It may take one of three forms: a referendum, a citizens' initiative or a recall vote.
Citizen observer	An individual or representative of an organization who is authorized and accredited to observe and assess the performance of the election process in her/his own country.
Donor	A country or intergovernmental or non-governmental organization that provides support in the form of money, in-kind contributions and/or technical assistance to the electoral process in another country.
Electoral activity	A portion of an election task that can be assigned to one or more persons. In some election operational plans, the term 'activity' is equated with or used interchangeably with the term 'task'.
Electoral administration	The measures necessary to conduct or implement any aspect of an electoral process.
Electoral administrator	A person who directs, manages and/or implements any of the operations of an EMB on a day-to-day basis.
Electoral commission	A title often given to an independent EMB under the Independent Model or to the component independent EMB under the Mixed Model of electoral management.
Electoral court	Court of justice or other body before which an electoral actor may dispute the validity of an election or challenge the conduct of candidates, political parties or the EMB. See also *Electoral tribunal*.

Electoral cycle	The full series of steps involved in the preparation, implementation and evaluation of an election or direct democracy instrument, which is viewed as one electoral event in a continuing series. In addition to the steps involved in a particular electoral process, it includes pre-electoral activities such as the review of relevant legal and procedural provisions and electoral registration, as well as post-electoral evaluation and/or audit, the maintenance of institutional memory, the process of consultation and the planning of the forthcoming electoral process.
Electoral dispute resolution	The process of hearing and adjudicating any complaint, challenge, claim or contest relating to any stage of the electoral process.
Electoral district	One of the geographic areas into which a country or region may be divided for electoral purposes. See also *Constituency*.
Electoral event	An election or direct democracy instrument.
Electoral law	One or more pieces of legislation governing all aspects of the process for elections to the political institutions defined in a country's constitution or institutional framework.
Electoral management	The process of conducting the activities, tasks and functions of electoral administration.
Electoral management body (EMB)	An organization or body that has been founded for the sole purpose of, and is legally responsible for, managing some or all of the essential (or core) elements of the conduct of elections and direct democracy instruments. These elements include determining who is eligible to vote, receiving and validating the nominations of electoral participants (for elections, political parties and/or candidates), conducting balloting, counting votes and tabulating votes. They are normally headed by a chairperson or president.
Electoral network (international or regional)	A mechanism, which may be formal or informal, through which EMBs in different countries share knowledge, expertise and/or resources.
Electoral observation	A process by which observers are accredited to access an electoral process, and may assess and report on the compliance of the electoral process, with relevant legal instruments and international and regional obligations.
Electoral period	The central part of the electoral cycle containing a series of steps involved in the implementation of a particular electoral process, usually starting with the official announcement of polling day and ending with the announcement of final results.
Electoral process	The series of steps involved in preparing and conducting a specific election or direct democracy instrument. The electoral process usually includes the enactment of the electoral law, electoral registration, the nomination of candidates and/or political parties or the registration of proposals, the campaign, voting, counting and tabulation of votes, resolution of electoral disputes and the announcement of results.

Electoral register	The list of persons registered as qualified to vote. In some countries it is known as a *Voters' list* or *Electoral roll*.
Electoral regulations	Rules subsidiary to legislation made, often by the electoral management body (EMB) or the ministry within which an EMB is located, under powers contained in the electoral law that governs aspects of the organization and administration of elections.
Electoral roll	See *Electoral register*.
Electoral system	A set of rules and procedures that allows the electorate to cast votes, and which translates these votes into seats for parties and candidates in the legislature.
Electoral tribunal	A judicial or other institution whose specific competence is to hear disputes on electoral matters. In Latin America, such a body is often also an electoral management body. See also *Electoral court*.
Electronic voting	Any method of voting using electronic means, including the use of electronic machines, the Internet, telephones, mobile phones or digital television. Often referred to as e-voting.
Evaluation	An independent assessment of the relevance of an organization's strategic objectives to its stakeholders' needs, and the economy, efficiency and effectiveness with which the organization and its legal framework have met those needs.
Expert-based EMB	An independent EMB under the Independent or Mixed Model of electoral management, all of whose members are chosen and appointed because of their expertise, reputation or standing in the community. Also referred to as a *Non-partisan EMB*.
External accountability	The requirements and/or methods through which an EMB reports to external stakeholders or a constitutional authority.
External audit	Audit of an organization's financial records or operational activities by an independent person or body that is outside the structure of the organization being audited.
External voting	A mechanism by which voters who are permanently or temporarily absent from a country are enabled to cast a vote. Also called out-of-country voting.
Financial audit	An independent examination of an EMB's accounting records to determine whether they are maintained accurately and in accordance with accepted accounting standards and legal and regulatory requirements.
Financial regulations	Rules subsidiary to legislation, often made by the electoral management body or the ministry responsible for public sector financial management, which govern financial management issues.
Full-time EMB	An EMB all or most of whose members serve on a full-time basis during their term of office.

General election	An election at which all those seats in an elected assembly at the national level that are subject to an election are filled simultaneously.
Government audit agency	A government body that conducts a process of external audit to examine the financial transactions, and in some cases the operational activities, of other public sector bodies.
Governmental Model of electoral management	An electoral management model in which elections are organized and managed by the executive branch of government through a ministry, such as the Ministry of the Interior, and/or through local authorities.
Horizontal communication	The passage of information, communication or instructions between different parts of an organization that are at the same level in its hierarchy.
Incremental budget	See *Baseline budget*.
Independent candidate	A candidate for an elected position who is not nominated by a political party.
Independent Model of electoral management	An electoral management model in which elections are organized and managed by an electoral management body that is institutionally independent of and autonomous from the executive branch of government, and which has and manages its own budget.
Indirect costs	See *Diffuse costs*.
Institutional memory	An organization's ability to retain understanding, expertise and physical records in order to be able to access and use these after the passage of time or after a major or total change of personnel.
Integrity costs	Those costs, over and above the core costs, which are necessary to provide safety, integrity, political neutrality and a level playing field for an electoral process. They are particularly relevant for electoral events in post-conflict societies or emerging democracies.
Internal accountability	Mechanisms by which the lower-level structures within an organization account to higher structures on their performance.
Internal audit	An audit conducted by or on behalf of an organization for internal control purposes. Also used to describe the unit within an organization that is responsible for internal audits.
International observer	Representative of an international organization, association, government or professional body who is authorized and accredited to observe and assess the preparation for or conduct of an electoral process in a foreign country. See also *Observer*.
Jurisdiction	The competence and geographic scope of an organization's direction-making, decision-making and implementation powers.

Legal framework	The collection of legal structural elements that define or influence an electoral process. The major elements are constitutional provisions; electoral laws; other legislation affecting electoral processes, such as political party laws and laws structuring legislative bodies; subsidiary electoral rules and regulations, and codes of conduct.
Liaison ministry	For an independent EMB under the Independent or Mixed Model of electoral management, the government ministry through which the EMB can channel its views and representations to the government, and vice versa.
List proportional representation (PR)	A system in which each participant party or grouping presents a list of candidates for an electoral district. Voters vote for a party, and parties receive seats in proportion to their overall share of the vote. Winning candidates are taken from the lists. Often referred to as 'list PR'. Common variants include 'closed-list PR', in which electors are restricted to voting only for a party or grouping and 'open-list PR', in which electors can express their preference for a party or grouping and for one, or sometimes more, candidates from that party or grouping. See *Proportional representation*.
Local authority	A body established as the legislative and/or executive arm of government at any subnational level lower than a province, region or equivalent.
Lower-level EMB	An EMB formed at any subnational level, for example a province, region, district or commune.
Member (of an EMB)	A person appointed or elected to serve on the body or committee that directs the conduct of elections and the implementation of the powers and functions of the EMB.
Mixed Model of electoral management	An electoral management model with a dual structure: (1) a policy, monitoring or supervisory EMB that is independent of the executive branch of government (e.g. Independent Model EMB) and (2) an implementation EMB located within a department of state and/or local government (e.g. Governmental Model EMB).
Multi-member district	An electoral district from which more than one representative is elected to a legislature or elected body.
Multiparty-based EMB	An EMB consisting of members nominated by political parties.
National Election Commission	A common title for an independent EMB under the Independent or Mixed Model of electoral management, which has competencies over the entire territory of a country.
Needs assessment	A method of addressing institutional sustainability, in which an organization examines its current management capabilities and the resources, financial, technological and human, necessary to organize and conduct its activities.
Nominating authority	A body that puts forward a candidate or candidates for election, selection or appointment to another body or position.

Non-partisan EMB	See *Expert-based EMB*.
Non-partisan member	An EMB member who has been appointed to the EMB other than as a representative of a political party.
Observer	A person accredited to witness and assess, but not intervene in, the proceedings of an electoral process. See *Citizen observer* and *International observer*.
Open list	A form of list proportional representation in which voters can express a preference for both a party or grouping and for one, or sometimes more, candidates within the list presented by that party or grouping.
Operational plan	A plan that defines the responsibilities and time periods for all activities that need to be undertaken to meet an organization's strategic objectives.
Oversight body	A body charged with ensuring that an electoral process is correctly conducted in line with the provisions of the legal framework.
Paper audit trail	An audit trail in which records are kept in printed or written form and not solely in an electronic form.
Part-time EMB	An EMB all or most of whose members serve on a part-time basis during their term of office.
Party symbol	An identification figure or sign allotted to a candidate or political party in accordance with the electoral law.
Performance accountability	Methods by which an organization internally and externally accounts for its progress toward achieving its strategic objectives and meeting its stakeholders' needs.
Performance audit	Retrospective assessment of the economy, efficiency and effectiveness of electoral procedures, operations and financing against an EMB's strategic objectives within its legal and regulatory framework.
Performance evaluation	Objective assessment against expected benchmarks of the value added to an organization by an employee's efforts.
Performance standard	A statement of benchmark criteria to be achieved, without specifying how they are to be achieved.
Permanent EMB	An EMB that has a continuous existence throughout the whole electoral cycle and handles electoral matters both during and between electoral periods.
Political party-based EMB	See *Multiparty-based EMB*.
Political party registration	Compiling of a list of political parties that meet defined legal or regulatory qualifications and may thus qualify for privileges such as proposing the nomination of candidates for election.

Polling district	An area in which all electors are allocated to vote at a single polling station.
Polling official	A member of staff who participates in the administration of a polling station on polling day. Polling officials may or may not be members of the staff of an EMB.
Polling station	A venue established for the purpose of polling, which is controlled by polling officials.
Postal voting	A mechanism for voting in which a voter completes his or her ballot paper and returns it by post to an official designated to conduct the election.
Post-electoral evaluation	A retroactive evaluation of the conduct of an electoral process, or specified parts of that process, that is completed after the electoral period.
Post-electoral period	One of three periods of the electoral cycle, during which audit and evaluation take place and during which legislation, regulations and administration are reformed and developed.
Post-transitional elections	The second and subsequent elections held in a country after an initial election—following a period of, for example, dictatorship or civil war—which marked the commencement (or re-commencement) of democratic competition in elections.
Pre-electoral period	One of three periods of the electoral cycle, during which planning and preparation for the conduct of elections take place, and during which legal and procedural provisions are reviewed.
Primary election	A public election through which a political party chooses its candidates for a forthcoming electoral process.
Proportional representation (PR)	An electoral system family based on the principle of translating the overall votes of a party or grouping into a corresponding proportion of seats in an elected body. See *List proportional representation.*
Public servant	An employee of any organization whose core funding is provided by the treasury of a country.
Qualified majority	A proportion of the vote in excess of 50 per cent plus 1 (e.g. two-thirds or three-fourths), which is sometimes required for the passage of certain proposals.
Recall	A direct democracy instrument that allows a specified number of citizens to demand a vote of the electorate on whether an elected holder of public office should be removed from that office before the end of his/her term.
Referendum	A direct democracy instrument consisting of a vote of the electorate on an issue of public policy such as a constitutional amendment or bill. The results of the vote may be either binding or consultative.

Regional EMB	An electoral management body at a subnational level.
Registration of political parties and candidates	The act of accepting applications to participate in an election from political parties and candidates that meet defined criteria.
Registration of voters	The act of entering the names of eligible electors and other relevant information into a register or list of electors.
Screening process	A process through which checks are made to verify that a candidate for appointment as a member or staff of an EMB meets the required qualifications.
Secondary legislation	See *Subsidiary regulations*.
Secretariat	The structure below the policy-making EMB member level in the Independent and Mixed Models of electoral management that comprises the officials in the EMB who are responsible for policy implementation. In the Governmental Model, the secretariat is usually the sole component of the EMB, and may also have some policy-making functions.
Secretary general	A term often used for the head of an EMB secretariat, who may or may not be a member of the EMB.
Security of tenure	A legal measure to protect members and/or staff of an EMB from dismissal or adverse change to the terms and conditions of contract or employment without due cause and due process.
Selection process	The mechanism, procedures and conditions for appointment and/or employment of members or secretariat staff of an EMB.
Simple majority	A majority requirement that demands that the prevailing candidate in an election (or the prevailing option in a direct democracy instrument) obtains the highest number of valid votes cast.
Single-member district	An electoral district from which only one member is elected to a legislature or elected body.
Single-member EMB	An EMB in which the powers and responsibilities for implementing an EMB's mandate are vested by the legal framework in a single person.
Special voting	Procedures and facilities for electors who are unable to implement the voting procedures or access the polling station at which they are registered to vote.
Staggered membership	A system under which members of an EMB are not all appointed at the same time and their terms of office do not end at the same time, usually used to ensure continuity in the work of an EMB.
Stakeholders	Individuals, groups and bodies that have an interest or 'stake' in the operations of an organization and/or that affect or are directly affected by the activities, policies and practices of the organization.

Standing orders	A set of rules adopted by an organization to regulate its internal structures and procedures.
State	In the context of a federal constitution, often refers to a subnational unit of a country. In the context of supranational bodies or intergovernmental organizations, a member state refers to a country that has been accepted as a full member of that body or organization.
Strategic plan	A document used by an organization to state its vision, mission, values, priorities and objectives from which its structure and budget are derived.
Subsidiary EMB	An EMB that is not the primary or principal entity responsible for the organization of elections within a country, and that assists the primary EMB and implements electoral tasks at the local and regional levels.
Subsidiary regulations	Rules that are consistent with, and made under powers granted by, a law, which provide details of the manner in which the law is to be implemented.
Supranational body	An organization created by a number of countries by treaty in which power is held by independent appointed officials or by representatives elected by the legislatures or residents of the member states.
Tabulation	The process of compiling the result of counting of votes cast in an electoral process. Also known as the *Amalgamation of results*.
Task profiling	Analysis of the resources required to implement a specified task to meet specific parameters, such as time and quality.
Temporary EMB	An EMB that exists only for a specified limited period, often the electoral period.
Term of office	The period of time for which a member of an organization serves following their election or appointment.
Transitional EMB	An EMB that is set up temporarily to facilitate transitional elections. It is normally set up under the auspices of the international community, such as the UN, and may consist of or include international experts as members.
Trust fund	A mechanism for aggregating individual donor contributions into a single pool of funds, held in trust and administered by an external organization (e.g. the UNDP) for use in support of an electoral process.
Vertical communication	The passage of information, communication or instructions through an organization upwards and downwards through two or more hierarchical levels.
Voter	A person who casts a vote in an election or direct democracy instrument.
Voter education	A process by which people are made aware of the electoral process and the particulars and procedures for voter registration, voting and other elements of the electoral process.

Voter information	A short-term programme focusing on specific electoral information, which aims to give voters timely and relevant factual information about an electoral process.
Voter registration card	A card issued to identify a person registered as an elector in accordance with the provisions of the electoral law.
Voters' list	See *Electoral register*.
Zero-base budget	A budget formulation method that treats each funding period for an organization as a clean slate and estimates the funds required to achieve the planned outcomes for that period. See also *Baseline budget*.

Annex C

References and Further Reading

ACE Electoral Knowledge Network, <http://www.aceproject.org>

Association of Asian Election Authorities (AAEA) General Assembly, 'Transparency in Election Management, 2005', (Taipei: AAEA, 2005)

Beramendi, Virginia et al., *Direct Democracy: The International IDEA Handbook* (Stockholm: International IDEA, 2008)

Bibler, Sarah, Mohan, Vasu and Ryan, Katie, *Gender Equality & Election Management Bodies: A Best Practices Guide* (Washington, DC: IFES, 2014)

Birch, Sarah, 'Electoral Institutions and Popular Confidence in Electoral Processes: A Cross-National Analysis.' *Electoral Studies* 27, no. 2 (2008): 305–20

— *Electoral Malpractice,* Oxford University Press, 2011

Bland, Gary, Green, Andrew and Moore, Toby, 'Measuring the Quality of Election Administration', *Democratization* 20, no. 2 (2013), pp. 358–77

Boda, Michael D. (ed.), 'Revisiting Free and Fair Elections: An International Round Table on Election Standards Organized by the Inter-Parliamentary Union, Geneva, November 2004', (Geneva: IPU, 2005) available at <http://www.ipu.org/PDF/publications/ffelections_en.pdf>

BRIDGE Building Resources in Democracy, Governance and Elections, available at <http://www.bridge-project.org/>

Dahlerup, Drude et al., *Atlas of Gender Quotas,* (Stockholm, International IDEA/ Inter-Parliamentary Union/Stockholm University, 2014)

Debrah, Emmanuel, 'Measuring Governance Institutions' Success in Ghana: The Case of the Electoral Commission, 1993–2008', *African Studies* 70, no. 1 (2011), pp. 25–45

Dundas, Carl W., *The Lag of 21st Century Democratic Elections: In the African Union Member States* (Bloomington: Author House, 2012)

Council of Europe, *Supervising Electoral Processes,* (Strasbourg: Council of Europe, 2010)

Electoral Institute of Southern Africa (EISA), 'Promoting Principles for Election Management, Monitoring, and Observation in the SADC Region: As adopted on 6 November 2003 at the Kopanong Hotel and Conference Centre, Benoni, Johannesburg' (Johannesburg: EISA, 2004), available at <http://www.eisa.org.za/PDF/pemmo.pdf>

Elklit, Jørgen, 'Electoral Institutional Change and Democratization: You Can Lead a Horse to Water, But You Can't Make It Drink', *Democratization*, 6/4 (winter 1999/2000), pp. 28–51

— and Reynolds, Andrew, 'Analysing the Impact of Election Administration on Democratic Politics', *Representation*, 38/1 (2001), pp. 3–10

— and Reynolds, Andrew, 'Judging Elections and Election Management Quality by Process', *Representation*, 41/3 (2005), pp. 189–207

— and Reynolds, Andrew, 'The Impact of Election Administration on the Legitimacy of Emerging Democracies: A New Research Agenda', Working Paper no. 281, Kellogg Institute, Notre Dame, Ind., 2000

Ellis, Andrew, Gratschew, Maria, Pammet, Jon H. and Thiessen, Erin, *Engaging the Electorate: Intiatives to Promote Voter Turnout From Around the Word* (Stockholm: International IDEA, 2006)

— and Navarro, Carlos, Morales, Isabel, Gratschew, Maria and Braun, Nadja, *Voting from Abroad: The International IDEA Handbook* (Stockholm: International IDEA, 2007)

Elmendorf, Christopher S., 'Election Commissions and Electoral Reform: An Overview' , *Election Law Journal* 5, no. 4 (2006), pp. 425–46

Ernst & Ernst, *Election Administration, Volume I: Planning Elections* (Washington, DC: National Clearinghouse on Election Administration, 1979)

— *Election Administration, Volume II: Managing Elections* (Washington, DC: National Clearinghouse on Election Administration, 1979)

— *Election Administration, Volume III: Costing Elections* (Washington, DC: National Clearinghouse on Election Administration, 1979)

Gazibo, Mamoudou, 'The Forging of Institutional Autonomy: A Comparative Study of Electoral Management Commissions in Africa', *Canadian Journal of Political Science* 39, no. 03 (2006), pp. 611–33

International IDEA, *Electoral Management during Transition: Challenges and Opportunities* (Stockholm: International IDEA, 2012)

— *The Use of Open Source Technology in Elections* (Stockholm: International IDEA, 2014)

James, Toby S., 'Electoral Modernisation or Elite Statecraft: Electoral Administration in the United Kingdom 1997–2007', *British Politics* 5, no. 2 (2010), pp. 179–201

— 'Fewer Costs, More Votes? United Kingdom Innovations in Election Administration 2000–2007 and the Effect on Voter Turnout', *Election Law Journal* 10, no. 1 (2011), pp. 37–52

Kelly, Norm, *Directions in Australian Electoral Reform: Professionalism and Partisanship in Electoral Management* (Canberra: ANU E Press, 2012)

— 'The Independence of Electoral Management Bodies: The Australian Experience', *Political Science* 59, no. 2 (2007), pp. 17–32

Lijphart, Arend, 'Advances in the Comparative Study of Electoral Systems', *World Politics,* XXXVI/3 (1984), pp. 424–36

López Pintor, Rafael, *Electoral Management Bodies as Institutions of Governance* (New York: UNDP, 2000), available at <http://www.undp.org/governance/docs/Elections-Pub-EMBbook.pdf>

Makulilo, Alexander Boniface, 'Independent Electoral Commission in Tanzania: A False Debate?', *Representation* 45, no. 4 (2009), pp. 435–53

McMillan, Alistair, 'The Election Commission of India and the Regulation and Administration of Electoral Politics', *Election Law Journal* 11, no. 2 (2012), pp. 187–201

Merloe, Patrick, *Democratic Elections: Human Rights, Public Confidence and the 'Level Playing Field'* (Washington, DC: National Democratic Institute for International Affairs, 1997)

Mozaffar, Shaheen, 'Patterns of Electoral Governance in Africa's Emerging Democracies', *International Political Science Review,* 23/1 (2002), pp. 85–101

Neufeld, Harry, 'Computerizing Electoral Administration: Part One', *Elections Today,* May 1995, pp. 18–21

— 'Computerizing Electoral Administration: Part Two', *Elections Today,* October 1995, pp. 22–23

Norris, Pippa, Frank, Richard W., and Martinez i Coma, Ferran, *Advancing Electoral Integrity* (Oxford: Oxford University Press, 2014)

Okello, Edward Odhiambo, 'Guaranteeing the Independence of Election Management Bodies in Africa: A Study of the Electoral Commissions of Kenya and South Africa' , Faculty of Law, University of Ghana, 2006, available at <http://www.repository.up.ac.za/handle/2263/1227>

Open Society Initiative for West Africa (OSIWA), *Election Management Bodies in West Africa: A Comparative Study of the Contribution of Electoral Commissions to the Strengthen* (Dakar: OSIWA, 2011)

Orozco-Henríquez, Jesús, et al., *Electoral Justice: The International IDEA Handbook* (Stockholm: International IDEA, 2010)

Pastor, Robert A., 'A Brief History of Election Commissions', in A. Schedler, L. Diamond and M. F. Plattner (eds), *The Self-Restraining State* (Boulder, CO: Lynne Rienner, 1999)

Reynolds, Andrew, Reilly, Ben and Ellis, Andrew, *Electoral System Design: The New International IDEA Handbook* (Stockholm: International IDEA, 2005), available at <http://www.idea.int/publications/esd>

Rosas, Guillermo., 'Trust in Elections and the Institutional Design of Electoral Authorities: Evidence from Latin America', *Electoral Studies* 29, no. 1 (March 2010), pp. 74–90

Spinelli, Antonio, *Strategic Planning for Effective Electoral Management: A Practical Guide for Electoral Management Bodies to Conduct a Strategic Planning Exercise* (Washington DC: IFES, 2011), available at <http://www.ifes.org/~/media/Files/Publications/Books/2011/Strategic_Planning_Guide_2011.pdf>

Struwig, Jare, Roberts, Simon and Vivier, Elsa, 'A Vote of Confidence: Election Management and Public Perceptions Electoral Processes in South Africa', *Journal of Public Administration: Special Issue 1* 46 (2011), pp. 1122–38

Tokaji, Daniel P., 'The Future of Election Reform: From Rules to Institutions', *Yale Law & Policy Review,* 2009, pp. 125–54

Tuccinardi, Domenico, et al., *International Obligations for Elections: Guidelines for Legal Frameworks* (Stockholm: International IDEA, 2014)

United Nations Development Programme (UNDP), *Getting to the Core: A Global Survey on the Cost of Registration and Elections* (New York: UNDP Bureau for Development Policy; IFES, Center for Transitional and Post-Conflict Governance, 2005), available at <http://content.undp.org/go/cms-service/stream/asset/?asset_id=472992>

Van Aaken, Anne, 'Independent Electoral Management Bodies and International Election Observer Missions: Any Impact on the Observed Level of Democracy? A Conceptual Framework', *Constitutional Political Economy* 20, no. 3–4 (2009), pp. 296–322 (2009): 296–322

Annex D

EMB Websites and Social Media Platforms

Country	Website
Afghanistan	www.iec.org.af
Albania	www.cec.org.al
Algeria	www.interieur.gov.dz/Dynamics/frmCategories.aspx?htmls=13&s=23
American Samoa	www.americansamoaelectionoffice.org
Andorra	www.eleccions.ad
Angola	www.cne.ao
Anguilla	www.gov.ai/elections
Antigua and Barbuda	www.abec.gov.ag
Argentina	www.pjn.gov.ar
Armenia	www.elections.am
Aruba	www.overheid.aw/index.asp?nmoduleid=19&wgid=6&spagetype=21&nPageID=6002031&nCMSPageType=1
Australia	www.aec.gov.au
Austria	www.bmi.gv.at/cms/bmi_wahlen
Azerbaijan	www.cec.gov.az
Bahrain	www.bahrain.gov.bh

All the websites and social media platform links in this list were tested and operational in July 2014. While it is as comprehensive as possible, it is not guaranteed to contain all EMB websites which were functional at that date.

For governmental EMBs under the Governmental or Mixed Model of electoral management, the list shows the page of the website of the relevant ministry which gives the most clear link to electoral matters.

The list does not include websites from other public or private bodies which contain material about electoral administration.

Facebook	Twitter	YouTube
www.facebook.com/pages/Independent-Election-Commission-of-Afghanistan/346663142023192	twitter.com/IECAfghanistan	www.youtube.com/user/ElectionAfghanistan
www.facebook.com/KomisioniQendroriZgjedhjeve	twitter.com/KQZ_ALBANIA	www.youtube.com/user/KQZALBANIA/videos
www.facebook.com/pages/Central-Electoral-Commission-of-the-Republic-of-Armenia/1760666689121093		
www.facebook.com/pages/Conseho-Electoral-Aruba/165245133656977		
www.facebook.com/AustralianElectoralCommission?rf=124140624296232	twitter.com/AusElectoralCom	www.youtube.com/aecgovau
www.facebook.com/msk.gov.az	twitter.com/AzRes_MSK	www.youtube.com/user/TheCECaz?feature=plcp
www.facebook.com/egovbahrain	twitter.com/egovbahrain	www.youtube.com/egovbahrain

Country	Website
Bangladesh	www.ecs.gov.bd
Barbados	www.electoral.barbados.gov.bb
Belarus	www.rec.gov.by
Belgium	www.ibz.rrn.fgov.be/index.php?id=33&L=0
Belize	www.elections.gov.bz/
Bermuda	www.elections.gov.bm
Bhutan	www.election-bhutan.org.bt
Bolivia	www.bolivia.gob.bo
Botswana	www.gov.bw/en/Ministries--Authorities/Ministries/Independent-Electoral-Commission-IEC
Brazil	www.tse.jus.br
Brunei	www.gov.bn/bm/Pages/default.aspx
Bulgaria	www.cik.bg
Burkina Faso	www.ceni.bf
Burundi	www.ceniburundi.bi
Cambodia	www.necelect.org.kh
Cameroon	www.elecam.cm
Canada	www.elections.ca
Cape Verde	www.dgape.cv
Cayman Islands	www.electionsoffice.ky
Central African Republic	www.commissionelectoraleindependantederca.sitew.com
Chile	www.tribunalcalificador.cl
Colombia	www.cne.gov.co/CNE
Congo, Democratic Republic of the	www.ceni.gouv.cd
Costa Rica	www.tse.go.cr
Côte d'Ivoire	www.ceici.org
Croatia	www.izbori.hr
Cyprus	www.moi.gov.cy
Czech Republic	www.volby.cz/index.htm
Denmark	www.elections.oim.dk

Facebook	Twitter	YouTube
www.facebook.com/pages/Election-Commission-of-Bangladesh/34831783470		
www.facebook.com/pages/Election-Commission-of-Bhutan/379655075433303	twitter.com/electionbhutan/	
www.facebook.com/pages/Independent-Electoral-Commission/116929558378193		
www.facebook.com/egnc.gov.bn	twitter.com/EGNCTweet	
www.facebook.com/cikbg	twitter.com/@cikbg	www.youtube.com/user/cikbulgaria/videos
	twitter.com/TCEChile	
www.facebook.com/consejo.nacionalelectoral	twitter.com/CNE_COLOMBIA	
www.facebook.com/TSECR	twitter.com/TSECostaRica	www.youtube.com/TSECostaRica

Annex D. EMB Websites and Social Media Platforms

417

Country	Website
Djibouti	www.ceni.dj
Dominica	electoraloffice.gov.dm
Dominican Republic	www.jce.gob.do
Ecuador	www.cne.gob.ec
Egypt	www.elections.eg
El Salvador	www.tse.gob.sv
Estonia	www.vvk.ee
Ethiopia	www.electionethiopia.org
Fiji	www.electionsfiji.org
Finland	www.vaalit.fi
France	www.interieur.gouv.fr/Elections
Gambia, The	www.iec.gm
Georgia	www.cec.gov.ge
Germany	www.bundeswahlleiter.de
Ghana	www.ec.gov.gh
Greece	www.ypes.gr/en/Elections
Guatemala	www.tse.org.gt
Guernsey	www.gov.gg/elections
Guyana	www.gecom.org.gy
Honduras	www.tse.hn
Hungary	www.valasztas.hu/en/ovi/index.html
Iceland	www.landskjor.is
India	www.eci.nic.in
Indonesia	www.kpu.go.id
Iraq	www.ihec.iq
Ireland	www.electionsireland.org
Isle of Man	www.iomelections.com
Israel	www.knesset.gov.il/elections17/eng/cec/CecIndex_eng.htm
Italy	www.elezioni.interno.it
Jamaica	www.eoj.com.jm/

Facebook	Twitter	YouTube
www.facebook.com/jcegobdo	twitter.com/juntacentral	www.youtube.com/videosjce
www.facebook.com/cnegobec	twitter.com/cnegobec	www.youtube.com/user/cneecuador
www.facebook.com/Elections.eg	twitter.com/EGElections	
www.facebook.com/tse.gob.sv	twitter.com/tse_sv	www.youtube.com/user/tsecomunicaciones
www.facebook.com/valimiskomisjon	twitter.com/valimiskomisjon	
	twitter.com/ElectionsFiji	
www.facebook.com/vaalit.fi		
www.facebook.com/ministere.interieur	twitter.com/Place_Beauvau	
www.facebook.com/CentralElectionCommissionOfGeorgia		www.youtube.com/user/CeCGeorgia
www.facebook.com/#!/ECGOVGH	twitter.com/ECGhana	www.youtube.com/user/GhanaEC
	twitter.com/Govgg	
www.facebook.com/pages/Tribunal-Supremo-Electoral-Honduras/128781813825137	twitter.com/tsehonduras	www.youtube.com/user/tsehonduras
www.facebook.com/elsovalaszto2014		
https://www.facebook.com/pages/KPU-Republik-Indonesia/137473109756643	twitter.com/KPURI2014	
www.facebook.com/ihec2013	twitter.com/IHEC2013	www.youtube.com/user/Theihec
www.facebook.com/iomelections	twitter.com/iomelections	
www.facebook.com/electionsja	twitter.com/ecjamaica	www.youtube.com/electionsja

Annex D. EMB Websites and Social Media Platforms

Country	Website
Japan	www.soumu.go.jp
Jersey	www.electoralcommission.je
Jordan	www.moi.gov.jo/tabid/110/default.aspx
Kazakhstan	election.kz
Kenya	iebc.or.ke
South Korea	www.nec.go.kr
Kosovo	www.kqz-ks.org
Kyrgyzstan	cec.shailoo.gov.kg
Latvia	web.cvk.lv
Lebanon	www.electionslb.com
Lesotho	www.iec.org.ls
Liberia	www.necliberia.org
Libya	www.hnec.ly
Liechtenstein	www.landtagswahlen.li
Lithuania	www.vrk.lt
Luxembourg	www.elections.public.lu
Macedonia, Former Yugoslav Republic of	www.sec.mk
Madagascar	www.ceni-madagascar.mg
Malawi	www.mec.org.mw
Malaysia	www.spr.gov.my
Maldives	www.elections.gov.mv
Malta	www.electoral.gov.mt
Mauritius	www.gov.mu/portal/site/eco
Mexico	www.ine.mx
Moldova	www.cec.md
Mongolia	www.gec.gov.mn
Mozambique	www.stae.org.mz
Namibia	www.ecn.na

Facebook	Twitter	YouTube
www.facebook.com/IEBCpage	twitter.com/IEBCpage	www.youtube.com/user/IEBCpage
	twitter.com/KorElectionCom	
www.facebook.com/pages/Komisioni-Qendror-i-Zgjedhjeve/189786584428894	twitter.com/KQZKosova	www.youtube.com/user/kqzkosova
	twitter.com/CVK_zinas	
	twitter.com/LibyaElections	www.youtube.com/user/LibyaElections
www.facebook.com/pages/Elections-Commission-of-Maldives/364238940329760		
www.facebook.com/INEMexico	twitter.com/INEMexico	www.youtube.com/ifetv
www.facebook.com/pages/Comisia-Electorala-Centrala-Moldova/123504584374934		www.youtube.com/user/TheCECmd?feature=mhee
	twitter.com/gecmongolia	www.youtube.com/gecmongolia
www.facebook.com/pages/Electoral-Commission-of-Namibia/255670464471211		

Annex D. EMB Websites and Social Media Platforms

421

Country	Website
Nepal	www.election.gov.np
Netherlands	www.kiesraad.nl
New Zealand	www.elections.org.nz
Nicaragua	www.cse.gob.ni
Nigeria	www.inecnigeria.org
Norway	www.valg.no
Pakistan	www.ecp.gov.pk
Palestine	www.elections.ps
Panama	www.tribunal-electoral.gob.pa
Papua New Guinea	www.pngec.gov.pg
Paraguay	tsje.gov.py
Peru	www.jne.gob.pe
Philippines	www.comelec.gov.ph
Poland	pkw.gov.pl
Portugal	www.cne.pt
Puerto Rico	www.ceepur.org/es-pr
Romania	www.roaep.ro/en/index.php
Russia	cikrf.ru
Rwanda	www.comelena.gov.rw
Saint Lucia	www.electoral.gov.lc
Samoa	www.oec.gov.ws
San Marino	www.elezioni.sm
Senegal	www.interieur.gouv.sn
Serbia	www.rik.parlament.gov.rs
Seychelles	www.ecs.sc
Sierra Leone	www.nec-sierraleone.org
Singapore	www.eld.gov.sg
Slovakia	www.minv.sk
Slovenia	www.dvk-rs.si
South Africa	www.elections.org.za

Facebook	Twitter	YouTube
	twitter.com/kiesraad	
www.facebook.com/IvoteNZ		
www.facebook.com/inecnigeria		
www.facebook.com/CECPalestine		www.youtube.com/CECPalestine
www.facebook.com/tepanama	mobile.twitter.com/tepanama	
www.facebook.com/Justicia.Electoral.Paraguay	twitter.com/tsjepy	www.youtube.com/justiciaelectoral
www.facebook.com/JNE.Peru	twitter.com/jne_peru	www.youtube.com/eleccionesperu
www.facebook.com/CEEPuertoRico	twitter.com/ceepuertorico	www.youtube.com/ceedepuertorico
www.facebook.com/NationalElectoralCommissionOfRwanda	twitter.com/necrwanda2	
www.facebook.com/pages/Saint-Lucia-Electoral-Department/109563472405045		
	twitter.com/dvk_rs	
www.facebook.com/IECSouthAfrica	twitter.com/IECSouthAfrica	www.youtube.com/user/IECSouthAfrica

Annex D. EMB Websites and Social Media Platforms

Country	Website
Spain	www.juntaelectoralcentral.es
Sri Lanka	www.slelections.gov.lk
Sudan	nec.org.sd
Sweden	www.val.se
Switzerland	www.ch.ch/abstimmungen_und_wahlen/index.html?lang=en
Taiwan	engweb.cec.gov.tw
Thailand	www.ect.go.th
Togo	www.ceni-togo.org
Tunisia	www.isie.tn
Turkey	www.ysk.gov.tr
Uganda	www.ec.or.ug
Ukraine	www.cvk.gov.ua
United Arab Emirates	uaenec.ae
United Kingdom	www.electoralcommission.org.uk
United States	www.fec.gov
Uruguay	www.corteelectoral.gub.uy
Uzbekistan	elections.uz
Venezuela	www.cne.gov.ve
Zambia	www.elections.org.zm
Zimbabwe	www.zec.gov.zw

Facebook	Twitter	YouTube
www.facebook.com/chchportal	twitter.com/ch_portal	www.youtube.com/chchportal
www.facebook.com/pages/CENI-TOGO/264536459556	twitter.com/cenitogo	
www.facebook.com/isietn	twitter.com/isietn	www.youtube.com/user/isietn
www.facebook.com/pages/Electoral-commission-Uganda/365803510149905	twitter.com/ECUganda	
	twitter.com/electoralcommUK	
www.facebook.com/pages/Electoral-Commission-of-Zambia/130763663658535		
www.facebook.com/ZimbabweElectoralCommission		

Annex D. EMB Websites and Social Media Platforms

Annex E

About the Authors

Helena Catt has been working around elections for 28 years as a practitioner, academic and consultant. From 2004–2009 she was Chief Executive and Commissioner of the New Zealand Election Commission. During that time there were two elections and the introduction of new party political finance legislation. She also oversaw extensive work on voter and civic education and encouraging participation. Prior to that she was an academic in the Department of Politics at the University of Auckland, teaching and researching on comparative democratic practice. In 2009 she returned to her native Scotland and has been working as an international election consultant and BRIDGE facilitator.

Andrew Ellis is a senior international consultant on elections, constitutions and democracy building based in Falmouth, UK. He retired from International IDEA in early 2014 having served as Director for Asia and the Pacific, Director of Operations, and Head of Electoral Processes. He was Senior Adviser for NDI in Indonesia from 1999 to 2003, working on constitutional reform, electoral process and decentralisation issues. He is the co-author of the IDEA handbooks *Electoral System Design: The New International IDEA Handbook, Electoral Management Design Handbook, Direct Democracy, Voting from Abroad* and *Electoral Justice*, and has written numerous papers on institutional framework design questions. Other major assignments have included acting as Chief Technical Adviser to the Palestinian Election Commission for the 1996 elections and designing the European Commission's electoral assistance programme in Cambodia for the 1998 elections. Andrew is a former Vice Chair and Secretary General of the UK Liberal Party, leader of the party's group on a first tier local authority, and Chief Executive of the UK Liberal Democrats.

Michael Maley spent more than 30 years as an election administrator before retiring in November 2012 from the position of Special Adviser, Electoral Reform and International Services, Australian Electoral Commission (AEC). He has done extensive work internationally: managing the AEC's overseas programs for the better part of 20 years; taking part in UN peacekeeping, observation and electoral survey and needs assessment missions, including in Namibia, Cambodia, South Africa, Timor-Leste, Western Sahara, Eastern Slavonia and Lesotho; working at UN headquarters, and for the Commonwealth Secretariat, International IDEA and IFES; and initiating the development of the BRIDGE electoral administrators' course.

Alan Wall, IFES Chief of Party in Kosovo since September 2013, has 30 years of experience in electoral administration and as a democracy adviser. From 1985 to 1994 he held various management positions with the Australian Electoral Commission. He was Country Director for IFES in Azerbaijan in 1999/2000, Indonesia 2000 to 2004, and Nepal 2010 to 2013. He has been a senior electoral official for the United Nations in Eastern Slavonia in 1996 and Nigeria in 1998, and an adviser to the South African government for the 1995 local government elections. From 2005 to 2009 Alan was Senior Advisor to Democracy International, and directed their election assistance in Indonesia and opinion polling programs in Indonesia and Timor-Leste. He has also implemented reviews of voter registration and/or electoral management systems in Bhutan, Iraq, Malawi, Mozambique, South Africa and Ukraine.

Peter Wolf has focused on ICT applications in electoral processes since joining the Elections Department of the OSCE mission to Bosnia and Herzegovina in 1999, where he worked on voter registration and results databases. He was a consultant in voter registration projects in Albania, the Democratic Republic of the Congo and Iraq, and has served in various international election observation missions, amongst others as an electronic voting expert in France, Kazakhstan, Kyrgyzstan, Venezuela and the Philippines. As part of his work on elections and technology for International IDEA he authored the policy paper *Introducing Electronic Voting: Essential Considerations*. Peter holds a master's degree in Telematik/Computer Engineering from Graz University of Technology, Austria.

The Case Study Authors

Ileana Aguilar Olivares has a licentiateship in Political Sciences from the University of Costa Rica. She is a former Program Officer at CAPEL and at International IDEA, and is currently the Head of International and Inter-Institutional Cooperation for IFED, the Institute of Formation and Studies on Democracy of the Supreme Tribunal of Elections.

Olufunto Akinduro is the head of the Elections and Political Processes Department at the Electoral Institute for Sustainable Democracy in Africa (EISA) in Johannesburg South Africa. She oversees the institute's election-related programmes which include election observation and technical assistance to key stakeholders like electoral commissions, national civil society groups, continental and regional institutions. Prior to her work at EISA, she worked in the field of elections and democracy in Nigeria for five years. During this period she managed the secretariat of the Electoral Reform Network (ERN). She has observed elections in Nigeria and in many African countries under the auspices of the African Union, ECOWAS and EISA Observer Missions. She has a masters in Development Studies specialising in governance and democracy; and a masters in Peace and Conflict Studies.

Gabrielle Bardall is an academic and an electoral assistance expert with a decade of experience supporting electoral processes in transitional states. She has worked in more than 20 countries with international organizations including UNDP, UN Women, DPKO, IFES, DRI, the Carter Center and others. Gabrielle holds a BA from McGill University in Montreal and a master's degree from the Institut d'Etudes Politiques de Paris. Motivated by her professional work, Gabrielle is currently completing her PhD at the University of Montreal on the topic of election violence and democratization. She is a 2012 Trudeau Scholar and an expert BRIDGE facilitator.

Vake Blake is the Chief Returning Officer of the Tonga Electoral Commission. She has worked with the election unit of the Prime Minister's Office of Tonga since 2007 and with Tonga Electoral Commission since 2010.

Andy Campbell is the Managing Director of Asabiyya Consulting, which he co-founded in 2011, and has over 20 years' democracy experience in the Middle East, South Asia and the South Pacific. Before joining the AEC (1999-2004) he was an active member of a political party. His Afghan election experience includes Head of Office for the Afghanistan OCV with IOM (2004); Regional Elections Coordinator with the UN (2005) based in Kandahar; LTO with NDI in Jalalabad and Chief Analyst in Kabul (2009); Afghanistan Country Director of National Democratic Institute (NDI), where he also led the NDI EOM (2010). His EOM experience also includes being member of the ANFREL leadership delegation for the Thai general election (2011) and STO in Timor-Leste parliamentary election (2012). He remains active in the Afghan electoral and political process advising CSOs, NGOs as well as conducting assessments for donors. Andy is a deployable election specialist with the Australian Civilian Corps (DFAT) and serves as a Council of Experts member for Regional Dialogue (Uzbekistan). He has a master's degree in International Relations and Political Science, bachelor's degree in Social Anthropology and Comparative Religious Studies and a graduate certificate in Public Administration.

Eric des Pallières has worked in democracy and electoral support for over 15 years with the UN, the EU and the OSCE in South East Asia, Africa, Eastern Europe and the Maghreb. After a diversified experience in the design and implementation of international technical assistance projects, Eric has contributed to numerous election observation and assessment missions with the EU and ODIHR. In Cambodia, he served as the EU Legal Advisor to the National Election Committee from 2008 to 2010. He recently led EU-funded support to civil society organizations ahead of transitional elections in the field of election observation and electoral dispute resolution, in Tunisia (2011) and Madagascar (2013).

Arpine Galfayan works with the Institute for Democracy and Human Rights (IDHR), an NGO in Armenia, where she is involved in civil society organizing and active citizenship education. Between 2002 and 2008 she managed electoral and capacity development projects at International IDEA's program in the South Caucasus and office in Armenia. She is also a facilitator of BRIDGE, with experience in the South Caucasus, central and Eastern European and central Asian countries. She collaborates freelance with local and international organizations on democracy development and human rights related projects, including training, reporting, facilitation of legal reform recommendations, etc.

Irena Hadžiabdić graduated from the Belgrade Faculty of Law and she holds a master's degree in EU Policy, Law and Management from RGU, Aberdeen. She has spent 17 years in the field of elections, first in OSCE, then as Executive Director of the IFES in BiH. Until 2007 she was Executive Director of the Association of Election Officials in BiH (AEOBiH). In 2007 she was appointed by the BiH Parliamentary Assembly as a member of the BiH Central Election Commission (BiH CEC). From January 2010 to September 2011 she was president of the BiH CEC. She represents the BiH CEC at the Executive Board of the ACEEEO and at the moment she chairs the Oversight and Audit Committee of the Association of World Election Bodies (A-WEB). She has observed and assessed elections in 14 countries with OSCE/ODIHR, IRI and NDI. In 2013 she received the international award for outstanding achievements in electoral management.

Toby S. James is a lecturer in British Politics in the School of Political, Social and International Studies at the University of East Anglia, Norwich, UK. His research interests include the governance and implementation of elections, political leadership and the policy process. He has published a range of articles on election administration and is the author of Elite Statecraft and Election Administration (Palgrave, 2012). He was previously a lecturer at Swansea University and a British Research Council Scholar at the Library of Congress, Washington D.C., and holds a PhD from the University of York.

Claude Kabemba is a chief research manager in the Society, Culture and Identity Research Programme at the Human Sciences Research Council of South Africa. He holds a master's degree in international relations from the University of the Witwatersrand, South Africa, and is a PhD candidate in international relations at the same university. Previously he worked at the Electoral Institute of Southern Africa (EISA) as research programme manager and at the Centre for Policy Studies and the Development Bank of Southern Africa. He has also worked as a consultant for international organizations such as Oxfam, the United Nations High Commissioner for Refugees, Norwegian People's Aid and the African Union. His main areas of research interest include issues of democratization and governance, election politics, citizen participation, conflicts, the media, political parties, civil society, and social policies.

Shumbana Karume is the head of the Democracy and Electoral Assistance Unit at the Department of Political Affairs of the African Union Commission. She has wide experience in the areas of electoral democracy, regional integration and other issues that cover governance and democracy in Africa. Prior to working for the African Union, she worked for the Electoral Institute for Sustainable Democracy in Africa (EISA) in South Africa, the Southern African Research and Documentation Centre (SARDC) in Zimbabwe and the United Nations.

Jebeh Kawa has been an information technology generalist for 15 years, with interests in social justice issues including gender mainstreaming and child welfare since 2009. Since 1997 she has worked with multi-national companies such as Accenture, PFPC and Société Générale, supporting client-driven environments in meeting enterprise objectives and she has worked with national governments through her tenure as Gender Coordinator at Liberia's National Elections Commission. She has also supported the IT-related attributes of electoral management for a local district while undergoing and implementing training to carry out poll center operations—including poll-worker screening, training, supervision and payroll, delivering time-bound solutions to elections management issues. Originally from Liberia, West Africa, Jebeh currently resides in Philadelphia, Pennsylvania in the United States.

Jeong-Gon Kim is the Director General of the Association of World Election Bodies (A-WEB). He has worked at the National Election Commission of the Republic of Korea (NEC) for 18 years in various positions such as the Team Manager of Legal Affairs Division and Head of International Elections Department. Recognizing the need for strengthened solidarity among electoral management bodies in order to ensure transparent electoral process worldwide, he first proposed the establishment of A-WEB. He is currently involved in various activities that can develop democratic culture and environment for free, fair, transparent and participative elections worldwide.

Carlos M. Navarro is the Director of International Studies and Projects of the National Electoral Institute (INE) of Mexico. He has written several publications about the Mexican electoral regime, as well as diverse international comparative studies on political and electoral issues. He has participated in international technical assistance missions in different regions around the world and he is responsible for the design and conduct the specialization workshops that INE organizes twice a year for representatives of EMB's from around the world.

Marie-Thérèse Purvis is a member of the Seychelles Electoral Commission since July 2011. As such she is involved in a major electoral reform process that started in 2012. Prior to this she worked in various capacities for the Seychelles Ministry of Education over twenty years—as principal education officer, director of the teacher training institute and director of the national curriculum centre. She holds a master's degree in Applied Linguistics from Durham University (UK) and a PhD in Education from Warwick University (UK).

S.Y. Quraishi served as the 17th Chief Election Commissioner of India from 2010–2012. He was the Election Commissioner since 2006. He completed his postgraduate degree in history from St. Stephen's College in Delhi before joining the Indian Administrative Service in 1971. Later he did his doctorate in social marketing. Dr Quraishi is the author of the books *Social Marketing for*

Social Change and *An Undocumented Wonder: The Great Indian Election*. He has travelled widely to represent India at International conferences and dialogues and has figured in The Indian Express list of 100 Most Powerful Indians of 2011 and 2012 and India Today's High and Mighty Power List, 2012.

Mohamed Chafik Sarsar is the President of the Independent Higher Authority for Elections in Tunisia. He is a Ph.D. in Public Law, Associate Professor of Public Law at the Faculty of Law and Political Sciences of Tunis (Tunis El Manar University), Director of the Department of Political Science at the Faculty of Law of Tunis (2011-14), and member of the Committee of Experts in the High Commission for the Achievement of the Revolution, Political Reform and Democratic Transition (2011), member of the Commission of Inquiry into the events Place Mohamed Ali (December 2012) Secretary General of the Association of Research on Democratic Transition (2013), and a founding member of the Arab Association of Constitutional Law. He was a lecturer at the Faculty of Law and Political Sciences of Tunis, Higher Judicial Institute, He has authored several publications and contributions in constitutional law and electoral systems. He participated as an expert in shares of the Venice Commission, UNDP, the Arab Institute for Human Rights, Arab Foundation for Democracy, and the Independent High Authority for the Elections.

Luis Antonio Sobrado González is a Licentiate and Doctor of Law from the University of Costa Rica and the Complutense University of Madrid respectively. Incumbent Magistrate of the Supreme Tribunal of Elections (TSE) since 1999. President of the Costa Rican electoral body since 2007. Professor for over 25 years of Constitutional Law at the University of Costa Rica and since 1993, he coordinates that department at the School of Law. He is the Director of the Electoral Law magazine of TSE and he is the author of several books and articles on electoral justice, democracy and elections.

Vincent Tohbi has been with Electoral Institute for Sustainable Democracy in Southern Africa (EISA) since 2003. Prior to that he was a consultant in Rwanda for ERIS (Electoral Reforms for International Systems) and NPA (Norwegian People Aid). Responsible for Rwandan NGO networks in election observation and voter education. International consultant to TROCAIRE (Iris-based NGO) for the evaluation of a capacity building and funding programme of Rwandan civil society organizations. In 2004 he was the International consultant to the Norweign people's aid for the evaluation of the Rwandan electoral process and the involvement of NGO's in the electoral process and also the EISA Country Director, Democratic Republic of Congo office. Vincent has participated in several election observer missions.

Vasil Vashchanka was a Programme Officer with International IDEA's Electoral Processes team in 2012–2014. His professional interests include electoral management and electoral justice. Vasil previously worked at the Office for Democratic Institutions and Human Rights of the Organization for Security and Co-operation in Europe (2002–2011) as Rule of Law Officer, Adviser, and Deputy Chief of the Rule of Law Unit.

Kåre Vollan is Director and owner of the company Quality AS. He has been working on elections in more than thirty countries and territories, including Nepal, Zimbabwe, Kenya, Iraq, Palestine, Sudan, Armenia and Bosnia and Herzegovina. Since 2006 he has been advising the Election Commission and politicians in Nepal, in particular on the group representation system. In the period 1996 to 2009 he headed twelve OSCE/ODIHR and NORDEM international election observation missions or teams. From 2003 he has drafted opinions on election laws for the Council of Europe Venice Commission. Kåre has been teaching and supervising students in elections and power-sharing issues and he has published a number of articles and reports on electoral and decision-making issues, in particular related to post-conflict situations.

Case Study Authors of the Original Edition*

Peter Bartu was a political adviser to the Special Representative of the UN Secretary-General HE Terje Roed Larsen to the Middle East Peace Process. He has also worked for the UN in Timor-Leste and Cambodia and for the Australian Prime Minister's Department and the Australian Department of Foreign Affairs and Trade.

Carl W. Dundas is a former Director of Elections in Jamaica and a former Special Adviser (Legal) in the Commonwealth Secretariat, with responsibility for technical assistance in elections matters (1990–2001). He has been an election consultant. He was the Election Consultant for the European Commission in Liberia. Carl is a Barrister-at-Law (Gray's Inn) and holds a Master of Laws (LL.M) degree from London University, UK.

Ellie Greenwood worked for the UK Electoral Commission, helping to set up and launch the organization when it was established. She helped shaping and implementing the introduction of political finance legislation, as well as looking at policies on encouraging participation.

Rubén Hernández Valle, professor of constitutional law at the University of Costa Rica, and a doctorate professor at the University of Siena, Italy. Having extensive judicial experience, he was a substitute magistrate of the Supreme Court of Justice of Costa Rica. He has authored and/or contributed to many specialized publications on constitutional, judicial, legal and election-related subjects.

Ajay Jha was a member of the Indian Administrative Service with extensive experience and expertise in managing elections at national and provincial levels. He served as Deputy Election Commissioner in the Election Commission of India and headed the team for the conduct of general elections to the national Parliament in 2004 using electronic voting machines in all polling centres.

Claude Kabemba was a chief research manager in the Society, Culture and Identity Research Programme at the Human Sciences Research Council of South Africa. He holds an MA in international relations from the University

---

* For case studies of countries that are also included in this edition.

of the Witwatersrand, South Africa, and was a PhD candidate in international relations at the same university. His main areas of research interest include issues of democratization and governance, election politics, citizen participation, conflicts, the media, political parties, civil society, and social policies.

Robert A. Pastor was the Vice President of International Affairs, Professor of International Relations, and Director of the Center for Democracy and Election Management at the American University in Washington, D.C.

Vijay Patidar was a member of the Indian Administrative Service, and specialized in elections at national and provincial level in India and also internationally. He served as joint Chief Electoral Officer of the state of Madhya Pradesh, as a consultant in the electoral components of four UN peacekeeping missions, and as head of the Elections Team at International IDEA.

Domenico Tuccinardi is an electoral specialist and directed the external registration and voting programmes for the OSCE Mission to Bosnia. As OSCE Deputy Director of Elections in Bosnia he designed the transfer of election administration functions to the newly created Election Commission of Bosnia. He led the European Union project in support of the Iraq transitional elections and was Deputy Chief Observer for the EU Observation Mission in Venezuela. He holds a law degree and an MA in international law.

Annex F

Acknowledgements

This Handbook could have not been completed without the valuable contributions made by many individuals and organizations. We would like to express our sincerest gratitude to all the experts, practitioners and partners worldwide who have contributed their knowledge, insight and a range of crucial data.

Our special thanks go to Rafael López Pintor, whose initial work and ideas provided the basis for the development of this publication.

In addition to the authors of the case studies, we are especially grateful to the following people who have actively supported the authors throughout their endeavour to produce this book: Lina Antara, Reginald Austin, Ayman Ayoub, Jarrett Blanc, Jeannette Bolenga, Roly Davila, Jean-Jacques Descartes, Sean Dunne, Linda Ederberg, Rémegie Gahungu, Lourdes Gonzalez, Margot Gould, Ron Gould, Maria Gratschew, Bill Gray, Nadia Handal Zander, Pedro J. Hernando, Marie Hohwu-Christensen, Nana Kalandadze, Olha Karavayeva, Ray Kennedy, Jean-Pierre Kingsley, Kaz Kuroda, Sophie Lagueny, Fredrik Larsson, Johan Lindroth, Belinda Musanhu, Pierre-Louis Opont, Robert Patterson, Lesley Richards, Claude Rioux, Alessandra Rossi, Joram Rukambe, Maiko Shimizu, Abdurashid Solijonov, Sara Staino, Oksana Syroyid, Domenico Tuccinardi and Peter Wolf.

Thanks also go to editorial anchor Stina Larserud, to Kelley Friel for her highly professional editing of the texts and to Lisa Hagman, IDEA's Publications Officer for her excellent support.

Annex G

About International IDEA

What is International IDEA?

The International Institute for Democracy and Electoral Assistance (International IDEA) is an intergovernmental organization with a mission to support sustainable democracy worldwide.

The objectives of the Institute are to support stronger democratic institutions and processes, and more sustainable, effective and legitimate democracy.

What does International IDEA do?

The Institute's work is organized at global, regional and country level, focusing on the citizen as the driver of change.

International IDEA produces comparative knowledge in its key areas of expertise: electoral processes, constitution building, political participation and representation, and democracy and development, as well as on democracy as it relates to gender, diversity, and conflict and security.

IDEA brings this knowledge to national and local actors who are working for democratic reform, and facilitates dialogue in support of democratic change.

In its work, IDEA aims for:

- increased capacity, legitimacy and credibility of democracy;
- more inclusive participation and accountable representation; and
- more effective and legitimate democracy cooperation.

Where does International IDEA work?

International IDEA works worldwide. Based in Stockholm, Sweden, the Institute has offices in the Africa, Asia and the Pacific, Latin America and the Caribbean, and West Asia and North Africa regions.

Index

A

AAEA, Association of Asian Election Authorities, 172, 345, 409

ACE Electoral Knowledge Network (Administration and Cost of Elections Knowledge Network), 157, 346–48, 409

ACEEEO (Association of Central and Eastern European Election Officials), 16, 345, 429

accountability of EMBs. *See electoral management bodies (EMBs), accountability*

Administration and Cost of Elections (ACE) Electoral Knowledge Network, 157, 346–48, 409

AEA (Association of Electoral Administrators), 186, 307–8, 343

AEC (Australian Electoral Commission), 160–1, 186, 204, 225, 240–1, 374, 425–7, 431

AEOBIH (Association of Bosnia and Herzegovina Election Officials), 344

Afghanistan, EMBs in,
    case study, 61–70
    donor funding, 207, 211, 316
    Election Commission, 374
    Election Law, 64, 66
    elections, transitional, 62–4, 208, 328
    Electoral Complaints Commission (ECC), 62–8
    electoral dispute resolution, 81
    Fair Election Foundation (FEFA), 69
    fraud, electoral, 67–71
    gender equity, 89–90
    Independent Election Commission (IEC), 63–9, 154
    Independent Model, 374
    international electoral missions in, 62–3, 69, 207. *See also names of individual missions*
    online resources, 414
    professionalism, 68, 190
    refugee voting in, 62–4, 91, 324, 428
    United Nations electoral missions in, 62. *See also United Nations, names of individual missions*
    voting, electronic, 66

Algeria, 214, 374, 414

Andorra, 374, 414

ANFREL (Asian Network for Free Elections), 347

Africa, EMBs in. *See names of individual countries*

African Union (AU), 45

Angola, EMBs in,
    election campaigns, 81
    Electoral Commission, 374
    Independent Model, 374
    legal framework, 81
    legislative framework, 214–5
    online resources, 414

Anguilla, 374, 414

Antigua and Barbuda, 147, 374, 414
Argentina, EMBs in,
  gender equity, 87
  legal framework, 44
  Mixed Model, 374
  online resources, 414
Armenia, EMBs in,
  case study, 98–105
  Central Electoral Commission (CEC), 98–100
  constitution, 98–9
  gender equity, 88
  Independent Model, 7
  legal framework, 44, 84, 98
  legislative framework, 104
  media, 104
  voting, electronic, 104
Aruba, 374, 414
Asia. *See names of individual countries*
Asia Foundation, 69
Asian Network for Free Elections (ANFREL), 347
assessment mechanisms of EMBs, 161, 216, 220, 290
Association of African Election Authorities, 345
Association of Asian Election Authorities (AAEA), 172, 345, 409
Association of Caribbean Electoral Associations, 345
Association of European Election Officials (ACEEEO), 16, 345, 429
Association of Electoral Administrators (AEA), 186, 307–8, 343
Association of Electoral Institutions of Central America and the Caribbean (Tikal Protocol), 96, 344
Association of South American Electoral Organizations (Quito Protocol), 344
Association of World Election Bodies (A-WEB), 346, 348, 429–30
AU (African Union), 45
Australia, EMBs in,
  Australian Electoral Commission (AEC), 160–1, 186, 204, 225, 240–1, 374, 425–7, 431
  Electoral Council, 344, 374
  financing, 213, 289
  Independent Model, 374
  legal framework, 22, 78, 85, 87, 160, 230
  legislative framework, 18–9, 44, 49, 74, 85, 160–1, 232, 288
  online resources, 414
  political parties, 80
  professionalism, 204
  regional, 226, 345
  stakeholders, 240–1
  Tonga EMB, support for, 226
  United Kingdom, electoral observation of, 306
  United States electoral reform, influence on, 246
  voter access, 321, 324
  voting, electronic, 83, 85, 267, 324–5
Austria, EMBs in,
  constitution, 47
  Governmental Model, 374
  legislative framework in, 47
  online resources, 414
A-WEB (Association of World Election Bodies), 346, 348, 429–30
Azerbaijan, EMBs in,
  Independent Model in, 11, 374
  legal framework of, 119
  online resources, 414
  professionalism, 119
  regional, 98

B

Bahamas, 374
Bahrain, 374, 414
Baker-Carter Commission on Federal Electoral Reform (2005), 290
Bangladesh, EMBs in,
  constitution, 46–7
  Election Commission, 376
  Electoral Training Institute, 186
  identification (ID) cards, voter, 79
  Independent Model, 376
  legal framework, 47, 85, 108–9, 112
  online resources, 414–5
  overseas delegations from, 306
  professionalism, 186
  United Nations (UN), support for, 85

437

Barbados, EMBs in,
    Electoral and Boundaries Commission, 78, 376
    Independent Model, 376
    online resources, 416
BCEN (National Office of Electoral Disputes), 351
BEC (Bureau Electoral Communal), 350–1, 353–4
BED (Bureau Electoral Départemental), 350–1, 353–4
Belarus, EMBs in,
    Central Commission on Elections, 376
    Independent Model, 376
    online resources, 416
    transparency in, 25
Belgium, EMBs in,
    Federal Public Service Interior, 376
    gender equity, 87
    online resources, 416
    voting, electronic, 271, 325
Belize, EMBs in,
    Electoral and Boundaries Commission, 78, 376
    Mixed Model, 78, 376
    online resources, 416
Benin, 376
Bermuda, EMBs in,
    Governmental Model, 376
    online resources, 416
    professionalism, 146
Bhutan, EMBs in,
    Election Commission of Bhutan (ECB), 163, 376
    financing, 215
    Independent Model, 369
    legal framework, 74–5, 117, 120, 124, 163
    online resources, 416–7
    overseas involvement of, 85
    professionalism, 115, 117, 120, 178
    voter education, 82, 426
    voting, electronic, 321, 325, 371
BiH. *See Bosnia and Herzegovina*
Bill of Electoral Rights for People with Disabilities, 91
Bolivia, EMBs in,
    accountability, 287
    election dispute and, 285
    financing of, 214–5
    Independent Model, 376
    online resources, 416
    Plurinational Electoral Body, 376
BON (Broadcasting Organization of Nigeria), 133
Bonn Agreement, 61
Bosnia and Herzegovina, EMBs in,
    accountability, 284, 286, 291, 331
    Association of Bosnia and Herzegovina Election Officials (AEOBIH), 344
    case study, 328–33
    Central Election Commission (CEC), 330, 333, 376
    donor funding, 315, 331
    ethnic balance, 90
    Election Appellate Sub-Commission (EASC), 328
    electoral dispute resolution, 88
    financing, 211, 315, 331
    gender balance, 90
    Independent Model, 7, 328
    legal framework, 73–4, 82, 109, 124
    media, 80–2
    Media Expert Commission (MEC), 328, 330, 333
    Provisional Election Commission (PEC), 328, 330
    professionalism, 109, 119, 347–8
    refugee voting, 324
    transitional, 18
    transparency, 124, 344
    voter registration, 91, 426, 46
boundary delimitation, 78–9, 322. *See also names of individual countries*
Brazil, EMBs in,
    expert-based, 118
    judiciary and, 22
    High Electoral Tribunal, 376
    Independent Model, 376
    legislative framework, 215
    online resources, 416
    permanent, 12
    powers and responsibilities, 18
    voting, electronic, 325, 371
BRIDGE (Building Resources in Democracy Governance and Elections), 68–9, 135, 186, 191, 198, 204–5, 225, 409, 426–8

British Virgin Islands, 394
Broadcasting Organization of Nigeria (BON), 133
Brunei, 374, 414
Building Resources in Democracy Governance and Elections (BRIDGE), 68–9, 135, 186, 191, 198, 204–5, 225, 409, 426–8
Bulgaria, EMBs in
    Central Election Commission, 376
    Independent Model, 16, 376
    online resources, 416–7
Burkina Faso, EMBs in,
    financing, 215
    Independent Model, 7, 146, 376
    legal framework, 85
    legislative framework, 49
    National Legislative Commission, 376
    online resources, 416
    professionalism, 22, 146
Burma. *See Myanmar*
Burundi, EMBs in,
    Independent Model, 376
    National Election Committee, 376
    online resources, 414

C

CAA (Constitutional Appointments Authority), 28
Cambodia, EMBs in,
    accountability, 287, 321
    Cambodian National Rescue Party (CNRP), 55
    Cambodian People's Party (CPP), 54–9
    case study, 54–60
    code of conduct, 81
    Constitutional Council for National Assembly and Senate Elections, 58
    CORE project (Cost of Registration and Elections), 317
    donor funding, 80, 204–12, 317
    Electoral Reform Alliance (ERA), 60
    financing, 59
    FUNCINPEC (United Front for an Independent, Neutral, Peaceful and Cooperative Cambodia), 54–6
    Human Rights Party (HRP), 55
    Independent Model, 376
    international observation of, 84
    Khmer Rouge, 54
    Law on the Election of the Members of the National Assembly (LEMNA), 55, 57
    legal framework, 74, 84–5, 425–7
    legislative framework, 55–7
    National Election Committee (NEC), 54–8, 376
    online resources, 416
    Paris Peace Agreements, 54
    professionalism, 86, 115, 146, 188
    Sam Rainsy Party (SRP), 55–6, 60
    sustainability, 287, 318
    transitional, 18
    transparency, 80
    United Nations Transitional Administration in Cambodia (UNTAC), 54–5
    voter education, 83
Cameroon, EMBs in,
    accountability, 289
    Elections Cameroon, 376
    gender equity, 89
    Independent Model, 376
    legislative framework, 47, 84, 215
    online resources, 416
Canada, EMBs in,
    accountability, 289
    boundary delimitation, 78–9
    Chief Electoral Officer, 376
    donor funding, 80
    Elections Canada, 346
    Independent Model, 7, 108, 376
    international missions, 85, 161
    legal framework, 25, 49, 74, 78
    media regulation, 84
    online resources, 416
    permanent, 16
    political parties, 233
    polls, opinion, 82
    professionalism, 108, 115, 117, 147, 181, 300, 215
    transparency, 232–3
CAPEL (Centre for Electoral Promotion and Assistance), 344, 424, 427
Cape Verde, EMBs in,
    Mixed Model, 376
    National Elections Committee, 376

online resources, 416
Carter Center, 197, 199, 346, 428
Carter, Jimmy (President), 247
Cayman Islands, EMBs in,
  Governmental Model, 376
  online resources, 416
CEC (Central Election Commission). *See under Bosnia and Herzegovina, Georgia, Russia, Armenia, Ukraine*
CEMC (Central Election Management Council), 14
CEN (Commonwealth Electoral Network), 345
CENA (Commission Electorale Nationale Autonome—National Autonomous Electoral Commission), 167–70
Central African Republic, EMBs in,
  Independent Electoral Commission, 378
  Ministry of Territorial Administration and Decentralization, 378
  Mixed Model, 378
  online resources, 416
Central Election Commission (CEC). *See under Bosnia and Herzegovina, Georgia, Russia, Armenia, Ukraine*
Central Election Management Council (CEMC), 14
Centre for Electoral Promotion and Assistance (CAPEL), 344, 424, 427
CEP (Conseil Electoral Provisoire), 350–6. *See under Haiti*
Chad, EMBs in,
  Independent National Electoral Commission, 378
  National Commission for the Organization of Elections, 378
  legislative framework, 214–5
  Mixed Model, 8
Chile, EMBs in,
  Electoral Service Board, 378
  Independent Model, 378
  online resources, 416
China, 378
CNE (National Elections Commission), 201–5
CNRA (Commission Nationale de Recensement des Votes—National Commission for the Tallying of the Votes), 167–8
COE, (Council of Europe), 278, 325, 331, 432
Colombia, EMBs in,
  Independent Model, 378
  National Electoral Council, 378
  online resources, 416
  voter registration, 80
Commission Electorale Nationale Autonome (CENA), 167–70
Commonwealth, British, EMBs in,
  boundary delimitation, 78
  professionalism, 225
  Secretariat, 230, 427, 432
  voting rights initiatives, 160
Commonwealth Electoral Act (1918), 156
Commonwealth Electoral Network (CEN), 345
Comoros, 378
ConEC (Constituency Electoral Commissions), 100, 102
Congo, Democratic Republic of (DRC), EMBs in,
  civil society organizations, 237
  donor funding, 316
  EISA (Electoral Institute for Sustainable Democracy in Southern Africa), 431
  Independent Model, 15, 378
  National Electoral Commission, 378
  online resources, 416
  voter registration projects in, 431
Congo, Republic of (Brazzaville), EMBs in,
  Mixed Model in, 12, 378
  National Commission for the Organization of Elections, 378
Conseil Electoral Provisoire (CEP), 350–6
Constitutional Appointments Authority (CAA), 28
Cook Islands, 378
Cost of Registration and Elections (CORE), 208, 220, 317
Costa Rica, EMB's in,
  accountability, 288
  case study, 93–7
  Center for Electoral Promotion and Assistance (CAPEL), 344, 427

440

constitution, 47, 93
donor funding, 317
Electoral Code, 96
electoral dispute resolution, 85
gender equity, 87–8
Independent Model, 7, 47, 74, 378
Institute for Training and Education in Democracy, 83
judicial independence, 22, 112
legislative framework in, 214, 233
legal framework in, 17, 22, 47, 96, 109
online resources, 416
organizational structure, 149, 156
professionalism, 95, 112, 117, 149
Supreme Court of Justice, 432
Supreme Electoral Tribunal (TSE), 93–5, 378, 431
technology in, 317
voter education, 82–3
voter registration, 79
voting, electronic, 317
Cote d'Ivoire, EMBs in,
    Independent Electoral Commission, 378
    Independent Model, 378
    legal framework, 112
    online resources, 416
    professionalism, 112
Council of Europe (COE), 278, 325, 331, 432
CPP (Cambodian People's Party), 54–9
Croatia, EMBs in,
    Independent Model, 378
    judicial independence, 112
    online resources, 416
    State Election Commission, 378
CTCEP (Transitional College of the Permanent Electoral Council), 350–6
CTV (Centre de Tabulation de Vote—Vote Tabulation Centre), 352, 354
Cuba, 378
Cyprus, EMBs in,
    Governmental Model, 378
    online resources, 416
    professionalism, 146
Cyprus (Northern), 378
Czech Republic, EMBs in,
    constitution, 47
    Governmental Model, 378
    online resources, 416
    professionalism, 107, 146

D

Dayton Peace Agreement (1995), 328
DEC (District Election Commission), 338–9
democracies, emerging, EMBs and,
    accountability, 320
    donor funding, 211, 220, 233, 317, 326, 347
    election campaigns, 81
    electoral observation, 84
    ethnic balance, 91
    financing, 215, 220, 371
    Independent Model, 7
    integrity costs, 209, 402
    legal framework, 75, 81, 190
    legislative framework, 233
    observation, international, 367
    sustainability, 233, 314, 326
    technology, 233, 367, 370–1
    voter education, 81
democracies, established, EMBs and,
    donor funding, 238, 317
    education, 82, 235
    international support for, 239
    media, 235
    multiparty, 27, 110, 125, 366
    promotion of, 1, 27, 29, 31, 77, 83, 87, 94, 174, 238–9, 274, 288, 347
    sustainability, 313, 317
    technology, 262, 264, 288
    voting rights, 75
democracy, direct, EMBs and, 1, 5, 77, 171, 397, 399, 405–7. *See also direct democracy instruments*
Denmark, EMBs,
    Governmental Model, 7, 210, 378
    legislative framework, 84
    online resources, 416
Diouf, Abdou (President of Senegal), 165
direct democracy instruments, 5, 77, 400
    recall vote, 5, 77, 121, 172, 343, 399, 405

441

referendum, 1, 5–9, 14, 18, 27, 29, 46, 49–50, 77, 95, 98, 160, 171–2, 174, 183, 193, 198, 201, 203, 214, 233, 251–5, 274–6, 282, 303–7, 323, 335–6, 347, 399, 405

direct recording electronic voting machines (DREs). *See under voting machines, electronic*

Djibouti, EMBs in,
   Independent Model, 378
   Independent National Electoral Commission, 378
   online resources, 418

Dominica, EMBs in,
   Independent Model, 378
   Electoral Commission, 378
   online resources, 418

Dominican Republic, EMBs in,
   Central Electoral Board, 378
   Independent Model, 378
   online resources, 418
   professionalism, 114
   voter registration, 79

donor funding, 11, 13, 24, 59, 67, 69–70, 100, 103, 134, 159, 168, 195–6, 203–14, 217–21, 225, 229, 243, 282, 300, 313–7, 331, 353–4, 367, 369, 407, 428. *See also names of individual countries and electoral management bodies (EMBs), financing*
   advantages and disadvantages of, 212, 326
   democracy promotion and, 211, 220, 233, 238, 317, 326, 347
   sustainability and, 220, 326
   technology support and, 211–2, 220, 267–8, 279, 316–18

DRE (direct recording electronic voting machines). *See under voting machines, electronic*

E

EAC (Election Assistance Commission), 247–8

Eastern Europe, EMBs in,
   multi-party, 110
   permanent, 16

East Timor. *See Timor-Leste*

EBDC (Election Broadcasting Debate Commission), 172–3

EC (Election Commission). *See under Bosnia and Herzegovina, South Korea, Seychelles*

ECC (Electoral Complaints Commission), 62–8

ECI (Election Commission of India), 358–62

ECK (Electoral Commission of Kenya), 273, 277

Economic Community West African States (ECOWAS), 46, 198, 345, 427

Ecuador, EMBs in,
   accountability, 287
   expert-based, 115
   financing, 287
   Independent Model, 380
   online resources, 418

Egypt, EMBs in,
   electoral polling, 324
   Independent Model, 380
   National Elections Commission, 380
   online resources, 418

EISA (Electoral Institute for Sustainable Democracy in Africa), 46, 346, 427, 429–31

ELECT (Enhancing Electoral and Legal Capacity for Tomorrow), 63–70

Election Assistance Commission (EAC), 247–8

Election Broadcasting Debate Commission (EBDC), 172–3

election campaigns, EMBs and,
   audits, 80, 252, 360
   financing, 80, 82, 163, 252, 360, 371
   internet advertising, 175
   media access, 196, 338
   oversight of, 28
   regulation of, 51, 76–7, 80–2, 252, 331

Election Commission of India (ECI), 358–62

elections calendar
   electoral cycle and, 16, 62
   project management software and, 159

Electoral Complaints Commission (ECC), 62–8

Electoral Commission of Kenya (ECK), 273, 277
Electoral Institute for Sustainable Democracy in Africa (EISA), 46, 346, 427, 429–31
electoral management bodies (EMBs), accountability, 7, 9–11, 13, 22, 25, 29, 31, 49, 51, 85, 150–1, 158, 183, 190, 211, 213, 216, 219, 266, 270, 285–312, 325, 366–7, 401–2, 404
   Afghanistan, 67–8
   Armenia, 101
   audits, 292–4
   Bosnia and Herzegovina, 330–1
   Cambodia, 60, 211
   Costa Rica, 94
   external oversight, 299
   financial, 11, 85, 212–3, 288–9, 294, 299
   importance of, 285
   Kenya, 279
   legislative, 220
   Liberia, 195
   Nigeria, 131, 134
   performance review, 7, 11, 25, 85, 286, 298, 300, 404
   post-election, 296–7
   principles of, 285
   quality controls and, 291
   Senegal, 168
   Seychelles, 29–35
   stakeholders and, 286, 293
   technology-based systems and, 66, 300
   Timor-Leste, 203
   Tonga, 225
   Tunisia, 253
   Ukraine, 337
   United Kingdom, 302, 307
   United States, 248–9
electoral management bodies (EMBs), electoral observation,
   definition of, 340
   European Council (EC) and, 29, 433
   donor funding and, 314, 367
   external EMB and, 20, 29, 46, 85, 100–1, 103, 239, 427
   independent EMB and, 8, 20, 84, 204, 234, 274, 276, 347, 431
   media and, 367
   OSCE/ODIHR and, 100–1, 428, 432
   United Nations (UN) and, 46, 84, 239, 426. *See also names of individual countries*
electoral management bodies (EMBs), electoral reform,
   Afghanistan, 63–4, 70
   Armenia, 104
   Bosnia and Herzegovina, 333, 347–8
   Cambodia, 59–60
   commitment to, 1, 77, 230, 296
   definition of, 369–70, 372
   Costa Rica, 96
   Haiti, 358
   India, 361
   Kenya, 273–4
   Liberia, 192, 197
   Mexico, 35, 59
   Nigeria, 128–30, 134, 427
   risks, 372–73
   Seychelles, 27, 30–1, 430
   Senegal, 175
   stakeholders, 230, 233, 243, 298
   Tonga, 226
   Ukraine, 339
electoral management bodies (EMBs), equity and,
   access, 92, 183, 202, 275
   campaign funding, 252
   disabled persons, 70, 371
   ethnic balance, 87, 90–2, 119, 160, 168, 186, 330
   gender, 31, 52, 73, 80–1, 87–90, 92, 118–9, 168, 181, 191, 197–8, 314, 354, 366, 369, 371, 398. *See also gender equity and names of individual countries*
   media, 198
   promotion of, 43, 77, 92
   secret ballot, 250
   voter registration, 202
electoral management bodies (EMBs), financing, 207–22. *See also donor funding and names of individual countries*
electoral management bodies (EMBs), membership and functions of, 107–27
   centralized, 17, 26, 130, 320, 339, 397

443

combined, 112–3, 379–93, 398
decentralized, 26, 37, 130, 137, 140, 151, 399
expert-based, 19, 110–2, 114–6, 119–20, 377–95, 398, 401, 404
lower-level, 17–8, 57, 336–8, 340, 402–3
multiparty-based, 118, 122, 124, 126, 140, 398, 403–4
non-partisan, 401, 404
permanent, 12, 14–7, 26, 32, 34, 37, 40, 48, 57, 67, 69, 99, 111–2, 114–5, 128, 130, 140, 156, 173, 190–1, 212, 230, 250–1, 319, 326, 336, 349–55, 366, 389, 404
political party-based, 110–1, 367, 404
regional, 1, 6, 17–8, 29, 45–6, 85, 94, 150–1, 155, 167–9, 185, 232, 238–9, 251–2, 278, 307, 336, 343–8, 353, 368, 400, 406
single-member, 36, 318, 406
subsidiary, 49, 179, 407
temporary, 12, 14, 16–7, 113, 190–1, 319, 353, 407
transitional, 18–9, 407
electoral management bodies (EMBs), professionalism, 2, 20–1, 24, 26, 39, 68, 93, 95, 101–2, 104, 111, 113, 158, 169, 173, 177–92, 204, 225, 231, 236, 238, 243–4, 249, 276, 280, 299, 307, 332, 337, 346–7, 353, 367
ACE Electoral Knowledge Network and, 346–7
accountability and, 299
Afghanistan, 68
Armenia, 101–2, 104
Bosnia and Herzegovina, 332, 335, 337
Costa Rica, 93, 95
expert-based, 113
failing EMBs, role in, 367
guiding principles and, 22, 24, 26, 115, 177–8
Haiti, 373
Independent Model and, 20
inhibiting factors, 190
Kenya, 276, 280
media, role, 235–6
Mexico, 39
regulation of, 111
Senegal, 169
South Korea, 173
staff training, 183–4, 186, 231
stakeholders and, 243–4
suppliers, 238
Timor-Leste, 204
Tonga, 225
United Kingdom, 307
United States, 249, 253
electoral management bodies (EMBs), strategic planning, 145–52, 295
electoral management bodies (EMBs), voter education and, 6, 12, 24, 31, 48, 59, 77–8, 82–3, 90–2, 98, 103, 113, 129, 132, 140, 146, 149, 166, 168, 183, 212–3, 223, 230, 237–8, 243, 252, 265, 272, 274, 278, 296–7, 314, 322, 345, 347, 355, 362, 407, 431. *See also names of individual countries*
electoral management models. *See also names of individual countries*
Governmental Model, 6–10, 12–5, 17, 19–22, 24, 26, 77, 107, 123, 126, 137, 145–6, 148, 151, 179–80, 208–10, 215–6, 231, 302, 306, 376–94 , 402–3, 406, 415
Independent Model, 6–10, 12, 14–5, 19–22, 26, 79, 98, 107, 123, 125–6, 145–6, 148, 151, 179, 210, 216, 369, 372, 376–94, 399, 402–3
Mixed Model, 6–10, 12, 15, 17, 19–22, 26, 107, 123, 126, 145–6, 148, 151, 179, 208–10, 215–6, 376–94, 398–403, 406, 415
electoral materials, EMBs and, accessibility, 177, 219, 233–4, 320–1, 346, 353
distribution, 35, 353, 396
Electoral Reform Commission (ERC), 130
electronic voting. *See voting, electronic*
El Salvador, EMBs in,
Independent Model, 380
online resources, 418
Supreme Electoral Tribunal, 380
EMBs. *See electoral management bodies*
Enhancing Electoral and Legal Capacity for Tomorrow (ELECT), 63–70

Equatorial Guinea, EMBs and,
    Central Elections Board, 380
    Mixed Model, 380
ERC (Electoral Reform Commission), 130
Eritrea, EMBs in,
    Electoral Commission, 380
    expert-based, 115
    Independent Model, 380
Estonia, EMBs in,
    Independent Model, 7, 380
    internet voting, 324, 371
    National Electoral Council, 380
    online resources, 418
Ethiopia, EMBs in,
    Independent Model, 380
    National Electoral Board, 380
    online resources in, 418
    transparency in, 23
EU. *See European Union*
European Commission, 211, 246, 432
European Union (EU)
    observation missions, 433
    treaties and agreements with, 45
European Parliamentary elections, 50
EVMs (electronic voting machines),
    See voting machines, electronic

F

Falkland Islands, 380
FEC (Federal Election Commission), 6, 247–8
Federal Election Commission (FEC), 6, 247–8
Fiji, EMBs in,
    accountability, 237
    Electoral Commission, 380
    Independent Model, 380
    online resources, 418
    professionalism, 119
Finland, EMBs in,
    Governmental Model, 22, 380
    online resources, 418
First Past the Post (FPTP) electoral system, 36, 166, 275
France, EMBs in,
    Constitutional Council, 380
    election campaigns, 80
    financing, 80
    international cooperation, technical, 85, 427
    Mixed Model, 8, 14, 210, 380
    online resources, 418
    professionalism, 186
    validation of elections, 84
FUNCINPEC (Front Uni National pour un Camobdge Indépendant, Neutre, Pacifique, et Coopératif—United Front for an Independent, Neutral, Peaceful and Cooperative Cambodia), 54–60
FYROM. *See Macedonia, Former Yugoslavian Republic of*

G

Gabon, EMBs in,
    Autonomous and Permanent National Electoral Commission, 380
    Mixed Model, 380
Gambia, EMBs in,
    expert-based, 115
    financing, 214–5
    Independent Electoral Commission, 380
    Independent Model, 380
    online resources, 418
    professionalism, 114
    regulatory powers in, 51
gender equity
    Afghanistan, 70
    Armenia, 100
    Bosnia and Herzegovina, 330
    Botswana, 297
    Costa Rica, 96
    EMBs and, 31, 52, 73, 80–1, 87–90, 92, 118–9, 168, 181, 191, 197–8, 314, 354, 366, 369, 371, 398
    Georgia, 88–9
    Ghana, 88, 90
    Guatemala, 88
    Guinea, 88
    Guyana, 87
    Haiti, 350, 354
    Indonesia, 87
    Kenya, 275

Liberia, 195–8, 430
Nepal, 81
Senegal, 83
Seychelles, 31
Ukraine, 339
GEO (Global Electoral Organization) Network, 346, 348
Georgia, Republic of, EMBs in,
  accountability, 287, 296
  BRIDGE project in, 186
  Central Election Committee, 380
  electoral reform, 386
  financial, 214
  gender equity, 88–9
  geography, 98
  Independent Model, 7, 16, 380
  meeting protocols, 124
  online resources, 418
  permanent, 16, 147
  political parties, 230
  professionalism, 147, 181
Germany, EMBs in
  electoral dispute resolution, 85
  Governmental Model, 380
  online resources, 418
  professionalism, 118
Ghana, EMBs in,
  centralized EMB, 17
  constitution, 46–8
  Electoral Commission, 380
  financing, 210, 215
  gender equity, 88, 90
  Independent Model, 380
  international cooperation, technical, 85, 321
  leadership, EMB, 109, 114–5, 121, 178
  online resources, 418
  professionalism, 114–5, 121, 178
  regulatory powers, 74
  stakeholders, 237
  voter education, 82–3
Global Declaration of Principles and Code of Conduct for International Electoral Observation (UN Declaration, October 2005), 46, 84, 239
Global Electoral Organization (GEO) Network, 346, 348

Greece, EMBs in,
  Governmental Model, 380
  online resources, 418
  professionalism, 146
Grenada, 380
Guatemala, EMBs in,
  gender equity, 88
  Independent Model, 380
  judicial membership, 112
  membership restrictions, 114
  online resources, 418
  professionalism, 112, 114, 117
  regional, 344
  Supreme Electoral Tribunal, 380
Guernsey, EMBs in,
  Governmental Model, 380
  online resources, 418
Guinea, EMBs in,
  accountability, 122
  expert-based, 115
  gender equity, 88
  Independent Model, 380
  Independent National Election Committee, 380
  Mixed Model, 8
  multi-party, 110–1
  professionalism, 119
Guinea Bissau, EMBs in,
  Independent Model, 380
  National Election Committee, 380
Guyana, EMBs in,
  accountability, 218
  Elections Commission, 380
  electoral dispute resolution, 85
  financing, 214
  gender equity, 87
  Independent Model, 380
  online resources, 418
  professionalism, 117
  voter registration, 79

H

Haiti, EMBs in,
  case study, 349–57
  donor funding, 207, 211, 316–7, 353
  gender equity, 354
  Independent Model, 382
  Provisional Electoral Council, 382

transitional, 349
voter registration, 317
HAVA (Help America Vote Act), 245–8
Holy See (Vatican City), 382
Honduras, EMBs in,
    accountability, 287, 289
    election validation, 84
    Independent Model, 382
    online resources, 418
    permanent, 114
    professionalism, 114
    Supreme Electoral Tribunal, 382
Hungary, EMBs in,
    financing, 208
    global electoral organization (GEO) network conference, 346
    legal framework, 50
    Mixed Model, 17, 382
    National Electoral Committee, 382
    online resources, 418
    professionalism, 181, 189
    voter registration, 79

I

IACREOT (International Association of Clerks, Recorders, Election Officials and Treasurers), 344
ICCPR (International Covenant of Civil and Political Rights), 43, 45
Iceland, EMBs in,
    financing, 214
    Mixed Model, 382
    online resources, 418
IDEA. *See International IDEA*
identification (ID) cards, voter, 25, 36, 44, 79, 91, 94, 96, 218, 224, 321–2, 352, 362. *See also names of individual countries*
IEBC (Independent Electoral Boundaries Commission), 274–82
IEC (Independent Election/Electoral Commission). *See under Afghanistan, Timor-Leste, Botswana*
IEIS BiH (Integrated Election Information System—Bosnia and Herzegovina), 331, 333
IENDC (Internet Election News Deliberation Commission), 172–3
IFES (International Foundation for Electoral Systems)
    ACE project, 346
    Afghanistan, in, 69
    BRIDGE partnership, 186, 427
    CORE project, 208, 220
    Haiti, in, 355
    Nigeria, in, 134–5
    Ukraine, 340
Independent Electoral Boundaries Commission (IEBC), 274–82
India, EMBs in,
    accountability, 121, 145
    audits, electoral, 271
    boundary delimitation, 78
    case study, 358–62
    code of conduct, 82
    constitution, 46–7, 358–9
    Election Commission, 178, 358–60, 382
    electorate, 237, 360, 362
    ethnic balance, 47
    financing, 82, 210, 319, 325
    identification (ID) cards, voter, 362
    India International Institute of Democracy and Election Management (IIIDEM), 362
    Independent Model, 7, 382
    international cooperation, technical, 85, 321
    media, 80
    online resources, 418
    political parties, 80–1, 112
    professionalism, 108, 112, 114–5, 178, 180, 319, 359
    regulatory power, EMBs, 74
    single-member, 318
    state elections, 18, 359
    sustainability, 318
    voting machines, electronic (EVMs), 271, 321, 325, 371
Indonesia, EMBs in,
    accountability of, 119
    boundary delimitation, 78
    BRIDGE program, 186, 204
    constitution, 46, 48
    decentralized, 148

donor funding, 207, 211
election campaigns, 81
electoral dispute resolution, 85
financing, 210–1
gender equity, 87
Independent Model, 7
legal framework, 17, 19, 44, 50–1, 73, 81, 86, 114
member committees, 125–6
permanent, 12
political parties, 111–2
professionalism, 114, 118–9, 146–8, 151, 179–81, 204
regulatory powers, 51, 75, 81
stakeholders, 239
Timor-Leste and, 200
transitional, 19
transparency, 21
Integrated Election Information System—Bosnia and Herzegovina (IEIS BiH), 331, 333
Inter-American Union of Electoral Organizations (UNIORE), 96, 344
International Foundation for Electoral Systems (IFES)
  ACE project, 346
  Afghanistan, in, 69
  BRIDGE partnership, 186, 427
  CORE project, 208, 220
  Haiti, in, 355
  Nigeria, in, 134–5
  Ukraine, 340
internally displaced persons, 87, 91, 371
International Association of Clerks, Recorders, Election Officials and Treasurers (IACREOT), 344
International Covenant of Civil and Political Rights (ICCPR), 43, 45
International IDEA (Institute for Democracy and Electoral Assistance)
  Administration and Cost of Elections (ACE) Project, 346
  Bosnia and Herzegovina, in, 331
  BRIDGE program and, 186, 427
  Costa Rica, in 96–7
  description of, 435
  Electoral Management Design Database, 6, 375
  Electoral Management Design: The International IDEA Handbook (2006), 54, 61, 93, 128, 165, 302, 328, 358, 426
  Electoral System Design: The New International IDEA Handbook (2005), 322, 426
  International Obligations for Elections: Guidelines for Legal Frameworks (2014), 50, 53, 36
  Model Curriculum for Master Programmes in Electoral Policy and Administration (2014), 186
  NEC Gender Office (Liberia), partnership with, 198
  Nigeria, in, 135
  survey of electoral management (2014), 8
International Organization for Standardization, 290
International Republican Institute, 204
Internet and information technology (IT) systems, EMBs and,
  access, 160, 373
  accountability and, 166, 172, 209
  Afghanistan, 66
  Africa, 66
  Bosnia and Herzegovina, 332
  election campaigns, 175, 224
  Estonia, 371
  Internet Election News Deliberation Commission (IENDC), 172
  media monitoring, 236
  Norway, 141, 264
  recruitment, EMB, 182
  security concerns, 251, 262, 324
  social media, 236
  surveillance, 170, 172, 224
  sustainability, 317
  transparency, 94, 224
  Ukraine, 336
  voting, 141–2, 151–2, 256, 264, 266, 270–1, 317, 324, 371, 401. *See also names of individual countries*
Internet Election News Deliberation Commission (IENDC), 172–3
Iran, EMBs in,
  geography of, 98

Guardian Council, 382
Mixed Model in, 382
voting, refugee, 62
Iraq, EMBs in,
   donor funding, 207–8, 210
   financing, 208
   gender equity, 87
   Independent High Electoral
      Commission, 382
   Independent Model, 382
   online resources, 418
   professionalism, 116, 119, 190
   transitional elections, 208, 433
   voting, refugee, 91, 324, 427
Ireland, Northern (Ulster), EMBs in,
   Boundary Commission, 304
   Electoral Office, 304
   Independent Model, 22
   voter registration, 303
Ireland, Republic of (Eire), EMBs in,
   electoral dispute resolution and, 85
   Governmental Model, 382
   online resources, 418
   professionalism, 146
IT systems. *See Internet and Information Technology systems*
Italy, EMBs in,
   Governmental Model, 382
   online resources, 418

J

Jamaica, EMBs in,
   Electoral Commission, 382
   Independent Model, 7, 382
   online resources, 418
   professionalism, 114
Japan, EMBs in,
   Central Election Management
      Commission, 382
   Mixed Model, 8, 382
   online resources, 420
JEMB (Joint Electoral Management Body), 61–9
Jersey, EMBs in,
   Independent Model, 382
   online resources, 420
Jordan, EMBs in,
   Election Commission, 382

Independent Model, 382
online resources, 420

K

Kazakhstan, EMBs in,
   Independent Central Election
      Commission, 382
   Independent Model, 382
   voting, electronic, 427
Kenya, EMBs in
   accountability, 80, 326
   case study, 273–83
   Communications Amendment Act
      (2009), 281
   Democratic Governance Donor Group
      (DGDG), 279
   donor funding, 238, 316
   Electoral Commission of Kenya (ECK), 273
   electoral calendar in, 161
   financing, 80
   gender equity, 88, 90
   Independent Electoral and Boundaries
      Commission, 382
   Independent Model, 11, 382
   Law Society of Kenya, 277
   legal framework, 273
   legislative framework, 275
   media, 281
   National Accord and Reconciliation Act
      (2008), 273
   online resources, 420
   professionalism, 147, 178
   sustainability, 316
   violence, post-election, 273
   voter education, 82
Kiribati, EMBs in,
   Independent Electoral Commission, 382
   Independent model, 382
   permanent, 114
Korea Democratic People's Republic of
   (North Korea), 386
Korea, Republic of (South Korea), EMBs in,
   case study, 171–6
   Civic Education Institute for
      Democracy (1996), 171–3
   electoral reform, 175

financing, 214
Global Electoral Organization (GEO) Network, 346
history of elections in, 171
Independent Model, 171, 390
international observer programs, 185
legislative framework, 172
National Election Commission, 171, 390, 430
online resources, 420
professionalism, 109, 118, 173
Public Official Election Act (2009), 172
United Kingdom, relationship with, 306
voter registration, 79
Kuwait, 382
Kyrgyzstan, 384, 427

L

Laos, 384
Latin America, EMBs in,
    electoral tribunal, 401
    history of, 33
    legal framework, 93
    nomenclature, 108
    oligarchic governments, 74
    public law, 93
Latvia, EMBs in,
    accountability, 121
    Central Election Commission, 384
    Independent Model, 384
    legal framework, 44
    legislative framework, 117
    meeting protocols, 124
    online resources, 420
    professionalism, 114–5, 117–8, 121
    voter education, 82
Law on the Election of the Members of the National Assembly (LEMNA), 55, 57
Lebanon, EMBs in,
    gender equity and, 90
    Governmental Model, 384
    online resources, 420
legal framework, EMBs, 43–55, 80–7, 90–2. *See also names of individual countries*
    checklist, 51, 187, 189, 191, 198
    codes of conduct, 16, 23, 44, 49, 57, 81, 84, 86–7, 177, 196, 202, 220–1, 252, 293, 403
    constitution, 46–8
    electoral regulation, 39, 177, 202, 401
    secondary legislation, 49, 52, 409
    treaties and agreements, 45, 52, 84
LEMNA (Law on the Election of the Members of the National Assembly), 55, 57
Lesotho, EMBs in,
    accountability, 287–8
    election campaigns, 81
    electoral commission, 384
    electoral dispute resolution, 85
    financing, 214
    gender equity, 88
    Independent Model, 384
    legal framework, 367
    online resources, 420
    political parties, 230
    professionalism, 114
    voter education 82–3
Liberia, EMBs in,
    accountability, 121, 195
    case study, 192–9
    code of conduct, 85, 193
    Comprehensive Peace Agreement (2003), 192
    displaced persons, 91
    donor funding, 209, 316, 367
    election campaigns, 81
    electoral reform, 369
    ethnic balance, 119
    financing, 80, 195, 209, 214, 316, 367
    gender equity, 88, 119, 198
    Independent Model, 7, 384
    legal framework, 84, 192
    legislative framework, 85, 192
    media, 81
    National Elections Commission, 394, 430
    online resources, 420
    political parties, 80
    powers and responsibilities, 74
    professionalism 121, 193–6
    transparency, 23
    voter education, 83

voting, refugee, 91
Libya, EMBs in,
   donor funding, 211, 316
   Independent Model, 384
   National Elections Committee, 384
   online resources, 420
   sustainability, 314
Liechtenstein, EMBs in,
   Independent Election Commission, 384
   Independent Model, 384
   online resources, 420
   party-based, 115
Lithuania, EMBs in,
   accountability, 80, 124
   Central Electoral Commission, 324
   centralized, 17
   financing, 90
   Independent Model, 11, 384
   oath-taking, 122
   online resources, 420
   political parties, 80
   professionalism, 109, 118–9, 122, 124
   voter education, 82–3
Luxembourg, EMBs in,
   Governmental Model, 384
   online resources, 420

M

Macedonia, Former Yugoslavian Republic of (FYROM), EMBs in,
   gender equity, 89
   Independent Model, 384
   Independent State Election Commission, 384
   online resources, 420
Madagascar, EMBs in,
   constitution, 48
   financing, 214
   Independent Model, 384
   National Electoral Commission, 384
   online resources, 420
Malawi, EMBs in,
   election campaigns, 81
   Electoral Commission, 384
   Independent Model, 384
   legislative framework, 233
   online resources, 420

Malaysia, EMBs in,
   Electoral Commission, 384
   Independent Model, 384
   online resources, 420
   professionalism, 115, 117
Maldives, EMBs in,
   Elections Commission, 384
   Independent Model, 384
   online resources, 420
Mali, 8, 384
Malta, EMBs in,
   Electoral Commission, 384
   Independent Model, 384
   online resources, 420
   professionalism, 114
Man, Isle of, 384, 418
Marshall Islands, 384
Mauritania, 384
Mauritius, EMBs in,
   Electoral Commissioner, 384
   financing, 212
   Independent Model, 7, 384
   online resources, 420
   professionalism, 119
Mexico, EMBs in,
   accountability, 36, 74
   case study, 32–40
   electoral boundaries, 36
   Federal Electoral Institute (IFE), 32–9, 346
   failed EMBs, 367–8
   financing, 36, 80, 210, 214
   gender equity, 87–8
   Global Electoral Organization (GEO) Network and, 346
   historical background, 33–4
   Independent Model, 386
   international programs, 85, 185
   legal framework, 21, 32–3
   media, 36–7, 80
   National Electoral Institute (INE), 386, 430
   oath-taking, 122
   online resources, 420
   permanent, 12
   political parties, 36, 80, 112, 230
   power and responsibilities of, 6, 35–6, 74–5, 115, 125

professionalism, 37–8, 111–2, 115, 117, 119, 147, 178–80, 182–3, 186
voter registration, 36
voting, electronic, 38
Micronesia, Federated States of, 386
MINUSTAH (United Nations Stabilization Mission in Haiti), 352–4
Moldova, EMBs in,
accountability, 224
Central Electoral Commission, 386
Independent Model, 386
online resources, 420
professionalism, 109, 119
voter registration, 79
Monaco, 386
Mongolia, EMBs in,
financing, 214
gender equity, 87
General Election Commission, 386
Independent Model, 386
online resources, 420
Montenegro, 386
Montserrat, 386
Morocco, EMBs in,
Governmental Model, 386
professionalism, 146
Mozambique, EMBs in,
donor funding, 210
electoral dispute resolution, 85
Independent Model, 11, 386
multiparty, 118
online resources, 420
political parties, 111–2, 118
professionalism, 109, 111–2, 122, 190
Technical Secretariat for Election Administration, 386
Myanmar, 386

N

Namibia, EMBs in,
accountability, 287
constitution, 48
electoral commission, 386
financing, 287
gender equity, 88
Independent Model, 19, 386
legal framework, 51, 75
legislative framework, 232, 287

online resources, 420
professionalism, 148
National Commission of Television and Radio (NCTR), 103
National Electoral Board—Riksvalgstyret (NEB), 137–40
Nauru, 386
Navarro, Carlos, 32–40, 430
NCTR (National Commission of Television and Radio), 103
NEC (National Election Committee—Cambodia or National Election Commission—Liberia, Nigeria, South Korea). *See under Cambodia, Liberia, Nigeria, South Korea*
Nepal, EMBs in,
donor funding, 238
election campaigns, 81
Election Commission, 386
gender equity, 81, 88–9
IFES in, 427
Independent Model, 386
media, 81
online resources, 422
power and responsibilities, 75
professionalism, 114–5, 119, 146, 190
voter education, 83
Netherlands, EMBs in,
Electoral Council, 386
financing, 271
Mixed Model, 386
online resources, 422
voter registration, 79
voting, electronic, 271
New Zealand, EMBs in,
accountability, 80
Electoral Commission, 386, 426
electoral reform, 366, 369–70
financing, 80
Independent Model, 386
online resources, 422
organizational structure, 149, 155
Pacific Islands, Australia, New Zealand Electoral Administrators Network (PIANZEA), 345
professionalism, 118–9, 225
regional networks, 345
stakeholders, 161
sustainability, 226

Nicaragua, EMBs in,
    election (1990), 190
    electoral materials, 321
    Independent Model, 386
    National Electoral Commission, 366
    online resources, 322
    professionalism, 190
Niger, EMBs in,
    Independent Model, 16, 386
    National Electoral Commission, 386
    permanent, 16
    validation of election, 84
Nigeria, EMBs in,
    accountability, 80, 134–5, 218, 288
    case study, 128–35
    boundary delimitation, 78
    constitution, 129
    donor funding, 316
    election campaigns, 81
    electoral calendar, 161
    financing, 134, 218
    history of, 128
    Independent Model, 7, 386
    Independent National Electoral Commission (INEC), 128, 132–3, 386
    institutional structure, 130–1
    legal framework, 129–30
    legislative framework, 128–30
    media, 133–4
    oath-taking, 122
    online resources, 422
    political parties, 80, 117, 133–4, 161
    powers and responsibilities, EMB, 18
    professionalism, 108, 114, 117, 180
    sustainability, 318
Niue, EMBs in,
    financing, 214, 319
    Governmental Model, 386
    sustainability, 319
Norway, EMBs in,
    case study, 137–42
    elections, 137
    electoral reform 141
    gender equity, 138
    history, 138–9
    legislative framework, 139–40
    National Electoral Board, 140–1
    voting, internet, 141

O

OAS, *see Organization of American States*
OCV (out-of-country voting), 62, 428. See also voting, refugee
Office for Democratic Institutions and Human Rights (ODIHR), 16, 98, 100–5, 141, 337–8, 341, 428–9
Oman, 386
OMR (optical mark recognition), 269–71, 325. See also voting, electronic
Organization of American States (OAS)
    Costa Rica, assistance to, 96
    donor funding and, 211
    Haiti, assistance to, 352–3
    international observation and, 45
    regional observation and, 210–11
Organization for Security and Cooperation in Europe (OSCE)
    Armenia, recommendations to, 98, 100–2
    Bosnia and Herzegovina, assistance to, 328–9, 331, 337, 427
    donor funds and, 331
    Norway, recommendations to, 141
    Office for Democratic Institutions and Human Rights, 431
    permanent EMBs and, 16
    regional observation and, 44–5
    United Kingdom, observation in, 306
OSCE, *see Organization for Security and Cooperation in Europe*
out-of-country Voting (OCV), 62, 428. See also voting, refugee

P

Pacific Islands Australia New Zealand Electoral Administrators Network (PIANZEA), 225, 345
Pakistan, EMBs and,
    accountability, 214
    Afghanistan, assistance to, 62
    Election Commission, 386
    financing, 214
    gender equity, 90
    Independent Model, 386
    online resources, 422

professionalism, 108–9, 115, 117, 119, 121–2
Palau, EMBs and,
　Election Commission, 388
　Independent Model, 388
　professionalism, 114
Palestine, EMBs and,
　accountability, 287
　Central Elections Commission, 388
　donor funding, 190
　gender equity, 87, 90
　Independent Model, 388
　legislative framework, 232
　online resources, 422
　professionalism, 190
Panama, EMBs and,
　accountability, 289
　Electoral Tribunal, 388
　financing, 289
　Independent Model, 388
Papua New Guinea, EMBs and,
　Electoral Commission, 388
　electoral reform, 370
　expert-based, 115
　failure, EMB, 367
　financing, 215
　Independent Model, 388
　online resources, 422
　professionalism, 117
Paraguay, EMBs and,
　gender equity, 87
　Independent Model, 388
　online resources, 423
　Supreme Electoral Justice Tribunal, 388
Paris Peace Agreements (1991), 54
PEC (Precinct Electoral Commission or Provincial Election Committee). *See under Armenia, Bosnia and Herzegovina, Cambodia*
PEMMO (Principles for Election Management, Monitoring and Observation), 46
performance review of EMBs, 7, 11, 25, 85, 286, 298, 300, 404
Peru, EMBs and,
　accountability, 289
　constitution, 48
　election campaigns, 82

financing, 289
Independent Model, 388
online resources, 422
Philippines, EMBs and,
　audits, 271
　centralized, 17, 74
　Commission on Elections, 388
　expert-based, 115
　financing, 214
　Independent Model, 388
　legal framework, 17, 44
　online resources, 422
　permanent, 12
　professionalism, 115, 117, 119
　voting, electronic, 265
PIANZEA (Pacific Islands Australia New Zealand Electoral Administrators Network), 225, 345
Pitcairn Islands, 388
Poland, EMBs and,
　gender equity, 87
　Independent Model, 7, 388
　National Electoral Commission, 388
　online resources, 422
　professionalism, 111–2, 119
　responsibilities, 5
　validation, electoral, 84
Political Parties Liaison Committee (PPLC), 281
polling, opinion, 82, 427
polling process, 323
Portugal, EMBs and,
　accountability, 289
　financing, 289
　Mixed Model, 388
　National Election Commission, 388
　online resources, 422
　professionalism, 118–9, 204
PPLC (Political Parties Liaison Committee), 281
Principles for Election Management, Monitoring and Observation (PEMMO), 46
professionalism, EMB, *see electoral management bodies, professionalism, and names of individual countries*

Q

Qatar, 388
Quito Protocol (Association of South American Electoral Organizations), 344

R

REC (Resident Electoral Commissioner), 130
recall vote, 5, 77, 121, 172, 343, 399, 405
referendum, 1, 5–9, 14, 18, 27, 29, 46, 49–50, 77, 95, 98, 160, 171–2, 174, 183, 193, 198, 201, 203, 214, 233, 251–5, 274–6, 282, 303–7, 323, 335–6, 347, 399, 405
refugees
  Afghan, 62, 66
  voting and, 62, 66, 91, 324, 371
Republika Srpksa (RS), 328–30, 334
Resident Electoral Commissioner (REC), 130
Romania, EMBs in,
  BRIDGE project and, 186
  constitution, 48
  Independent Model, 7, 16, 388
  online resources, 422
  professionalism, 115, 118
  voter registration, 79
Russian Federation, EMBs and,
  accountability, 80, 287, 289
  Armenia, influence on, 98
  BRIDGE project and, 186
  centralized, 18
  electoral dispute resolution, 82
  financing, 80, 289
  Independent Model, 388
  media, 80
  National Electoral Commission, 388
  online resources, 422
  permanent, 16
  polling, opinion, 82
  powers and responsibilities of, 73–4, 80
  professionalism, 109, 115, 119, 184
  Ukraine, relationship with, 340
Rwanda, EMBs in,
  Electoral Commission, 388
  financing, 214

Independent Model, 388
online resources, 422
permanent, 114

S

SADC (Southern African Development Community), 30, 46, 211, 345–7, 410
Saint Helena, Ascension and Tristan da Cunha, 388
Saint Kitts and Nevis, 388
Saint Lucia, 388
Saint Vincent and the Grenadines, 388
Samoa, EMBs in,
  Electoral Commissioner, 388
  Independent Model, 388
  online resources, 422
  sustainability, 319
Sam Rainsy Party (SRP), 55–6, 60
San Marino, 388, 422
Sao Tomé and Principe, 388
Saudi Arabia, 390
Senegal, EMBs in,
  accountability, 168
  case study, 165–70
  constraints, 170
  electoral dispute, 168
  financing, 168, 215
  gender equity, 83
  history of, 165–6
  internet technology (IT), 170, 323
  legal framework, 168
  media, 167
  Mixed Model, 8, 14, 390
  National Autonomous Electoral Commission, 167
  National Commission for the Tallying of the Votes, 167
  oath-taking, 122
  online resources, 422
  political parties, 168–9
  professionalism, 115, 119, 122, 169–70
  voter identification cards (IDs), 169
Serbia, EMBs in,
  Electoral Commission, 390
  Independent Model, 390
  online resources, 422

Seychelles, EMBs in,
 accountability, 29
 case study, 27–31
 electoral reform management, 30–1
 financing, 29
 gender equity, 31
 history, 27
 Independent Model, 390
 legislative framework, 27–8
 media, 29–30
 National Electoral Commission, 390, 430
 online resources, 422
 professionalism, 29
 voting, electronic, 30
Sierra Leone, EMBs in,
 access, 88
 Central Electoral Committee, 390
 donor funding, 210
 electoral dispute resolution, 85
 financing, 215
 gender equity, 88
 Independent Model, 390
 online resources, 422
 refugees, 88
Singapore, EMBs in,
 code of conduct, 82
 financing, 210
 Governmental Model, 7, 390
 online resources, 422
 voter information, 82
Slovakia, EMBs in,
 centralized, 17
 Electoral Commission, 390
 Mixed Model, 390
 online resources, 422
Slovenia, EMBs in,
 Independent Model, 390
 online resources, 422
 Republic Electoral Commission, 390
Solomon Islands, EMBs in,
 Electoral Commission, 390
 financing, 215
 Independent Model, 390
 legislative framework, 232–3
 professionalism, 109
Somalia, 390

South Africa, EMBs in,
 accountability, 287
 civil service organizations (CSOs), 237
 code of conduct, 86–7
 constitution, 46
 donor funding, 211–2
 election campaigns, 81
 Electoral Commission, 153, 390
 electoral materials, 320
 electoral reform, 368
 expert-based, 19
 financing, 80, 85, 321
 gender equity, 88, 182
 Independent Model, 7, 153, 390
 international EMB, 19, 85
 legal framework, 21, 44, 73–4, 84
 online resources, 153, 422
 permanent, 12
 political parties, 80, 230
 powers and responsibilities of, 73–4
 professionalism, 115, 118–21, 124, 147, 180–1, 186, 190, 318
 structure charts, organizational, 149
 sustainability, 318
 validation, electoral results, 84
 voter education, 82
 voter registration, 79
 voting, electronic, 321
Southern African Development Community (SADC), 30, 46, 211, 345–7, 410
Spain, EMBs, in,
 Electoral Census Office, 79
 Mixed Model, 8, 15, 22, 390
 online resources, 424
 political parties, 80
 professionalism, 182
 regional, 6
 voting, postal, 324
Sri Lanka, EMBs in,
 Department of Elections, 390
 Independent Model, 390
 online resources, 424
SRP (Sam Rainsy Party), 55–6, 60
STAE (Technical Secretariat for Electoral Administration), 201–5
stakeholders, EMB, 229–44, 285–315
 Afghanistan, in, 64, 70

Armenia, in, 100–1
  Cambodia, in, 54–8
  commitment to, 45, 48, 51–2, 109, 141,
      144, 150–1, 160–1, 177–8, 187–8,
      252, 262, 369
  confidence, 19, 24–5, 52, 85, 109, 113,
      116, 133, 141, 144, 158, 164,
      177–8, 187–90, 285, 366–7
  definition of, 406
  electoral reform and, 365–8
  Haiti in, 355
  Kenya, in, 275, 279, 281–2
  Liberia, in, 196–8
  multiparty, 113, 159, 189, 285
  Nigeria and, 133
  performance accountability and, 25,
      51–2, 152, 158, 216, 219, 258,
      286–90, 368, 401, 404
  professionalism and, 319
  Senegal in, 169
  Seychelles, in, 31, 34
  suppliers, 86, 212, 215–6, 231, 238,
      240, 242–3, 263–4, 270–1, 290–2,
      316
  technology and, 263–5, 325, 326
  Ukraine and, 338
Sudan, EMBs in,
  expert-based, 120–1
  gender equity, 118
  Independent Model, 390
  National Elections Commission, 390
  oath-taking, 238
  online resources, 424
  professionalism, 114, 120–2
Suriname, 390
sustainability of EMBs, 2, 17, 20, 59, 67, 69,
    104, 180, 183, 188, 196, 211, 220–1,
    226–7, 257, 259, 267–8, 290, 293–4,
    297, 307, 313–27, 338, 346, 353–4,
    365, 403. *See also names of individual
    countries*
Swaziland, 390
Sweden, EMBs in,
  decentralized, 7, 17, 22
  electoral dispute resolution, 85
  electoral reform, 366, 369
  Governmental Model, 7, 12, 392
  online resources, 424

  voter education, 82–3
  voter registration, 79, 323
  voting, electronic, 323
Switzerland, EMBs in,
  Governmental Model, 7, 392
  local election, 17–8
  online resources, 424
Syria, 392

T

Taiwan, EMBs in,
  Central Election Commission, 306, 392
  gender equity, 88
  Independent Model, 306, 392
  international observation, 306
  online resources, 424
Tajikistan, 392
Tanzania, EMBs in,
  Election Commission, 392
  ethnic balance, 90
  financing, 215
  gender equity, 89–90
  Independent Model, 392
  professionalism, 119, 146–7
TCO (total cost of ownership), 261–2, 268
Thailand, EMBs in,
  Election Commission, 392
  electoral dispute regulation, 85
  Independent Model, 7, 392
  legal framework, 44, 51, 74–5
  online resources, 424
  political parties, 80
  professionalism, 109, 112, 126, 146
  voter education, 82
Tikal Protocol (Association of Electoral
    Bodies of Central America and the
    Caribbean), 92, 344
Timor-Leste (East Timor), EMBs in,
  accountability, 203, 296
  case study, 200–5
  donor funding, 210–2, 316–7
  electoral dispute resolution, 85
  electoral reform, 396
  financing, 203
  gender equity, 88, 181
  history of, 200–1
  legislative framework, 233

media, 204
Mixed Model, 392
National Election Commission, 392
professionalism, 148, 190, 204, 238
sustainability, 314, 316–7
United Nations missions, 200–3. *See also names of individual UN missions*
Togo, EMBs in,
    National Election Commission, 392
    Independent Model, 392
    online resources, 424
Tokelau, 392
Tonga, EMBs in,
    BRIDGE project and, 223, 225
    case study, 222–6
    election campaigns, 82
    Electoral Commission, 222, 392, 428
    electoral reform, 369
    ethnic balance, 226
    financing, 214
    Independent Model, 366, 369, 392
    legal framework, 74, 148–9, 157, 222–3
    legislative framework, 222–3
    organizational structure, 149
    Pacific Islands, Australia, New Zealand Electoral Administrators Network (PIANZEA), 223
    professionalism, 118–9, 146, 148–9, 189, 319
    sustainability, 226
    voter education, 82–3
Tribunal Supremo de Elecciones—Supreme Electoral Tribunal (TSE), 93–6, 378, 431
Trinidad and Tobago, EMBs in,
    Elections and Boundaries Commission, 392
    Independent Model, 392
    professionalism, 114–5, 117
TSE (Tribunal Supremo de Elecciones—Supreme Electoral Tribunal), 93–5, 378, 431
Tunisia, EMBs in,
    accountability, 253
    case study, 250–5
    financing, 254–5
    history, 250

Independent High Authority for Elections (ISIE), 250–3
    legal framework, 250–1
    professionalism, 253–4
Turkey, EMBs in,
    accountability, 289
    expert-based, 114
    financing, 289
    Independent Model, 392
    geography and, 98
    professionalism, 114–5, 119
    Supreme Electoral Council, 392
Turkmenistan, 392
Turks and Caicos Islands, 392

U

Uganda, EMBs in,
    accountability, 215
    boundary delimitation, 78
    Electoral Commission, 392
    expert-based, 115
    gender equity, 89
    Independent Model, 392
    professionalism, 115
Ukraine, EMBs in,
    accountability, 337
    case study, 335–41
    Central Election Commission, 339–40, 392
    expert-based, 115
    financing, 337
    gender equity, 89, 339
    history, 335
    Independent Model, 392
    legal framework, 74, 335–6
    oath-taking, 122
    online resources, 341, 424
    professionalism, 109, 111–2, 115, 117, 119, 122, 336–8
    transparency, 23
UN, *see United Nations*
UNAMA (United Nations Assistance Mission in Afghanistan), 62
UNDESA (United Nations Department of Economic and Social Affairs), 346
UNDP (United Nations Development Programme), 61, 66–70, 96, 134–5,

186, 198–9, 208, 211, 220, 279, 346, 352–3
UNEAD (United Nations Electoral Assistance Division), 62–3, 186, 346
UNIORE (Inter-American Union of Electoral Organizations), 96, 344
United Arab Emirates, EMBs in, Governmental Model, 392
online resources, 424
United Front for an Independent, Neutral, Peaceful and Cooperative Cambodia (FUNCINPEC), 54–6
United Kingdom, EMBs in, accountability, 307
Association of Electoral Administrators (AEA), 186, 307–8, 343
Boundary Commissions, 304
case study, 302–9
financing, 307
Governmental Model, 392
international collaboration, 161
local elections, 6
online resources, 424
professionalism, 307
sustainability, 307–8
United Nations (UN)
Afghanistan and, 61–2, 65, 67, 69
Bangladesh and, 85
Cambodia and, 54
codes of conduct and, 46, 84
donor funding and, 204, 210–1
Global Declaration of Principles and Code of Conduct for International Electoral Observation, 84, 238–9
Haiti and, 352–3
Liberia and, 316
Nepal and, 238
professionalism, and 186
Timor-Leste, and, 200, 238, 296
treaties, 45
transitional, 18, 200–1
United Nations Assistance Mission in Afghanistan (UNAMA), 62
United Nations Department of Economic and Social Affairs (UNDESA), 346
United Nations Development Programme (UNDP), 61, 66–70,

96, 134–5, 186, 198–9, 208, 211, 220, 279, 346, 352–3
United Nations Electoral Assistance Division (UNEAD), 62–3, 186, 346
United Nations High Commissioner for Refugees, 66, 429
United Nations Office of Project Services (UNOPS), 62
United Nations Resolution 940 under Chapter VII (1994), 352
United Nations Stabilization Mission in Haiti (MINUSTAH), 352–4
United Nations Transitional Administration in Cambodia (UNTAC), 54
United States Agency for International Development (USAID), 211, 331
United States of America
accountability, 80
American University, 186, 247, 433
Baker–Carter Commission on Federal Electoral Reform (2005), 290
Bosnia and Herzegovina, in, 347
boundary delimitation, 75
Campaign Finance Act (1976), 246
case study, 245–7
decentralized, 17
donor funding, 211
Election Assistance Commission, 247
financing, 80
Global Electoral Organization (GEO) Network, 346
Governmental Model, 7–8, 392
Help America Vote Act (HAVA), 245
international assistance, 347
information technology (IT) and, 267
history, 245
legal framework, 44, 75
local elections, 44, 344
National Association of Clerks and County Recorders (NACRC), 344
National Association of State Election Directors and the National Association of Secretaries of State, 344
online resources, 424
political parties, 181–2, 290

459

presidential election (2000), 247
primary elections, 80
professionalism, 287
voting, electronic, 249, 290, 325
voting, verified audit paper trail (VVAPT), 271
UNOPS (United Nations Office of Project Services), 62
UNTAC (United Nations Transitional Administration in Cambodia), 54
Uruguay, EMBs in,
    accountability, 288
    constitution, 46
    Electoral Court, 392
    electoral dispute resolution, 85
    financing, 288
    Independent Model, 7, 21, 392
    legal framework, 51, 74–5
    online resources, 425
    professionalism, 109, 117, 147, 182
USAID (United States Agency for International Development), 211, 331
Uzbekistan, EMBs in,
    Central Election Commission, 392
    gender equity, 89
    Independent Model, 392
    legal framework, 44
    online resources, 424
    professionalism, 109

V

Venice Commission, 272
voter education and information, 6, 12, 24, 31, 49, 58, 77–8, 82–3, 90, 92, 98, 113, 129, 132, 140, 146, 149, 166, 168, 183, 213, 223, 230, 237, 243, 252, 265, 272, 274, 276, 278, 296, 324, 322, 347–8, 355, 362, 371, 407. *See also names of individual countries*
voter registration, 6, 12, 16–7, 28, 44, 47, 49, 51, 55, 57, 59–60, 63, 65–70, 78–80, 89, 91–2, 113, 129, 134, 146, 151, 153, 156, 159, 161, 181–2, 187–9, 195, 198, 201–4, 208–9, 212–3, 225–7, 266, 268, 282, 290, 317–8, 321–3, 325–8, 339, 351–2, 360–1, 366, 369–72, 399, 407–8, 427. *See also names of individual countries*

voter-verified paper trail audit (VVPTA), 249, 271–2
voting, *see also names of individual countries*
    absentee, 76, 96, 104, 173, 208, 271, 324, 371, 396, 406
    age, 165
    displaced persons, 91
    donor funding and, 70, 317
    electoral cycle and, 16
    electronic, 104, 207–9, 212, 248–9, 258, 264, 269–71, 282, 290, 300, 313, 351, 325, 327, 370–1, 401
    gender equity and, 44–5, 91, 103, 138, 366, 406
    identification (ID) cards and, 36, 38–9, 249, 257, 325, 327–8
    information technology (IT) and, 141, 258, 264, 269–71, 290, 317, 324
    local election, 62
    materials, 91, 165–7, 321
    mechanisms, definitions of, 396–406
    member voting, EMB, 38, 108, 111, 117, 123, 126, 230
    Open Source Digital Voting Foundation (OSDV), 264
    postal, 91, 173, 231, 271, 302, 324, 405
    procedures, 105, 151–3, 226, 266, 324
    security, 133
    transparency, 49, 183
    Venice Commission, 272
voting machines, electronic, 214, 246, 248–9, 257–8, 270–1, 321, 370–1
    direct recording electronic (DRE), 270
    Open Source Digital Voting Foundation (OSDV), 264
Vanuatu, EMBs in,
    Electoral Commission, 394
    Mixed Model, 394
    professionalism, 117, 119
Venezuela, EMBs in,
    European Union Observation Mission, 427
    financing, 214
    Independent Model, 394
    National Electoral Council, 394
    online resources, 424
    political parties, 110
    recall vote, presidential (2014), 77
    voting, electronic, 371

voter verified paper trail audit
(VVPTA), 271–2
verification of electoral process, 15, 16, 37,
66, 162, 257, 330, 357
VVPTA (voter-verified paper trail audit),
249, 271–2

W

Western Europe, Governmental Model in,
208

Y

Yemen, EMBs in,
accountability, 288
donor funding, 238
Independent Model, 394
legal framework, 51, 117
political parties, 117
professionalism, 147
Supreme Council for Elections, 394